CENSORING
SEX RESEARCH

CENSORING SEX RESEARCH

The Debate over Male Intergenerational Relations

Editors

Thomas K. Hubbard and Beert Verstraete

Walnut Creek, CA

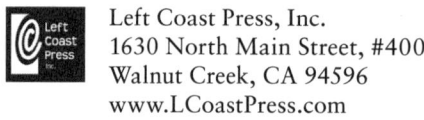
Left Coast Press, Inc.
1630 North Main Street, #400
Walnut Creek, CA 94596
www.LCoastPress.com

Copyright © 2013 by Left Coast Press, Inc.
Foreword © 2013 Daniel C. Tsang

All rights reserved. No part of this publication may be reproduced, stored in a retrieval system, or transmitted in any form or by any means, electronic, mechanical, photocopying, recording, or otherwise, without the prior permission of the publisher.

ISBN 978-1-61132-338-2 hardcover
ISBN 978-1-61132-339-9 paperback
ISBN 978-1-61132-340-5 institutional eBook
ISBN 978-1-61132-724-3 consumer eBook

Library of Congress Cataloging-in-Publication Data

  Censoring sex research : the debate over male intergenerational relations / edited by Thomas K. Hubbard and Beert Verstraete.
    pages cm
  Includes bibliographical references and index.
  ISBN 978-1-61132-338-2 (hardback : alk. paper)
  ISBN 978-1-61132-339-9 (pbk. : alk. paper)
  ISBN 978-1-61132-340-5 (institutional ebook)
  ISBN 978-1-61132-724-3 (consumer ebook)
  1. Homosexuality—Research. 2. Pedophilia—Research. 3. Sexology—Research—Censorship. I. Hubbard, Thomas K. II. Verstraete, Beert C.
  HQ76.25.C385 2013
  306.76'6072—dc23
                                                          2013010024

Printed in the United States of America

∞ ™ The paper used in this publication meets the minimum requirements of American National Standard for Information Sciences—Permanence of Paper for Printed Library Materials, ANSI/NISO Z39.48–1992.

Cover design by Piper Wallis

Contents

Foreword — vii
Daniel C. Tsang

Introduction — xvii
Thomas K. Hubbard

1. Pederasty: An Integration of Empirical, Historical, Sociological, Cross-Cultural, Cross-Species, and Evolutionary Perspectives — 1
   Bruce Rind

2. More Speech or Less? Censoring Social Science — 91
   Patrick O'Neill and Janice Best

3. Intergenerational Sexualities: A Case Study on the Colonization of Late Modern Sexual Subjects and Researcher Agendas — 107
   Richard Yuill

4. Blinded by Science: A Critique of Rind's Views on Pederasty — 139
   Richard D. McAnulty and Lester W. Wright Jr.

5. A Critique of the Academic Process and Application of Evolutionary Theory in Pederasty: An Integration of Empirical, Historical, Sociological, Cross-Cultural, Cross-Species, and Evolutionary Perspectives by Dr. Bruce Rind — 145
   L. Eric Alcorn

6. Same Sex, Different Ages: On Pederasty in Gay History — 161
   D. H. Mader and Gert Hekma

7. "Here's to You, Mr. Robinson": Men Who Have Sexual Relations with Male Minors — 193
   David F. Greenberg

8. Harming Children in the Name of "Child Protection": How Minors Who Have Sex with Other Minors are Abused by the Law and Therapy — 235
   Andrew Heller

9. The Sex Offender System: Punishing *homo sacer*, the New Internal Enemy 251
Thomas K. Hubbard

10. Blinded by Politics and Morality—A Reply to McAnulty and Wright 279
Bruce Rind

Index 299

About the Contributors 303

Foreword

Taboo Sex Research: Thinking Outside the Box

Daniel C. Tsang

The essays in this important book challenge readers to think outside the box. Instead of viewing all sex across the age of consent as abuse, the authors address this topic without prejudgment. Thinking outside the box may be a tall order, and I leave it up to you as to whether the book succeeds in challenging prevailing norms of sex research and helps change any minds.

Myth of Pure Scientific Research

Ideally scientific research is done objectively, without politics or politicians intervening, but in the real world, all sorts of complications arise—the more so in such a taboo area such as this. Thus "pure" scientific research is still a sometimes unachievable goal.

As I write, the US Congress has recently passed, and the president has signed, legislation banning National Science Foundation funding of political science—unless the proposed research relates to national security or is of economic interest to the United States (Nelson, 2013). Thus even mainstream disciplines—let alone sexual science—can be arbitrarily subjected to the constraints of the political process. This follows an earlier attempt, most notably in 2011, by a Republican from California, Darryl Issa, to bar funding of specific sex-related research by the National Institutes of Health. (See the anti-censorship Coalition to Promote Research website: http://www.cossa.org/CPR/cpr.html). Earlier Congress also moved to condemn a scholarly article by Bruce Rind and his cowriters (addressed elsewhere in this volume).

In contemporary Western societies, the drive to "protect" children has meant that any taboo sex across the age of consent means automatic criminalization of that behavior and the attendant categorization of the adults as "sexual predators" and the minors as "victims." The adults are further assumed to be "pedophiles" (thus conflating pedophilia—sexual attraction to preadolescents—with hebephilia—attraction to adolescents), and all minors are assumed to be "children," without any agency. Of course, if America is really interested in helping children and truly protecting them, Congress would not cut off benefits to children or dismantle Head Start programs and would offer a single-payer health plan for everyone within the United States. Nor would drones be used to kill children abroad.

Increasing the criminal penalties on such behavior (see the Reform Sex Offender Laws website: http://nationalrsol.org/) has meant that the only research that is of interest to state-funded agencies is that which relates to criminal justice. Thus, the typical research looks at how to prevent pedophiles from abusing more children rather than depicting the complex realities of interactions between adult and adolescents.

According to the 2011 Youth Risk Behavior Surveillance System, conducted by the CDC, 47.4 percent of secondary school students have engaged in heterosexual vaginal sexual intercourse (it was 60 percent for black students), with more than 6 percent before the age of 13 (CDC, 2012, Table 63, p. 111). In addition, the National Survey of Family Growth 2006–2008 found that heterosexual oral sex was engaged in by under 45 percent of females and 48 percent of males aged 15–19 (Copen et al., 2012, p. 1). Gay teens seeking encounters with peers as well as adults are also common on gay dating sites.

Given the many instances where teenagers already engage in tabooed sexual behavior—and the prevalence of teen pregnancy—does society really mean to criminalize such behavior and turn so many teenagers into criminals? Compared with Europe for example, which has much lower ages of legal consent, the United States is arguably still stuck in the more puritanical, earlier historical period. What is different in the set of essays presented here is the attempt to challenge the prevailing notions of perpetrator versus victim and look closely at the empirical evidence about what is actually going on in these tabooed relationships, contacts, and attractions.

The reader will make up his or her own mind about how successfully this collection manages to challenge the prevailing norms.

Legacy of Alfred Kinsey

Sex research over the years has also faced similar challenges from puritans, moralizers, and politicians willing to exploit the topic, while proclaiming their intent to "save" society, especially its children.

Alfred Kinsey released his pioneering sexual studies of the human male and female in the late 1940s and early 1950s, at a time when homosexuality was taboo and homosexual acts were illegal. Kinsey also found, as further addressed in this book, that minors frequently engage in illegal but non-abusive sex play.

It is generally forgotten that, as a result, Kinsey faced tremendous difficulties, which continue decades later. The researcher himself came under scrutiny, not just his methods. His funding was cut, his research methods criticized, and his own credibility attacked. Vern Bullough, in his study of the history of sex research, *Science in the Bedroom* (1994, 181), notes that "[o]ne result of the mounting criticism was that Kinsey lost his financial support from the CRPS and the Rockefeller Foundation." CRPS stands for the Committee for Research in Problems of Sex, within the National Research Council.

The attacks on Kinsey have continued. The state legislature in Indiana, where the Kinsey Institute is based, routinely lashes out at Kinsey, accusing him of being a pedophile and dismissing his earlier studies. One author, Judith Reisman, has gone on an anti-Kinsey crusade, coming out in 1990 with a coauthored book, *Kinsey, Sex and Fraud: The Indoctrination of a People: An Investigation into the Human Sexuality Research of Alfred C. Kinsey, Wardell B. Pomeroy, Clyde E. Martin, and Paul H. Gebhard,* whose title says it all (Reisman et al., 1990). She has continued her attack with a series of books, among them: *Kinsey: Crimes and Consequences: The Red Queen and the Grand Scheme* (Reisman, 1998, with a third, expanded edition by 2003), and *Sexual Sabotage: How One Mad Scientist Unleashed a Plague of Corruption and Contagion on America* (Reisman, 2010).

The Indiana state legislature has also jumped into the act, given that the Kinsey Institute is based in Bloomington, Indiana, at Indiana University, a state-funded institution. In 1998, for example, the Indiana House of Representatives passed House Concurrent Resolution No. 16, which mandated "No public funds should be used to operate or support institutions that further the claims made by Alfred Kinsey's research," according to another Kinsey critic (Newman, 1998). The critic also asked, "Q: Should state funding of the Kinsey Institute's sexual research end? Yes: Research that mainstreams sexual perversity does not serve the public good." Her strident lead paragraph begins: "Deep in America's heartland is the heart of one of history's biggest cover-ups. Hundreds, perhaps thousands, of sex crimes undoubtedly have been committed in the name of science, and yet a major state university continues to battle for the sake of protecting the name and the reputation of a callous, maniacal scientist who blithely collected data obtained as results from massive sexual experimentation on babies and children."

The Kinsey Institute was compelled to respond on its website ("Further Response to Allegations, 2003") to some specific allegations made by detractors, including these:

> *The act of encouraging pedophiles to rape innocent babies and toddlers in the names of "science" offends. The act of protecting them from prosecution offends. The act of falsifying research findings which, in turn, open the floodgates for the sexual abuse of children, offends. (from Dr. Laura's (Schlesinger) website)*

"This would be a cause of great concern if it were true. Kinsey was not a pedophile in any shape or form. He did not carry out experiments on children; he did not hire, collaborate, or persuade people to carry out experiments on children. He did not falsify research findings and there is absolutely no evidence that his research 'opened flood gates for the sexual abuse of children'. Kinsey did talk to thousands of people about their sex lives, and some of the behaviors that they disclosed, including abuse of children, were illegal. In fact, many sexual behaviors, even some between married adults, were illegal in the 1940's and 1950's. Without confidentiality, it would have been impossible to investigate the very private lives of Americans then, and even now."

Where did Kinsey's information about children's sexual responses come from?

"Kinsey clearly stated in his male volume the sources of information about children's sexual responses. The bulk of this information was obtained from adults recalling their own childhoods. Some was from parents who had observed their children, some from teachers who had observed children interacting or behaving sexually, and Kinsey stated that there were nine men who he had interviewed who had sexual experiences with children who had told him about how the children had responded and reacted."

Legacy of the Catholic Church's Sex Scandal

The political climate that encourages such anti-sex research crusades today is not helped by the media's obsession with the Catholic Church's sex scandal. Routinely, news accounts on the transgressing priests confuse pedophilia with other forms of sexual attraction, and even supposedly more objective studies fall into the trap of assuming that every cross-generational sexual attraction is abusive.

One nuanced study did emerge, however. In May 2011, researchers from the John Jay College of Criminal Justice at the City University of New York released a report, *The Causes and Context of Sexual Abuse of Minors by Catholic Priests in the United States, 1950–2010* (Terry et al., 2011). Although the 143-page study, submitted to the U.S. Conference of Catholic Bishops, uses the prevailing, loaded "abuse" terminology, its principal investigator, Karen Terry, found that only a small percentage of the cases involving priests could be called "pedophilia." Only 5 percent of the priests were "pedophiles" (sex with prepubescents), with the majority of the cases relating to sex with pubescent or adolescent boys. Shortly after the report was released, I interviewed her on the KUCI *Subversity* radio program.

I also interviewed, separately, but on the same 2011 program, a critic of the way such sex research is normally conducted, Bill Andriette, who has for decades fought as an activist to challenge the "abuse" categorization for consensual relationships across the age barrier.

Interview with Bill Andriette

My interview with Bill Andriette has been transcribed online, and it is worth quoting at some length here, because the issues discussed are pertinent.

BA: Well, I have to say that, listening to Karen, the phrase that comes to mind is "the banality of evil," and I mean that in a sense that most listeners wouldn't grasp on first hearing it. You know, listening to her talk about this whole phenomenon—it's so cold-blooded. She could be talking about, say, Jewish sex-fiends for an academic study in 1930s Germany; she could be talking about Black rapists in Georgia in the 1930s. She's just missing the whole human dimension here, the many layers, the many dimensions of what went on here, the many different kinds of phenomena. It's all hidden behind this thick, clouded rhetoric, these supposedly scientific terms of "offender" and "pedophile priest" and "abuse." But we never get to the human reality.

Certainly the priests are never allowed to speak in this, and the words of the victims have been filtered through what is a massive hysteria and a massive looting of the church. We're talking, like, two billion dollars that the U.S. church has handed out. When sums like that are involved, and when you're hitting raw cultural nerves, as you are inevitably with (quote unquote) "deviant sex," a term that appears in the report a lot, reality just gets warped. So there's no recognition of that. It's just sort of breathtaking that someone who could call herself a social scientist could be so clueless as to the context, so unaware of the broad view that you need to take when you are dealing with an issue that is very inflamed at a given time in a given society.

DT: I think she's taking the legal definition and considering everything abuse. She did concede that there could be some emotional attachment between a priest and an adolescent, but then she said that was wrong.

BA: Right, and after damning the report, let me say that I think also that it is a fascinating document and shows in some respects wisdom and nuance compared to what we hear typically in the media. Yet the sort of voice that is just not heard here at all, that can be heard ever so slightly elsewhere, is totally missing from the report...

DT: I think you bring up the issue that a lot of gay men had positive sexual relationships with older guys when they were growing up, but that testimony of that voice is totally obliterated in the media when they label all this type of interaction "abuse."

BA: Right. We're dealing with a whole range of phenomena, but we do know some things. We know that the kinds of activities that went on were typically very mild: they were touching, fondling; they were, as far as anyone can tell from the lugubrious descent into the empirical data that the folks at John Jay have treated us to, that they involved activities that were very often oriented toward pleasuring the younger partner. Now, was all of this consensual? Are there issues involved when priests make approaches to youngsters? Absolutely, it's a complex thing, but the question is: is this best handled through ordinary human smarts about what's appropriate, about how boundaries of what's appropriate change as people get to know each other, about overall affect? Is it best handled that way, or with a technical vocabulary which, in reading this report, I find immensely dehumanizing?

DT: But were you pleased that they did try to distinguish between the different terms, at least?

BA: Right, and they've gotten into a lot of trouble for that, or they've gotten a lot of criticism. I know that the *Boston Globe* had an editorial damning this report, the *Globe,* which has been behind a lot of the hysteria.

DT: Yeah, especially in the Boston cases.

BA: I think the John Jay report does some very interesting things. It is very nuanced. It tries to makes some distinctions that are completely lost in the media. It makes a big distinction between pedophilia, attraction to pre-adolescents, and hebephilia, attraction to adolescents. One trouble with this report is that it takes all these term that sound like they refer to absolute, clear, crystalline things, and it misses how fuzzy and hazy they are in relation to the actuality of people's erotic lives.

DT: It reminds me of studies in the 1950s or before that that looked at homosexuals as criminals. They were talking about all these deviant acts, but with the benefit of hindsight you see that they were actually human beings. So that's important to bear in mind.

BA: Right, and the other thing to bear in mind here is that the pedophilic and hebephilic interest, that is, adult male sexual attraction to children and adolescents is incredibly common. We know this from some scientific studies that have been done with community samples, that is, people not in prison, not in trouble for anything, completely normal people. In one study from 1995, 25% reported pedophilic interest or showed plethysmographic arousal—you know, that's when they strap a meter on the male's penis to judge his arousal when exposed to some sort of stimulus.

Another study, done in Czechoslovakia back in 1970, looked at 48 young Czech soldiers; all 48 showed penile response to adult females; 40 of the 48 did to adolescent females; and 28 of the 48 showed penile response to females aged 4 to 10, with penile responsivity to the last category, female children, intermediate to adolescent and adult females.

So we're dealing with feelings that are just basic to male sexuality. I mean, not every male has them, but a huge proportion of the people in the population do, and that's fodder for this sort of hysteria. It's long been known that people who crusade against homosexuals are much more likely to have some sort of homosexual feelings that they're struggling with themselves. So rather than use the tragedy of this abuse crisis as an opportunity to have a wise discussion of the fact of this desire and ask why it exists, in what forms can it be expressed, what role does this sort of desire have in ordinary adult male affection for children. You know, there's no question that young mothers have enormous erotic connections with their infants. Why can't we talk about the possible good ways in which these erotic feelings can feed, not into sexual acts, but into affection and attention?

DT: It seems that, because everything is considered abuse, there's no room for this other kind of observation or discussion.

Bill Andriette also noted in the interview: "You know, there's always been sort of an erotic dimension to adult interaction with young people.

I'm inclined to think that if something is that common, it's probably natural and we should not be so quick to condemn it. We should ask: what function does it serve? What function did it serve? How can we mobilize and contain these impulses today? Rather than demonizing the impulses, rather than demonizing people who show them."

Another recent study that provides a more nuanced and tolerant portrayal is Sarah Goode's *Understanding and Addressing Adult Sexual Attraction to Children* (2010). Her evolving position is reminiscent of the Christian ethos of hating the sin but loving the sinner. As she herself explains in her preface her message "in a nutshell" is this: "[A]dult sexual contact with children should be prevented but punishing an individual for his sexual attraction rather than his actual behavior is counterproductive; all of us adults need to behave in a much more mature and responsible way, so that all of our children can have happy childhoods, free from harm. Hating paedophiles seems easier, but doesn't keep children safe" (p. x). The irony is that Goode's book is published by Routledge, owned by Taylor & Francis, the corporate publishing giant that declined to put out a follow-up publication on intergenerational relationships after it acquired *Journal of Homosexuality* from Haworth Press. Some of those banned articles are now gathered in this very collection from Left Coast Press. The Haworth pederasty controversy (Durber, 2006) is covered as well elsewhere in this volume.

Sexual Movements Turn Mainstream

Before the recent mainstreaming of the social and sexual movements from the 1960s and beyond, there was a brief period of sexual freedom, when all sorts of sexualities were explored and celebrated (see for example, Tsang, 1981; the seminal Gayle Rubin essay, "Thinking Sex, " Rubin, 1984; Brogersma, 1986 and 1990; and Sandfort, Brongersma, & van Naerssen, 1990). As the politics of accommodation took over and as gay and lesbian leaders sought respectability in marriage recognition and mainstream acceptance, this flourishing of sexual liberation was blocked and new laws were enacted to further punish sexual contacts across the age barrier. Such voluntary, noncoercive sexual transgressions became more and more legally perilous and dangerous, to be treated by society only as abuse.

Options for the Future

What then are the options for scientific, empirically based research of the lived experience? First off, given the political constraints facing state and federal funding agencies, it will be some time before the authorities will fund any research of the type covered in this book. The only research that the authorities will permit will continue to be couched in the "abuse" rhetoric, but may become more nuanced as researchers encounter sexual situations—the lived experience—that go counter to their preconceived notions.

More optimistically, I suspect the move toward open access in terms of scholarly communication and the deposit of research materials in digital scholarly repositories—both for published articles as well as the associated research data—offers an opening for researchers with unconventional research interests to have their findings "published" in such scholarly open-access institutional and discipline-based repositories. Given constraints on federal funding, it is likely that only small studies be funded, hopefully to produce innovative or nuanced research findings. One area missing from much sex research is more granular ethnicity data so that smaller groups of ethnic minorities will show up in the findings, such as the many Asian ethnicities as well as those of multiple ethnic backgrounds. Liberating scholarly publishing from corporate control will likely also free up researchers to tackle more unconventional areas of interest.

That adolescents seek out adults for sexual contact is well covered in literature and nonfiction (see for example, Lotringer and Moffett, 1981, about a 15-year-old boy's quest for a man, as well as elsewhere in this volume). Additionally, films are frequently where such taboo topics are addressed, often sympathetically. The synopsis of the film, *Absent*, directed by Marco Berger, released in 2012 as a DVD from TLA Releasing (*Absent*, n.d.), begins as follows: "Knowingly, even aggressively sexual, 16-year-old Martin (newcomer Javier De Pietro) locks his seductive sights on Sebastian (Carlos Echevarria), his recently engaged, 30-something swimming instructor." Sex researchers need to lift their blinders and conduct more nuanced research that go beyond addressing issues of teen HIV and pregnancy and look at the diversity of sexual behaviors teenagers and adults engage in.

References

Absent (synopsis). n.d.. TLA Releasing. URL: http://tlareleasing.com/films/absent/ (Accessed April 29, 2013).

Andriette, B. (Interviewee). 2011. KUCI *Subversity Show,* Catholic priests and sex: The research, May 23. Interviewer: Daniel C. Tsang. Audio: http://kuci.org/~dtsang/subversity/Sv110523b.mp3 Transcript: Church abuse crisis John Jay report interview. URL: http://williamapercy.com/wiki/index.php?title=Church_abuse_crisis_John_Jay_report_interview (Accessed April 25, 2013].

Brongersma, E. 1986. *Loving boys,* Vol. 1. Elmhurst, NY: Global Academic Publishers.

_____. 1990. *Loving boys,* Vol. 2. Elmhurst, NY: Global Academic Publishers.

Bullough, V. L. 1994. *Science in the bedroom: A history of sex research.* New York: Basic Books.

CDC. 2012. Youth risk behavior surveillance—United States, 2011. *Mortality and Mortality Weekly Report, Surveillance Summaries,* 61/4, June 8. URL: http://www.cdc.gov/mmwr/pdf/ss/ss6104.pdf (Accessed April 28, 2013).

Copen, C. E., Chandra, A., & Martinez, G. 2012. Prevalence and timing of oral sex with opposite-sex partners among females and males aged 15–24 years: United States, 2007–2010. *National Health Statistics Reports 56,* August 16. URL: http://www.cdc.gov/nchs/data/nhsr/nhsr056.pdf (Accessed April 28, 2013).

Durber, D. 2006. Haworth's end to the pederasty debate. *Sexualities,* 9/4, October. URL: http://sex.sagepub.com/content/9/4/487.short (Accessed April 29, 2013).

Goode, S. D. 2010. *Understanding and addressing adult sexual attraction to children: A study of paedophiles in contemporary society.* London: Routledge.

Kinsey Institute. 2003. "Further Response to Allegations." URL: http://www.indiana.edu/~kinsey/about/contro-03.html (Accessed May 23, 2013).

Lotringer, S., & Moffett, M. 1981. Loving men. In D. Tsang (Ed.), *Age taboo: Gay male sexuality, power and consent* (pp. 14–24). Boston, MA: Alyson Publications.

Nelson, L. A. 2013. Money for military, not poli sci. *Inside Higher Education*, 21 March. URL: http://www.insidehighered.com/news/2013/03/21/senate-votes-defund-political-science-research-save-tuition-assistance-budget-bill (Accessed April 29, 2013).

Newman, B. R. 1998. Q: Should state funding of the Kinsey Institute's sexual research end? Yes: Research that mainstreams sexual perversity does not serve the public good. *Insight on the News*, March 30, Symposium, 24. (Accessed on Lexis Nexis Academic, April 25, 2013).

Reisman, J. A. 1998. *Kinsey: Crimes and consequences: The red queen and the grand scheme.* Arlington, VA: Institute for Media Education. (Third, revised, expanded edition in 2003, from Crestwood, KY: Institute for Media Education).

———. 2010. *Sexual sabotage: How one mad scientist unleashed a plague of corruption and contagion on America.* New York: Midpoint Trade Books, 2010

Reisman, J. A., et al. 1990. *Kinsey, sex and fraud: The indoctrination of a people: An investigation into the human sexuality research of Alfred C. Kinsey, Wardell B. Pomeroy, Clyde E. Martin and Paul H. Gebhard.* Lafayette, LA: Huntington House Publishers.

Rubin, G. 1984. Thinking sex: Notes for a radical theory of the politics of sexuality. In Carole S. Vance (Ed.), *Pleasure and danger* (pp. 267–319). Boston, MA: Routledge & Kegan Paul.

Sandfort, T., Brogersma, E., and van Naerssen, A. (Eds.). 1990. Male intergenerational intimacy: Historical, socio-psychological, and legal perspectives. *Journal of Homosexuality 20* 1–2. Also published as a monograph with the same title, in New York and London by Harrington Park Press, 1991.

Terry, K. (Interviewee). 2011. Catholic priests and sex: The research. KUCI *Subversity Show*, May 23. Interviewer: Daniel C. Tsang. Audio: http://kuci.org/~dtsang/subversity/Sv110523a.mp3

Terry, K. J., et al. 2011. *The causes and context of sexual abuse of minors by Catholic priests in the United States, 1950–2010.* Washington, DC: United States Conference of Catholic Bishops. URL: http://www.usccb.org/issues-and-action/child-and-youth-protection/upload/The-Causes-and-Context-of-Sexual-Abuse-of-Minors-by-Catholic-Priests-in-the-United-States-1950-2010.pdf (Accessed April 28, 2013).

Tsang, D. (Ed.). 1981. *The age taboo: Gay male sexuality, power and consent.* Boston, MA: Alyson Publications.

Introduction

Thomas K. Hubbard

The story of how this volume came into existence, despite corporate cowardice in the face of preemptive attacks by right-wing media and screwball special interest groups, is also an explanation of why the volume is necessary in an era when even the most restrained and balanced academic discussions are too often silenced by the demands of political correctness. The question of the sexually active "child," and particularly the child who is sexually active with an adult, stirs strong emotional reactions not only in the self-proclaimed champions of "family values," but even among many feminists, therapists, and social liberals who are sensitive to relationship structures of social inequality and power imbalance and aware of the very real harm that coercive or manipulative relationships can inflict upon young children. Ordinary parents, inflamed by media sensationalism, understandably cringe at the thought of their own children becoming too intimate with adults different from themselves.

Moreover, we live in a time when the definition of "child" is continually extended, covering sexually mature adolescents, college students dependent on parents' financial support, underemployed college graduates still living at home, and even young adults who are now covered by their parents' health insurance through the age of 26. The coincidence of extended "childhood" with a public culture saturated by images of youthful sexiness engenders a tangled web of troubling questions about the permeability of our socially constructed separation of *child* and *sex* as incompatible and mutually exclusive terms. To what extent should financial dependency on parental support shade over into parental control of a sexually mature young person's body and its most intimate acts? When does family "protection" become family tyranny? Is the exercise of such sexual control over children itself a form of incestuous domination? What are the special dynamics of this relationship as it may affect the "queer" (i.e., sexually nonconforming) child and his or her search for extra-familial role models?

These problematic family issues pale before the even broader social dilemmas. Do the simultaneous trends toward ever-lower ages of biological puberty (see Moller 1987) and ever-higher ages of legal consent to sexual activity (at least in North America) exacerbate problems of social maladjustment? Is the young person's individuation and emergence as an independent, responsible adult retarded by these bifurcating trends? How do these issues differ for male and female children? Do boys have a greater need for establishing early independence of parental control than girls? Is biological age really the best indicator of a child's level of maturity, sexual understanding, and decision-making capacity? Are children who willingly engage in sexual acts helped or harmed by a legal regime of severe punishment for childhood sexual experimentation and by therapeutic protocols or popular dogma that tell them they have been "victimized" and scarred for life? Does age- or class-difference in a relationship necessary entail a "power imbalance," or does youthful vigor and attractiveness give the less well-established partner a power of their own? Why do we legally sanction relations between an affluent 50-year-old and a needy 20-year-old, but punish those between a cash-poor 19-year-old and a 15-year-old, if all power imbalances are inherently exploitive? Are teenage boys necessarily more fragile and less resilient than young adults of both genders? How can legal regimes best balance the need of developing adolescents for bodily autonomy and the concerns of well-meaning parents for protection of the young? All of these are serious and difficult questions with major implications for public policy and family counseling. They need to be dealt with on the basis of scholarly research and sober discussion among professionals from various disciplines, not within the prisms of moral ideology and emotional intuition.

In recent times, scientific concern over child sexual abuse (CSA) began in the 1970s (see Rush 1974; Finkelhor 1979) and accelerated during the 1980s amid exaggerated reports in the popular media alleging widespread abuse of very young children in day care centers and satanic rituals. The public was also treated to a spate of reports that therapists and prosecutors had found widespread incestuous abuse of children by their own parents even in placid rural communities like Jordan County, Minnesota; adults in therapy were invited to produce "recovered memories" of childhood abuse by their own parents, leading to the destruction of many formerly intact family relationships (see Maran 2010, for a journalist's moving account of how her own family was destroyed by such iatrogenically induced false "memories"). The sexual revolution of the 1960s seemed to have spawned evil twins in the plagues of AIDS and CSA, which appeared to have become suddenly ubiquitous and terrifying in the eyes of a general public longing for a return to "normality" after two decades of sexual and social experimentation. Even though the transmission of AIDS eventually came to be better understood and effective therapies were developed, and the sensational media accounts of ritualized abuse, sexual torture in day care centers, and repressed memories were eventually debunked (albeit with far less media fanfare), the specter of dangerous sexuality violating childhood innocence continues to haunt the imagination in later decades with a new set of predators among sexually confused Catholic priests and attractive 20-something female teachers.

Amid the noise and multimedia tumult, a few quiet scholarly voices dared to pose inconvenient questions, beginning in the 1990s, once many of the most sensational claims about incidents of organized CSA had been exposed as frauds. James Kincaid, an English professor and Victorian specialist at the University of Southern California, sat through many days of testimony in the infamous McMartin Preschool case and was moved to inquire about the historical aetiology of popular conceptions of childhood sexual innocence that led so many adults who should have known better to believe the most fantastic scenarios of child abduction and torture, underground zoos, and elderly women playing the piano naked. Contrary to usual stereotypes, his study of Victorian child-rearing manuals (Kincaid 1992) showed that such a sentimentalized view of childhood was far from universal or even dominant among the Victorians. However, what began as a fringe viewpoint in the nineteenth century gradually inserted itself into mainstream opinion, owing to a variety of factors, at the very same time that unsentimental depictions of naked or semi-naked children became ubiquitous in advertising and popular media. In two books (Kincaid 1992, 1998), he explored this paradox, which he explained as a fetishization of childhood innocence: by elevating child purity to cult-like status, that purity itself became a focal point for repressed sexual desire, which always finds its way to transgression of the highest taboo as the most intense pleasure. For proposing such theories, Kincaid's first book was labeled "obscenity" by a member of the British House of Lords, who argued that its distribution within the UK should be banned (see Yuill, Chapter 3 in this volume).

Kincaid's work was followed by several other historically oriented studies that also demonstrated, based on different evidence sets, how "protection" of children from sexuality had its origins in paternalistic regimes for controlling children's sexuality. Odem (1995) and Alexander (1995) examined the ideological assumptions behind raising the "age of consent" and exploiting other vaguely worded moral laws in Progressive Era-America to regulate the newly found sexual freedom of young women, who became independent of parental control because of the increased economic independence offered by employment opportunities in a rapidly urbanizing nation. Jackson (2000), Robson (2001), and several of the essays in Rousseau (2007) further explored evolving attitudes toward childhood and legal regimes governing children's sexuality in Victorian and Edwardian England. In a book titled *Moral Panic: Changing Concepts of the Child Molester in Modern America,* Philip Jenkins (1998) critically surveyed the diachronic evolution of moral and legal responses from the 1890s to the 1990s. Political scientist Carolyn Cocca (2004) devoted a detailed study to the legislative updating of statutory rape laws during the 1970s and 1980s; she demonstrates that broad and sweeping changes in these laws, hatched in messy legislative compromises with little or no expert scientific input, inadvertently expanded them to regulate adolescent male sexuality in ways that the laws had never done before; Waites (2005) does much the same for the UK. Literary scholars (Ohi 2005, Stockton 2009) and art historians (such as Mavor 1995, Halpern 2006) have also expanded our consciousness of the erotic child and adult responses to it from artists, including Lewis Carroll and Norman Rockwell, both of whose works simultaneously construct and fetishize childhood innocence.

A second strand of critical inquiry that shows the influence of Kincaid's seminal insights is in the emerging field of "Queer Theory." The year 2004 saw the publication of two significant works: Steven Bruhm and Natasha Hurley's *Curiouser: On the Queerness of Children* (2004) collected several essays from scholars, including Kincaid, philosopher Richard Mohr, and feminist literary scholar Kathryn Bond Stockton (see now Stockton 2009), suggesting that our society constructs all childhood sexual feeling as "queer" and that our social construction of child sexuality as harmful is what in fact makes it harmful, rather than any essential qualities of harm. In the same year, the Australian social theorist Steven Angelides published an award-winning article in *GLQ*, the periodical that has come to define the discipline of Queer Theory, under the title "Feminism, Child Sexual Abuse, and the Erasure of Child Sexuality." Angelides (2004) complains that feminist victimological theory has effectively erased a long tradition of studying child sexual agency in its own right by positing as orthodoxy an overly simplistic binary axis of empowered adult vs. helpless child; coupling historical overview with powerful Foucauldian critique, he deconstructs this radical feminist rhetoric of power inequality by emphasizing that the most damaging abuse of power comes from well-intentioned adult efforts to control children's sexual knowledge rather than exploitation of their bodies for ends of adult pleasure.

Sex education and noneducation have long been a flash point of political conflict in America (for a history of the struggles, see Irvine 2002). In a book that gained some media attention (and attacks), *Harmful to Minors: The Perils of Protecting Children from Sex*, journalist Judith Levine (2002) condemns the essentially negative bias of American sex education, which she sees as consistent with the full range of evidence for our collective cultural denial of underage sex—draconian legislative and juridical regimes, sensationalistic media exploitation, and therapeutic/legal orthodoxy that sometimes labels children themselves as "sex offenders" (on which, see also Heller in this volume). Rather than teaching confused adolescents sex-positive attitudes geared to achieving mutual pleasure and respect, or providing teens with credible parameters for decision making, even the more liberal American sex-education curricula still frame adolescent sex as a problematic undertaking fraught with multiple risks to health, education, and livelihood. Others, of the "abstinence-only" variety, even prohibit discussion of prophylactic technologies except in terms of "failure rate." Inevitably, curricular decisions are driven by moral and ideological agendas rather than by sound public health policy, with the result that America continues to experience higher rates of teenage pregnancy and STDs than Japan and most EU nations (Singh & Darroch 2000; Panchaud, Singh, Feivelson, & Darroch 2000). Exposed to negative messages from parents and school, while also being bombarded with an outpouring of videos, music, and other popular media associating youth with sexual allure, teens understandably feel even more confused and conflicted about sex than they were already.

Just as American sex education arguably does more harm to teens than good, it has been argued that therapeutic responses to CSA often have the long-term effect of worsening the self-esteem of victims more than the initial impact of the events themselves. Such was the conclusion of Harvard research psychologist Susan Clancy (2009), who conducted in-depth interviews of nearly 200 CSA victims over several years. Contrary to her initial expectations, she found that most respondents who reported childhood sexual encounters with adults felt no trauma at the time the events occurred, when the sexual and social meaning of the acts performed was not yet clear to them. Rather, the harm stemmed from much later retrospective feelings of shame traceable to the victims' perception that they might have been too acquiescent or cooperative as children. This sense of shame and its attendant psychological maladjustments are exacerbated by the popular stereotype of CSA as a traumatic event that is supposed to create immediate fear and aversion in the victim; too many victims simply felt that because this model clearly did not apply to them, they were themselves abnormal and perhaps responsible for what happened. The real harm of CSA is thus in many cases iatrogenic, as victims find their own experiences out of synch with the prevailing social narratives engendered by outmoded clinical orthodoxies about children never cooperating with or enjoying their "abuse," even in the many cases when it occurs at the hands of a beloved family member or friend. Clancy indicts the clinical consensus on CSA for being profoundly out of touch with victims' own mixed feelings about what happened.

Also important is the book of Sarah Goode (2010), whose research project complemented Clancy's by interviewing adults who feel pedophilic attractions. Goode (2010, pp. 18–20) cites multiple clinical studies establishing that anywhere from 17 percent to 58 percent of "normal" adult men are capable of sexual arousal in response to prepubescent children of either sex; the number is likely even higher if one were to count arousal in response to adolescent children. In view of such numbers, Goode reasons that not all pedophiles can be classified as dangerous social "deviates," but must be recognized as ordinary humans. Because it is hardly practical to incarcerate such a large percentage of the male population, institutional responses are better directed toward providing support systems and networks to prevent the many adults who sometimes conceive such desires from acting in a manner that does harm to minor children.

Case studies of notable pedophiles who have attracted recent media attention, such as Penn State football coach Jerry Sandusky or the late entertainers Michael Jackson and Jimmy Savile, reveal a curious mixture of charitable generosity with predatory license. That they will be remembered primarily for the latter should not blind us to the reality of the former. Although all three unquestionably molested some children, it is easy to forget that their enthusiasm for kids benefited many as well. Rather than condemn them as one-dimensional monsters, we should attempt to learn from their human tragedies how easily noble instincts can become perverted into self-destructive obsessions. As Goode emphasizes, simple demonization is not a very effective therapeutic protocol; clinical psychologists and social workers should be encouraged to develop strategies for channeling or sublimating pedophilic tendencies into a more Platonic form of love.

Arguably the creative medium of film has over the last two decades explored adult-child relations and their consequences with greater sensitivity to individual nuance and detail than therapeutic orthodoxy. Mel Gibson's *Man Without a Face* (1993) humanizes an ex-teacher suspected of being a pedophile and portrays him as a successful mentor to a fatherless teenage boy. An actual suburban pedophile is portrayed sympathetically in *L.I.E.* (2001); *For a Lost Soldier* (1994) shows a brief affair between a 13-year-old Dutch boy and a Canadian soldier in the waning days of World War II as a formative life experience for the boy. *Notes on a Scandal* (2006) centers upon a married female schoolteacher seduced by one of her 15-year-old male students. Films such as Larry Clark's *Kids* (1995) or *Thirteen* (2002) debunk any illusions about the sexual innocence of young teens. Even child prostitutes are revealed as willing existential agents in films like the German *Street Kid* (1991) and the Danish *Pretty Boy* (1995). For other examples, see the work of Ohi (2000) and Davies (2007), as well as Goode (2010, pp. 92–93).

Amid this scholarly and artistic ferment taking place independently across different disciplines and media, a trio of young scholars sought in the mid-1990s to review all the quantitative studies they could find concerning the long-term effects of CSA, subjecting them to a rigorous statistical technique known as "meta-analysis," whereby variables are controlled to pool commensurable data from a much larger sample size than is commonly possible in individual surveys. They distrusted clinical samples of patients involved in some form of psychotherapy, because this population was statistically biased toward individuals with severe adjustment problems, whether because of CSA or some other causation. Instead, they preferred to use the many studies of college students (the most readily available group for academic researchers to survey), whom they regarded as more likely to be representative of the general population. They found that females rated early sexual experiences with an adult (or significantly older child) far more negatively than males and that most male respondents rated their sexual experiences as either neutral or positive, as long as no force or coercive abuse of authority was involved. However, the age of a child's first experience or the age of their abuser appeared to have little correlation with positive or negative outcomes. The detailed paper that emerged from their collaboration (Rind, Tromovitch, & Bauserman 1998) integrated the results of fifty-nine separate studies and appeared in *Psychological Bulletin,* the journal of the American Psychological Association and generally regarded as the most prestigious American serial in the field of academic psychology.

This result was discomfiting to some moral conservatives, who argued that these academics were excusing and even encouraging pedophilia. First, a local radio talk-show host in Philadephia, the home of two of the study's authors, and later a syndicated national radio personality, "Dr. Laura" Schlessinger, denounced the study's authors and questioned their motives. Stimulated by other right-wing organizations and media sources, including James Dobson's Focus on the Family, a member of the House leadership, Rep. Tom DeLay (R-TX), cosponsored a resolution condemning the study; on July 12, 1999, the House voted 355–0 to pass this resolution, with the Senate concurring by a 100–0 vote later that month. This is the first and only time in US history that the Congress has ever seen its role as passing judgment on the merits of a specific peer-reviewed scientific study.

The study was subsequently reviewed by the American Association for the Advancement of Science (publisher of the journal *Science*) and by a special issue of the *American Psychologist* (March 2002), both of which upheld the scientific validity of its approach and methodology (for a more complete review of these events, see Rind 2006). However, the study's lead author, Dr. Bruce Rind of Temple University, had not heard the last from the right-wing media and their allies within the therapeutic community (principally proponents of the long-discredited notion of recovered memory syndrome and the National Association for the Research and Therapy of Homosexuality [NARTH], a group founded by the psychoanalyst Dr. Charles Socarides, who believed his methods could cure patients of homosexual attraction). Dr. Rind had been invited to contribute a short essay to a special issue of the *Journal of Homosexuality,* slated to appear as Volume 49, Number 3-4 (2005), and copublished as a book under the title *Same-Sex Desire and Love in Greco-Roman Antiquity and in the Classical Tradition of the West.* The purpose of Rind's contribution was to propose that other social scientists like himself needed to understand pederasty as a social phenomenon within a broadly interdisciplinary context, including the study of historical cultures in which it was commonplace like Greece and Rome. The issue had been peer-reviewed, approved by the *Journal*'s regular editor, Prof. John DeCecco, himself a psychologist, and was about to go to press when the for-profit publisher of this and a number of other scholarly journals in the field of LGBTQ studies, Haworth Press, suddenly announced in late September 2005 that it was withdrawing the special issue and book because it had received numerous letters of complaint and even threats of cyber-attacks from irate members of the public.

The apparent source of this letter-writing campaign was two Web postings, both dated September 19, 2005: one was a story on NARTH's website titled "Haworth Press Publishes Book Promoting Pederasty" (http://www.narth.com/docs/pederasty.html), and the other was a news story published by *World Net Daily,* a Web-based news magazine closely affiliated with the Religious Right, with the even more inflammatory title, "New book promotes sex with children: Ph.D. 'expert' claims pederasty good for 'nurturing,' 'mentoring' young boys" (http://worldnetdaily.com/news/article.asp?ARTICLE_ID=46394). Neither the editors nor authors had been informed of the issue's cancellation until some of them began receiving telephone calls from various media outlets, including the *Chronicle of Higher Education.*

Some of the authors in that special issue, including Hubbard, and both of the editors (Verstraete and Provençal) began our own campaign of letter-writing and telephone calls to the publisher, pointing out to Haworth what a fundamental assault on academic freedom it was to allow fringe pressure-groups to intimidate presses into censoring peer-reviewed journal articles. Ultimately, the American Library Association wrote to the publisher to protest the censorship, and after considerable negotiation with the publisher's management, we obtained an agreement to proceed with the special issue as long as the Rind article, which was the chief focus of outside attacks, was omitted. As part of the agreement, Haworth promised to publish a longer and better documented version of Rind's article in a later special issue, where it would be accompanied by several essays in response from specialists in the various fields Rind touched on, including both scholars critical of and sympathetic to Rind's approach.

Rind's present essay and the others in this volume, as well as two others that had to be dropped, were to have constituted this second special issue, originally slated to go to publication in spring 2009. In this essay, Dr. Rind contextualizes his earlier analyses of psychological data through an aggressive interdisciplinary approach, showing that his earlier finding that male intergenerational relationships are usually not harmful is not as surprising or implausible as critics claim. The volume has also assembled an interdisciplinary group of scholars representing a range of different disciplines, including anthropology, sociology, criminology, clinical psychology, zoology, history, gay/queer studies, and communication studies, as well as a practicing criminal defense attorney. Each, from his or her special perspective, responds to Rind's essay: some are critical, some supportive, others mixed in their assessment of his argument. All agree, however, that the issues are significant and should be the object of engaged interdisciplinary dialogue, not fearful of censorship or political demagogy.

In 2007, Haworth sold its business to a large multinational publishing syndicate, Taylor and Francis, Inc. Some, although not all, of Haworth's employees went to work for the new owner, including employees who were aware of the earlier controversy and the ensuing agreement. After the editors of the second special issue (Verstraete and DeCecco, who was also the general editor of the *Journal of Homosexuality*) had collected and reviewed the essays, and Prof. DeCecco's editorial assistant formatted them and submitted them to the publisher's production department in the manner customary for all issues of the journal, the editors were suddenly notified by Ms. Kathryn Rutz, one of the former Haworth employees hired by Taylor and Francis, that Taylor and Francis did not feel bound by Haworth's agreement and did not wish to publish this special issue. No explanation was offered beyond the mere statement that the publisher had exercised its "judgment." Repeated inquiries yielded no further justification from the publisher.

Taylor and Francis's actions in overruling the judgment of a journal's general editor and his peer evaluators thus replicated the initial response of Haworth to the first special issue; so far as we have been able to determine, Taylor and Francis, like Haworth, never employed its own peer evaluators, but made the decision at the level of corporate management. Whereas Haworth had withdrawn the first special issue in response to angry letters inspired by sensationalistic and distorted accounts of the issue's contents in Internet media, Taylor and Francis appears to have canceled the second special issue mainly out of fear that such a letter-writing campaign might develop. Such preemptive corporate censorship out of anxiety about hypothetical (not yet actualized) threats from fringe sources like NARTH and the *World Net Daily* raises many disturbing questions about the commitment of for-profit academic publishers to upholding academic freedom on sensitive or controversial topics.

Accordingly, Hubbard, who at this point had been invited by Verstraete to join the editorial team, filed a formal protest of Taylor and Francis's actions to the Professional Matters Committee of the American Philological Association, which in turn sent a letter of inquiry about the matter to an executive of Taylor and Francis. After some correspondence back and forth, the APA's Vice President for Professional Matters wrote Taylor and Francis on January 15, 2010, to convey the finding that Taylor and Francis was in violation of the APA's Statement on Professional Ethics and to suggest that "the most suitable remedy" was for Taylor and Francis either to resume negotiations with the editors of the special issue or at least provide a detailed explanation of their reasons for declining to publish the special issue that had been promised as part of the resolution of the earlier dispute with Haworth. Taylor and Francis declined any response to the APA's admonition; after three months, the Professional Matters Committee referred the matter to the APA's Board of Directors to determine whether any type of sanctions were appropriate. After a final letter from one of the editors (Hubbard) to the President of Taylor and Francis's US Journals Division on May 21, 2010, describing the type of sanctions the APA might be asked to consider and the potential negative consequences for the publisher's business, Taylor and Francis offered to consider the project as a book submission, but still refused to publish it as a special issue of the *Journal of Homosexuality*. Doubting this publisher's sincerity and commitment to open discussion of sensitive issues, the editors of this volume decided to submit it to another publisher that seemed genuinely interested.

During the two years that our collection of papers was left hanging in limbo, Dr. Rind continued to revise and streamline his original anchor essay, cutting it to about one-half its original length. He observes that over the last three decades, age-discrepant sex with minors has increasingly been enveloped in moral panic, manifested in the passionate resistance to critical analysis of basic assumptions and claims concerning this type of sex. Based on a brief review of empirical, historical, cross-cultural, and cross-species data, he argues that beliefs that pederasty is injurious and pathological by nature are not scientifically sustainable; on the contrary, pederasty's social integration in numerous other cultures and commonness in nonhuman primates suggest non-pathological (e.g., evolutionary) origins. He emphasizes that his work neither advocates nor condemns pederasty, but describes and explains it—the proper stance for scientific analysis. The study concludes that advocates' efforts to promote pederasty are likely to fail, given that it so strongly misfits current social structures. Despite this misfit, he argues that more comprehensive and nuanced analysis of pederasty is needed to mitigate moral panic and ameliorate scientific neglect concerning this behavior.

The first essay of comment comes from Canadian psychologist Patrick O'Neill and literature professor Janice Best, who contextualize the attempts at suppression of Rind's work by studying similar censorship controversies. This historical view of censorship aims to show why it fails and, in fact, draws attention to what it would hide. Based on three other examples of recent attempts to suppress information or opinion in socially sensitive research, they conclude that censorship of "offensive" material limits the sort of debate that is essential for decision making in a democratic society.

In a related paper, Scottish sociologist Richard Yuill applies Foucauldian insights to explain how victimological CSA (child sexual abuse) perspectives have effectively colonized both experiential accounts of intergenerational sexualities and any critical research. Yuill examines the male "survivor" literature and contrasts it with two case studies from his own research, to highlight the current epistemological hierarchy governing narrative presentations of intergenerational sexualities. The paper then examines eight case studies of researchers on this topic who have faced a series of attacks from Christian fundamentalists, conservatives, CSA professionals, certain mainstream feminists, and the media. The paper concludes that the various strategies used to impose a monolithic victimological schema on child and intergenerational sexualities represent a concerted attempt to present CSA as an immutable sexual truth.

The next two papers take a more critical view of Rind's study. Clinical psychologists Richard McAnulty and Lester Wright fault Rind for ignoring clinical and forensic samples, but instead relying on other sources, such as autobiographies and unscientific surveys, to conclude that the practice of pederasty is not inherently harmful and may actually be beneficial to the younger males. By resorting to such unscientific sources, Rind is, in their view, guilty of the same kind of bias and ideology for which he denounces supporters of victimology.

Evolutionary biologist Eric Alcorn critiques Rind's survey of male–male age discrepant sexual relations (ADSR) in other animal species and his mentoring-enculturation evolutionary hypothesis, which maintains that ADSR in general, and pederasty in particular, evolved and were refined in humans to allow for the mentoring and enculturation of adolescent males into adult society. Alcorn finds that the mentoring-enculturation model fails to justify an evolutionary origin of pederasty, because there are fundamental errors concerning evolutionary theory in some of the model's assumptions: specifically, that natural selection selects for traits, that selection takes place at the group level, that selection pressure can influence the development of a phenotype, and that a pederasty gene or gene complex can be regulated by social norms. As well, Alcorn's review does not support the assumption that ADSR are a subtype of homosexuality and questions the non-contextual use of animal behavior data. However, Alcorn also concludes that the debate concerning ADSR has been hampered by dogmatic thinking; the role of science is to inform debate, and concerns about advocacy should not deter honest researchers from scientific inquiry.

The Dutch clergyman Donald Mader and gay studies scholar Gert Hekma add relevant historical evidence from late premodern and modern Europe to Rind's survey. They review evidence from legal documents, popular and elite visual culture, historical research, and ego documents to conclude that indeed age-structured relations have been a major, if not always the major, strand in male homosexuality in this period. They claim that the use of the term *child abuse* by anti-gay activists as a blanket designation for all such age-structured relations is anachronistic and unjustified. Although the potential for abuse exists in any human relationship, the historical and cultural record they examine also indicates that age-structured male homosexual relations have the potential to be experienced as consensual, enjoyable, and beneficial for both parties.

David F. Greenberg, a prominent sociologist and criminologist, critiques Rind's article on several fronts, with special emphasis on the social policy issues raised by Rind's theorizing about sexual relations between men and adolescents below the legal age of consent. He argues that an activity does not have to be universally harmful to be made illegal: the law has a responsibility to avert potential consequences of harm as well. He is unconvinced that the considerations raised by Rind can lead to substantive legislative reform, but he does advocate more thoughtful use of prosecutorial discretion in dealing with such cases and points to several areas where further research is needed.

The last two responses to Rind also examine the practical legal consequences of contemporary public policy with regard to child sexual abuse. Criminal attorney Andrew Heller documents numerous recent cases in which criminal justice authorities have charged teens and preteens with heinous crimes, including rape, for sexually experimenting with kids more-or-less their own age. The Sex Offender Registration and Notification Act (SORNA) forces children found guilty to register as lifelong sex offenders, wear electronic monitoring devices, live in remote places, and even undergo forms of aversion therapy deemed cruel and inhumane a half-century ago. In his view, neither politicians, psychologists, police officers, nor parents have raised the necessary cautions about the consequences of this change in legal regime and enforcement.

Similarly, classicist and queer historian Thomas Hubbard examines contemporary treatment of adult sex offenders as analogous to the ancient Roman concept of the *homo sacer*. His survey of legal developments and specific cases spotlights punitive trends, including life sentences, the death penalty, civil commitment up to life, lifetime registration, and onerous zoning restrictions regarding living arrangements. He argues that the force and effect of this regime of perpetual surveillance is to construct the sex offender as a special category of internal enemy that is subhuman and even anti-human, and whose crimes are defined not just by antisocial acts, but even by mere fantasies of transgression.

Finally, Dr. Rind adds a response to the essays responding to his own initial essay. He particularly focuses on the most critical essay, that of McAnulty and Wright.

It is the editors' hope that the long-delayed publication of this volume will help generate more scholarly and public interest in the dilemmas posed by our society's ambivalent construction of the sexual child, boys' sexuality, and the queer child. Dr. Rind, the editors, and various authors in this volume do not aim to advance any one point of view or solution, but we do all agree on the importance of academic freedom, interdisciplinary dialogue, and open discussion of politically or socially sensitive topics by qualified scholars and professionals, without the interference of morally driven ideology that would silence such discourse.

References

Alexander, R. (1995). *The "girl problem": Female sexual delinquency in New York, 1900–1930*. Ithaca, NY: Cornell University Press.

Angelides, S. (2004). Feminism, sexual abuse, and the erasure of child sexuality. *GLQ 10*, 141–177.
Bruhm, S., & Hurley, N. (Eds.). (2004). *Curiouser: On the queerness of children.* Minneapolis: University of Minnesota Press.
Clancy, S. A. (2009). *The trauma myth: The truth about the sexual abuse of children—and its aftermath.* New York: Basic Books.
Cocca, C. E. (2004). *Jailbait: The politics of statutory rape laws in the United States.* Albany: State University of New York Press.
Davies, J. (2007). Imagining intergenerationality: Representation and rhetoric in the pedophile movie. *GLQ, 13,* 369–385.
Finkelhor, D. (1979). *Sexually victimized children.* New York: Free Press.
Goode, S. (2010). *Understanding and adressing adult sexual attraction to children: A study of paedophiles in contemporary society.* London: Routledge.
Halpern, R. (2006). *Norman Rockwell: The underside of innocence.* Chicago, IL: University of Chicago Press.
Irvine, J. M. (2002). *Talk about sex: The battles over sex education in the United States.* Berkeley: University of California Press.
Jackson, L. A. (2000). *Child sexual abuse in Victorian England.* London: Routledge.
Jenkins, P. (1998). *Moral panic: Changing concepts of the child molester in modern America.* New Haven, CT: Yale University Press.
Kincaid, J. R. (1992). *Child-loving: The erotic child and Victorian culture.* London: Routledge.
_____. (1998). *Erotic innocence: The culture of child molesting.* Durham, NC: Duke University Press.
Levine, J. (2002). *Harmful to minors: The perils of protecting children from sex.* Minneapolis: University of Minnesota Press.
Maran, M. (2010). *My lie: A true story of false memory.* San Francisco, CA: Jossey-Bass.
Mavor, C. (1995). *Pleasures taken: Performances of sexuality and loss in Victorian photographs.* Durham, NC: Duke University Press.
Moller, H. (1987). The accelerated development of youth: Beard growth as a biological marker. *Comparative Studies in Society and History, 29,* 748–762.
Odem, M. E. (1995). *Delinquent daughters: Protecting and policing adolescent female sexuality in the United States, 1885–1920.* Chapel Hill: University of North Carolina Press.
Ohi, K. (2000). Molestation 101. *GLQ, 6,* 195–248.
_____. (2005). *Innocence and rapture: The erotic child in Pater, Wilde, James, and Nabokov.* Houndmills, UK: Palgrave-Macmillan.
Panchaud, C., Singh, S., Feivelson, D., & Darroch, J. E. (2000). Sexually transmitted diseases among adolescents in developed countries. *Family Planning Perspective, 32,* 24–32.
Rind, B. (2006). Meta-analysis, moral panic, congressional condemnation, and science: A personal journey. In D. Hantula (Ed.), *Advances in social and organizational psychology: A tribute to Ralph Rosnow* (pp. 163–193). Hillsdale, NJ: Erlbaum.
Rind, B., Tromovitch, P., & Bauserman, R. (1998). A meta-analytic examination of assumed properties of child sexual abuse using college samples. *Psychological Bulletin, 124,* 22–53.
Robson, C. (2001). *Men in Wonderland: The lost girlhood of the Victorian gentleman.* Princeton, NJ: Princeton University Press.
Rousseau, G. (Ed.). (2007). *Children and sexuality: From the Greeks to the Great War.* Houndmills, UK: Palgrave-Macmillan.
Rush, F. (1974). The sexual abuse of children. In N. Connell & C. Wilson (Eds.), *Rape: The first sourcebook for women* (pp. 65–75). New York: New American Library.
Singh, S., & Darroch, J. E. (2000). Adolescent pregnancy and childbearing: Levels and trends in developed countries. *Family Planning Perspectives, 32,* 14–23.
Stockton, K. B. (2009). *The queer child, or growing sideways in the Twentieth Century.* Durham, NC: Duke University Press.
Waites, M. (2005). *The age of consent: Young people, sexuality, and citizenship.* Houndmills, UK: Palgrave MacMillan.

Chapter 1

Pederasty: An Integration of Empirical, Historical, Sociological, Cross-Cultural, Cross-Species, and Evolutionary Evidence and Perspectives

Bruce Rind

Introduction

Pederasty, defined as sexual relations between men and adolescent boys, is severely condemned in our society. It is generally seen as just another type of child sexual abuse with equivalent effects. In particular, it is widely assumed to be a highly dysfunctional interaction between a youth and a man, intrinsically traumatizing and damaging for the former, and a reflection of severe pathology and dangerousness in the case of the latter. This thinking is strongly emotionally held and culturally entrenched, and to challenge it is to invite disbelief and attack. Yet, from a scholarly and scientific point of view, there is substantial basis for such challenge. In many other cultures across time and place, pederasty was viewed as functional, youths' successful development was attributed to the practice, and men's disposition for the behavior was considered normal and even noble. In our own society, substantial empirical evidence shows that positive response on the part of the youth does occur and is not uncommon. Finally, cross-species evidence suggests that pederasty has an evolved basis, because it is common in primates and a variety of subprimate species.

In 2005, in an invited article written for the *Journal of Homosexuality*, I provided a brief sketch discussing these points. The article was attacked by a right-wing website, whereupon the publisher quickly censored the article before it was put into print. But the censoring came, as well, from pressure exerted by left-leaning personnel connected with other scholarly or scientific journals, which the publisher also published. Attacks from like-thinking colleagues in my own department at the university followed, in which the article was described as "beyond the pale," even while "academic freedom" was reaffirmed as a sacred value. As anticensorship counterattacks by other scholars mounted, the publisher eventually agreed to publish a revised, more detailed article by me. When the article was completed in 2009, the new publisher of the *Journal of Homosexuality* refused to publish it, declining to say why, despite repeated requests, except to assert that its decision was one of "judgment," not censorship.

The politically charged atmosphere surrounding the censoring of these articles is a blot on the scientific enterprise and on scientific publishing. The articles were descriptive and explanatory, not prescriptive. They were scholarly, drawing upon widely diverse academic sources, including many articles in previous volumes of the *Journal of Homosexuality*. The current chapter was devised not merely to publish the suppressed evidence and conclusions, but to oppose censorship that stems from panic or political correctness. Such censorship corrupts any science topic it touches.

Caveats

The study presented in this chapter, as well as the previous two versions, deals with functional explanations for pederasty. This approach follows not only the evidence but previous scholarship, where such explanations have already been introduced. Offering functional explanations for pederasty can prompt people to write them off as advocacy for the behavior, rather than valid science. This is what happened in response to the first version of the current study. It is important to emphasize, however, that functional explanation falls in the domain of science, advocacy falls in the domain of politics, and the two are distinct and have no necessary connection. For example, Zeitzen (2008) reviewed polygamy from a cross-cultural perspective and documented that its frequent practice in many other cultures was functional under the circumstances of those cultures. Gat (2006) reviewed war from zoological, historical, anthropological, and evolutionary perspectives and concluded that, in humans, it has an evolved adaptive function. Neither author was advocating the behavior for our society, but each was offering a functional explanation for an age-old phenomenon to improve scientific understanding relative to earlier explanations that were inadequate, in part, because they were explicitly or implicitly tied to prevailing values and morals. The same applies to functional explanations for pederasty. It is an age-old phenomenon. Much evidence indicates that it has been functional within particular cultural settings, which suggests that function is an element of its nature. This conclusion takes us beyond moral discourse to improve our objective understanding of the behavior. But the conclusion is not an advocacy for the behavior in our society, whose cultural setting is very different.

To clarify these points further, it is useful to consider three fallacies discussed by Cardoso and Werner (2004). The *naturalist fallacy* is showing that a behavior occurs in other species and concluding that it is, therefore, moral for humans. The *relativistic fallacy* cites a behavior's occurrence in other cultures as morally acceptable and then concludes that it, therefore, should be moral in ours. The *moralistic fallacy* is the reverse of the naturalistic fallacy in that it derives what "is" from what "ought to be," but frequently in contradiction to what actually *is*. Accordingly, it would be fallacious to show that pederasty is commonplace in other species and other cultures and to conclude that it should be seen as moral in our society (naturalistic and relativistic fallacies). On the other hand, it is no less fallacious to begin with the fact that pederasty is seen as immoral in our society and then to read into it all sorts of pathologies that may well not be objectively true (moralistic fallacy).

For practical purposes, our society is currently so vehemently opposed to pederasty that there is little chance that it could be influenced into changing its attitudes, values, or practices regarding this behavior by arguments committing the naturalistic or relativistic fallacies. On the other hand, the moralistic fallacy is a serious problem, because it has had a dominating, biasing impact on scientific understanding of pederasty (as discussed later), which is an important rationale for this study.

Methodology

How do we judge *scientifically* whether a particular class of sexual behaviors is normal or abnormal, healthy or pathological? In our society several centuries ago, this task was assigned to clerics, but with the advance of medicine, clinicians became the designated authorities. As Foucault (1978) and Szasz (1990) noted, however, when the clinician replaced the cleric in this role, he merely substituted sickness for sin and did little or nothing to bring science into the classifications. Similarly, Kinsey, Pomeroy, and Martin (1948), writing decades earlier, complained that clinicians' classification of normal and abnormal sexual behavior, still in the mid-twentieth century, too often was "little more than a rationalization of the mores masquerading under the guise of objective science" (p. 203). They sharply criticized clinicians for drawing upon morals coupled with anomalous clinical and legal case studies to deduce what constituted abnormal sexual behavior across the human species.

Kinsey et al.'s (1948) remedy was to expand the database with large numbers of individuals from widely divergent segments of the general population, individuals who did not have problems by definition, as clinical patients do. Ford and Beach (1951) then argued that the scope needed even further broadening because culture so profoundly affects sexual behavior. To determine whether a pattern obtained for a particular type of sexual behavior, they conducted an extensive cross-cultural review. To determine whether observed human sexual behavior patterns were reinvented from one culture to the next or had deeper biological roots, they argued for and then conducted an extensive cross-species analysis. Bullough (1976) added that historical analysis is also essential, because it can help correct for the all-too-common bias in both lay persons and professionals of assuming that dominant sexual behavior patterns in present-day society, as well as personal preferences, are not only natural but inevitable whereas other variations are abnormal, when historical perspective may show otherwise.

The broader perspectives and approaches of Kinsey et al. (1948), Ford and Beach (1951), and Bullough (1976) contradicted clinical theorizing on abnormal sexual behavior in many areas (e.g., masturbation, homosexuality, sexual behavior among immature individuals). The broad perspective is more compatible with valid science, because it directly deals with issues of external validity (i.e., generalizability) and improves internal validity (i.e., causation) by taking into account multiple relevant factors that can influence sexual behavior patterns. Additionally, the broad perspective understands that morals are culturally constructed[1] and therefore does not conflate morality with normalcy, as the narrow clinical approach too often has done (Foucault, 1978; Szasz, 1990).

To illustrate the shortcomings of the clinical approach, consider the case of homosexuality. Half a century ago, both lay persons and professionals generally reacted to homosexual behavior in adulthood with "disgust, anger, and hostility" (Hooker, 1957, p. 18), reactions deeply rooted in antihomosexual sentiments indoctrinated through centuries of Christian moral teachings (Crompton, 2003). The mainstream clinical view was that this behavior represented a "severe emotional disorder," which clinicians claimed to have verified through examinations of homosexuals obtained almost entirely from clinical, forensic, and prison settings (Hooker, 1957, p. 18). As Kinsey et al. (1948) did, Hooker argued for the need to study homosexuals outside these settings, where they were not maladjusted by definition. She recruited a convenience sample of homosexuals who had not had clinical or legal dealings, along with a matched sample of heterosexuals, and administered to them a battery of tests of psychological adjustment. She found that her homosexual subjects were as well adjusted as her heterosexual controls. She acknowledged straightforwardly that her homosexual sample was highly selected, but noted that this posed no problem, because her goal was to test the repeated claim of clinicians that *all* homosexuals were maladjusted. Citing Ford and Beach's (1951) cross-cultural and cross-species survey, she speculated that homosexuality may be a sexual deviation that is "within the normal range" (p. 30), and she criticized clinicians for being unable to consider or accept this possibility.

Notably, Hooker's thesis came to be more and more supported, and clinicians' pronouncements of pathology more and more discredited, as research on homosexual behavior greatly expanded after gay liberation four decades ago. This research came from nonclinical empirical, sociological, historical, cross-cultural, cross-species, and evolutionary perspectives, and its emergence was enabled by the new cultural attitude that researchers were no longer expected or obligated to verify pathology regarding homosexual behavior and to support the intervention engine of the state. That is, researchers were freed from reliance on clinical-forensic samples, where conclusions of pathology were preordained. Some of the more significant examples of this research include Dover's (1978) study of ancient Greek homosexuality, Bell, Weinberg, and Hammersmith's

(1981) large-scale nonclinical empirical study critically assessing a multitude of causal explanations for homosexuality, Herdt's (1984) survey of ritualized homosexuality in Melanesia, Greenberg's (1988) historical, anthropological, and sociological review of homosexuality, Bagemihl's (1999) zoological review of homosexual behavior in hundreds of species of mammals and birds, Crompton's (2003) historical review of homosexual behavior in high civilizations, and Sommer and Vasey's (2006) collection of zoological studies accompanied by evolutionary analyses.

The studies and reviews by Hooker (1957), Kinsey et al. (1948), Ford and Beach (1951), and Bullough (1976), as well as the multitude of post–gay liberation research just discussed, offer several important lessons for examining any form of sexual behavior, even and especially those disapproved of today. First, it is erroneous to extrapolate from clinical samples to the general population (i.e., the *clinical fallacy*). Second, when a form of sexual behavior is shrouded in disgust stemming from moral disapproval, before assuming that disgust is a primary reaction, that the behavior is a primary pathology, and that negative correlates associated with the behavior constitute primary damage, it is important to examine other cultures with different sexual moralities and practices. Third, the broader the perspective and the empirical database are, the better the scientific judgment will be regarding the pathological or non-pathological nature of a particular sexual behavior pattern. Fourth, understanding human sexual behavior patterns can be improved through cross-species comparisons, especially with primates, particularly when there is continuity or overlap in these patterns.[2] And fifth, the last point leads directly to evolutionary considerations in examining dysfunction, function, or neutrality in particular types of sexual behavior (cf. Wakefield, 1992).

Finally, it is important to emphasize that, in light of cross-cultural research on male homosexuality in societies tolerating or encouraging this behavior, and in view of the radically changed environment of widespread tolerance in our society today regarding this behavior, in which homosexual persons are often normal in adjustment or untroubled by their sexuality, it becomes clear that homosexual patients' difficulties with their sexuality in the past were not the primary effects of their homosexuality but interaction effects with a culture that severely stigmatized and disadvantaged them. For currently disapproved sexualities, it is important to take into account and distinguish between primary and interaction negative effects.

The "Harmful Dysfunction Approach" to Mental Disorder

In addition to the preceding discussion regarding the evaluation of sexual pathology, another approach, which is relevant to the fifth point previously mentioned on evolutionary considerations, and which will be useful for the current study, is that developed by Wakefield (1992, 1999, 2007). Wakefield has significantly sharpened conceptual approaches to understanding abnormal behavior and mental disorders, including those of a sexual nature, by adding an evolutionary psychological framework. He argues that the "pure values approach" to disorder, which has dominated the mental health field and which holds that behaviors at odds with important norms and morals are disordered, is flawed, because if valid, then runaway slaves in the antebellum South really did suffer from drapetomania,[3] and Soviet political dissidents really were in need of confinement and treatment, because these persons violated the dominant values of their society.

Wakefield noted that natural selection has produced many physical mechanisms that perform needed functions for the body. When a physical mechanism breaks down and can no longer perform its function, it is called a *dysfunction* and may be harmful to the individual. When a dysfunction is harmful, it is called a *disorder*. Drawing upon evolutionary psychology, he noted that the same applies to mental mechanisms. Natural selection has also produced many mental mechanisms, designed to perform particular functions, and they become dysfunctions when they break down, which can be harmful to the individual. When a mental mechanism does break down, causing harm to the individual, it is a *harmful dysfunction*, which properly defines the concept of *mental disorder*, he argued.

What constitutes harm is a value judgment in a particular society, Wakefield argued. His definition of mental disorder is a hybrid, consisting of an objective component (i.e., is it a dysfunction?) and a value component (i.e., is it harmful?). Importantly, mechanisms were naturally selected in distantly past environments, referred to as the environments of evolutionary adaptedness, to serve functions useful in those environments. In a novel environment, a mechanism that is still performing its designed function may actually be harmful rather than helpful to the individual. A moth's white-color-producing mechanism may be functioning as designed, but if the moth finds itself in a changed, black-sooted environment, this healthy functioning mechanism may well be harmful for the moth, because it will be more likely to be preyed upon. The mechanism has become mismatched with the current environment, and so is an *evolutionary mismatch*. As Wakefield emphasized, an evolutionary mismatch is not a disorder, because it is functioning as designed. The individual is not disordered, just "unlucky," he argued.

For present purposes, sexual desires or behaviors that were naturally selected in distantly past environments to perform useful functions in those environments, but which are mismatched with the current environment, in which they are judged immoral or criminal because of values peculiar to this environment, are not objective disorders. If they cause harm for the individuals or their partners, they are of social and professional concern, but they are not pathologies or sexual disorders, because they are not dysfunctions; they are functioning as designed, but in an incompatible environment.

Plan for the Current Review on Pederasty

Because the goal of this chapter is to study pederasty scientifically, the foregoing points will structure the approach to follow. First, it is important to discuss the relevant clinical data. The clinical reports that have come out over the last three decades presenting cases of men who reacted negatively to or were traumatized by boyhood sexual events with older males, and felt or were judged to have been damaged long term as a result, are taken here as no more than suggestions for what may obtain in the general population, rather than as evidence for what actually does occur throughout this population. As discussed previously, unsupported extrapolation from clinical case studies to the entire population constitutes the clinical fallacy. When homosexual patients half a century ago evidenced disturbance over their sexuality, was this a primary reaction independent of other factors or secondary in nature, such as: (a) a response to intense social hostility and discrimination, (b) an internalized, harm-producing belief about being diseased as a result of dominant social views (i.e., nocebo reaction), or (c) the same kind of belief, but clinically rather than socially induced (i.e., iatrogenic harm)? The same questions can be raised in clinical cases of pederasty, which has been highly problematized in our society, especially since the rise of sexual victimology in the 1970s, which successfully instated among the lay public and professionals alike strong expectations that all instances of adult-minor sex are highly injurious, setting up the conditions for problems such as nocebo reactions and iatrogenic harm. In short, recent clinical reports of negative effects of pederasty are not probative with respect to the effects in the general male population. Hence, what is needed is an examination of nonclinical samples, which forms the first part of this review.

Previously in discussing homosexuality, some of the more significant examples of historical, sociological, anthropological, zoological, and evolutionary approaches to understanding it were mentioned (i.e., Bagemihl, 1999; Crompton, 2003; Dover, 1978; Greenberg, 1988; Herdt, 1984; Sommer & Vasey, 2006). Most, if not all, of these works were undertaken to understand *homosexuality*—that is, understood to mean the gay pattern in the modern West. But in each of these works, pederasty or pederastic-like behavior was prominent or even predominant (which is the general rule in such research). Given this copious source of relevant, broad-based evidence, along with the general guidelines discussed previously emphasizing the importance of using such evidence for assessing sexual behavior, the current study will examine evidence from each of these broader disciplines after the nonclinical empirical review.

Definitions

Before proceeding, it is important to establish a precise working definition of pederasty. Although popular definitions have tended to define pederasty as "unnatural" anal intercourse, generally between a man and a boy of any age (e.g., *The Compact Edition of the Oxford English Dictionary*, 1971; *West's Encyclopedia of American Law*, 2008), scholarly sources have tended to define it as an erotic relationship between a man and an adolescent boy, regardless of whether actual sex occurs, taking into account nonsexual interpersonal and cultural aspects in addition to the erotic elements. Examples of such definitions include sexual relations of some duration between men aged 18 or more and boys from puberty through age 15 (Tindall, 1978), the erotic attraction of men aged 18 and over to boys from puberty to age 16 (Rossman, 1976), an erotic relationship between an adult male and a boy, generally between ages 12 and 17 (Bullough, 2004), the love between a man and youth 12 to 18 years of age (Thorstad, 1998), and age-graded homosexual relations with younger partners not fully mature, most commonly from puberty up to age 18, but sometimes somewhat younger or older (Menasco, 2000). In these definitions, the beginning and ending ages of the boys differ somewhat, as do the criteria for the involvement (e.g., attraction, sexual contact, love). But the definitions have in common adolescence (both emerging and unfolding) as a focal point for the interests and behaviors. For this reason, they essentially conform, whereas popular definitions do not, to the original meaning and usage of the term in ancient Greece, where *paiderastia* literally meant "boy love," from *pais* (boy) and *eros* (love, of a sexual nature). Greek pederasty involved a relationship that, though with *eros* at its core, went far beyond sex and was not tied to any particular sex act (Fone, 2000), and which involved boys generally from ages 12 to 17 (Lear & Cantarella, 2008).

In the present study, the definition of pederasty is based not just on the ancient Greek tradition and scholarly usage, but on the broader historical and cross-cultural record, as well as newer, improved understandings of puberty. Among the numerous societies to be reviewed later in this study, in which these relations were commonplace, data regarding typical beginning and ending ages of the boys involved were averaged, producing means of 10.72 and 16.35, and medians of 12 and 17, respectively.[4] These empirical findings support using the age range of 12 to 17 in the definition of pederasty, but suggest allowing for some variability at the extremes, especially the lower end. Regarding the lower boundary, the designation of the onset of puberty (i.e., appearance of pubic hair in boys) has been used in definitions of pederasty (e.g., Rossman, 1976; Tindall, 1978), but is problematic in view of research evidence showing that puberty is not a sudden event but a continuous process preceding the appearance of secondary sex characteristics by several years, during which sexual maturation (e.g., emergence of sexual attractions) under the influence of increased hormones is already occurring (Herdt & Boxer, 1993; McClintock & Herdt, 1996). Consequently, in the present study, pederasty is defined as erotic attractions, behaviors, or relationships involving older males and boys or youths in their second decade of life, mainly from 12 to 17 (cf. Bullough, 2004), but up to two years below and above this range (cf. Menasco, 2000).

What is important in this definition of pederasty is its central focus on emerging and unfolding adolescence in males, which distinguishes it from pedophilia, which centers on attractions to prepubescent persons, who can be either male or female, and which tends to end abruptly with the visible onset of adolescence.

Empirical Review

Finkelhor (1979) discussed two camps of professionals as of the late 1970s, with very different views on the effects of adult-minor sex. The first camp, consisting of researchers tending to infer from nonclinical cases and data (e.g., Kinsey et al., 1953), believed that such contacts are generally "innocuous" or only a "minor hazard" (p. 29). The second camp, consisting of therapists inferring from the severe consequences of the rape of women (e.g., Burgess & Holmstrom, 1974) or the fact that incest was in the background of so many of their patients (e.g., Herman & Hirschman, 1977), believed adult-minor sex causes trauma and leaves permanent scars. Though Finkelhor sided ideologically with the latter camp—he was one of the chief architects of sexual victimology—he discussed weaknesses in their inferences. Because of this, he remained agnostic on the issue, remarking that "Many comments have been and will be made about this controversy before it is settled" (p. 32). Contrary to this forecast predicting protracted scholarly debate, the issue was virtually settled by 1981 or so, when nearly the whole field came to side with the therapists. As Jenkins (1998) later observed, this shift in beliefs came about because of politics, not science; it occurred virtually overnight, far too quickly for the proper research to have been done. The idea of minors being seriously psychologically injured from sex with men is something that resonated with the times because of the new gender politics of the day (Angelides, 2004, 2005; Nathan & Snedeker, 1995).

The new belief of pervasive and intense harm from sex between men and their prepubescent daughters was soon generalized to sex between men and unrelated pubescent girls, and then to sex between men and both prepubescent and pubescent boys. Eventually the belief extended to sex between women and boys. Soon after the new belief was culturally instated in the early 1980s, moral panics broke out in more than one hundred day care centers across the United States, where staff were accused of satanic ritual and sexual abuse, and in the "recovered memories" of thousands of adult patients in psychotherapy, who believed they had just remembered long-repressed episodes of incestuous abuse in their childhood (Jenkins, 1998; Nathan & Snedeker, 1995). What is significant here is that these sensationalistic cases, later to be discredited during the 1990s, convinced a whole society of the extreme, inevitable harm of all forms of adult-minor sex, a belief that stayed intact after the discrediting of these particular cases and which continues to the present day.

For present purposes, the goal is to examine whether the pederastic form reliably has these assumed effects. But because sexual victimology has succeeded in convincing society that even sexual relations between adolescent boys and women are psychologically destructive, it will be instructive to start there to test the general theory of sexual victimology. Are sexual relations between adolescent boys and women comparable to the rape and incest involving female victims just cited, which formed the basis for the general theory? Are these youths generally unwilling, coerced, and otherwise overpowered, and do they generally react traumatically at the time and suffer negative long-terms effects? The review that follows addresses these questions.

Boy-Women Sex: An Initial Test of Sexual Victimological Theory

For this analysis, nonclinical studies were sought that reported men's remembrances of their reactions to boyhood sexual encounters with women, as well as their perceptions of the effects of these encounters and their willingness to participate. Many studies to date have reported on boys' reactions to sex with adults, but few have separately reported responses by gender of the older participant. Table I presents a summary of nine studies where men's boyhood reactions, self-reported effects, or perceived consent specifically to sexual episodes with women could be extracted.

Based on $n = 325$ cases or experiences in the nine studies, for which reaction data were provided, boys' reactions to sexual episodes with women were most often positive (62%) and only occasionally negative (14%). Based on $n = 279$ cases or experiences, only a small minority (19%) felt harmed in some way by the episodes, whereas twice as many men felt benefited (41%). Based on $n = 357$ cases or experiences where relevant data were provided, boys' level of willingness or consent was quite high (87%), with only 13 percent reporting lack of consent.

Not displayed in the table, the studies also revealed the following. The sexual episodes often involved oral sex and vaginal intercourse, rather than superficial interactions. In general, experiences were less positive when the boys were prepubescent, but tended to be more positive and consenting as the boys were beginning adolescence (e.g., Coxell et al., 1999; Okami, 1991; Woods & Dean, 1984). Furthermore, the longer the duration, the greater the frequency, and the more intense the nature of the sexual contacts (e.g., intercourse as opposed to fondling), the more positive the boys' reactions tended to be (e.g., Okami, 1991; West & Woodhouse, 1993). Finally, men with consenting sexual relations as boys with women were as well adjusted as controls in measures of adult psychological functioning (Coxell et al., 1999; Fromuth & Burkhart, 1987, 1989; Okami, 1991; Sandfort, 1988, 1992).

Table 1: Reactions, Self-Reported Effects, and Consent in Sexual Relations Between Boys and Women.

Study	Sample	Country	Ages of Boys	n	Reaction (%) pos	Reaction (%) neut	Reaction (%) neg	Effect (%) pos	Effect (%) neut	Effect (%) neg	Consent (%) yes	Consent (%) no
Condy et al. (1987)	college, prison	US	mean, first contact = 12.5	144	65	22	14	43	36	21	88	12
Coxell et al. (1999)	general medical practice	GB	mean, first contact = 11 (non-consent), 14 (consent)	195							87	13
Fishman (1991)	college	US	<13 (60%), 13–16 (40%)	13	46	54	0	n/a	n/a	0		
Fromuth & Burkhart (1987)	college	US	<13 (62%), 13–16 (38%)	76	55	32	13	39	46	15	82	18
Nelson & Oliver (1998)	college	US	<14 (54%), 14–15 (45%)	11								
Okami (1991)	convenience	US	mean = 11.2 (pos cases), 9.7 (neg cases)	17	82	12	0					
Sandfort (1988, 1992)	community, convenience	NL	first contact: <12 (37%); 13-15 (63%)	7							86	14
West & Woodhouse (1993)	college	GB	<10 (39%), 11–15 (69%)	29	83	8	8					
Woods & Dean (1984)	convenience	US	mean = 11.4 (5 to 16)	46	50	20	30	38	38	24		
Totals/Means				**538**	**62**	**24**	**14**	**41**	**39**	**19**	**87**	**13**

Note. US = United States, GB = Great Britain, NL = The Netherlands. Pos = positive, neut = neutral, neg = negative. Sample size (n) is either number of persons or experiences. "n/a" indicates data not available. In bottom row, total N is given, followed by weighted mean percents for reactions, effects, and consent (i.e., weighted by sample size). Conservative estimates were made for positive and neutral reactions in Fromuth and Burkhart (1987) and neutral and negative reactions in West and Woodhouse (1993). Ages of boys refer to the whole set of experiences, which could include boy-woman and boy-man sex in some studies. Total Ns = 325 for reactions, 279 for effects, and 357 for consent.

Reinforcing these findings are the results from a recent analysis of the Kinsey data, in which males' reactions to first coitus after reaching puberty—often an especially significant life event—were assessed (Rind & Welter, 2012). Reactions to first coitus were very positive just as often when it occurred as an adolescent (10 to 17) with an adult woman (*n* = 548; 41%) as when it occurred as an adult (18 or over) with an adult woman (*n* = 2,546, 41%). The highest rate of positive reactions among all groups was among younger adolescent boys aged 10 to 14 with adult women (*n* = 116, 63%).[5]

The foregoing results dramatically contradict sexual victimological theory, specifically its strongly held assumptions that all minors are overpowered and traumatized by sex with much older persons. Notably, sexual victimologists have responded by arguing that boys who view their relations as consenting and positive have been deceptively indoctrinated and manipulated (see Rind et al., 2001, for discussion), implying that the natural, innate response *is* one of feeling exploited and traumatized. However, if we turn to nature (i.e., other species closely related to humans), we do not find evidence that such response is innate. In humans' closest relatives, bonobos and chimps, juvenile males frequently and preferentially solicit adult females and attempt to copulate with them. In most cases, they show sexual arousal with erections. Adult females are usually tolerant and even cooperative, but when they are not, the juvenile males frequently protest with whimpering or tantrums (Bagemihl, 1999; Hashimoto, 1997; Kano, 1980; Kollar, Beckwith, & Edgerton, 1968). Similar patterns have been observed in many other primate species (Bagemihl, 1999). Anderson and Bielert (1990) noted that "Among nonhuman primates ... sexual interaction between adult females and immature males is universal" (p. 192). It may be that primate patterns do not extend to humans, but the similarity of the observed human and primate patterns in juvenile male-adult female sex suggests a phylogenetic continuum (cf. Ford & Beach, 1951). The data are completely inconsistent with sexual victimological assumptions of innate exploitation and trauma.

In short, the above empirical results contradict the broad sweep of sexual victimological theory to such an extent as to expose the theory as ideological and scientifically defective, points that have been made conceptually by various critics (e.g., Angelides, 2004, 2005; Jenkins, 1998; Nathan & Snedeker, 1995). These results demonstrate that boys, especially in adolescence, are not *in essence* the sexually fragile beings that the sexual victimological models based on rape and incest involving females have been used to suggest. These findings do not imply the same for pederasty, the chief interest here, but they conceptually pave the way for a consideration of pederasty conducted without being tied down by the ideological assumptions of sexual victimology, which dominate current popular and professional views of pederasty.

Gay Boy-Man Sex: An Initial Examination of Pederastic Correlates

Despite sexual victimological influence, popular writers have long recognized that adolescent boys can be erotically drawn to adult women and often are not simply "passive victims" when sexual interactions occur (e.g., Heffernan, 2004; Hoffman, 1994; Macklin, 1997; Zernicke, 2005). But many gay writers have voiced the same idea with respect to gay adolescent boys' attractions to and relations with adult men (e.g., Kramer, 1981; Schulman, 2007; Tuller, 2002). Empirically speaking, is the gay boy-man dyad a good analog of the heterosexual boy-woman dyad? To examine this question, and as a first attempt to empirically evaluate beliefs that pederastic interactions are innately toxic, nonclinical studies were gathered that presented reaction and related data on gay and bisexual boys' sexual experiences with older males. Table II summarizes the eight studies obtained.

Like their heterosexual counterparts reviewed in Table I, these sexual relations were often of an intensive nature, frequently involving some type of penetration (oral or anal). Mean positive, neutral or mixed, and negative reactions were, respectively, 56 percent, 19 percent, and 27 percent.[6] Reactions were most positive in the national recruitment studies, where volunteers provided details about their gay experiences, including boyhood sexual encounters, the Brazilian study, notable for being the only non-Anglophone and developing-nation study in this set, and in the Rind (2001) study, which summarized data obtained from Savin-Williams (1997) on middle- and upper-middle-class gay and bisexual men who had their sexual contacts with men between ages 12 and 17, where incest and use of force were absent.[7] Reactions were most negative in the one quasi-clinical study involving lower socioeconomic subjects, who most often had their age-gap sexual experiences before age 12, which often involved incest or force (Doll et al., 1992). Two of the studies contrasted non-abusive and abusive boyhood sexual experiences with older males—based on self-perceptions or definitional criteria—and found that boys having non-abusive experiences were older on average (Ms = 10 and 11.6) than boys having abusive experiences (M = 8) (Dolezal & Carballo-Diéguez, 2002; Stanley et al., 2004).

In terms of psychological adjustment, men categorized as having had non-abusive sexual experiences with older males were as well adjusted as controls, whereas those categorized as having had abusive relations were slightly less well adjusted (Dolezal & Carballo-Diéguez, 2002; Stanley et al., 2004). The Rind (2001) study found that gay/bisexual men with boyhood pederastic experiences were as well adjusted as controls on some measures and better on others. Recently, Arreola et al. (2008) replicated this result in a multi-city community sample study of gay and bisexual men regarding consenting homosexual sex (peer and age-gap) under age 18—subjects not consenting to these contacts were slightly less well

Table II: Reactions in Sexual Relations Between Gay or Bisexual Boys and Older Males.

Study	Sample	Country	Ages of Boys	n	Reaction (%) pos	Reaction (%) neut, mixed	Reaction (%) neg	Study features
Carballo-Diéguez, Balan, Dolezal, & Mello (2009)	convenience	BRAZIL	mean age of boy = 9, of partner = 19	155	57	29	14	Used respondent-driven sampling in Campinas, Brazil; obtained n = 517 (439 men, 78 transgenders); 30% had sex with older partner (almost all male).
Dolezal & Carballo-Diéguez (2002)	convenience	US	overall mean = 8.5; mean of self-perceived abused = 8, not abused = 10	100	32	33	34	Latino men of low SES. Cases (<13, 4+) were 91% with males, 34% incest, 39% force.
Doll et al. (1992)	quasi-clinical	US	mean = 10; <12 (61%); 12-15 (33%)	336	27	15	58	Subjects recruited at STD clinics, of lower SES. Cases (<19, older/more powerful) were 95% with males, 43% incest, 49% force.
Jay & Young (1977)	non-random national	US, CAN	5-10 (56%), 11 to 14 (33%), 15 to 17 (11%)	18	83	5	11	Subjects recruited with ads across US and Canada. Authors presented cases they deemed typical. Cases (<18, 4+) were analyzed here.
NGLS (1993)	convenience	GB (50%)	9-14 (50%), 15-17	16	50	31	19	Subjects responded to request from national gay organization to describe early sexual experiences. Cases (<18, 4+) were analyzed here.
Rind (2001)	convenience	US	12-15 (42%), 16-17 (58%)	26	77	8	15	Mostly middle- to upper-middle class whites. Cases (<18, 5+ and >17) involved no incest or force.
Spada (1979)	non-random national	US	5-10 (33%), 11-14 (28%), 15-17 (39%)	18	67	11	22	Subjects recruited with ads across US. Author presented cases he deemed typical. Cases (<18, 4+) were analyzed here.
Stanley, Bartholomew, & Oram (2004)	community	CAN	overall mean = 10.10 (2 to 16); mean abusive sex = 8.17; mean non-abusive sex = 11.64	48	n/a	n/a	42	Community sample from Vancouver. Reactions to sex (<17, 5+) were classified as negative if any aspect was negative.
Totals/Means				717	56	19	27	

Note. US = United States, GB = Great Britain, CAN = Canada. Pos = positive, neut = neutral, neg = negative. Predominantly positive or negative reactions were classified as positive or negative, whereas reactions with a greater mix of positive and negative aspects were classed as neutral-mixed reactions. "n/a" indicates data were not available. In the bottom row, total N is given, followed by unweighted mean percents for reactions. (Unweighted means were used owing to the overweighting of the quasi-clinical sample.) In the study features column, age relations between the boys and their older partners are defined in parentheses. For example, (<18, 4+) means that the sex occurred when the subject was under 18 and the partner was four or more years older. SES = socioeconomic status.

adjusted. Bartholow et al. (1994) analyzed the Doll et al. (1992) data and found that boyhood homosexual experiences with older males were associated with poorer adjustment—but, only slightly so when converted to effect sizes.

Research into the gay male experience has often revealed boyhood sexual attractions and desires for much older males (e.g., McClintock & Herdt, 1996; Savin-Williams, 1997). Spada (1979) provided eighteen illustrative examples of the emergence of boyhood crushes for other males, which were directed at older males and men as opposed to peers by a margin of four to one. Jay and Young (1977) provided thirty-three illustrative examples, of which 61 percent were directed at men or much older youths and only 27 percent directed at male peers. In The National Lesbian and Gay Survey (1993), of the twenty-five illustrative examples of early boyhood crushes and erotic desires provided, 68 percent were directed at men. In a recent compilation of gay anecdotes concerning first boyhood erotic attractions, from the twenty cases providing enough information, 90 percent were directed at adult men (Trachtenberg, 2005). Anecdotally, gay commentators have frequently noted how common it has been in their experience to hear tales of gay friends and acquaintances who had boyhood crushes on, as well as positive sexual experiences with, adult males (e.g., Giovanni's Room Press Release, 1999; Kramer, 1981; Schulman, 2007; Tuller, 2002).

In sum, these results suggest that the gay boy-man dyad *is* an analog of the heterosexual boy-woman dyad, in which sexual orientation-consistent boyhood sexual encounters with much older persons are for the most part positively experienced. These results add force to the heterosexual data in undermining the sexual victimological theory that all adult-minor sexual contacts are inherently toxic. The data just reviewed demonstrate that reactions (negative or positive) are not innate, but depend on contextual factors. Negative reactions are associated with incest, use of force, lack of willingness, and younger ages of contact. That is, pederastic encounters, the focus of the present review, are likely to be positively experienced and not problematic in terms of later adjustment in this population if participated in willingly. Finally, the predominance of positive reactions is likely to be related to the tendency for early boyhood homosexual attractions to be preferentially directed at older, more mature males.

Pederastic Sex More Generally: A Further Empirical Examination

As an initial evaluation of youths' reactions to pederastic sex more generally, data were extracted from the five nonclinical empirical studies in Table I, in which reactions to man-boy sex could be isolated. Reactions were estimated via unweighted means as 27 percent positive, 34 percent neutral, and 42 percent negative.[8] These estimates are crude with respect to pederastic experiences, because many pedophilic experiences were included. All of these studies were Anglophone (4 U.S., 1 British). In a different society and cultural climate, when age-gap sex involving minors was temporarily more tolerated, Sandfort (1988, 1992) found that most of his Dutch male subjects with boyhood sexual experiences with older males were willing participants (69%), who reacted on average positively, in contrast to the unwilling participants (31%) who reacted on average negatively. Willing participants were as psychologically well adjusted as controls, and unwilling participants were slightly less well adjusted.

In two important forensic studies, conducted outside the sexual victimological framework, results were that harm and coercion were quite uncommon. Baurmann (1983), in a large-scale study conducted for the German government, found no evidence for psychological injury in his nearly one thousand cases of boys who had sexual encounters with men before age 14. He noted that use of force or coercion was rare in these cases, occurring instead mostly in heterosexual offences with female victims. Gebhard et al. (1965) examined ninety-one cases of boys aged 12 to 15 who had sexual encounters with men, and found that, according to the boys' official court accounts, they were encouraging in 70 percent of the cases, passive in 11 percent, and resistant in 16 percent. In these cases, they added, use of force or threat was quite rare. They attributed the youths' generally receptive response to libidos that are well activated in males by the early teens (which is in contrast to females). They remarked that if "twelve- to fifteen-year-old girls had as developed libidos as boys of the same age, our penal institutions would burst at the seams" (p. 299). They argued that a boy of this age is still flexible sexually, and if he can be persuaded, "he exhibits an intensity of response matching or frequently surpassing that of an adult" (p. 299).

In a number of interview studies based on convenience samples, positive reactions to pederastic encounters predominated (Bernard, 1981; Ingram, 1981; Leahy, 1992; Money & Weinrich, 1983; Sandfort, 1984; Sandfort & Everaerd, 1990; Tindall, 1978). In each of these studies, the boys were mainly in their preteens or early teens during the contacts, which occurred within friendship relationships of significant duration, in which the boys' positive responses were tied in part to willingness in participation and to their perception of attainment of important nonsexual benefits (e.g., a mature friend who listens to them). For example, Tindall (1978) followed nine cases of boys over three decades, who had sexual relations with men starting between the ages of 12 and 15, and found normal psychological development and adjustment in all cases, and negative signs (i.e., lingering guilt) in just one. He reported mentoring effects in more than half the cases, in which the youths' later direction (i.e., career choices) reflected their adult partner's profession and influence.

As with the heterosexual boy-woman and gay boy-man reviews, this review undercuts sexual victimological theory. Since its rise to dominance three decades ago, sexual victimology has succeeded in framing all adult-minor sex as necessarily coercive, which has heavily biased lay and professional views since (Malón, 2011). The forensic and interview studies just reviewed, conducted outside the sexual victimological framework, consistently found coercion to be rare but encouraging participation to be common. This pattern was even more pronounced in the nonclinical interview studies, where most cases were pederastic and involved willing participation within durable friendships, in which the sexual contacts were generally intimate (e.g., oral sex) and the relationships yielded valuable nonsexual benefits. By contrast, in the studies extracted from Table I, which combined had a plurality of cases with negative reactions, sexual episodes frequently were pedophilic and often included one-time approaches or fondling, which were generally unwanted. In short, assumptions of coercion and trauma as properties of pederastic relations do not hold under empirical examination. Reactions to these events reflect the circumstances under which they occur, as other types of sexual relations do.

In the three reviews just presented, what needs to be emphasized is that all these relations occurred in a society that views them as having no worth or legitimacy and that is quite hostile toward them both attitudinally and legally—especially the pederastic relations because of their homosexual nature. It is reasonable to assume that if these relations had been socially sanctioned, invested with value, and encouraged—as they have been in numerous other cultures to be reviewed later—they would have been experienced even more positively on average. The rather high levels of positive reactions under the conditions of our culture, therefore, should be taken as a strong indication of not only the incorrectness of sexual victimological theory, but its wrongheadedness as well, because it has strongly biased the objective appraisal of these relations, clinical perceptions of them, and views more generally throughout our society. As per Bullough (1976) and Ford and Beach (1951), historical, cross-cultural, and cross-species considerations are indicated to remedy these biases.

Two Case Studies

Before considering the broader data beyond our culture, two case studies are presented next to illustrate what positive pederasty can look like, given that it does occur with some frequency, as per the review just presented. Putting a face on positive cases can be valuable, given their counterintuitive nature for a society whose main source for such anecdotes is the mainstream media, whose strong filter permits only presentation of negative cases, often of sensationalistic nature (West, 1998). Both cases concern men (one gay, one straight) of accomplishment, to which their boyhood pederastic experiences (based on friendship and mentoring) contributed.

Case 1

Gavin Lambert (1924–2005) was a screenwriter, novelist, and biographer, who came from an upper-middle-class home in England. At age 10, he showed musical talent and won a scholarship to St. George's Preparatory School at Windsor Castle (Rapp, 2005). Toward the end of his long life, Lambert (2000) described his early homosexual unfolding and his pederastic relationship at the prep school.

After entering St. George's, Lambert developed a friendship with another boy named Rammelkamp who was also "already adjusted to a homosexual future" (p. 13). Lambert commented on the positive nature of each of their sexual initiations with adult men:

> We once compared notes on our sexual initiations, Rammelkamp's at the age of ten with a workman when he was on summer holiday with his parents in Cornwall, mine at the age of eleven with a [music] teacher at my preparatory school [St. George's], and agreed that we'd felt no shame or fear, only gratitude. (p. 13)

Lambert provided a lengthy description of his own initiation. He noted that, before entering the boarding school and meeting the teacher at age 11, he already knew his homosexual orientation "and never questioned it" (p. 28). He recalled that his "teacher-lover" made what happened between them seem completely natural, telling him that "they understood in ancient Greece" (p. 29). Lambert wrote that the sexual relationship "not only made me feel superior to the people who wouldn't or couldn't understand. Having to sneak out the dormitory to my teacher's bedroom was exciting, and made him even more attractive" (p. 29).

He added that "soon after falling in love with him, I fell in love with the movies" (p. 29). The teacher gratified his new appetite for the movies by taking him to one every Thursday afternoon, which constituted the beginnings of his eventual career as a screenwriter. The affair continued for the next eighteen months. Then, when returning from Christmas holidays, he found his teacher-lover gone—the new headmaster fired him and several other teachers thought to be sexually involved with pupils. The headmaster interrogated young Lambert, who "lied with a clear conscience" about whether he was sexually involved with the teacher and who felt "violated when [the headmaster] spoke of 'violation'" (p. 30). Initially afterward, he felt abandoned by his teacher-lover, who was by then far more important to him emotionally than his parents were. But he didn't feel betrayed, just disappointed not to have at least received a letter—until one of the other abandoned boys explained that that would have been too risky. Lambert summed up his feelings at the time and more than sixty years later:

> For several years I had fantasies of a passionate reunion when we met again by chance. It never happened. Perhaps he was killed in the war. Just possibly he has survived to read this after turning ninety. In any case he is still remembered, an unfaded photograph in the mind's eye, as my first love and the first love I lost. (p. 31)

Some years later, he read Plato's *Symposium* and was especially moved by Agathon's praise of Love, whom Agathon described as the most blessed of all gods, who empties us of all unneighborliness, fills us with intimacy, in wreck is a pilot, in time of dread is a shipmate, is the best of drinking companions, and is the noblest champion in debate. Upon reading this passage, Lambert recalled that it "brought to mind my music teacher, and made me realize exactly what he meant by saying 'They understood in ancient Greece.'" (p. 44)

Case 2
Heinz Kohut (1913–1981) was a leading theorist and practitioner of psychoanalysis, known for his work on narcissism and the self, as well as his writings on his patient "Mr. Z," who was actually Kohut himself (Strozier, 2001). In his biography of Kohut, Strozier (2001) discussed young Kohut's pederastic experience in a chapter entitled "The Tutor." Kohut grew up in Vienna in the 1920s. When he was age 11, his parents' marriage was deteriorating, but he "survived the fragmentation of the family quite well, in no small part due to the lucky presence of a warm-hearted tutor named Ernst Morawetz, who entered his life just as his mother left it" (Strozier, 2001, p. 23). His mother hired Morawetz, a university student in his early 20s, to be young Kohut's companion and provide him with intellectual stimulation. Most afternoons after school, Morawetz took Kohut to a museum, an art gallery, or the opera, or they simply read together and talked about interesting subjects. As Kohut later put it:

> I had this private tutor, who was a very important person in my life. He would take me to museums and swimming and concerts and we had endless intellectual conversations and played complicated intellectual games and played chess together. I was an only child. So it was in some ways psychologically life-saving for me. I was very fond of the fellow. (p. 24)

Kohut found in Morawetz companionship, connection, and deep empathy. He later described those years with his tutor as extremely happy ones, perhaps the happiest years of his life. He idealized his tutor, who was a "'spiritual leader,' able to share his 'almost religious' love for nature, as well as teach him about literature, art, and music" (p. 24), thereby making him appreciate nature and culture far ahead of his age or his peers. The relationship became sexual, at first kissing and hugging, then tender mutual fondling, and mutual oral sex. Kohut put his relationship with Morawetz into the context of the ancient Greeks, about whom he was beginning to read in depth. In retrospect, he felt that the sexual aspect had no effect on his own sexual identity, which was firmly heterosexual. What was important was the emotional connection. This experience formed the basis for his later theorizing, in which he contradicted Freud, who had said that the self is constructed by vagaries in development of the sex instinct. Kohut reversed this, saying that the need for emotional connection precedes sex. Sexuality just symbolizes and concretizes our deepest needs.

Summary

These cases represent the opposite end of the spectrum from clinical and media reports. Both men's experiences fit the ancient Greek model of mentoring to be discussed later. Importantly, each man interpreted his experience in this way, not through the lens of the incest and rape models, which only permit perception of victimization. For Lambert, the relationship launched his career in movies; for Kohut, it built his intellect and underlay some of his later theorizing. For each, it was a source of deepest friendship. For the gay boy, the man was his first love; for the heterosexual boy, the man was his spiritual hero. Lambert felt only gratitude toward the man for the sexual initiation and remembered him decades later in lofty poetic terms; Kohut was unconcerned about the homosexual aspect, considering the emotional connection all that mattered. Though sexual victimologists and others may reject these cases and others like them as "cognitive distortions," such cases are just as real as the negative cases uniformly accepted without question. The scientific study of pederasty needs to include these cases, too, or else it is a pseudoscience.

HISTORICAL AND CROSS-CULTURAL PERSPECTIVES

In the previous section, pederasty was examined within the Western (mainly Anglophone) culture, with focus on assessing the clinical assumption of intrinsic pathology by studying nonclinical evidence. Not only was this evidence contradictory, it indicated that sometimes pederasty could be functional (i.e., useful or beneficial to the youth), as exemplified in the Lambert and Kohut cases. This finding segues with the present section, which examines pederasty from historical and cross-cultural perspectives, where researchers have often described functional manifestations (i.e., useful for the youth, man, and social group). The goal here, then, is to review this broader evidence and use it to reconsider Western assumptions of pathology. This evidence will be useful in examining assumed pathology at the level of both the individual (older, younger partner) and group (society).

Numerous reviews examining male homosexual behavior from historical and cross-cultural perspective have been conducted (e.g., Adam, 1985; Cardoso & Werner, 2004; Carrier, 1980; Crapo, 1995; Ford & Beach, 1951; Greenberg, 1988; Gregersen, 1983; Herdt, 1991, 1997; Murray, 2000; Murray & Roscoe, 1998; Werner, 2006). These reviews have described a multitude of societies in the recent and distant past, in which pederastic behavior was commonplace or institutionalized.[9] For the present review, thirty-three of them from across the globe were selected for illustration and analysis (see Table III): Europe ($n = 5$), North Africa, Western and Central Asia ($n = 2$), Sub-Saharan Africa ($n = 4$), Southeast Asia ($n = 6$), Melanesia-Australia ($n = 9$), Polynesia ($n = 1$), and the Americas ($n = 6$). Some of these societies were small in territory and number of inhabitants (e.g., the various Melanesian tribes), whereas others were vast geographically and in population (e.g., the Muslim culture across North Africa and into Western and Central Asia). Many other pederastic societies have been described and could have been included. For example, beyond the nine Melanesian-Australian cultures in Table III, at least fifty others with institutionalized pederasty have been studied (Herdt, 1997); Murray (2000) reviewed eighteen Sub-Saharan African cultures beyond the four included here; five Southeast Asian societies were included, but many others also had a tradition of pederasty (Greenberg, 1988; Herdt, 1997); given that Amazonia had a pattern of pederasty similar to that in Melanesia (Herdt, 1987), many more examples from the Americas could have been included. Importantly, the current list, with its varied examples, is likely to be representative of other societies with institutionalized or culturally widespread pederasty, because all of these societies tended to have much in common structurally and in the way pederasty occurred (Adam, 1985; Crapo, 1995; Murray, 2000).[10]

In column two of Table III, the typical beginning and ending ages of boys' participation in pederasty are provided, where they were available or could be estimated. The mean beginning and ending ages were, respectively, 10.72 ($n = 25$, $SD = 1.77$) and 16.35 ($n = 20$, $SD = 2.74$) and the corresponding median ages were 12 and 17. One society (East Bay) was mostly pedophilic in form (ages 7–11). In the several other societies with beginning ages under 10, these lower ages represented extremes rather than norms. For example, Sambian boys began somewhere from 7 to 10, but generally toward 10 (so 7 was an extreme) (Herdt, 1997), and boys in Muslim cultures could begin as young as 8, but the most common interest was in boys from about 11 to 15 (Rouayheb, 2005). In short, the typical age pattern in these societies generally indicates that the interest or practice began with peripubescence and ended with later adolescence.

Pederastic Interest/Behavior in Men: Examining Assumptions via the Broad Perspective

Western clinical, victimological, and popular thinking generally holds that adult male erotic attraction to males in the pederastic range is highly abnormal, a condition that necessarily pertains to a small minority of men, whose attractions must have resulted from abnormal circumstances such as disturbed development (e.g., brain injury) or deformed personality (e.g., poor self-esteem). Notably, the same thinking used to apply to gay attractions, but that eroded in the aftermath of gay liberation, when such attractions came to be seen by liberal society as normal and non-pathologically caused. The rule that came to dominate thinking

Table III: Examples of Historical/Cross-Cultural Societies (or Subgroups) with Institutionalized or Widespread Pederasty

Society	Ages of Boys Involved	Characteristics of Pederasty	Sources
Europe			
Ancient Greece	12–17	Had mentoring function (prepared elite boys for adult roles as warriors, citizens). Boyish beauty repeatedly valorized in the arts (e.g., love poetry, pottery); body hair (face, legs) ended boys' attractiveness; bisexual interests (women, boys) widespread; attraction to other adult men scorned. Notables with pederastic interests: poets (e.g., Alcaeus, Ibycus, Anacreon, Theognis, Pindar); playwrights (e.g., Aeschylus, Sophocles, Euripides); political leaders (e.g., Solon, Demosthenes, Agesilaus, Philip, Alexander); philosophers (e.g., Socrates, Plato, Zeno, Chrysippus). Eroded with rise of Christianity.	Crompton (2003); Hubbard (2003); Lear (2004); Lear & Cantarella (2008)
Ancient Rome	12–20	No social function. Boyish beauty thematic in love poetry; attractions were to smooth, hairless bodies regardless of gender (for boys, from puberty to start of beard); exclusive attraction to one gender seen as eccentric; relations with other adult men seen as disgraceful. Notables with pederastic interests: poets Catullus, Horace, Juvenal, Martial, Tibullus, and Virgil, and emperors Trajan and Hadrian. Tradition eroded with consolidation of Christian sexual morality.	Cantarella (1992); Crompton (2003); Lambert (1984); Williams (1999)
Renaissance Italy	12–18	The majority of younger men and adolescent boys in all classes (working to elite) in Florence and other Tuscan cities were involved. This practice represented an unbroken continuation of the ancient Roman practice. Despite severe penalties (e.g., torture, death) based on belief in God's retribution, cases were often treated leniently (e.g., fines) through much of the Renaissance, a pragmatic response to its pervasiveness. Notables with pederastic interests: Donatello, Verrocchio, da Vinci, Botticelli, Pontormo, Bronzino, Cellini, and Caravaggio. The tradition was eroded through stepped-up religiously based anti-sodomy campaigns, especially Savonarola's in the 1490s, along with harsher penalties with more determined enforcement. The tradition was also entrenched in other areas such as Venice.	Crompton (2003); Moulton (2003); Rocke (1996); Ruggiero (1985); Saslow (1986, 1989)
Albania	12–17	Highly romanticized pederasty still found in latter half of twentieth century, owing to isolation from outside world (it was institutionalized during Ottoman rule); nineteenth and early twentieth century visitors confirmed that younger men frequently cultivated passionate, enthusiastic erotic relations with boys (12 to 17); Muslim Albanian custom of "boy-brides" also spread to Albanian Christians.	Greenberg (1988); Murray (1997, 2000); Williams (1992)
English Boarding Schools	11–14	Deeply sentimentalized, erotically based attachments were common in many all-male private boarding schools before 1970s between older (about 17–18) and younger (about 12–13) boys; older teens sought "cute" boys, calling them "talent," "crushes," or "tarts;" younger boys competed to be selected (for the many favors, privileges it entailed); older/younger pairs exchanged notes, poetry, and other items of endearment; after graduating, most moved on to heterosexuality.	Chandos (1984); Gathorne-Hardy (1978); Lambert & Lambert (1968); Lewis (1955); Nash (1961)
North Africa, Western & Central Asia			
Muslim Societies	8–20	Pervasive in Muslim societies (North Africa, Western-Central Asia) eighth to nineteenth centuries; pederastic attractions seen just as normal as heterosexual ones; main interest in boys was early to mid-teens, peaking at	Baldauf (1988); Crompton (2003);

Table III: (continued)

Society	Ages of Boys Involved	Characteristics of Pederasty	Sources
North Africa, Western and Central Asia (continued)			
	about 14	appeal vanished with beard (about 16, 17); adult men scorned if passive partners in homosexual relationships; manly behavior was to be active (partner gender did not matter); staggering amount of love poetry shows obsession with boyish beauty, seen as comparable to women's; poets attracted to boys constitutes a Who's Who; desire for boys, but not behavior or lust, was permissible under Islam, but behavior was common nevertheless; tradition ended in late nineteenth century, because of Western colonialism, with its abhorrence of the tradition and the local embarrassment this created, along with local assimilation of European concepts and efforts to modernize.	Massad (2007); Murray & Roscoe (1998); Patanè (2006); Rahman (1989); Rouayheb (2005); Schild (1988); Wright & Rowson (1997)
Siwans of Libya	12–18	Pederasty was a well-entrenched custom from antiquity to at least 1950s; matchmakers made marriage-like arrangements between men and boys; the boy got a gift larger than brideprice for females; man and boy then entered into alliance with family approval; prominent men lent each other their sons for sex; love affairs and jealousies over boys were common; Robin Maugham said: "They will kill for a boy. Never for a woman."	Adam (1985); Herdt (1997)
Sub-Saharan Africa			
Azande of Northern Congo	12–20	Under polygynous system, women were scarce; warriors married boys aged 12 or older; commanders might have more than one boywife; man and boy addressed each other with terms such as my love and my lover; boy performed wifely duties and apprenticed for man; on reaching adulthood, the boy typically joined a military company, taking a boywife of his own; tradition faded when practice of military service discontinued under British colonialism.	Evans-Pritchard (1971); Murray & Roscoe (1998); Seligman & Seligman (1932)
Mossi of Burkina Faso (W. Africa)	8–15	All chiefs (ca. late nineteenth century) had large groups of pages, boys aged 8 to 15 chosen for attractiveness (some were thought to be quite beautiful); on Friday nights, because heterosexual intercourse was forbidden, a chief would engage in sex with a boy instead (he could also on other nights). Upon reaching maturity, a boy was given a wife by the chief.	Murray & Roscoe (1998); Tauxier (1912)
Tsonga of Southern Mozambique	?–?	Common practice in twentieth century among native men, used as miners by colonialists, was taking boys as wives (with wedding feast, brideprice payment); boy performed domestic, sexual duties; was given presents, money in exchange; fidelity was expected; relationships were marked by intense feelings and jealousy; marriage could be terminated in divorce; some men took boywives home after mining, where they were accepted by men's other wives and tribal leaders. Asked if boys desired being wives, an elderly Tsonga man answered, "Yes: for the sake of security, for the acquisition of property and for the fun itself." A beard indicated the boy was no longer a sex object but a competitor for boys.	Murray & Roscoe 1998); Wallace ((2006)
Bantu-Speaking	12–18	Male peer homosexual behavior was universal from puberty until age 18 or 20, and adult-youth sexual interactions were common as well. The older men disposed to form such relationships were described as bian	Wallace (2006)

Table III: (continued)

Society	Ages of Boys Involved	Characteristics of Pederasty	Sources
Tribes in Central Africa		nku'ma (having a heart for boys). In various Central Bantu groups, boy initiates resided at a sex-segregated lodge during their initiation phase and were required to manipulate the phalluses of the lodge-keeper and other adult male visitors, a practice that was seen as instrumental in helping the boys' phalluses grow large and strong.	
Southeast Asia			
Dynastic China	10–18	Multiple forms of male homosexuality (especially pederasty) occurred across 2 millennia of dynasties; cut sleeve became term for homosexual love (ca. 0 CE) when emperor cut his sleeve rather than waking up his boy favorite, who was on it; poetry after 220 CE often discussed beauty, charms of boys; marriage to boys was a common Fujian practice (ca. 1000 CE); key seventeenth century author (Li Yu) wrote a book illustrating popular interest in pederasty; Western visitors in nineteenth century expressed shock at prominent Chinese men openly courting boys (aged about 14-15); tradition ended in later nineteenth century with embarrassment at Western repugnance and efforts to modernize.	Crompton (2003); Hinsch (1990); Leupp (1995)
Pre-Meiji Japan	10–18	From eleventh to nineteenth centuries, bisexuality (women, boys) was pervasive; over time pederasty appeared in three contexts (monastic, samurai, kabuki theater), the first two as mentorships with boys of ranking families, the last as prostitution; among samurai, it fostered loyalty and sacrifice in youths training to be warriors; shoguns and warlords from twelfth to eighteenth centuries involved in pederasty reads like a Who's Who of military-political history; key seventeenth century author (Saikaku) illustrated its pervasive presence; another described typical ages of interest (10–13 = "blossoming flower," 14–17 = "flourishing flower," 18–21 = "falling flower"); tradition ended in late nineteenth century in response to Western abhorrence and efforts to modernize.	Crompton (2003); Leupp (1995); Watanabe & Iwata (1989)
Ancient Korea	?–?	Pederasty at times common in the imperial realm. By sixth century CE, imperial court had hwarang ("flower boys"), a corps of young warriors made up of aristocratic youth chosen for beauty, education, and martial prowess. Various kings through the fourteenth century known to have had pederastic relations at the court. Monastic pederasty was widespread. Popularity of "beautiful boys" in seventeenth century entertainment indicates pederasty was common among the gentry. It was especially common among provincial gentlemen, some of whom kept boy-wives, a practice openly acknowledged in their villages.	Leupp (1995)
Tibet	?–?	Monasteries had a strong reputation for master-novice sexual relations, which participants viewed without shame as they made no attempt to conceal them to Westerners upon early contacts.	Prince Peter (1963)
Batak of Northern Sumatra	12–?	In late childhood, boys moved into all-male houses with about a dozen other boys and young men. From puberty until marriage, homosexual behavior was prescribed and constant. Pederasty and age-equal sex were both common. Sequestering the sexes ensured girls remained virgins until marriage (premarital sex for girls was highly taboo). With outside cultural contact, the tradition began to change.	Money & Ehrhardt (1972)
Java	8–14	In Ponorogo area, all-male folk dance was a major cultural institution (before 1990s); spectating men admired beauty of dancing youths; boy dancers aged 8–14, called gemblaks, often had culturally approved sex with	Weiss (1974); Williams (2011)

Table III: (continued)

Society	Ages of Boys Involved	Characteristics of Pederasty	Sources
Java (continued)		men; interviewees who had been gemblaks all viewed the sex positively; all got married; some had long-term sexual relationships with the dance troupe directors (the Waroks). Waroks were spiritual guides, valorized by the community. Each Ponorogo village had a formalized male group for unmarried males; the group did socially constructive work for the community; heterosexual sex before marriage was disapproved, so members had sex with gemblaks; this practice was seen as benefiting the gemblaks, who got gifts, the group members, who got a sexual outlet, the community, which got good works. Under Western influence, educated Ponorogo people began seeing all this as an embarrassment (relic from an "uncivilized" past); have since worked to end the practice.	
Melanesia-Australia			
Sambia of New Guinea	7–14	Boys between 7 and 10 taken into men's society; until age 14 fellated older bachelors up to age 25; semen viewed necessary for growth to be strong warrior; after age 25, most men stopped being semen "donors" to get married (some men continued who preferred boys); relations were not just duty for the boys, who were often complicit in arousing bachelors through bawdy enthusiasm; as boys matured, they tended to express more desire for insemination, became more aggressive in soliciting it.	Herdt (1991, 1997)
Gebusi of New Guinea	11–14	Boys in early adolescence "coquettishly" initiated sexual relations with older, unrelated males. As with the Sambia, the belief was that insemination grew the boys into men. The sexual relations were based on personal affection rather than obligation.	Herdt (1991, 1997)
Keraki of New Guinea	12–14	All boys were sodomized for about a year, seen as essential for their development; adult informants repeatedly answered, when asked whether they submitted as boys, "Why yes! Otherwise how should I have grown?" Bachelors saw some boys as more attractive, gave them more attention; they sodomized boys until marriage, then engaged mostly in heterosex, but continued to have relations with boys on occasion.	Williams (1936)
Marind-Anim of New Guinea	12–20	Upon reaching puberty, a boy moved in with a mentor and his wife; he assisted the mentor in gardening, hunting, and other chores; their relation was sexual and lasted about seven years until boy's later marriage; bond between them was extremely strong; the sexual contacts seemed to contribute to the strength of this bond; insemination was regarded as helpful to boy's growth.	Van Baal (1966)
Kaluli of New Guinea	10–13	From 8 to 28, males resided in sex-segregated hunting lodge; daily, boys accompanied older males on grueling hunting trips, learning essentials of the practice; at 10 or 11, a boy's father chose for him an older male to inseminate him for months or years; some boys chose their own inseminator; insemination thought essential for growth. Men looked back on youth in hunting lodge with nostalgic excitement, zest; remembered continual hunting, growth-stimulating insemination, ritual discipline, unity of purpose, vigorous manly ethos as highlight of their lives; whole practice was one of prestige for them. Tradition ended in 1960s by colonial administration and missionaries, who policed against it.)	Schieffelin (1982)

Table III: (continued)

Society	Ages of Boys Involved	Characteristics of Pederasty	Sources
Big Nambas of Malekula, Melanesia	?–?	Society had rampant warfare, chiefs had near monopoly on women; father chose man to circumcise his son; this man then became boy's "husband," and the boy his "wife;" intercourse believed to strengthen boy's penis; relationship was very close; boy followed the man everywhere, participating with him in daily chores; man was intensely jealous if other men took interest in the boy; if man or boy died, the other would mourn deeply; some men were so deeply homosexual in affections that they would seldom have intercourse with their wives, preferring the boy; every chief had several boy lovers.	Herdt (1993); Layard (1942)
East Bay Islanders (Santa Cruz)	7–11	Nearly every male engaged in extensive homosex; men had sexual relations with boys (7 to 11); it was obligatory to give boy presents in return; the boys discussed these contacts freely and without shame in presence of parents, friends. Upon marriage, only a few men became exclusive heterosexuals; most continued to have sex with boys as well; only one man in the study preferred exclusively boys.	Davenport (1965)
Aranda of Australia	10–14	Typically, an unmarried man (late teens) would take a boy from 10 to 12 years old to be his wife and live with him for several years until he (the older partner) got married to a woman. Aside from sex, the man served as the boy's mentor (e.g., in hunting).	Strehlow (1913–15)
Nambutji of Australia	?–?	Every boy became a boywife to a man, who circumcised the boy and whose daughter became the boy's wife when he reached adulthood. In the intervening time, the man and boy were homosexually involved.	Roheim (1945)
Polynesia			
Marquesas Islands in Polynesia	?–?	Adolescent boys frequently had sex with each other. Married men rarely had homosex, but would when conditions prevented heterosexual intercourse; they preferred boys for this purpose, whose bodies they said were soft, like females; contacts with boys were casual, fleeting, and without stigma.	Suggs (1966)
Americas			
Mayans, Aztecs, and Incas	?–?	Among sixteenth and seventeenth century Mayans, missionaries reported a custom of youth–younger boy marriages. In field work, Williams (1992) found pederastic behavior still common in late twentieth century Yucatan. Missionaries reported religious-based pederasty as common among the Aztecs and Incas.	Greenberg (1988); Williams (1992)
Coerunas Indians of Brazil	?–?	An apprentice healer would go into the woods for an extended time with an older healer, who would transmit his special powers to the youth through sexual relations and also directly instruct him on the art of curing illnesses.	Greenberg (1988)
Zapotecs of Mexico	12–?	Boys entering puberty commonly had sexual relations with men.	Williams (1992)
Various Indian tribes in southern Mexico	12–?	Married men would adopt an adolescent boy, who was proud to have been chosen and saw it an honor to be the man's lover; the boy would help the wife, her children, and the household, and would take a boy of his own when later an adult and married	Ross (1991)

Table III: (continued)

Society	Ages of Boys Involved	Characteristics of Pederasty	Sources
Pirates	12–?	Lived in all-male arrangements with mixed ages from young adolescents or younger through older men. Sexual relations between men, especially pirate captains (e.g., Blackbeard), and adolescent boys were common.	Burg (1995); Williams (1992)
Hobos	12–?	Between 1880 and 1930, sexual relations between men and adolescent boys were commonplace among transient workers in the Pacific Northwest. Developing industries (e.g., lumber, mining) drew in large numbers of unmarried men and male youths from other parts of the United States to perform backbreaking work. They lived and worked in all-male societies, which fostered intergenerational sex (rather than age-equal sex). Their relations were social, not just sexual—the boys often served domestic functions for the men. In return, they got various benefits (e.g., advice, apprenticing, emotional support, safety, protection). By the 1930s, these all-male societies eroded, owing to mechanization (which reduced brute-strength work) and population expansion (with more women). These changes, along with constant policing activity (the middle class saw pederasty as a threat to their youth and the family), helped to dissolve the tradition.	Boag, (2003); Flynt (1927); Williams (1992)

Note. Age ranges of boys involved in pederasty are explicitly stated in sources in most cases, estimated from sources' descriptions in others (e.g., if beginning of puberty or adolescence is noted, age 12 was used).

was that sexual attractions are normal when they are directed at other fully mature persons, whether the same or opposite sex; however, when directed primarily at less than fully mature others, such attractions are disorders (e.g., Blanchard et al., 2009). The unarticulated assumption in this thinking is that adult sexual attractions have been "designed" (e.g., by evolution) to be directed only at other adults, and pederastic attractions are therefore "against design," and consequently unnatural and abnormal (cf. Wakefield, 1992). A counterpoise to this assumption is that it is culturally constructed, that "unnatural" and hence "abnormal" are conflations with "uncultural," and that judgment as to facts of nature have been biased by hegemonic cultural values (cf. Vanggaard, 1972; Williams, 1999). The historical and cross-cultural evidence in Table III, the related scholarly source material, and the many literature reviews on homosexuality across time and place are probative regarding these competing accounts.

In society after society in the table, it was the typical adult male, not the deviant one, who had erotic interest in immature males, an interest that usually ended shy of attainment of full sexual maturity by the younger males, a stage in development that pervasively represented a sexual turn-off for the adult males. In most of these societies, erotic attractions to fully mature males were rare and scorned. In ancient Greece and Rome, adult males were generally attracted to smooth, young bodies—boys in the "flower of youth" (beginnings of puberty until beard growth) and women in their prime (Hubbard 2003; Williams, 1999). Body hair (e.g., on face and legs) was decisive in ending boys' attractiveness. Not only women, but boys, too, were frequently seen as beautiful, as repeatedly expressed in love poetry written by Greece and Rome's premier poets. Men exclusively attracted to only one gender were considered "eccentric," although it was common for them to be more inclined to one gender than the other (Williams, 1999, p. 228). Men's sexuality was energized by difference—women's different gender, boys' different age and level of maturity, and sometimes other adult men's different gender orientation (i.e., cross-gendered). Williams laid out this pattern of difference as a principle of mature male eroticism across time and place, except for the modern West, with its unique emphasis on egalitarian sexual relations. Cross-cultural reviews of male homosexuality support Williams's thesis (e.g., Adam, 1985; Greenberg, 1988; Herdt, 1997; Murray 2000).

The essentials of ancient Roman adult male erotic attractions applied to most of the other literate civilizations in Table III (e.g., ancient Greece, Renaissance Italy, pre-Meiji Japan, Muslim societies of North Africa and Western, Central Asia). In Muslim societies from the eighth to nineteenth centuries, particularly extensive documentation shows that "men's attraction to boys was considered as natural as their attraction to women" (Rowson, 1997, p. 159) and that it was widely taken for granted that "beardless youths posed a temptation to adult men as a whole, and not merely to a small minority of deviants" (Rouayheb, 2005, p. 115). Monroe (1997) illustrated these common beliefs by quoting a twelfth century religious jurist, who remarked that "He who claims that he experiences no desire when looking at beautiful boys or youth[s] is a liar, and if we could believe him, he would be an animal, not a human being" (p. 117). Though pederastic *behavior* was condemned by Islam (a carryover from its Judeo-Christian roots), pederastic *desire* was not disapproved, unlike in Judeo-Christian culture, a circumstance that contributed to its flourishing.

As in Muslim societies, pederasty was pervasive in China and Japan until the nineteenth century. Much evidence remains of its practice and prevalence in these cultures, owing to the extensive legacy of writings and other source materials dealing with it (Hinsch, 1990; Leupp, 1995; Watanabe & Iwata, 1989). For example, in Japan's Tokugawa period (1603–1868), the overwhelming majority of sexual or romantic references attests to a culturally entrenched bisexuality in men directed at women and boys, the latter aged 10 to 18 with 14 to 17 being the prime (Leupp, 1995). Important with respect to drawing inferences about pederasty is the complete cultural independence between societies of the Far East and the Mediterranean and Near Eastern societies, coupled with a common pervasiveness of pederastic interests in both. Likewise, the many nonliterate cultures in Table III, which were independent of the high civilizations and often each other as well, and in which pederastic desire and behavior were similarly pervasive, add force to inferences about mature males' potential for pederasty.

Beauty and intensely passionate feelings concerning peripubertal and adolescent boys were recurring themes in both the literate and preliterate cultures in Table III. In the former, traditions of love poetry focused particularly on boyish beauty and strong passions, and were crafted not merely or necessarily to express personal feelings but to feed the demands of a literate audience, where such perceptions and feelings were commonplace (Hinsch, 1990; Lear & Cantarella, 2008; Leupp, 1995; Rouayheb, 2005; Williams, 1999). These traditions are indicators of widespread genuine pederastic desire for boys in those cultures, rather than mere role playing in response to custom and cultural expectations. Notably, men in these cultures saw beauty in both women and boys: a parallel love poetry genre existed for both. Just as men eroticize women in all human societies in connection with their perceived beauty, so they often eroticized boys in the societies in Table III in connection with perceptions of boyish beauty. This is an important point, because part of sexual victimological theory is that erotic attractions to minors are based essentially on power, not sex (cf. Paglia, 1992). This view, however, was never based on empirical evidence, but instead derived from ideological assumptions coupled with clinical impressions. The empirical evidence in the present historical and cross-cultural review, however, locates pederastic desire in genuine eroticism rather than in "power needs."

In short, contrary to Western thinking, in these cultures pederasty was not confined to men on the fringes, but applied alike to typical men, high-status men (e.g., chiefs), and esteemed men (e.g., the *Who's Who*). The clinical, victimological, and popular assumption in the West that pederastic desire is intrinsically deviant for the entire human species is both incorrect and clearly a social construction, as the historical and cross-cultural perspective amply reveals. The assumption that if a "normal" man is going to be attracted to another male, then that male *must* be an adult, is a late twentieth century Western construction, not an empirical induction based on the historical record of what "normal" men have actually found attractive. Later, the issue of pederasty and "design" is examined (cf. Wakefield, 1992), but for now it seems clear that Western assumptions about unnaturalness and intrinsic abnormality are conflations with unculturalness (cf. Bullough, 1976; Vanggaard, 1972; Williams, 1999).

A theoretically important point is the repeated finding across the societies in Table III that individual males differed in their pederastic inclinations, inasmuch as few men had particularly enduring attractions focused mostly on boys, many had a mix of attractions to both boys and women (but often somewhat inclined toward one or the other), and some others were concentrated mostly on women (e.g., Davenport, 1965; Herdt, 1997; Leupp, 1995; Rouayheb, 2005; Williams, 1999). This pattern suggests a natural variation in pederastic tendencies along a continuum. In societies tolerating or approving the behavior (e.g., ancient Greece, Samurai Japan), or in environments encouraging it (e.g., the all-male English boarding schools or pirate and hobo societies), the continuum appears to be normally distributed. But in antagonistic societies or environments, such as ours, this normally distributed potential is highly constrained in its actualization, such that only individuals presumably above a certain threshold on the continuum are likely to express the potential, producing a highly skewed distribution, with the strong modal outcome being no expressed interest at all. This speculation is consistent with the historical and cross-cultural data, as well as with the pattern in our own society, and suggests approaching pederasty as a normally distributed behavioral tendency that interacts with the cultural environment at hand to produce the phenotypic distribution. Contemporary Western assumptions that locate the cause of pederasty in idiosyncratic pathology, which describes dominant professional opinion well, rather than in the interaction between preexisting potentials and cultural-environmental inputs, fail in light of the historical and cross-cultural evidence.

Pederasty and Boys: Examining Assumptions via the Broad Perspective

Anthropological studies on preindustrial societies with culturally institutionalized or widespread pederasty provide reports on how the younger males responded to sexual contacts with older males (see Table III). Among the Javanese, men remembered their boyhood pederastic experiences entirely positively, despite the researcher's probing to uncover negative cases (Williams, 2011). Sambian boys showed much initiative in these contacts, especially at older ages (Herdt, 1991, 1997). Keraki men believed that they could not have developed properly without these relations as boys (Williams, 1936). Kaluli men looked back on the complex of grueling hunting, living in a sex-segregated men's lodge, ritual discipline, unity of purpose, vigorous manly ethos, *and* growth-stimulating insemination by older males as the highlight of their lives (Schieffelin, 1982). East Bay boys discussed their sexual experiences with men freely and without shame in the presence of their parents and friends (Davenport, 1965). Gebusi boys aged 11 to 14 initiated sexual relations with older males based on personal affection rather than obligation (Herdt, 1991). The bond between Marind-Anim boys and their adult male partners was extremely strong, which was apparently facilitated by the sexual interactions (Van Baal, 1966). Likewise, pederastic relations were extremely close among the Big Nambas (Layard, 1942). Among the Kiman, pederastic behavior would stop after adolescence, but "nevertheless, a lifelong emotional relationship often" resulted (Serpenti, 1984, p. 305). In various southern Mexican Indian tribes, adolescent boys were proud to have been chosen for pederastic relationships, seeing it as an honor to be their men's lovers (Ross, 1991). And being a Tsongan boy-wife was not just good for security, but for the "fun" it afforded (Murray & Roscoe, 1998).

What is important to point out about these reactions, which are diametrically opposite to clinical characterizations and popular suppositions in the modern West, is that they came from boys in cultures in which pederasty was acceptable and often esteemed. Even in Western society, as the empirical review presented previously showed, pederastic relations have frequently been experienced positively by youths when these relations occurred under certain circumstances (e.g., within friendships, depending on the perception of willingness and receiving important nonsexual benefits). Notably, these Western relationships all occurred within a cultural atmosphere highly condemning of pederasty, a circumstance that was likely to influence the boys' perceptions of their experiences to some degree negatively, depending on the extent to which they were exposed to the moral negatives about pederasty or homosexuality and had actually absorbed them (cf. Constantine, 1981). The net positive response in these cases implies that the perceived benefits outweighed the perceived moral negatives. If this latter factor were turned into moral positives, as it would have been in cultures approving and encouraging pederasty, then it follows that net positives in the population of experiences would increase sizably. Culture contributes significantly to the interpretation of personal experiences, sexual or otherwise, and must be taken into account for valid understanding of reactions (Herdt, 1997; Williams, 1999). Western professional thinking, not to mention lay thinking, has been quite neglectful or oblivious in this regard, rarely taking into account cultural influence, locating negative reactions instead entirely in the experience itself.

Pederasty and the Group: Examining Assumptions via the Broad Perspective

In our society, pederasty is not simply considered pathological in the case of the adult actor and damaging in the case of the youth involved, but harmful to society as well. A frequent claim included within media commentaries, for example, is that *no* society that permits this behavior can survive. Given this thinking, it is noteworthy that many of the cultures listed in Table III held diametrically opposite views and lasted for centuries or even millennia. Many of them considered pederasty necessary for their boys to develop properly so as to enable their culture to function adequately. This section reviews pederastic functioning according to accounts by historians, anthropologists, and the societies themselves and then reconsiders our society's view of *intrinsic* malfunction not just at the individual but also the group level.

Sexual victimologists and others have compared adult-minor sex, including pederasty, to slavery, and when they have considered societies such as ancient Greece, they have dismissed claims of pederasty's social role there, arguing that these societies had slavery, too. Slavery can be described in many ways, but for present purposes what is relevant is that it retards or prevents another's development and realization of potential by forcing him or her to sacrifice effort that instead advances the slaveholder's interests. In ancient Greece, pederasty was institutionalized among the elite in order to advance, not hinder, elite boys' development, so as to recreate adult male citizens who functioned well according to the society's needs (Hubbard 1998; Lear, 2004; Rice, 2005). That is, the social custom was viewed as functional at the level of the adult male lover (*erastes*), the beloved youth (*eromenos*), and society: the *erastes* had a dedicated apprentice; the *eromenos* learned manly skills and virtues; the society as a whole had a stronger citizenry. In the warrior culture of early Greece, manly skills (e.g., martial) and virtues (e.g., courage, loyalty, self-sacrifice) were needed, and one-on-one mentoring with its emotional connection was an efficient means of transmitting these characteristics (Neill, 2009). The slavery analogy is a projection of current dominant ideologies and obfuscates the actual character of pederasty in ancient Greece and many other cultures across time and place—that is, societal benefit, owing to building, not thwarting, youths.

It is relevant to add that this social custom in ancient Greece came as a package involving beauty, desire, sexual excitement, and pedagogy (Lear, 2004). Boyish beauty was thematically valorized in vase paintings, with the inscription *kalos* (beautiful) frequently inscribed (Lear & Cantarella, 2008). In philosophy, Plato's *Phaedrus* held boyish beauty to be that which most closely resembled the Form of Beauty (i.e., the ideal of beauty) in high heaven. Numerous Greek poets from the seventh century BCE to the triumph of Christianity in the fourth century CE wrote of the bewitching power that boys' beauty held over them or other men (Hubbard 2003; Lear, 2004). A leitmotif from the archaic period (before 480 BCE), which was imitated repeatedly in later times, was the power of a beautiful boy's eyes, which were said to induce a state of helplessness in the adult male admirer (Hubbard, 2002). The point is, as with the earlier discussion on beauty, that Greek pederasty was driven by a genuine erotic energy tapped for the benefit of the social group, not the neurotic energy of satisfying personal "power needs" in opposition to the group's well-being (cf. Hubbard, 2000; Paglia, 1990).

In medieval and premodern Japan, pederasty was also institutionalized for its social utility (Leupp, 1995). By the thirteenth century it was prevalent in Buddhist monasteries. Boys from ranking families entered around age 10 to train for the clergy or to learn scripture and by their early teens may have formed a pederastic relationship with a monk, serving as his acolyte. The relationship was acceptable in the culture, being understood as facilitating the pedagogic process, and thus serving to maintain the institution. It was eventually formalized in a "brotherhood bond," resembling man-boy marriages in many other pederastic societies (see Table III). Monastic pederasty influenced the development and institutionalization of feudal pederasty practiced by samurai warriors. Feudalism developed by the twefth century, when centralized state institutions collapsed. Rule was then organized in a hierarchical military class made up of lords and samurai warriors, who exchanged service for land. By the late sixteenth century, the samurai population had reached the hundreds of thousands. The practice of pederasty was pervasive among them and was recognized to serve the mentoring function of transmitting martial skills and virtues to the youths, to aid the warriors by giving them devoted apprentices, and ultimately to maintain the functioning of the ruling order and thus the social whole.

A revealing view into the nature of premodern Japanese pederasty comes from the writings of Saikaku, one of the world's literary giants, who first achieved national recognition with his 1687 book on *shudo* (i.e., pederasty), entitled *The Great Mirror of Male Love* (with subtitle *The Custom of Boy Love in Our Land*) (Schalow, 1989). His book became an instant success, owing to the contemporary popularity of pederasty as well as his novel approach—he combined the three main forms of pederasty (monastic, samurai, and kabuki) into a single prose work. His forty short stories reflect and reveal the ideals of pederasty as viewed in his day. Pederasty involved mutual emotional exchange between man and boy, embodying *ikiji* (shared masculine pride), an element not obtainable from male-female relations. A youth was deemed worthy of the love of a man if he possessed *nasake,* a form of empathy that involved emotional sensitivity to the suffering of a potential lover, as well as the desire to relieve that suffering. In the case of the samurai, the man was expected to give social backing to the youth and to provide a model of manliness. In exchange, the youth was expected to be a good student of samurai manhood, which meant vowing to be loyal, steadfast, and honorable in his actions. Both were expected to sacrifice for the other, even the ultimate sacrifice of life if honor required it (Schalow, 1989; Saikaku, 1990). This practice is unimaginable to our society, where pederasty is conceived of only in terms of exploitation and harm. But in premodern Japan, with its very different social structure, pederastic relations were an efficient means, owing to their intimate nature, of transmitting culturally needed masculine skills and emotional readiness to the next generation in service of the wider society (cf. Neill, 2009).

In most preliterate cultures in Table III, pederasty was also institutionalized for its mentoring value. In the anthropological literature, these cultures are referred to as "mentorship" societies, in recognition of the social function that pederasty was serving for them (Crapo, 1995). The form of mentorships could be one-on-one mentor-apprentice arrangements of the type in ancient Greece or communal arrangements, as in many of the Melanesian societies (Adam, 1985). In Table III, examples of the ancient Greek (one-on-one) form were the Azande warriors of the Northern Congo, the Marind-Anim of New Guinea, the Aranda of Australia, and the Coerunas Indians of Brazil. Examples of the Melanesian (communal) form were the Sambia, Gebusi, and Keraki of New Guinea. In this latter form, boys would interact sexually with many older males, taking in their semen orally or anally, with the belief being that the semen "grew" the boys, without which they would not mature (Herdt, 1987, 1993). In these societies, pederasty was one of a number of cultural rituals involved in transforming boys into cultural producers of socially needed activities, particularly warfare, by instilling in them the skills, emotional readiness (e.g., courage), and group orientation (e.g., loyalty, sacrifice) required for these activities. It was a mechanism for reproducing the male group, so vital to the way of life in these societies (Herdt, 1987, 1991, 1993, 1997; Keesing, 1982).

In our society today, the male group is far less present or important compared with the societies just discussed. One key reason why is unprecedented advances in technology, which have enabled women to take on many jobs or tasks that traditionally only men could do. But in the low-tech environs before the modern age, only males could undertake war and big-game hunting (Gat, 2006; Gilmore, 1990). As Gat argued, war was often not a choice, but a necessity throughout our species' existence, as enemy tribes posed a constant threat to invade at night and kill everyone: this pattern of warfare has been ubiquitous among extant and historical hunter-gatherer and primitive horticulturalist societies, and inferentially can be assumed to extend throughout prehistory.[11] Warrior responsibilities and big-game hunting necessarily fell on males, being twice as physically strong as females on average, such that in low-tech environs females could not have competed with male enemies. Because of this, in past low-tech societies where warfare or big-game hunting were priorities, the male group was also a priority, as was its maintenance, which behooved adult males to recruit and train boys continually (Mackey, 1990; Weisfeld, 1979; Weisfeld & Billings, 1988). It was in such environs that pederasty was one of the mechanisms to facilitate boys' enculturation to maintain the male group, as the historical and cross-cultural review just presented shows. Later, it will be considered whether pederasty was a naturally selected mechanism designed to serve this function (cf. Mackey, 1990).

In short, pederasty is pervasively portrayed in our society as *intrinsically* disordered in the case of the man, harmful in the case of the boy, and destructive in the case of society. The historical and cross-cultural review just presented adds much weight to the previous nonclinical empirical review in undermining these assumptions. Moreover, the present review supports the radically (from our society's point of view) different conceptualization of pederasty, already suggested in some of the nonclinical empirical data and in the case studies of Lambert and Kohut presented previously, that it can be functional at both the individual and group levels rather than necessarily dysfunctional. Importantly, function, culture, and environment interact, which is considered in greater detail next.

Sociological Considerations

Cultural ideologies and social structures are closely linked, and either may causally influence the other (Gilmore, 1990). The social structure composing the Greco-Roman world (e.g., sharp gender-role divisions; mentorships institutionalized within a warrior culture) was favorable to the expression of pederasty (Crapo, 1995), as were key cultural ideologies (e.g., manly sex was rigidly defined by the active role; the gender of acceptable partners was irrelevant) (Williams, 1999). Cultural ideologies, in turn, may be encoded in myths that validate them. For the Greeks, many of their most important male gods sought sexual relations with both women and boys. Examples of pederastic affairs included Zeus with Ganymede, Apollo with Hyacinthus, Poseidon with Pelops, Dionysus with Ampelus, and Hercules with Hylas (Pequigney, 2002). Premodern Japan had similar social structure, cultural ideologies, and validating myths. Pederasty was supported by the beliefs that Kūkai, founder of the Shingon Buddhist sect and one of the great religious figures in Japanese history, imported it from China in the ninth century CE, that one of the gods of Happiness indulged in it, and that a number of Shinto gods were guardians of it (Leupp, 1995). In Melanesia, pederasty always had religious sanctification (Herdt, 1991). In this section, cultural ideologies and social structures, as they influence the expression of pederasty, are examined.

Cultural Ideologies

The Greco-Roman tradition of pederasty, lasting at least a millennium, gradually decayed as Christianity, which was intensely hostile to it, rose to dominance (Crompton, 2003). Christianity brought in the Old Testament (Genesis 18–19) tale of God's destruction of Sodom and Gomorrah and the other cities of the Plain as punishment for a variety of sins, one being the attempted homosexual rape of two angels appearing as male youths: this sin is the one that came to define the entire tale in the Western mind (Crompton, 2003; Rice, manuscript in preparation). The Sodom myth served to morally invalidate pederasty, as well as any type of homosexual behavior between adults, because it instated the belief that all homosexual behavior was wicked and dangerous, a belief that lawmakers for centuries afterward helped to institutionalize through draconian legislation (punishments often included torture and execution), lest cities yet again be destroyed by God (Crompton, 2003; Greenberg, 1988; Rice, manuscript in preparation).[12] The ideology of pederastic and other homosexual behavior as evil was implanted in the Western mind, conditioning in the populace concomitant emotional feelings of revulsion in reaction to instances of this behavior.

When Westerners visited the Far East or Muslim societies much later and encountered pederastic relations, their reactions, under the influence of centuries of this potent ideology, were ones of unfathomable disbelief and deepest abhorrence. An Englishman visiting China in 1806 recorded his reactions, writing of "detestable and unnatural" acts that are "attended with so little sense of shame." He complained that the first officers of the state did not hesitate to show off their interests, with each "constantly attended by his pipe-bearer, who is generally a handsome boy, from fourteen to eighteen years of age" (quoted in Hinsch, 1990, p. 141). Another Englishman visiting Baghdad, when learning that his Iraqi guide's beloved was a boy, later recounted that he "shrunk back from the confession as a man would recoil from a serpent on which he had unexpectedly trodden" (quoted in Rouayheb, 2005, p. 92). By the middle of the nineteenth century, this attitude of unyielding revulsion from Westerners worked to undo a millennium or more of pederastic traditions in China, Japan, and the Muslim world, as the elite of these cultures, embarrassed by Western reactions and yet wanting to modernize in line with the West to get its goods and technology, sought to discard permissive ideologies concerning pederasty and institute Western-style heterosexual exclusivity (Hinsch, 1990; Leupp, 1995; Massad, 2007; Rouayheb, 2005).

Notably, even within the West with these ideologies already instated, the fall of pederasty was slow to occur (Boswell, 1980; Oberhelman,

1997). In certain pockets, particularly Renaissance Florence and neighboring regions, it lasted in unbroken form from Greco-Roman times as a pervasive pattern, falling only with renewed energized efforts by church and state to suppress it (Rocke, 1996). For present purposes, the point is that cultural ideologies strongly affect the expression of pederasty among a populace. If supportive, the practice can be widely distributed across the male population. If antagonistic, the practice will be or become uncommon. The Sodom myth has been a particularly potent antagonistic ideology, with direct and indirect effects across the globe.

Social Structures

Cross-culturally, as reviews have repeatedly shown (e.g., Ford & Beach, 1951; Greenberg, 1988; Murray, 2000; Werner, 2006), when male homosexual behavior has occurred in a society as an acceptable pattern, it has generally fallen into three basic forms: (a) age-stratified (i.e., pederasty), (b) gender-stratified (i.e., a masculine male with a transgendered male), and (c) egalitarian (usually between adolescent boys, who give up the practice when they become adults). The pederastic and gender-stratified forms have both frequently occurred cross-culturally and historically, with the former often being practiced society-wide but the latter being restricted to much smaller numbers of individuals (Adam, 1985; Ford & Beach, 1951; Gregersen, 1983). Notably, the gay pattern (i.e., exclusively same-sex relations between relatively equal adults), a subtype of the egalitarian form, has been restricted to the modern West and is exceptional from a cross-cultural and historical perspective (e.g., Adam, 1985; Cardoso & Werner, 2004; Gregersen, 1983; Herdt, 1987; Werner, 2006).

Crapo (1995) and Murray (2000) examined the moderating effects of social structure on the appearance of the different forms of homosexual behavior by conducting cross-cultural statistical analyses. Combining their results, they found that mentorship (i.e., pederastic) societies had greater sex role distinctions, greater adolescent sex-segregation, greater tendency to consider virginity to be necessary for brides, less paternal effort in rearing the very young, less female political power, less occurrence of husbands and wives sleeping together, and more polygyny (limited to older and wealthier men). Crapo added that mentorships were commonly embedded in exclusively male settings (e.g., military, religious), where young males were initiated into the skills and symbolism of warfare, religion, politics, and male social dominance. According to Crapo, in mentorship societies, younger males needed the training offered by their elders to climb the male status ladder. Conversely, gender-stratified societies had greater equality between the sexes in political matters, in principal subsistence work and in sex roles more generally, and were less likely to segregate adolescent males. Murray found that egalitarian systems were most likely where premarital sex was most permissible and fewer wealth distinctions existed. Crapo concluded that the social traits commonly associated with gender-stratified homosexuality were also present where homophilia (e.g., the gay pattern in the modern West) was found.

In Western culture, the pederastic form dominated from classical times through the Renaissance, being openly and widely practiced early on, though more hidden and sporadic later (Greenberg, 1988). Sometime after the Renaissance, the homophilic, or gay, form began emerging as a significant pattern in the West. At the same time, the pederastic form lessened, owing to the industrial revolution, which acted to create greater distance between the generations, and thus to reduce older male-younger male social interactions, which beforehand had been extensive. Nevertheless, well into the twentieth century, both forms, though derogated and criminalized, appeared in various underground contexts with regularity (for the former, see Reiss, 1961; Rossman, 1976). By the 1970s, a series of major social structural changes set in, which helped to alter the trajectories of the pederastic and gay forms substantially, rendering the former even more deviant, but the latter relatively normal. These changes included most of the elements analyzed by Crapo (1995) and Murray (2000). Tendencies toward sex-segregation during adolescence began to disappear, virginity until marriage was no longer emphasized, sex-role distinctions weakened considerably, women gained more significant political power, fathers exerted more child-rearing efforts with young children, and all-male societies weakened and disappeared as men began spending free time mostly with female companions and nuclear family units rather than men's groups (cf. Coontz, 2006; Mackey, 1986, 1990).

These structural changes were all related to major advances in technology throughout the twentieth century, increasingly reducing or eliminating the purely muscular nature of many male occupations, while opening up many occupations that were not physically demanding at all (e.g., white collar, tertiary, service sector). These changes helped to erode sex-role distinctions, because women could do most of these jobs as well. Another technological advance, the invention of the pill in 1960, removed pregnancy as a major obstacle in women's securing careers (Gibbs, 2010). It also helped usher in the sexual revolution, in which virginity lost its cultural importance. Cross-culturally, manhood has been valued to the extent that the social and physical environment is dangerous and physically demanding, as in warrior and big-game hunting societies (Gilmore, 1990). With the significant reduction in brute-strength male activities, however, manhood has weakened in our society as a cultural ideal or necessity, paving the way for women's gains in political power. Moreover, cross-culturally, males generally congregate with other males in all-male groups in cultures where brute-strength male activities predominate, but associate mainly with women and nuclear families when these activities do not (Mackey, 1986). Increasingly, all-male groups have thinned out or disappeared in our culture with the advances in technology, and the genders mix much more regularly outside the workplace as well, such that former practices of sex-segregation have all but vanished and new practices, such as fathers' greater involvement in child-rearing of young children, have grown.

In short, cross-cultural and sociological considerations provide an important means for attempting to understand trends and fluctuations in pederasty and homophilia. The supplanting of former dominant social structures with the current one has altered the practice and perception of both the pederastic and gay forms. As we shall show, associated changes in cultural ideologies have been important as well.

Additional Considerations: Cultural Ideologies Revisited

As just discussed, changes set in beginning around 1970 that heightened pederasty's deviant status, rendering it considerably more derogated than previously, while virtually eliminating the deviant status for androphile gay sexuality, which quickly became not simply tolerated but acceptable in many circles. For example, across states in the United States, pederastic behaviors that might have brought probation or minimal prison sentences half a century ago today are routinely subject to decades or life in prison (Hubbard, in this volume), whereas gay relations that subjected the participants to prison half a century ago are now increasingly becoming eligible for marriage. The discussion of cultural ideologies and social structures up to this point needs supplementing to adequately account for the intensity of this altered cultural thinking with respect to pederasty.

An older cultural ideology that formed an important foundation for the changes after 1970 was "childhood innocence," the conviction that children are asexual and need to avoid sex for healthy development. This notion emerged during the Enlightenment and formed the basis for the masturbation hysteria from the mid-eighteenth to early twentieth centuries, in which childhood masturbation was claimed to cause a long list of maladies from acne to death (Hare, 1962). It also influenced Freud's early theory that childhood seduction is the cause of all neuroses (Foucault, 1978). As Foucault showed, these beliefs developed in response to changing social conditions and relations between the state and individuals, in which it was useful for the state to asexualize children, and in which clinicians accommodated the state in their theorizing. That childhood innocence is a Western belief, not a scientific fact, was empirically demonstrated by Ford and Beach (1951) in their cross-cultural and cross-species review of child sexual development.

Another older cultural ideology was that sex was for procreation. By the 1970s, in consequence of the sexual revolution, this older ethos was replaced by "consenting adults" as the legitimate basis for sexual relations (Levine & Troiden, 1988), which helped enable gay liberation to occur and succeed. At the same time, various feminists were raising consciousness about rape of women, making quick gains in changing social views and response. Following this success, they moved on to incest, attributing to it the same motives (e.g., power) and effects (e.g., trauma, lasting maladjustment), which they observed in or attributed to rape. Sexual victimology, consisting of a loose network of mental health and law enforcement professionals concerned with sexual victimization, arose in response to the campaigns against rape and incest. It appeared as a scientific discipline on the surface, but adopted as axiomatic the assumptions, theorizing, and ideologies espoused by the antirape and anti-incest feminist advocates. By the early 1980s, the rape and incest models became the basis for sexual victimological understanding of all forms of adult-minor sex (Jenkins, 1998, 2006).

From a scientific point of view, what is problematic is that many feminist advocates in the 1970s focusing on sexual abuse were given to hyperbole in service of political aims (Angelides, 2004, 2005; Sommers, 1995). Their goal was to uproot the "patriarchy," in which challenging or undermining ideologies of masculinity was instrumental. Using male sexual transgressions of all types became a chief tactic, and freely mixing hyperbolized claims with valid ones became routine (Jenkins, 1998; 2006). Angelides (2004) referred to these advocates as "radical feminists," whereas Sommers (1995) referred to them as "gender feminists." Such activists did not represent all types of feminists in the 1970s or afterward (e.g., prominant feminist writers such as Camille Paglia or Gail Rubin opposed their ideology, message, and tactics). Importantly, however, their point of view came to dominate throughout the West. Sexual victimology emerged, incorporated their point of view, and gave it a "scientific" face. In other words, hyperbole and ideology were built into the foundations of sexual victimology. Though it has never been a valid science, its assertions have been taken as scientific and have substantially influenced public policy (Malón, 2011).

In terms of adult-minor sex, the hyperbole of these activists and sexual victimologists was readily accepted by professionals and the public, in part because it was built on top of the already existing ideology of childhood innocence. Freud's seduction theory was revived by sexual victimologists, and adult-minor sex came to be invested with all the pathogenic agency that had once been attributed to masturbation (Jenkins, 1998; Malón, 2010). In the 1980s, the results of this 1970s thinking were dramatic, as moral panic spread across the United States with satanic-sexual-ritual abuse by staff in day care and recovered memories by adult patients in therapy (Jenkins, 1998; Nathan & Snedeker, 1995). These false claims, repeatedly sensationalized in uncritical media coverage, firmly implanted in social thinking the belief that adult-minor sex is the ultimate crime with the most extreme negative psychological effects.

In short, building upon earlier assumptions about childhood innocence, reflecting the new ideology of anything goes provided it involves "consenting adults" and proceeding from radical feminist discourse, all adult-minor sex became equated with rape and incest, accompanied by assumptions of invariable imposition of power, lack of consent, and extreme harm (Jenkins, 1998; Malón, 2011). Pederasty, being a type of adult-minor sex, came to be fully invested with this ideology. In 1980, the National Organization for Women issued an opinion, clarifying its view on pederasty to remove any previously existing ambiguity. It resolved that pederasty is "an issue of exploitation or violence, not affectional/sexual preference/orientation" (quoted in Jenkins, 2006, p. 125). Such thinking has since been an entrenched social belief.

An early paradigmatic illustration of this thinking was a 1984 editorial in a major US newspaper, in which the writers decried a series of recently uncovered sexual relations between men aged 18 and over and boys aged 12 to 17—that is to say, pederastic relations (*Philadelphia Inquirer*, 1984, 22A). The writers asserted that "there can be no question" that such relations "are among the most brutalizing [crimes] known to civilized society." They claimed that all credible psychological and psychiatric theory recognized that all relations of this sort are "profoundly damaging" and "leave emotional scars, distrusts, [and] self-contempt that last through lifetimes." They further claimed that this theorizing rested on "the truth that such contacts invariably involve the imposition of power and exploitation, in the most fearfully private of ways." They emphasized that these relations had nothing to do with homosexuality, and that homosexuals, who deserved dignity, should not be confused with "pathological, and criminal, pedophiles." What is notable in this diatribe is its point-by-point adherence to radical feminist discourse, even while presuming to be scientific. In 1984 the large bulk of scientific literature on pederasty actually reported it to be benign or beneficial (see empirical review earlier in this article). But the editorial, driven by ideological fervor, committed the moralistic fallacy by strongly reading into the pederastic relations many of the talking points of this ideology. From this time frame to now, there has been an unbroken chain in mainstream media coverage, in which the view, tone, and hyperbole in this editorial have been repeated. Notably, the editorial writers' journalistic forebearers a generation earlier, under a different set of cultural ideologies, were given to similar tirades against gay men, rather than advocating dignity for them.

In sum, cultural ideologies and social structures have strongly influenced both the practice and perception of pederasty across time and place. These influences in the modern West over the last four decades have been especially potent in this regard. It is important in scientific analysis to take such influences under consideration. By contrast, relying on current cultural ideologies and the social structure as final reference points in making claims about factual matters (e.g., pederasty is "profoundly damaging") is to invite commission of the moralistic fallacy.

Cross-Species Perspective

Pederasty has repeatedly appeared in different societies in institutionalized form for its mentoring and enculturation value (Crapo, 1995), as well as in many other societies on a more casual, but still widespread, basis (Murray, 2000). As Ford and Beach (1951) argued, when a sexual pattern recurs across societies, evolutionary roots should be considered, and cross-species comparisons are useful to this end. In this section, other species are examined for pederastic-like behavior, referred to here as "age-discrepant homosex," which stands for age-discrepant homosexual relations between older males and immature males.[13] First, primates are considered, which have direct relevance for humans, who are primates as well. Next, subprimate mammalian and then avian species are examined for additional perspective. The review relies on four basic sources: (a) Vasey's (1995) review of primate homosexual behavior in about three dozen species; (b) Bagemihl's (1999) review of homosexual behavior in several hundred species of mammals (including primates) and birds; (c) Sommer and Vasey's (2006) edited collection of extensive recent field studies of homosexual behavior in various mammalian and avian species, and (d) many of the primary studies on primates.

Before proceeding, it will be helpful to consider in more detail the logic behind this sort of comparative analysis. In the social sciences, there has been much resistance to drawing inferences from animal behavior to human behavior, as if humans are discontinuous with respect to the rest of the animal kingdom and different laws of evolution apply to them. This is a fallacy. Humans are evolutionarily continuous with prehuman and nonhuman ancestors, and the same evolutionary processes that apply to other animals apply to humans as well. In particular, what we learn about animal sexual behavior can be informative about human sexual behavior (Vasey & Sommer, 2006). Human heterosexual mating was not "specially" created for humans, but derives, with modification, from primate and mammalian patterns. By studying mating in other primates or subprimate mammalian species, we can learn about general principles that may apply to humans, even if the details in mating patterns in other species are different. The same applies to patterns in homosexual behavior (Bagemihl, 1999; Ford & Beach, 1951; Vasey & Sommer, 2006). Rather than imagining that human homosexual behavior is "against nature," as some conservatives might argue, or was specially created in humans, as some liberals might believe, an informed scientific approach is to analyze patterns across species, especially those more closely related to humans. Even though the details of these patterns in other species (e.g., form, function) may not transfer to the human pattern, nonetheless general principles may be inferrable. This inference is stronger the more similar the cross-species patterns are to the human pattern. To repeat Ford and Beach (1951), when a human pattern recurs often, cross-species analysis is called for to consider an evolutionary basis for this pattern. This principle applies as well for pederasty.

Primates

Bagemihl (1999) provided extensive descriptions of twenty-one primate species, in which male homosexual behavior has been documented (in all these species, age-discrepant homosex was one of the forms). In Table IV, these species along with three additional ones are listed, for a total of twenty-four species.[14] In the table, each species is rated along three dimensions based on Bagemihl's (1999) ratings and descriptions, Vasey's (1995) ratings, and the descriptions in the primary studies themselves. The three dimensions, appearing in columns 2–4, are: (a) frequency of male homosexual activity, (b) dominant type of age pairings involved, and (c) receptivity regarding the younger partners in age-discrepant homosex. The last column presents brief summaries of the male homosexual behavior, including age-discrepant homosex, in each species. The ratings and the summaries will be useful for reconsidering human pederasty from a comparative approach. For example, if pederasty is *innately* pathological, as believed in our society, it might be expected to find evidence in the primates pointing in the same direction. If pederasty has functions, as other cultures believe, and if such functions have an evolutionary basis, then evidence of utility and benefit rather than harm in primates would be informative.

Male homosexual activity occurred frequently in 42 percent of the listed species and moderately in another 50 percent. Mature-immature contacts (i.e., age-discrepant homosex) dominated in 29 percent of the species, immature-immature relations in 13 percent, and mixed relations, with non-dominant occurrences of mature-immature, immature-immature, and mature-mature relations, in 58 percent of the species—in no species did relations between two adults dominate.[15] Receptivity, rather than resistance, on the part of immature animals involved in age-discrepant homosex predominated in most of the species (83%). The summaries provided in the last column in the table flesh out the ratings and provide information useful for assessing pathology, neutrality, and function.

Consent/assent by younger partner. In many species, the younger animals involved in age-discrepant homosex were frequently observed not simply assenting to the sexual interactions but actually initiating them (e.g., bonobos, chimps, gorillas, gibbons, Hanuman and Nilgiri langurs, crab-eating macaques, rhesus macaques, Tibetan macaques, patas monkeys). Specific examples include juvenile Tibetan macaques jumping up to the faces of adult males to be fellated (Ogawa, 1995), an adolescent gibbon repeatedly soliciting sex from his father (Edwards & Todd, 1991), and juvenile rhesus macaques fiercely competing to be the one mounted by an adult male (Kempf, 1917). In a number of species,

Table IV: Homosexual Behavior Between Mature and Immature Males in Primates.

Species	Freq	Age	Rec	Researcher Observations/Summaries
Great Apes				
Bonobos (Pan paniscus)	3	1	3	Mature males frequently performed thrusts on much younger males who might actively solicit the mounting (Kano, 1980). Common also is an adult male masturbating an adolescent male lying on his back with legs spread apart. Sex serves to reduce social tension (de Waal, 1997).
Chimpanzees (Pan troglodytes)	2	2	3	Male homosex varies considerably across and within chimp populations (Bagemihl, 1999). Kollar et al. (1968) described multiple age-gap encounters (e.g., a young juvenile male interrupted copulation of an adolescent male and female, then presented to the older male, who mounted him).
Gorillas (Gorilla gorilla)	3	4	3	In all-male groups, adults are most attracted to adolescents; mounting can be initiated by either (Harcourt, 1979; Yamagiwa, 1987, 2006). Courtship and copulation occur daily (Bagemihl, 1999). Age-gap sex may help group cohesiveness (Harcourt, 1979).
Orangutans (Pongo pygmaeus)	2	2	3	Homosex is often consensual (heterosex often not), often occurs within a special friendship (Bagemihl, 1999). Example: An adolescent male that received fellatio from a young adult male became very attached to him, and followed him wherever he went (Rijksen, 1978).
Lesser Apes				
White-handed gibbons (Hylobates lar)	2	4	3	Homosex occurs sometimes in father-son pairs (Bagemihl, 1999). Edwards and Todd (1991) observed fifty-five episodes between father and adolescent son, always without tension or aggression, initiated by both; seemed to provide reassurance to the adolescent.
Siamangs (Hylobates syndactylus)	2	1	2	Father-son sex occurs (like gibbons), but is sometimes accompanied by threats, when the younger partner wants to end it before the older one does (unlike gibbons) (Bagemihl, 1999).
Old World Monkeys				
Hanuman langurs (Presbytis entellus)	3	1	3	Immature males frequently engage in mounting, often with like-aged males, but also with mature males (Sommer et al., 2006). Immature males increase their touching, mounting, and embracing of adult males as they mature (Jay, 1965). Weber (1973) found that male-male age-gap mounting was usually initiated by the immature partner, with apparent function of securing social acceptance (juveniles are no longer protected by mothers and turn to other adults; mounting and other physical contact are mechanisms to achieve social integration).
Nilgiri langurs (Presbytis johnii)	2	1	3	Dominant males (alphas) mount subordinate males (juveniles, adolescents, younger adults) in dominance displays, which the subordinates may initiate by presenting. Mounts are brief, with several thrusts but no penetration, and are part of a communication matrix that maintains troop harmony (Hohmann, 1989; Poirier, 1970).
Proboscis monkeys (Nasalis larvatus)	1	2	2	Homosexual mounting occurs in younger males (adolescents and juveniles); it tends to stem from play wrestling. It is resisted by the younger male in some cases (as females sometimes also do in heterosexual mounting). Its frequency is low, as is heterosexual sex (Bagemihl, 1999; Yeager, 1990).
Bonnet macaques	3	1	3	Males of all ages are frequently involved in a wide variety of homosex. Younger males often masturbate

Table IV: (continued)

Species	Freq	Age	Rec	Researcher Observations/Summaries
Old World Monkeys (continued) (Macaca radiata)				other males to orgasm, sometimes eating the semen. Some do only a little homosex, others a great deal (Bagemihl, 1999).
Crab-eating macaques (Macaca fascicularis)	2	1	2	Males can develop intense sexual friendships, especially between older and younger males (with affection, arousal, mounting). Homosexual mounting is both consensual (54%) and nonconsensual (46%). In the former, the mountee fully cooperates and may initiate the mounting (Bagemihl, 1999).
Crested black macaques (Macaca nigra)	2	4	3	Younger males often mount older ones (Bagemihl, 1999). Dixson (1977) frequently observed the oldest male in one troop presenting to younger males, who invariably responded by mounting him, often with erections. Also, ritualized "greeting" gestures (e.g., penis-grabbing), especially by younger males, are common practice (Bagemihl, 1999).
Japanese macaques (Macaca fuscata)	3	1	3	All adult and juvenile males were seen presenting to another male (aggression was rare, <3%) (Hanby & Brown, 1974). Takenoshita (1998) observed free-ranging adult-juvenile consort relationships (adults ejaculated, juveniles erected; they foraged, groomed, and attacked others together).
Pig-tailed macaques (Macaca nemestrina)	3	1	3	Age-equal and age-gap male-male mounting (juveniles, adolescents, adults) occurs frequently, is not associated with force (as heterosexual mounting sometimes is), and makes up from 8% to 67% of individual males' overall mounts (Bagemihl, 1999). Dominants invite subordinates to mount them as an elaborate display of tolerance toward subordinates (Oi, 1990) or mount subordinates as a rank maintenance mechanism (Tokuda et al., 1968).
Rhesus macaques (Macaca mulatta)	3	1	3	Age-gap consort relationships occur, highly affectionate (Bagemihl, 1999). Kempf (1917) observed two juvenile males competing to be mounted by an adult male. Homosex helps juveniles get protection, integrate into group (Carpenter, 1942). Older, younger both show sexual excitement; mature-immature relationships are frequent, seem to have sexual basis (Hamilton, 1914). Redican et al. (1974) observed an immature male taking the sexual initiative with an adult male in an intensive relationship.
Stumptail macaques (Macaca arctoides)	3	1	3	Chevalier-Skolnikoff (1976) reported mutual excitement and affection in several intense friendship-based mature-immature sexual relationships. These were "rewarding" to all participants (e.g., protection for younger partner). Homosex seemed to foster greater social cohesion.
Tibetan macaques (Macaca thibetana)	3	4	3	Ogawa (1995) found that male adult-juvenile homosex occurs on a regular basis; either may initiate oral sex on the juvenile; it is never aggressive; both are excited; context is friendly. It seems to serve to reduce tension.
Savanna baboons (Papio cynocephalus)	2	1	3	All males, from juvenile to adult, greet one another via ritualized sexual behaviors. These behaviors (presenting, mounting, fondling) occur briefly (a few seconds), constitute "greetings," and appear to serve in part formation of coalitions (Bagemihl, 1999; Smuts & Watanabe, 1990).
Hamadryas baboons (Papio hamadryas)	2	4	3	Zuckerman (1932) observed a three-year sexual relationship between an adult and immature male. When ever the immature was threatened, the adult immediately rescued it.

Table IV: *(continued)*

Species	Freq	Age	Rec	Researcher Observations/Summaries
Old World Monkeys *(continued)*				
Gelada baboons (*Theropithecus gelada*)	2	4	3	Bernstein (1975) found that mounting occurs between bachelors and immature males in the all-male group. When a bachelor successfully challenges a harem leader, he switches entirely to heterosex (the deposed leader switches to homosex).
Mona monkeys (*Cercopithecus mona*)	3	1	3	Glenn, Ramsier, and Benson (2006) found that homosex, with oral sex (often with orgasm), is universal in all-male groups, where males spend most of their lives. It involves all combinations from juveniles to adults; aggression is extremely rare. It seems to function to help younger males' immigration and social skills, as well as the groups' social cohesion.
Patas monkeys (*Erythrocebus patas*)	2	4	3	Adolescent or younger males often fondle and nuzzle the genitals and scrotum of adult males (Bagemihl, 1999).
New World Monkeys				
Squirrel monkeys (*Saimiri sciureus*)	2	1	3	Denniston (1980) frequently observed male homosexual behavior, the commonest form being between adults and adolescents. Baldwin (1969) frequently observed sexual mounting and sometimes consortships between older adolescents and much younger juveniles (of both sexes); older adolescents, unlike younger adolescents, were gentle with their younger partners, who consequently allowed the interactions to take place (by contrast, they tended to resist the much rougher initiatives from younger adolescents).
Prosimians				
Verreaux's sifaka (*Propithecus verreauxi*)	1	1	1	Homosexual behavior is rare in prosimians. In this lemur species, adult males sometimes mount younger adults or adolescents, who often snap and struggle to wriggle free (Bagemihl, 1999).

Note. Freq = frequency, based mainly on Vasey's (1995) and Bagemihl's (1999) ratings (1 = incidental or rare; 2 = moderate; 3 = frequent or primary). Age = age class (dominant age pairings that occur), based mainly on Vasey's (1995) ratings (1 = mixed ages; 2 = between immatures; 3 = between adults; 4 = mature with immature). Rec = receptivity based on researchers' descriptions (1 = mostly unwilling with resistance or aggression; 2 = mix of receptive and nonreceptive encounters; 3 = mostly receptive with no or little aggression). Researcher observations/summaries provide illustrations from research on typical encounters and overall nature of mature-immature male homosex.

the researchers noted the sexual excitement exhibited by the immature partners in age-discrepant homosex (e.g., rhesus, stumptail, and Tibetan macaques). In several species, sometimes immature males were assenting and sometimes not (e.g., siamangs, proboscis monkeys, crab-eating macaques, and squirrel monkeys). In siamangs, sometimes the younger animal assented but then wanted to end the contact earlier than the older animal did (Bagemihl, 1999), and in squirrel monkeys juvenile males tended to resist sexual approaches from younger adolescent males, who were rough, although they accepted these approaches from older adolescent males, who were more gentle (Baldwin, 1969). In only one species (Verreaux's sifaka) was age-discrepant homosex, as well as adult-adult sex, predominantly or always non-consensual, where the approached animal resisted aggressively (Bagemihl, 1999). In the other examples in the table, as well as in most primate species in general, aggression in connection to homosexual behavior of any sort is rare or absent; when it occurs, it typically is associated with heterosexual interactions between mature animals (Bagemihl, 1999; Vasey, 1995).

Adult male interest. Adult male primates frequently exhibited a bisexual orientation, with interests often directed at both mature females and immature males. Mature male bonobos frequently directed thrusts on immature males (Kano, 1980), adult male gorillas were primarily and intensely aroused by immature males in their all-male groups (Harcourt, 1979; Yamagiwa, 1987), and adult male rhesus, stumptail, and Tibetan macaques showed excitement in their sexual interactions with immature males (Chevalier-Skolnikoff, 1976; Hamilton, 1914; Ogawa, 1995). Being in all-male groups contributed to the expression of these interests by adult males (e.g., gorillas, mona monkeys, gelada baboons), although adult males also exhibited interest in younger males in the presence of sexually receptive females (e.g., bonobos, rhesus macaques, stumptail macaques). Adult males' interest in immature males could switch to females with a change in social environment or status. For example, adult male gorillas in mixed groups generally directed erotic attentions to mature females instead of immature males (Yamagiwa, 1987, 2006), and adult male gelada baboons who moved from all-male groups to become harem leaders switched from interests in immature males to interests in mature females (Bernstein, 1975).

Special friendships. Intense sexually based friendships or consort relationships between older and younger animals have been documented in various species, including gorillas, orangutans, macaques (crab-eating, Japanese, rhesus, stumptail), Hamadryas baboons, and squirrel monkeys. Takenoshita (1998) observed consort relationships between adult and juvenile male Japanese macaques, where these pairs, in addition to engaging in homosexual interactions, foraged together, groomed one another, and attacked other monkeys together. Chevalier-Skolnikoff (1976) described intensely affectionate relationships between mature and immature stumptail male macaques, in which both older and younger partners responded with sexual excitement to the sexual interactions. Zuckerman (1932) observed a three-year sexual relationship between an adult and an immature male Hamadryas baboon. Redican, Gomber, and Mitchell (1974) observed an intense attachment between an adult male rhesus macaque and a much younger male, in which the latter took strong initiative in establishing the relationship and sexual interaction. Hamilton (1914), also studying rhesus macaques, reported that he "found that friendships between immature males and mature males are of frequent occurrence, and that they seem to have a sexual basis" (p. 308). In one illustrative case, Hamilton reported, when a separated mature-immature pair was allowed to reunite, the two rushed into an embrace, smacking their lips. Both animals showed marked sexual excitement, and the older mounted the younger, who rotated his head to achieve lip contact with the older partner.

Frequency and variability. As indicated in Table IV, the frequency of age-discrepant homosex and other homosexual interactions varied both between and within species. In some, these interactions occurred incessantly (e.g., gorillas, mona monkeys, Tibetan macaques). In gorillas, as Yamagiwa (1987) noted, courtships and copulations between older and younger participants occurred daily. In general, Vasey (1995) noted a trend across the primate order in frequency of homosexual behavior from rare or absent in prosimians, to somewhat more common in New World monkeys, to frequent in Old World monkeys and apes, with the former two groups being more distantly, and the latter two more closely, related to humans. Researchers have also noted the variability of age-discrepant homosex and other homosexual behavior among individuals within particular species (e.g., chimpanzees, bonnet macaques, pig-tailed macaques). In pig-tailed macaques, for example, 8 percent to 67 percent of individual males' mounts are homosexual (Bagemihl, 1999).

Real versus pseudo/proto-homosexual behavior. Homosexual behavior in primates can look like human homosexual behavior (e.g., masturbation, oral sex, penetration) or it can look superficial (e.g., dominance rituals with very little contact). Age-discrepant homosex, in particular, frequently is of the former type (e.g., bonobos, gorillas, orangutans, gibbons, bonnet macaques, Japanese macaques, Tibetan macaques, mona monkeys). In bonobos, adult males commonly masturbate adolescent males, who display full erections (de Waal, 1997). In gorillas, adult males anally penetrate younger males (Yamagiwa, 1987). In mona monkeys, oral sex accompanied by orgasm is frequent (Glenn, Ramsier, & Benson, 2006). In other species, homosexual interactions are often ritualistic, as in dominance mounts (e.g., Hanuman langurs, Nilgiri langurs, savanna baboons). In a study sample of Hanuman langurs, male homosexual behavior included no manual stimulation, oral sex, or anal penetration, but instead mounts in which erections were rare and in which ejaculations occurred less than 1 percent of the time (Sommer, Schauer, & Kyriazis, 2006). In Savanna baboons, mounting and fondling occur frequently among males from juveniles to adults, but last only a few seconds (Smuts & Watanabe, 1990).

Functions. Finally, researchers have frequently inferred or speculated that male primate homosexual relations, including and often specifically age-discrepant homosex, serve positive functions for the participants, such as overcoming social tension (bonobos, Tibetan macaques), communicating or acknowledging rank to express or seek tolerance or to avoid conflict (pig-tailed macaques, Nilgiri langurs), facilitating social cohesion (gorillas, stumptail macaques, mona monkeys) and social integration (Hanuman langurs, rhesus macaques, mona monkeys), providing reassurance (gibbons) and protection (rhesus macaques, stumptail macaques, hamadryas baboons), initiating cooperation (savanna baboons), and helping the young to acquire social skills (mona monkeys).

Summary and conclusions. Immature males in many of the primate species reviewed, especially those more closely related to humans, frequently assented to, and even initiated, sexual contacts with mature males. In general, assent predominated over non-consent across these species, and aggression in connection to the latter was quite rare. Adult males in these species generally showed the capacity to respond erotically to younger males, and they frequently expressed it. In many of these species, older-younger pairs formed special friendships, which included affection, intense bonds, and sexual interactions. Species varied from common to infrequent in homosexual behavior, as did individuals within the species. Age-discrepant homosex often included forms of sexual behavior that, in human terms, would be called genuine sex. In many species age-discrepant homosex appeared to serve one type of function or another. Taken together, these findings lend no support to the notion that homosexual behavior between mature and immature males is an intrinsic pathology in the primate order, but instead point to neutral or functional value. The parallels with the human nonclinical empirical, historical, and cross-cultural data are fairly strong and suggest that human pederasty has evolutionary roots that are shared by many other species in the primate order. The primate data add to the nonclinical human data in contradicting the view that pederasty is an intrinsic pathology.

Subprimate Mammals and Birds

Animal species from different orders or classes are more removed from humans in evolutionary terms, but a brief look at them can be useful. Given the prevalence of primate age-discrepant homosex, it becomes of interest to examine whether and to what extent this behavior occurs elsewhere in nature. If its occurrence is frequent rather than rare, for example, locating human pederasty in the context of nature and evolution, rather than idiosyncratic pathology, is further indicated. In the review to follow, most of Bagemihl's (1999) case studies that involved age-discrepant homosex are included, and the list is updated with some of the primary studies in Sommer and Vasey's (2006) collection.

Mammals
The twenty-six species listed in Table V include eleven marine mammals, thirteen hoofed mammals, and two other types. The descriptions below summarize key themes from the table.

Dolphins and whales. In the dolphin and whale species, male homosexual behavior was frequent, sometimes exceeding heterosexual behavior. It generally occurred in all-male settings, was most characteristic of younger males, often involved intimate (e.g., penetrative) and lengthy interactions, and could involve extensive mutual affection and bonding (as in some age-discrepant boto and bottlenose relations). In orcas, the age-discrepant type predominated, where adolescents typically were involved with much older or younger males, courting was frequent, and sexual interactions were usually reciprocal. In Mann's (2006) extensive field study on bottlenose dolphins, immature males were hypersexual, frequently behaving homosexually with peers, but with older males as well. More than half of adult males' sexual activity was directed at immature males. Mann concluded that immature males' homosexual behavior was functional, serving later male-male alliance formation, which facilitates male-female consortships.

Seals and manatees. In the seal and manatee species in Table V, male homosexual behavior was generally quite common. It usually involved all ages, and age-discrepant relations were common. Although resistance was characteristic in adult-immature relations in northern elephant seals, consent, including initiative from the younger animal, predominated among age-discrepant homosexual relations in the other species. For example, younger males mounted older ones among Australian and New Zealand sea lions. Affection was common in manatees, where males of all ages intensively interacted in a homosexual way. Walruses were notable for their nearly universal male homosexual behavior, which usually occurred between adolescents or between adults and adolescents, and in which adolescents frequently solicited adults, adults frequently courted adolescents, and adults and adolescents fairly often formed companionships.

Deer and moose. Male homosexual behavior occurs only occasionally in deer and moose. When it occurs, all ages can be involved, although it is more common among the young. In age-discrepant homosex, typically younger males mount older ones. Sometimes older and younger males form companionships, as in wapiti and moose. Bartos and Holeckova (2006) found that resistance to being mounted occurred mainly between immature bucks; it was not a factor between older and younger deer.

Antelopes and gazelles. In blackbucks and pronghorns, males of all ages frequently participate in homosexual behavior in their all-male

Table V: Homosexual Behavior Between Mature and Immature Males in Subprimate Mammals

Species	Summary of Descriptions from Bagemihl (1999) or Primary Researchers
Marine Mammals	
Dolphins and whales Boto or Amazon River dolphin (Inia geoffrensis)	Males participate in a wide variety of homosexual behavior, including various kinds of intercourse. When there is an age difference typically the older penetrates the younger. Pairs interacting sexually display a great deal of mutual affection, which Bagemihl (1999, p. 341) illustrates in a photo, in which an adult and immature partner are touching while swimming side by side.
Bottlenose dolphins (Tursiops truncates)	Homosexual behavior largely exceeds heterosexual behavior. Adolescents and younger males typically live in all-male groups, where homosexual behavior is common and exclusive. Only as full adults do they attempt to father calves via heterosexual contact. Younger adolescents form homosexual pair-bonds with like-age males, which often last throughout life. When there is an age difference in homosexual sex, either party may penetrate the other—adolescents have been observed penetrating adults (Bagemihl, 1999). McBride and Hebb (1948) observed adult males repeatedly interacting sexually with younger males and described an intense, affectionate bond in one pair. In an extensive ten-year field study, young, immature males were found to be the most sexual (most often with male peers, but also with all other age-sex classes); most of adult males' sexual interactions were with immature males (Mann, 2006).
Orca or killer whales (Orcinus orca)	Orcas are the largest in the dolphin family. Homosexual behavior is integral to male social life. During salmon feasting, males of all ages spend afternoons courting, being affectionate, and engaging in overt homosexual behaviors, with 90% being reciprocated. Sessions last an hour on average. Most involve adolescents and an age difference of at least five years. At least half of all males get involved.
Sperm whales (Physeter macrocephalus) & Bowhead whales (Balaena mysticetus)	3–5% of males may be homosexually bonded, with couples consisting of two adults or an older and younger male. Sexual interactions leading to orgasm can take place in groups of primarily younger males. Intensive male homosexual sessions lasting up to forty minutes occur, involving mainly groups of adolescents and young adults.
Seals and Manatees	
Gray seals (Halichoerus grypus)	Male homosexual behavior is common; males of all ages mount each other on shore after molting.
Harbor seals (Phoca vitulina)	Male homosexual behavior is common, involving males of all ages, but mainly adolescents and adults.
Northern elephant seals (Mirounga angustirostris)	Adolescent and young adult males do same-sex mounting during the molting season. Adult males sometimes mount younger adolescent or juvenile males, but the younger males usually struggle to escape.
Australian sea lions (Neophoca cinerea) & New Zealand sea lions (Phocarctos hookeri)	Male homosexual mounting is common. All ages may be involved, but usually a younger partner mounts an older one. As mating is polygynous, many males never mate heterosexually.
West Indian manatees (Trichechus manatus)	Males can form bachelor herds. Males of all ages intensively interact homosexually, involving embracing, kissing, mouthing, caressing, genital rubbing, and frequent ejaculation.

Table V: (continued)

Species	Summary of Descriptions from Bagemihl (1999) or Primary Researchers
Marine Mammals (Seals and Manatees) (continued)	
Walruses (Odobenus rosmarus)	Males are segregated during the nonbreeding summer months. Here, homosexual courtship, affection, and sex are common. Typically, a younger male will display to an older one, and each may mount the other. Groups of younger males may crowd an adult male, making body contact. An adult may sing a courtship song to a group of younger males or a specific younger male companion that accompanies him. Younger and older males also pursue each other during the breeding season. Homosexual behavior is very common if not universal among male Walruses, even during the breeding season, where up to a third of mounting is between younger males or between an adult and a younger male.
Hoofed Mammals	
Deer and Moose	
White-tailed deer (Odocoileus virginianus)	Males are sex-segregated most of year. Mounting sometimes occurs between two adults, two yearlings, or an older-younger pair, where the younger mounts the older one (Bagemihl, 1999). Most commonly, it is young males that mount others. Mounting is not based on dominance; no specific function is apparent. Mountees generally do not oppose being mounted if age-discrepant, but do so more if two immature males are involved (Bartos & Holeckova, 2006).
Wapiti (Cervus elaphus)	They are sex-segregated most of year. Mounting occasionally occurs between two adult or adult-yearling males. Male pairs may form companionships, either older-younger or age-equal.
Père David's deer (Elaphurus davidianus)	Males sometimes mount each other, with the younger mounting the older one.
Moose (Alces alces)	They are often solitary. Yearling males sometimes mount adult males. Sometimes adult males associate with younger male companions called satellites.
Antelopes and Gazelles	
Pronghorns (Antilocapra americana)	Some males get territories and breed. The rest live in bachelor herds, where homosexual mounting occurs to a moderate degree. Males of all ages participate, but adult males usually direct their attentions to adolescents. Mounting is preceded by courting. Most males (70%) never breed.
Blackbuck (Antilope cervicapra)	Males with territories mate with females. The rest live in bachelor herds, where most engage in mounting. This follows friendly sparring. Adult males often perform courtship displays to adolescent males before mounting them. Blackbuck males are predominately homosexual, leaving the group only once or twice in their lives attempting to breed.
Grant's gazelles (Gazella granti)	They live in mixed or all-male groups. Homosexual behavior is rare. Adult males usually attack other males trying to mount them.
Wild Sheep, Goats, Buffalo	
Bighorn sheep (Ovis canadensis) & Thinhorn sheep (Ovis dalli)	Males live in homosexual societies in sex-segregated bands. Only during the rutting season do they meet females. Older males court younger, smaller males and mount them. The mountee facilitates by assuming lordosis. Interactions are non-aggressive; the younger male is usually willing. So pervasive is this, that females will mimic younger males to attract older males. Geist (1975) views older/younger male homosex as an adaptation, allowing the younger males to live in the group.
Musk-oxen (Ovibos moschatus)	They are in mixed or all-male groups. Adult males court and mount adolescent and juvenile males. Younger males do the same with each other. Mountees sometimes resist (as females do), but sometimes assent. About 40% of courting and 10% of mounting are homosexual.

Table V: (continued)

Species	Summary of Descriptions from Bagemihl (1999) or Primary Researchers
Hoofed Mammals (Wild Sheep, Goats, Buffalo) (continued)	
Mountain goats (*Oreamnos americanus*)	They are often sex-segregated. Adult males court younger males, using the species-typical approach used in courting females. Typically, the yearling male reacts aggressively. Almost one-fifth of courtships during the breeding season occur between adult and yearling males.
American bison males (*Bison bison*)	Male bison spend most of their time alone or in bachelor herds. In these herds, homosexual mounting, including full penetration, is prevalent, especially among younger males (i.e., adolescents), and exceeds heterosexual mounting in frequency. The mounted animal often facilitates the mounting. Younger males also sometimes form tending bonds with other males, involving following, defending, and mounting or being mounted by their partners (Bagemihl, 1999). Homosexual behavior is not based on dominance, but may serve a bonding function (Vervaecke & Rodin, 2006).
Other Hoofed Mammals	
Giraffes (*Giraffa camelopardalis*)	They are often in all-male groups. Sparring between males is almost always gentle, begins as calves and juveniles, and is most common among adolescents. Participants are often of different sizes, with the smaller, younger one usually initiating. Mounting sometimes accompanies sparring, and mostly involves older adolescents mounting younger ones. These behaviors are not associated with dominance. Homosexual behavior occurs mainly among the young (Pratt & Anderson, 1985).
African elephants (*Loxodonta africana*) & Asiatic elephants (*Elephas maximus*)	African and Asiatic male elephants often form all-male herds. Breeding males associate only temporarily with females. Male homosexual mounting occurs regularly, especially among younger males. In African elephants, homosexual mounting may be preceded by extensive affectionate interaction, and both adult and younger males participate. Males also form long-lasting bonds called companionships, mainly between older and younger "attendants"—heterosexual couples do not form long-lasting bonds. The attendant male and adult male often help each other in various ways, and they are constant companions. Sometimes an older male will have two attendant males. In Asiatic male elephants, almost a fifth have a male companion.
Other Mammals	
Dwarf cavies (*Microscavia australis*)	Dwarf cavies are small rodents that live in colonies of twenty to fifty individuals. Adult males are sexually attracted to juveniles of both sexes. A typical homosexual encounter begins with an adult male and juvenile male sitting together quietly, often in front of the juvenile's mother, who is not visibly bothered. The two males then engage in affectionate contact, which eventually escalates to sexual behavior. Adult males often have favorite younger males, and will actively seek them out while ignoring other juvenile males. More than half of adult male-juvenile sexual interactions are same-sex. Most males are homosexually involved. Occasionally, an adult male will have an adolescent male companion, who feeds with him and is physically affectionate with him. The adult may allow the adolescent to mount a female he is courting. Adult males in two other species, mocó or rock cavies (*Kerodon rupestris*) and préa (*Galea spixii*), sometimes also court juvenile males.
Feral cats (*Felis catus*)	In an extensive field study, a quarter of males did homosexual mounting, but only occasionally. It always occurred in the presence of estrus females. Mounters were adults, and mountees were adolescents, smaller in size, comparable to adult female size. Mounters bit the backs of mountees' necks, as they do when mounting females. Older-younger male homosexual mounting appears to be an outlet for heterosexual mountings that were recently frustrated (Yamane, 2006).

Note. The descriptions are based mostly on Bagemihl's (1999) summaries. Only when based on other authors instead or as well, citations are given.

groups. Adult males direct their attention mainly to adolescent males, which involves courtship before mounting them. These interactions may occur following friendly sparring. In contrast to these mainly consensual interactions, mountees in Grant's gazelles generally are not consenting, and mounted adults usually attack their mounter. Blackbucks live in essentially homosexual societies, leaving only once or twice to attempt mating heterosexually.

Wild sheep, goats, and buffalo. Like blackbucks, bighorn and thinhorn sheep live in male groups that are essentially homosexual societies. Adult males court adolescent males, which are generally willing to be mounted and cooperate by assuming lordosis. So common is this practice that adult females mimic adolescent males—they are the same size—to attract adult males. Geist (1975) argued that the age-discrepant homosex is an adaptation allowing younger males to remain in the male group. Musk oxen court and mount adolescent and younger males, who sometimes resist (as females do), and sometimes assent. Adult male mountain goats also court and try to mount young males, who usually react aggressively in response. In American bison, homosexual behavior, including penetration with facilitation by the mountee, is prevalent and frequent among younger males (i.e., young adolescents to young adults).

Giraffes and elephants. In giraffes, male homosexual behavior occurs among the young in all-male herds. Typically, a younger adolescent male initiates friendly sparring with an older adolescent. The latter then sometimes mounts the younger male. Male elephants also live in all-male herds, where homosexual mounting is frequent. This may be accompanied by affectionate behavior. Adults and younger males partake, but it is especially common among younger males. Adult males fairly often form companionships with younger males, which are long-lasting bonds.

Other mammals. Adult male dwarf cavies, a type of rodent, often engage in affectionate, then sexual, contact with juvenile males, and often have favorites among them. Sometimes they have adolescent male companions. In an extensive field study of feral cats, adult males who were frustrated in pursuing estrous females sometimes mounted adolescent males, who were the same size as adult females, and whom the adult males treated as they treat females during mounting (e.g., biting the neck).

Summary and conclusions. The foregoing summaries of the species in Table V show that age-discrepant homosex extends beyond the primate order to many other species in the mammalian class. Within these species, it was always part of the mix of male homosexual behavior, oftentimes one of the dominant forms. Homosexual behavior among the young was also very common. In other words, young male mammals were often homosexually involved, whether with age-mates or older males. The pattern of age-discrepant homosex, which emerges from these summaries, contradicts the notion of its being pathological in mammals. Such relations often involved mutual participation, even initiative by the younger males. Resistance, occasionally with aggression, sometimes occurred but was not characteristic across the species. Notably, resistance occurs in other age-pairings between males, and even more so in heterosexual interactions, such that age-discrepant homosex does not stand out in this regard. Additionally, in many species age-discrepant homosex included affection and bonding. Several researchers endorsed adaptively functional or neutral explanations for this behavior; none suggested malfunction. In short, the subprimate mammalian evidence suggests that age-discrepant homosex is a variant that recurs across mammals, that many adult males in certain species have the capacity for it, and that it is often a friendly rather than antagonist interaction. This pattern adds to that in primates in countering the view of pathology and suggesting neutral or functional alternative explanations for this phenomenon in mammals, including humans.

Birds
Evidence for age-discrepant homosex in birds can further extend the evolutionary implications already suggested by the primate and mammal reviews. Table VI presents summaries of seventeen avian species included in Bagemihl's (1999) review, in which age-discrepant homosex occurred. Because birds are quite distantly related to humans, and the main point here is to consider possible deeper evolutionary roots of this behavior, a brief overview rather than a case-by-case analysis follows.

Among the species in the table, male homosexual behavior, including age-discrepant homosex, varied from occasional (e.g., blue-backed manakins, black-billed magpies) to frequent (e.g., Guianan cock-of-the-rock, acorn woodpeckers). In various species, half or more of the male population participated in this behavior (e.g., ruffs, Guianan cock-of-the-rock, superb lyrebirds). Adult male courtships and displays to adolescent, and sometimes juvenile, males were pervasive across the species. Typically, adult males also courted and displayed to females as part of a bisexual orientation. Displays to young males were elaborate, matching those typically directed toward females. Superb lyrebird adult males, for example, might follow an adolescent male for hours, periodically performing a wing display and serenading the adolescent. Sometimes adolescent males courted each other (e.g., superb lyrebirds), and in one species, juvenile males courted adult males in bowers they had built (i.e., regent bowerbirds—adult males also courted younger males in bowers they built). In some species, adult males formed long-lasting pair-bonds with other males, who could be other adults or adolescents or juveniles (e.g., Canada geese, bicolored antbirds). In some species, adolescents and juveniles were active, consenting partners in mounting behavior with adult males (e.g., Guianan cock-of-the-rock, acorn woodpeckers). In Guianan cock-of-the-rocks, adolescent males visited multiple adult males' leks in a season and mounted the adults with their full cooperation, and in acorn

Table VI: Homosexual Behavior Between Mature and Immature Males in Birds

Species	Summary of Descriptions from Bagemihl (1999)
Aquatic and shore birds	
Canada geese (Branta canadensis)	18 % of adult males form homosexual bonds with partners, who may be other adults or juveniles.
Ruffs (Philomachus pugnax)	About half of males are involved predominantly in same-sex. Certain adult males acquire a territory called a lek, where they display to potential sex partners, male as well as female. Male visitors may be those without leks or younger males, who have not yet developed adult plumage. The younger males rarely are heterosexually involved, but instead do mounting with each other and with adult lek residents.
Perching and song birds	
Guianan cock-of-the-rock (Rupicola rupicola)	Male homosexual mounting between two adolescents and between an adult and adolescent is routine, accounting for about half of all copulations and involving about 40 % of the total male population and 64 % of the adolescent male population. Certain adult males acquire leks, which females and young males visit to see whether they want to mate. In a typical homosexual encounter, while an adult male is displaying his colorful plumage, an adolescent male will land nearby. The adult keeps his back to the adolescent, showing off his plumage and inviting the adolescent to mount him. The adolescent climbs onto the adult's back, achieves genital contact, and then mounts several times in succession. Adolescents usually visit the display courts of numerous other adult males and may have relations with up to seven adults in a season, including some adults without leks. Adult males who avoid heterosexual contacts are the ones most often mounted by adolescent males
Swallow-tailed manakins (Chiroxiphia caudata)	Several adult males will form long-term associations and display together on their leks to attract both females and adolescent males. When a young male arrives, the adult males perform a group courtship ritual, in which they take turns jumping up and hovering in front of him. The young male sits motionless as he watches the spectacle. Same-sex sexual behavior likely makes up a sizable proportion of all sexual activity.
Blue-backed manakins (Chiroxiphia pareola)	Pairs of adult males behave similarly to swallow-tailed manakins, displaying to a third male, which is sometimes an adolescent, performing leapfrogging and cartwheels to impress the other male.
Bicolored antbirds (Gymnopithys bicolor)	Male homosexual pair-bonds make up 4–6% of all pair-bonds; partners may be two adults or an older and younger bird. The bonds are initiated by courtship-feeds, in which one offers the other a spider or an insect. The receiving male, unlike a female, then passes it back. Once paired, they become constant companions.
Red bishop birds (Euplectes orix)	In their nesting territories, adult males court both females and males, the latter being younger males who look like females in terms of their plumage coloring. When a younger male approaches, the adult male performs a distinct bumble-flight and displays his plumage to attract the oncomer.
Orange bishop birds (Euplectes franciscanus)	In captivity, both adult and younger males attempt to mount young males, who usually reject the attempt or react indifferently at most.
Redshouldered widowbirds (Euplectes axillaris)	Adult males sometimes court younger males.

Table VI: (continued)

Species	Summary of Descriptions from Bagemihl (1999)
Aquatic and shore birds	
Black-billed magpies (*Pica pica*)	Homosexual behavior involving adult males with adolescent or juvenile males occurs occasionally. A typical courtship begins with one male ritually begging the other, followed by the second hopping around the first. Afterward, the two might form a pair-bond, in which they stay near one another, preen one another, and cooperate in evicting intruders.
Gray-breasted jays (*Aphelocoma ultramarina*)	Adult males have been observed to courtship-feed younger males.
Victoria's riflebirds (*Ptiloris victoriae*)	Adult males sometimes court younger males, using spectacular displays that are also used in heterosexual interactions. Male-male courtships occur frequently, although mounting is rarer and is likely to drive the mountee away.
Regent bowerbirds (*Sericulus chrysocephalus*)	Males build bowers, tunnels of twigs decorated with a variety of colors (e.g., from berries). Adult males display in their bowers to both females and younger males, sometimes ritually offering gifts to their guests. Juvenile males also build bowers and court males and females. When an adult male arrives, the juvenile male behaves in a ritual manner to attract the adult into the bower. Adult males spend 15% of their time displaying to other males, and juvenile males spend 28% of their time doing the same.
Satin bowerbirds (*Ptilonorhynchus violaceus*)	Adult males have been observed to court younger males.
Superb lyrebirds (*Menura novaehollandiae*)	Adult males often court adolescent males upon encountering them alone or in groups. The adult may closely follow the adolescent, even for hours, periodically performing a wing display accompanied by serenading the younger male with a variety of vocalizations. Adults will occasionally mount the adolescents, but genital contact may not occur because the younger male does not facilitate the interaction. Adolescent males also court and mount one another, behavior that is usually mutual. Occasionally, an adult and adolescent male will engage in a mutual display to one another. Adult males approach groups of adolescents fairly often during breeding season and twice as often outside of it. They spend more than half their time away from their display mounds associating with adolescent males. Most males are bisexual, courting both females and adolescent males. Adolescent males appear to be exclusively homosexual in their behavior and often form companionships with like-aged males. Male and female lyrebirds live largely separate lives aside from brief encounters during breeding season.
Other birds	
Anna's hummingbirds (*Calypte anna*)	Both females and juvenile males visit an adult male's territory to feed on his supply of currant and blossoms. If a juvenile male visits, the adult male will perform a dive display several times, in which he climbs 150 feet, dives toward the visitor, and makes loud shrieking sounds. After the display, the visitor will usually fly off, with the adult in pursuit, singing at him. If the adult succeeds in attempting to mount the younger male, the latter usually strongly resists, and the adult may attempt to use force. About 25% of sex in this species is between males.
Acorn woodpeckers (*Melanerpes formicivorus*)	A ritualized group display occurs involving courtship and sex. At dusk, the members of a group gather and begin mounting one another in all combinations. Males mount females and other males, females mount males and other females, young woodpeckers mount older ones, and older woodpeckers mount younger ones. Reciprocal mounting is common. This mounting display is a regular feature in this species, occurring daily all year around.

woodpeckers, younger and older males reciprocated mounting. In other species, the adolescent was typically resistant or indifferent to being mounted by an adult male (e.g., orange bishop birds, Anna's hummingbirds). Additionally, in a number of species adolescent males mounted each other (e.g., ruffs, superb lyrebirds).

In short, adult male interest in younger males was common across these species, taking the form seen across human societies in which pederasty was commonplace—that is, bisexual interest in adult females and male youths. The actual age-discrepant homosexual interactions were sometimes like those described earlier in the review of primates (i.e., cooperative and completed), and other times fragmentary (e.g., the adult male shows extensive interest, but the younger male does not cooperate, and mounting is not achieved). Notably, however, the latter pattern in birds may be common between adult males as well (e.g., Kotrschal, Hemetsberger, & Weiss, 2006). On the whole, the bird species in this sample showed the rudiments of the homosexual, including age-discrepant, interactions seen in the higher primates. Together, the primate, mammalian, and avian evidence just reviewed shows that male age-discrepant homosexual behavior frequency occurs in nature, not just in humans.

EVOLUTIONARY SYNTHESIS

The historical and cross-cultural review showed that pederasty has been a recurring behavioral pattern across time and place. The cross-species review, which also showed a wide distribution across a diverse set of species, suggests that the human pattern has a phylogenetic basis, with roots in primates, other mammals, and even birds. Even deeper roots might be suggested by looking at other animal classes. For example, Trivers (1976) described pederastic behavior in anolis lizards (*Anolis garmani*). In this reptilian species, adult males control territories, where they mate with females. Sometimes adolescent males are allowed on the territory, because they resemble females (e.g., in their smaller size) and allow the adult males to mount them. Trivers argued that this female mimicry is adaptive for the adolescents, as it permits them access to females, which they otherwise would not get. Analogous behavior has also been observed in some fish species (Werner, 2006). In short, it is reasonable to locate pederastic behavior in evolution. Ford and Beach (1951), using the cross-cultural and cross-species approach, did so with homosexual behavior—notably, much of their human and most of their primate evidence was pederastic in form. Various researchers since, using this approach, similarly located homosexual behavior in evolution, while relying substantially on evidence involving pederastic behavior (e.g., Bagemihl, 1999; Kirkpatrick, 2000; Muscarella, 2000). In this section, the notion that human pederasty is not simply an evolved behavior, but actually an adaptation, is examined.

Evolutionary Considerations and Previous Hypotheses

Adaptations are mechanisms (physical or behavioral) that have been naturally selected (i.e., produced by natural selection) in some past environment (i.e., the environment of evolutionary adaptedness, or EEA) because they had fitness-enhancing effects; the functions served by adaptations are the solutions produced in response to recurring adaptive problems in the EEA (Buss et al., 1998; Cosmides & Tooby, 1999). Evolved behaviors or physical traits (i.e., characters) are not necessarily adaptations—they can also be adaptively neutral or maladaptive (Buss et al., 1998; Thornhill, 1997; Vasey & Sommer, 2006). Natural selection selects out maladaptive characters, but allows adaptively neutral ones to persist in descendent populations. Adaptively neutral (i.e., functionless) characters can evolve in a number of ways, including as by-products of some adaptive character (referred to as "spandrals"),[16] as vestigial traits (i.e., traits that were adaptive in an ancestral species, but that have lost their function in the current species),[17] or as evolutionary noise (i.e., random effects via non-harmful mutation). In the following analysis, under the assumption that pederasty is an evolved behavior based on the phylogenetic evidence just reviewed, maladaptation, non-adaptation, and adaptation are all considered.

Background on Evolutionary Hypotheses for Homosexual Behavior
The assumption that all homosexual behavior is maladaptive was firmly entrenched before the 1950s. Ford and Beach's (1951) analysis was an initial challenge to this view. Hutchinson (1959), the noted evolutionary biologist, took the next step, proposing that homosexual behavior is actually adaptive, arguing that it must have some evolutionary function, because it occurs too frequently to be a biological "mistake." Nineteen years later, E. O. Wilson (1978) proposed an adaptive function (i.e., yielding kin-selection benefits). Since then, numerous evolutionary explanations for homosexual behavior have been offered, most of them proposing adaptive value, with several others proposing neutral value (for reviews, see Bagemihl, 1999; Vasey & Sommer, 2006).

Illustrative of the latter hypothesizing is Bagemihl's (1999) proposal. Bagemihl firmly concluded that homosexual behavior is evolved—he asserted that "anyone looking at the prevalence and elaboration of homosexual behavior ... in the animal kingdom will be led, eventually, to this conclusion" (p. 64)—but proposed that it is adaptively neutral, arguing that homosexual behavior arose because nature is exuberant or plentiful in what it produces, including sexual behavior. He showed that heterosexual behavior across species is exuberant in nonreproductive forms, far in excess of any apparent functional utility, which he used to support his inference regarding homosexual behavior. Once homosexual behavior evolves in a given species, he argued, it can be passed along to future generations, as well as to descendent species, because selective pressures will not act against it.

Regarding pederasty, a number of hypotheses to be reviewed shortly have offered functional explanations to account for it. This review will be useful in further consideration of pederasty's possible adaptive value. But it will also be important to keep in mind non-adaptation as an alternative explanation, as Bagemihl (1999) did for homosexual behavior in general. For example, though the primate record amply points to phylogenetic roots for human pederasty, the primate forms of this behavior could all be adaptively neutral, and the human form may be nothing more than a continuation of this functionless primate pattern. Its functional uses in various cultures, then, would simply represent "cultural exaptations," which are co-optations of traits of neutral value for positive cultural purposes (Buss et al., 1998).

Previous Evolutionary Hypotheses for Pederasty

Before considering adaptation, it will be useful to comment on the possibility of maladaptation. The extensive reviews presented earlier in the present article (i.e., nonclinical empirical, historical and cross-cultural, sociological, and cross-species) combine to substantially contradict the possibility that pederasty is a maladaptation. Goethe observed that pederasty is as old as humanity and must therefore lie in nature (Hirschfeld, 1914), which the historical/cross-cultural record supports with regard to humanity (e.g., Greenberg, 1988; Herdt, 1997) and the cross-species record supports with respect to nature. If pederasty were maladaptive in an evolutionary sense, it should not have such longevity in nature or in humanity. And if maladaptive, it would be tightly associated with harm. The nonclinical empirical review presented earlier clearly indicates that pederasty is not perforce associated with harm—this outcome is an interaction of culture, circumstances, and the individual, rather than the behavior itself.[18] The cross-cultural data, coupled with sociological considerations, reinforce this conclusion, as do the primate data, which give no reason to assume pederasty is innately harmful among higher primates, including humans.

A number of hypotheses having indirect or direct bearing on possible adaptive value for pederasty are now considered. Werner (2006) proposed what he called the hierarchy/cooperation theory of human male homosexual behavior. He argued that male homosexual behavior evolved in stages. Drawing upon extant species, he argued that in primitive species in the distant past, adult males controlled territories for mating, chasing away other adult males. Adolescent males or transvestite adult males, both mimicking females in morphology or behavior, could get on the territories and get access to females through their mimicry, including homosexual submission. As species grew more complex, male homosexual behavior exapted (i.e., changed function), as males in various species shifted from solitary to group living and evolved higher cognitive functioning, such that female mimicry no longer deceived other males. Now male homosexual submission served to elicit tolerance from more dominant males, upholding the dominance hierarchy, which in turn facilitated group living. The last stage in the evolution of male homosexual behavior was when groups of males did not simply live together but also formed alliances and cooperated on shared tasks. Citing baboons (cf. Smuts & Watanabe, 1990), Werner argued that homosexual behavior exapted once again, such that it facilitated alliances and cooperation. Because human males form cooperative alliances to such a great degree, he argued, homosexual behavior coevolved in elaborated form to serve alliance formation and cooperation. Werner's argument on stages fits the cross-species data in relation to social complexity well and so can be useful in any functional analysis of male homosexual behavior.

A shortcoming of Werner's hypothesis is that it was directed at accounting for androphilia (i.e., man-man homosexuality), while never adequately explaining how androphilia contributes to human male alliances and cooperation. He never considered how pederasty might fit this explanation, despite having discussed mentorship societies in his article. But the fit is strong, as the cross-cultural review presented previously indicates. Pederasty in mentorship societies was widely practiced to instill team spirit in boys so as to reproduce the coordinated male group (Herdt, 1991), whose highly dangerous and demanding activities, particularly warring and big-game hunting, depended heavily on cooperative male alliances (Gat, 2006; Gilmore, 1990; Weisfeld & Billings, 1988). Thus, human pederasty clearly fits in with the last stage in Werner's stage theory, because it was ultimately directed at teamwork. In short, as Werner argued, alliance formation and cooperation seem to be important for understanding the evolution of human male homosexual behavior—but it is for pederasty that these behaviors seem especially relevant.

Four hypotheses have been offered that did consider the evolutionary relationship between cooperative alliances and pederasty (i.e., Kirkpatrick, 2000; Mackey, 1990; Muscarella, 2000; Neill, 2009). Muscarella (2000) and Kirkpatrick (2000) both presented functional hypotheses for human homosexual behavior in general, but drew much or most of their evidence from cross-cultural pederasty, so their hypotheses are especially relevant to pederasty. Modeling from various cross-species and cross-cultural examples, Muscarella posited that male hominid adolescents were likely to have been peripheralized, that alliances with older males would thus have benefited them, and that these alliances were likely to have been facilitated by homoeroticism (i.e., through the bonds it created). He argued that the adolescents would have benefited from increased protection, greater access to resources, and valuable assistance in moving up the male hierarchy. He argued further that the older males would have benefited by expanding their social alliance networks.

Kirkpatrick reached similar conclusions regarding the adaptive mediating role of homoeroticism, but focused on alliances as the chief benefit, which he argued were needed for resource competition and cooperative defense. In age-discrepant alliances, he posited that older males benefited from younger males' assistance, whereas younger males benefited through acquisition of knowledge and resources. Mackey (1990), based on field research in sixteen countries from five continents, found that the adult male-peripubertal male dyad is especially common. He attributed this pattern to humans' unique evolutionary history, in which the male group became a well-coordinated warring and hunting unit, an adaptation that behooved adult males to continually recruit peripubertal boys to replenish the male group and its network of reciprocal alliances. He speculated that pederasty functioned to facilitate this recruitment and then foster the boys' enculturation. Neill (2009) argued that pederastic relations work to produce emotional bonds between younger and older partners, which benefit youths by enhancing role modeling tendencies, which in turn facilitate their acquiring skills and traits and assimilating beliefs and norms that they will shortly need to function successfully when fully grown. He further argued that clans would have benefited in the evolutionary past by this process, being strengthened in their competition with other clans.

Mentorship-Bonding/Enculturation-Alliance Hypothesis

The articles just reviewed form a foundation for further hypothesizing on the evolutionary origins of pederasty. In their hypotheses, the articles variously discussed benefits for the boys involved in pederastic relations (e.g., protection, resources, knowledge, enculturation), for the men involved (e.g., expanding alliances, getting assistants), and for the male group concerned (e.g., replenishment, bonding, maintenance of functioning). In this section, aspects of these hypotheses are combined with evidence from the multiple in-depth reviews presented earlier in this article, along with additional evolutionary considerations, to arrive at a refined adaptation-based explanation for pederasty. Unlike the previous studies just considered, the current hypothesizing focuses just on pederasty. Different forms of homosexual behavior are likely to have had different origins, evolutionary or otherwise, such that hypothesizing should be narrow rather than general and take care to limit cited evidence to that which is relevant (Dickemann, 2000; Jones, 2000; Vasey, 2000). In the hypotheses just discussed, for example, pederastic evidence was prominently tapped, but then applied to other homosexualities, sometimes not even to pederasty itself.[19] Pederasty should be isolated in hypothesizing because of the abundance of data relevant specifically to it, its clear relation in many other cultures to male group functioning, its likely role in this regard in evolutionary times, and, hence, its plausible adaptive origins that would be specific to it.

Environment of Evolutionary Adaptedness (EEA)
A fundamental principle in evolutionary biology or psychology is that adaptive physical or behavioral traits are products of past environments, in which recurring adaptive problems created selection pressures, which caused these traits to be naturally selected (Buss et al., 1998). For different adaptive traits, different past environments may have been involved in their natural selection. Such an environment for a given adaptive trait is referred to as its environment of evolutionary adaptedness (EEA). To examine whether a trait is adaptive, it should be assessed in terms of its usefulness not in the current environment but in the environment in which it is posited to have evolved, its proposed EEA.

That pederasty may sizably mismatch our social environment today is irrelevant to whether it is an evolved adaptation. What matters is how it fit in some past environment, its EEA, in which it was naturally selected, if that is what occurred. Primate pederastic tendencies are common enough that it can be inferred that early humans acquired these tendencies from primate ancestors. But the primate and human forms are different, with only the latter intimately connected to the male group and its shared goals or tasks, rather than simply consisting of private relations between individuals generally with no broader purpose. Additionally, only the human form is intimately connected to mentoring. Therefore, to understand human pederasty in evolutionary terms, it is necessary to look at the unique evolutionary history of humans, which requires looking at early human environments, those in which the human form of pederasty may have been naturally selected.

Big-game hunting emerged and became increasingly important among early human males—it was a male prerogative—setting in motion selective pressures for coordinated hunting units (Mackey, 1990). The hunting-gathering lifestyle defined humans for more than 90 percent of their existence, until the agricultural revolution ten thousand years ago, meaning that key aspects of male human nature were naturally selected in relation to the requirements of big-game hunting (Buss, 2007; Gat, 2006). But intergroup tribal warfare also emerged as a central component of early human environments (Gat, 2006; Holmes, 2008; Wade, 2008; Wrangham, 1987), which likewise produced strong selective pressures for the evolution of well-coordinated male groups along with facilitating psychological mechanisms (Buss, 2007; Gaulin & McBurney, 2004; Tooby & Cosmides, 2005; Wilson & Wilson, 2007). Owing to the brute-strength requirements of primitive warfare, it also became a male preserve (Gat, 2006). Among the psychological mechanisms facilitating male group behavior was male bonding, which produced such effects as loyalty, self-sacrifice, and courage, needed particularly and especially in warfare (Gat, 2006; Weisfeld & Billings, 1988). Given the significance of big-game hunting and warfare for the male group, and ultimately for the survival and welfare of the entire group, it behooved adult males to continually recruit younger males in order to replenish the male group (Mackey, 1990; Weisfeld & Billings, 1988). Because years of practice and training were needed to acquire the skills and patterns of primitive hunting and warfare (Savin-Williams & Weisfeld, 1989), peripubertal boys, being at the right stage to be prepared for the difficult teamwork soon to be demanded of them, were sought out as recruits (Mackey, 1990).

The view that intergroup aggression was common in early human environments is controversial in anthropology (Gat, 2006) and thus needs further comment. Holmes (2008) reported on a recent conference involving anthropologists, archeologists, primatologists, psychologists, and political scientists, who assembled to examine warfare and its role in shaping human evolution. The emerging consensus was that warfare is quite ancient, not a product of the agricultural revolution, and that it was central in shaping the evolution of human traits such as coalitional aggression and super-high levels of cooperation. Gat (2006), in his evolutionary analysis of warfare, provided compelling evidence for these ancient origins of human warfare. After reviewing cross-species evidence to show the commonness of lethal aggression in the animal world (e.g., chimpanzees), he reviewed evidence on hunter-gatherer societies, which best reflect ancient humans. In one comparative study of ninety-nine extant hunter-gatherer bands in thirty-seven different cultures, almost all had engaged in warfare within a year of when the study was conducted; in another study, most of their hunter-gatherer societies engaged in warfare at least every two years (Divale, 1972; Ember, 1978; Otterbein, 1991). From the simplest hunter-gatherer societies (e.g., Australian and Tasmanian aborigines) to the more complex (e.g., coastal Northwest American Indians and Eskimos), warfare was rife and bloody, Gat noted. Deadly conflict, if not endemic, was always threatened, forcing a constant state of preparedness, often with aggressive territorial behavior and xenophobic attitudes. The Australian, Tasmanian, and coastal Northwest examples are significant, because they were "pure" in the sense that these societies had been little affected by agriculturalists and pastoralists before being studied. From this evidence, both cross-species and hunter-gatherer, Gat concluded that tribe-on-tribe warfare stretched back to the evolutionary formative years of humankind, substantially shaping its character.

For present purposes, in examining the importance of peripubertal recruits, mentoring, and group bonding to the male group's functioning, it is relevant to consider the nature of primitive warfare. As Gat (2006) documented, the pattern of primitive warfare, from hunter-gatherers of all levels of complexity to primitive agriculturalists, is remarkably uniform and manifests itself regularly. It ordinarily consists of ambuscade carried out in night raids, often with the goal of committing the greatest slaughter. Sometimes whole tribes are exterminated; other times, women are taken home by the victors, but the men and boys are killed. Most men bear scars of warfare, and mortality rates are commonly around 15 percent of the entire group, but 25 percent of men. Anthropologists studying New Guinea and Australian tribes, for example, have noted that the inhabitants faced a constant threat or the actuality of warfare, creating a perpetual state of insecurity and preparedness. Elaborate ritualistic activity, invoking supernatural support before, during, and after battles, was pervasive in hunter-gatherer and primitive agriculturalist tribes to cope with losses (and pray for gains). This pattern, recurring as it has across numerous independent societies, can be inferred to extend back through human prehistory, which was entirely hunter-gatherer in nature, and it, rather than the recent invention of agriculture and the lifestyle changes it produced, determined the core of evolved male human nature (Gat, 2006).[20] It created powerful selection pressures for the strengthening of both the need and capacity for male bonding, the mainstay of troops' cohesion and fighting spirit, as well as for the evolution of associated mechanisms of preparedness, including recruiting boys, instilling group allegiance in them, and mentoring them in the skills and emotional readiness to be required of them as men (Gat, 2006; Mackey, 1990; Weisfeld & Billings, 1988).

Manhood Ideologies
Gilmore (1990) reviewed manhood cross-culturally and found that in culture after culture manhood was viewed as something that boys must achieve; it did not develop simply through maturation, as womanhood was ubiquitously thought to. In most cultures, boys had to pass tests on the way to manhood, and the harsher the environment and the more scarce the resources, the more manhood was stressed as important and the harsher the boys' tests were for being recognized as having achieved it. In warrior society after warrior society, peripubertal boys were subjected to extreme ordeals. Among the Masai and Samburu of East Africa, boys had to react stoically to excruciatingly painful circumcisions in front of the male group; the slightest flinching shamed them for life. Among the Amhara in nearby Ethiopia, all able-bodied adolescent boys had to engage in whipping contests, which lacerated faces and tore ears open; any sign of weakness was derided with taunts and mockery. Among the Tewa Indians of New Mexico, young adolescent boys were purified by ritual, then stripped naked and whipped mercilessly by men dressing up as spirits, inflicting permanent body scars; the boys were expected to bear up to it impassively, or else their manhood was in doubt. In many cultures in the New Guinea Highlands, boys were subjected to a series of brutalizing rituals, including whippings, flailing, and beatings, which they had to endure stoically; if they could not, it was believed, they would not mature into real men. In at least two-thirds of the world's cultures that have been studied, harsh ordeals for boys in these rites have been commonplace (Weisfeld & Billings, 1988).

In our society, these rituals would be seen as senseless acts of cruelty. But their pervasive occurrence in independent cultures around the world clearly indicates some sort of function. The function was to harden boys for the far greater ordeals that awaited them shortly when they reached adulthood, as well as to emotionally bind them to the male group, so that they would be effective, loyal, and courageous team members (Gilmore, 1990; Weisfeld & Billings, 1988). The problem is that, if not pushed into manhood, boys and young men will find eschewing difficult and dangerous manhood tasks congenial, as Gilmore (1990) found in several exceptional cultures, where manhood was not needed or valued. In Tahiti, for example, there was no concept of manhood when Europeans first arrived in the 1770s. Men and women had exactly the same roles, boys were never tested in their masculinity, and the men were generally effeminate in demeanor and quite content in their status. Tahiti was a paradise, with no natural enemies because of isolation; food could be picked from trees and fish snatched from shallow waters. Gilmore (1990) argued that these exceptional cases show that manhood is socially constructed, not an obligate endpoint. As he noted, manhood ideologies are adaptations to particular social and physical environments. The correlation between the harshness of environment and the degree that manhood is stressed in different cultures "could not be more clear, concrete, or compelling," he emphasized (p. 224).

Interpreting Gilmore's (1990) findings in light of two additional decades of research and theorizing in evolutionary psychology, it can be concluded that manhood is an evolved capacity, not an irresistible drive. It evolved among ancient humans as an adaptation in response to the commonly harsh and dangerous social and physical environments confronted (Gat, 2006). As an innate capacity, it emerges in relation to environmental contingencies. The more pressing the contingencies, the more extensively manhood emerges. Cultures with extreme manhood ideologies (e.g., Melanesian societies) therefore should not be simplistically reduced to examples of oppressiveness, while those without any (e.g., Tahiti) are classified as liberated. Rather, these variations should be looked at in relation to the forces producing them (i.e., social and physical environments) interacting with the evolved capacity for manhood.

Manhood ideologies are a type of cultural ideology and are interwoven with social structures (see earlier section on sociological considerations). For present purposes, the importance of the manhood embedded within these ideologies is that it is reflective of an EEA, whose selective forces naturally selected a complex of facilitating behavior patterns, including those directed at replenishing manhood when it was culturally needed: for example, recruiting boys, reorienting them psychologically and emotionally to meld into the male group, and mentoring them. It has been the contention of several researchers (e.g., Mackey, 1990) that pederasty was part of this complex as well. In short, in evaluating adaptive functions for pederasty, manhood and manhood ideologies need to be taken into account.

Individual Versus Group Selection

Up to this point, this chapter has inferred from the cross-species data that early humans inherited pederastic tendencies. It has noted that previous hypotheses have connected these tendencies to benefits for boys, men, and groups where pederasty was practiced. It was argued that early human environments were extremely harsh and perilous, such that male bonding and mentoring boys often would have been needed. It was argued further that manhood tendencies are evolved capacities stemming from selective pressures from past harsh environments, such that particular societies' efforts in "manning up" boys are moderated by the degree of environmental stress in those societies. These elements allow for presenting a more refined version of the previous hypotheses concerning pederasty's adaptive value. First, however, one additional consideration will be useful.

Notably, the hypotheses presented by Muscarella (2000), Kirkpatrick (2000), and Neill (2009) focused on individual benefits, mostly for the youths, but also for the men, involved in pederastic relations. Mackey's (1990) focus was directed at benefits to the male group; Neill (2009) also explicitly touched on group benefits. Distinguishing between individual and group benefits is directly related to the evolutionary processes of individual and group selection, which none of these authors discussed, but which are important for evolutionary hypothesizing. Individual selection holds that physical and behavioral traits are naturally selected in relation to the survival and reproductive fitness they confer on individuals possessing these traits. Group selection, on the other hand, holds that traits are naturally selected in relation to benefits to the group, even when individual fitness is lessened in individuals with these traits.

Group selection as a legitimate evolutionary process has been in disfavor since the 1960s. Wilson and Wilson (2007), however, noted that the dismissal of group selection came only through argumentation, not through a distinguished body of empirical evidence. Since the 1960s, they continued, a number of key biologists who had rejected group selection later reverted back to it as a supplemental process (e.g., George C. Williams, William D. Hamilton, John Maynard Smith). More importantly, growing evidence for it has emerged in microbes, plants, insects, and vertebrates, in which various species (a small minority of all species) have crossed an evolutionary threshold to include this process as part of their evolutionary nature. Once crossed, group selection has been a powerful evolutionary force in shaping the concerned species, they argued, and it has contributed to their dominance over other species. Group selection in ants, for example, is now considered a model instance (Wilson & Hölldobler, 2008). Wilson and Wilson (2007) and Wilson and Hölldobler (2008) argued that humans, being unusually groupish, are partly products of group selection, an argument that is suggested by parallels with ants: hyperaggressiveness between groups, hyper-cooperativeness within groups, and extreme evolutionary success (all hallmarks of group selection). In terms of evolutionary success, ants and humans are the two most dominant animal species on earth.[21] In various interviews, E. O. Wilson argued that group selection helps to explain human males' level of bravery, innovativeness, sacrifice, and loyalty, traits all necessary in human intergroup competition (*Discover*, 2006; Wade, 2008).

In short, group selection appears to be an important supplement to individual selection in evolutionary thinking regarding humans. Gat (2006) saw its obvious value in his attempt to account for warfare across human existence, given that warfare is centrally about group-on-group competition. Pederasty has so often occurred in societies in connection with group behavior and in service of it, that group selection appears useful in analyzing pederasty. The hypothesis to follow makes use of individual selection, but considers group selection as well.

Current Hypothesis
The refined adaptation-based explanation for pederasty is entitled the "mentorship-bonding/enculturation-alliance hypothesis," which corresponds to how pederasty has actually occurred in societies in which it served explicit cultural functions. In the narrow context between individual men and boys, *mentorships* transmitted culturally needed skills (e.g., hunting, warring) and emotional readiness (e.g., bravery, courage) to the boys, and they also yielded apprentice benefits to the men. The *bonding* produced by the intimate nature of the pederasty facilitated these mentorships (cf. Kirkpatrick, 2000; Muscarella, 2000; Neill, 2009). In the broader group-level context, pederasty served as a mechanism, among others, to immerse boys in the ways of the male group (i.e., *enculturation*) and to bond them with the group and its members in strong *alliances* needed for well-coordinated group behavior in difficult and dangerous activities, particularly big-game hunting and warfare (cf. Mackey, 1990).

Formally, this hypothesis holds that pederasty evolved in the early human hunter-gatherer EEA as an adaptation (i.e., exaptation), whose function it was to reproduce the male group by facilitating the mentoring and enculturation of boys from peripubescence through adolescence, as well as their emotional and psychological binding with the group. This function was a solution to the recurring adaptive problems in the EEA of surviving and exploiting an extremely dangerous and competitive social and physical environment, which frequently involved the serious risks and valuable rewards (e.g., nutritional) of big-game hunting, as well as the extreme (i.e., lethal) risks and sizable rewards (e.g., material) of warfare.

Individual and group selection. In the narrow context just discussed, individual selection is the evolutionary process assumed to have driven the proposed exaptation. Here, pederastic relations facilitated mentoring and bonding, which helped to enhance boys' development and secure assistance for the men involved. Boys and men benefited as individuals in the near term and later on. Regarding the latter, the maintenance of the male group over time would have fed back positively on the now grown up boys and their former older partners.

Notably, however, sizable proportions of males would have been seriously injured or lost through their male group activities in the harsh EEA, meaning that the male group also imposed significant costs on many individuals involved. Under these circumstances, in order for the male group to function successfully, it had to be prioritized over the individual. As in the social insects, individuals mattered less than the group and could be sacrificed. The history and prehistory of warfare clearly attest to this relation (Gat, 2006). Group selection is the evolutionary process indicated here. Pederasty is inferred to have exapted in early humans in service of the group, not just the individual. Following its actual practice in mentorship societies, it is inferred that pederasty facilitated enculturation and group allegiance in the EEA, which could override individual benefit in favor of the group when needed.

Design features. Humans have designed many devices for particular purposes. A reading lamp, for example, is designed to produce light (i.e., its function), which its various design features (e.g., filament, vacuum, glass encasement) enable. Heat is emitted, but this is incidental (i.e., a by-product). The same reasoning applies to adaptations, designed instead by natural selection. If a trait is an adaptation, it will have special design features that are tightly tied to the function it is serving. By documenting a trait's design features and showing their fit to the function being proposed for the trait, confidence can be built that the trait is an adaptation serving the proposed function. As in the lamp analogy, traits can also be by-products of adaptations, rather than adaptations themselves (Buss et al., 1998; Tooby & Cosmides, 2005).

If pederasty is an adaptation that serves reproducing the male group, aspects of it (i.e., design features) should fit this function well. Cross-culturally, boys are brought into male groups at peripubescence, and by later adolescence they are well-integrated, participating members (Mackey, 1990; Weisfeld & Billings, 1988). It is during this period that mentoring and enculturation occur, the direct means of group reproduction. Notably, pederastic attractions typically emerge at the beginning of this period (i.e., peripubescence) and terminate at the end (i.e., later adolescence), suggesting that these attractions are design features, which act to switch on and then switch off older males' interest in putting special effort into the boys' development, thereby replicating the group. In the historical and cross-cultural review, in society after society, pederastic interests not only emerged, but surged at the peripubescent stage, but then were completely shut off by later adolescence with boys' development of body hair on the legs and especially the face. Nonclinical empirical data in our own society reveal the same pattern, in which attractions surge around ages 12 to 14, but then vanish with the emergence of boys' facial hair and macho behavior (Lautmann, 1994; Wilson & Cox, 1983).

Not only is boys' initial pubertal development a likely design feature that switches on pederastic attractions, but so is their adventuresome demeanor at this stage. Lautmann (1994) reported that the men attracted to boys in his sample were not only attracted to the "blooming of the flower" (i.e., puberty), but that they found a boy particularly appealing when he was a "burst of energy," and when he was "no angel," but a "rascal." Men in his sample attracted to girls were not drawn to such characteristics in girls. These boy-specific attributes appear also to be design features that not only activate the pederast's interest, but that are useful for the rough male role that awaits boys in harsh environments, to which mentoring and enculturation are geared.

During peripubescence, boys become decidedly team-oriented and readily hero-worship older males, whereas by later adolescence a firm sense of independence generally emerges in them (Neill, 2009; Weisfeld & Billings, 1988). As well, nonclinical empirical research indicates that, when they have not absorbed the moral negatives about sex with other males or with older males, boys can be open to pederastic relations until later adolescence, at which point they usually lose all interest in favor of pursuing females (e.g., Lautmann, 1994; Money & Weinrich, 1983; Rossman, 1976; Tindall, 1978). In the pederastic cultures in the historical and cross-cultural review, boys in later adolescence similarly lost this interest, at which point they frequently became sexually interested themselves in younger boys, in addition to females. These early and later characteristics are coordinated and appear to be additional design features that promote boys' receptiveness to and even enthusiasm about mentorships and enculturation, as well as pederastic relations, for a limited time, as needed to achieve the developmental milestones that will serve them in becoming adults and will serve the male group as well.

In short, the ages of boys sought out as recruits in male groups, the period in which they are mentored and enculturated, the ages of boys that men in such societies (and our own) find erotically appealing, the ages at which boys are especially open to being mentored (and capable as well, owing to an emergent adult-cognitive capacity), and the ages at which they are open to pederastic relations appear to be part of a single package, in which each of these characteristics seems to be a design feature and element of a larger design, whose function is reproducing the male group.

Adaptation versus by-product. It has frequently been suggested that, when females are not available, boys can become their substitutes for older males, such that older males' erotic interests in boys are essentially a by-product of their adaptive attractions to females. For example, in English boarding schools prior to the 1970s, older teens frequently developed intense erotic crushes on peripubertal boys, only to become exclusively heterosexual upon graduation when they reentered sexually mixed society (Gathorne-Hardy, 1978; Lambert & Lambert, 1968). The problem with this argument is the assumption that living mostly in sex-segregated settings while a youth is intrinsically artificial, when the cross-cultural data show otherwise. In particularly harsh environments, sexual segregation at this stage of life has been common, and likely was so stretching back into the EEA. In numerous mammalian species, sexual segregation for youthful males is also common, showing that such arrangements are part of nature, not intrinsically against it. In such settings in the case of humans, as the earlier historical and cross-cultural review suggests, older male erotic interest in boys appears to be an emergent attraction, not simply a substitute for females, arising as part of a functional package supporting the maintenance and continuation of the male group. Sexual segregation is not an arbitrary arrangement, but one generally associated with societal needs at the time—for example, when the male group is especially needed for its contributions (e.g., hunting, warfare) to the wider group. In this context, mentoring, enculturation, and male bonding become important, and emergent pederastic interests can be awakened. In short, the by-product alternative explanation to adaptation, though likely valid in particular cases, does not appear to be valid across a significant part of the domain of pederastic interests.

Obligate versus facultative traits. Finally, it is important to note that genetically based traits may be obligate or facultative. Barring major disruptions, obligate traits will always be expressed. The expression of facultative traits, on the other hand, is contingent on environmental and other inputs (Gaulin & McBurney, 2004). Social behaviors that are adaptations generally fall into the second category. Their activation may crucially depend on various inputs during development, for example. Moreover, other types of input during development can disrupt or completely block their emergence (Buss et al., 1998). Another reason why adaptations may not be expressed is that other adaptations can be in conflict with them, such that their expression is suppressed by the expression of the other adaptations (Wilson & Wilson, 2007). Though Kirkpatrick (2000) argued that homosexual behavior is adaptive, he emphasized that its expression is variable, being contingent on environmental conditions such as social and family structures. Under certain conditions, homosexual behavior is associated with benefits (e.g., as when alliance formation is important), and so will tend to be expressed. Under other conditions, it may be associated mainly with costs, and so will rarely find expression.

Notably, Kirkpatrick's (2000) evidence for facultative homosexual expression specifically concerned pederasty, which has been widespread in certain environments (e.g., Melanesia, ancient Greece, premodern Japan) but rare in others (e.g., the modern West). It is important to emphasize that pederasty's relatively infrequent expression in societies such as ours does not imply that it is not an adaptation. In our society, developmental inputs have traditionally been intensely hostile toward homosexual behavior, often accompanied by severe social sanctions, including public disgrace and punishment, which can be expected to have had a significant dampening effect on the emergence and activation of pederastic desire and the expression of pederastic behavior. On the other hand, developmental inputs, as well as social and family structures, have been entirely encouraging of exclusive heterosexual interests and behavior, generally producing this outcome. Cross-culturally, as well as in other species, pederasty and heterosexuality have often resided in the same individual, rather than being characteristic only in separate individuals. Therefore, when the one behavior is punished and the other is rewarded, as is very much the case in our society, it follows that the latter is the one that will be activated and expressed in most individuals.

In our society, pederastic desire and behavior nevertheless still do occasionally surface. The explanation that best fits the evidence presented throughout this chapter is that pederastic tendencies are naturally variable across the male population, probably forming a normal distribution from little to high potential, with most males having moderate potential. These tendencies are presumably genetic, the result of primate heritage, natural selection, and pederasty's functional utility in the EEA. As well, heterosexual tendencies probably form a distribution of potential, perhaps negatively skewed (i.e., few have a low potential in the direction of the negative end of the scale, most have a high potential in the direction of the positive end). Given our society's cultural ideologies and social structure, for males with high heterosexual potential (i.e., most males), exclusive heterosexuality is the likely outcome, even if the pederastic potential is also high. For males with high pederastic potential, but lower heterosexual potential, a pederastic outcome may be likely. Thus, even though adaptive in the EEA, pederasty, being a facultative trait, is nevertheless rare in our environment. On the other hand, in cultures with cultural ideologies and social structures facilitative of pederastic desire and expression, its occurrence has been widespread across the male population, which is consistent with the assumptions that most males have at least a moderate potential for the behavior and that such potential is sufficient for the behavior to emerge, provided other factors are not inhibitory.

DISCUSSION

Clinicians, psychologists, journalists, and other influential opinion-makers who comment on the nature of pederasty nearly unanimously state or imply that it is innately pathological in the adult male, intrinsically disturbing for the youth, and always damaging for society. Their epistemological approach, however, is the same as that formerly used to judge masturbation, homosexuality, and other sexual behaviors as pathologies: values, ideologies, and clinical cases. This approach, however, is not scientifically sound. Such generalizations require broader evidence and perspectives to be valid (Bullough, 1976; Ford & Beach, 1951; Kinsey et al., 1948). Broader evidence (e.g., anthropological, sociological, zoological) is copious. The present chapter employed such evidence to critically assess the dominant generalizations about pederasty.

The current view that pederasty is intensely psychologically harmful for the youths involved derives most directly from sexual victimological theory (SVT), which emerged in the 1970s (Jenkins, 1998, 2006; Nathan & Snedeker, 1995). SVT, using rape and incest as its model, implanted the view by the early 1980s that all forms of adult-minor sex, including pederasty, are characterized by coercion, trauma, and long-term maladjustment. As well, SVT fostered and amplified general views that pederastic desires are intrinsically pathological and that society is badly damaged by pederastic behavior. In the nonclinical empirical review in the present article, SVT was clearly refuted with respect to adolescent boys, where consent, positive reactions, and normal adjustment were common, particularly in age-discrepant sexual relations that were sexual orientation consistent (i.e., heterosexual boys with women, homosexual boys with men) and in pederastic relations occurring within special friendships (i.e., typically involving heterosexual boys with men). Moreover, within these special friendships, the evidence suggested function rather than dysfunction for the youths involved.

A historical and cross-cultural review was conducted next, because sexual behavior is profoundly influenced by culture, and so any valid generalizing about sexual behavior needs to take culture into account (Bullough, 1976; Ford & Beach, 1951). Thirty-three societies with institutionalized or wide-spread pederasty were considered. In these societies, pederasty was often characteristic of the typical man, contradicting our society's assumptions that locate this behavior necessarily in idiosyncratic disturbance. The evidence from these societies suggested that pederastic propensities are normally distributed across males, ranging in potential from weak to strong, with most in the moderate range. The evidence also indicated that males perceived their pederastic involvements as youths in positive terms, consistent with the positive ideologies of these cultures. In the many mentorship societies examined, pederasty was seen by the natives themselves and described by visiting anthropologists as being functional, acting to reproduce the male group, which in these societies usually performed dangerous but vital services (e.g., big-game hunting, warring) in the interests of the wider society. Pederasty served to create bonds between younger and older males as well as allegience to the male group. These bonds, in turn, facilitated the transmission of culturally needed skills and emotional readiness to the youths.

Sociological considerations then showed that pederastic expression across time and place has varied as a function of cultural ideologies and social structures. In general, these factors feed back on one another, and each reflects the material needs of a given culture as well as its social constructions stemming from politics. In the present-day West, all these factors have combined to position pederasty as an unfathomable deviance in both lay and professional thinking, which helps to account for its negative-halo, in which all sorts of harms and pathologies are readily attributed to it. Importantly, the sociological perspective, along with the other perspectives in this chapter, reveals the social constructionist nature of this Western thinking, which, far from being equivalent to scientific thinking, is quite at odds with it.

The cross-species review was the next logical focus, given the argument that deeper (i.e., evolutionary) roots should be considered when a human sexual behavior pattern recurs cross-culturally (Ford & Beach, 1951). In this review, twenty-four primate, twenty-six subprimate mammalian, and seventeen avian species were considered. The review showed that pederastic-like tendencies are common in the primates most closely related to humans (Old World monkeys and apes), as well as in many other higher mammals. In these species, the evidence indicated that this behavior is not a pathology but instead a normal variant, which is often associated with assent or even initiative on the part of the younger animal and may serve useful functions. The special friendships reported in many of these species show parallels with those reported in the human nonclinical and cross-cultural literature. Pederastic-like behavior also often occurs in subprimate mammals, sometimes with probable functionality (e.g., bighorn and thinhorn sheep), and it occurs in numerous bird species, where adult male courting of adolescent males was frequently observed. In short, the cross-species evidence shows that pederasty is part of nature and indicates that it is generally a benign and sometimes functional behavior, rather than a maladaptation. This evidence strongly suggests that benign or perhaps functional pederastic tendencies were inherited by human ancestors. Their trajectory in humans was then determined by humans' unique evolutionary history.

In the evolutionary synthesis, which built on the evidence in the earlier sections, a functional hypothesis for pederasty was proposed. In the censorship of the 2005 version of this chapter in the *Journal of Homosexuality,* the brief functional allusion in that article was received incredulously by critics. So it is important to emphasize here that discussing function is fully consistent with the scientific literature, in which: (a) cultural function for pederasty has repeatedly been discussed in the anthropological literature, (b) social or individual function for pederastic-like behavior has repeatedly been discussed in the zoological literature, and (c) at least four published scholarly studies to date have made use of the cross-cultural and cross-species evidence to hypothesize function for human pederasty. In this synthesis, the "mentorship-bonding/enculturation-alliance" hypothesis was proposed, directly reflecting the way that pederasty has appeared in the many societies across time and place institutionalizing it. In these "mentorship" societies, as they are referred to by anthropologists, pederasty was one of the means employed by the male group to replicate itself, which was effected through: (a) *mentoring* boys in specific skills and emotional demeanor to be needed later on, (b) facilitating this mentoring through *bonding,* to which pederasty's erotic character contributed, (c) *enculturation* of boys into the practices and ideologies of the group, and (d) cementing *alliances* with other male group members, which were essential in the teamwork needed in activities such as big-game hunting and warfare.

Support for this hypothesis came from various considerations, a few of which are recapped here for emphasis. First, human nature as an evolved set of behavioral adaptations was molded in ancient humans, not modern people, and understanding it therefore requires looking at ancient human environments (i.e., the EEA). In the EEA, conditions were harsh and demanding, more or less in line with Hobbes's (but not Rousseau's) "state of nature" (Gat, 2006). In these environments, with intergroup aggression, or the perennial threat of it, as well as frequent big-game hunting, the male group would have especially mattered, and so recruiting boys would have been continually needed, which entailed mentoring, bonding, enculturation, and alliance formation. Evolved mechanisms would have been needed for each of these behaviors or processes, and pederasty seems likely to have been one of them, given its role in mentorship societies. Second, cross-cultural manhood ideologies were reviewed, which indicated that "manhood" is an evolved capacity, whose degree of expression depends on the harshness of the environs. Significantly, manhood is not a drive—it does not emerge in paradises like Tahiti. Harsh environs create the need for it, boys have to be pushed into developing it, and so mechanisms facilitating this push then become important. Pederasty appears to be one of these mechanisms. Third, pederasty as an adaptation was supported by identifying various design features, including the correspondence in boys' ages for the emergence and termination of pederastic attractions with the period in which boys are generally recruited and eventually fully assimilated into the male group. In this age matching, pederasty appears to function as an activating or energizing mechanism. Finally, pederasty as a facultative trait was discussed, in which its degree of expression at the population level was argued to depend on the interaction between its assumed normally distributed potential and environmental inputs, including harshness of environs, the social structure, and cultural ideologies. In our society today, the environment is more like Tahiti than the New Guinea Highlands because of super-technology and strong statehood: acquiring food is a trip to the supermarket, combat is consigned to paid volunteers, and safety is usually ensured by the state. Our social structure, fashioned by the super-technology, favors mixed-sex socializing while disfavoring all-male groupings, which have lost much of their value. And cultural ideologies emphasize egalitarian sexual relations while derogating relations based on substantial difference, especially age differences involving minors. Given these inhibitory influences, pederastic expression is generally only likely to emerge among males with high genetically based propensities; hence, it is uncommon in our society.

Evolutionary Mismatch

From the evolutionary synthesis emerges the conclusion that pederasty is an evolutionary mismatch. That is, though it is a functionally evolved mechanism, well suited to ancient and other more recent human environments, it is ill-suited to our own. The modern-day pederast is like the moth with a light-coloring mechanism transported to an industrialized, sooted environment, in which the mechanism is functioning as designed, but this functioning now imperils the moth. The moth does not have a disease, because it does not have a dysfunction; the problem is external (cf. Wakefield, 1992, 1999, 2007). The pederast likewise does not have a disease, because he does not have a dysfunction. His erotic attraction mechanism is functioning according to design, but in the wrong environment. Attempts to classify such attractions as a pathology, as a mental disorder (see Blanchard et al., 2009), are misguided in the same sense that classification of masturbation and homosexuality in past were misguided. These misclassifications stem from value judgments, which serve dominant ideologies and interests of the day, but not science.

Many youths involved in pederastic relations have benefited from them—a finding well supported by the empirical literature. On the other hand, many other youths have reacted negatively, either during the relationships or later—as clinical studies report. The problem is that the latter findings receive 100 percent of media and professional attention, in service of the cultural view that pederasty is a crime against nature, which invariably harms and destroys. The current review, which is scientific (examines broad-based evidence, rather than focusing on a narrow slice), shows this view to be untenable. Missing from our cultural view is consideration of the evolutionarily mismatched nature of pederasty in the present environment. Pederasty is currently gravely at odds with the social structure and cultural ideologies, especially since their modifications in the 1970s. Therefore, when it occurs now in particular cases, it is likely to be occurring far outside the context associated with its design, devoid of mentoring, bonding, and group purpose. Its occurrence is prone to being tainted by opprobrium and a sense of exploitation and violation. It is this evolution-culture mismatch rather than the behavior itself that is a prime source for negative response. Neill (2009, p. 436) referred to pederastic behavior in such mismatched contexts as "distorted discharges."

Science Versus Advocacy

As previously noted, the study of adult-minor sex was commandeered by sexual victimology over three decades ago, a paradigm and movement essentially ideological and political in nature, given to unchecked hyperbole, and yet accorded immense powers to define the nature of these sexual relations in "scientific" terms (Malón, 2010, 2011; Money, 1979, 1988). Sexual victimology grew out of a particular strand within the feminist movement, which Angelides (2004, 2005) referred to as "radical feminism" and Sommers (1995, 2000) as "gender feminism." In contrast with other forms of feminism, this form focused on male misbehavior (sexual and otherwise) as a chief advocacy tactic. It did so not simply to right past wrongs, but specifically to weaken the male brand as a means of advancing women's power. The problem is not simply that hyperbole became entrenched in this advocacy—as it may in any political advocacy—but that it became absorbed into sexual victimology. The problem is that sexual victimology was received by professionals and the public as "scientific," as a legitimate authority on the topics under its purview. But it was not a science; it was the codification of an ideology, with extremist character. To wit, shortly after sexual victimology's rise to dominance, moral panics broke out across the United States in day care and recovered memories—a direct result of sexual victimology's extremist claims regarding the nature and effects of sexual misconduct (Jenkins, 1998, 2006; Nathan & Snedeker, 1995).

Notably, the Rind et al. (1998) meta-analysis was one important corrective to this extremism, documenting myriad methodological and hermeneutic flaws recurring in sexual victimological studies and demonstrating the value of the application of proper methods and interpretation. For example, along with related meta-analyses (Rind et al., 2001; Rind & Tromovitch, 1997, 2007), it showed that child sexual abuse is associated on average with small, not large, differences in psychological adjustment in the general population. In laymen's terms, if two of one hundred persons in the general population have clinically significant problems, only three of one hundred persons having experienced child sexual abuse do—far fewer than the large majorities implied by sexual victimologists.[22]

The Rind et al. (1998) meta-analysis was not conducted to advocate adult-minor sex, but rather a return to the scientific study of it, an important goal, given the moral panics sweeping through the United States during the 1980s and 1990s. Similarly, the current review was not conducted to advocate pederasty, but to advocate the scientific study of it. Whereas the foci of moral panics in the 1980s and 1990s were alleged abuse of very young girls and boys in day care centers and young girls in recovered memories of adult patients, new foci have emerged since, of which pederasty is one. For at least the last decade, pederasty has been constantly in the news, perhaps as the most often discussed form of child sexual abuse. The rhetoric follows the radical feminist ideology illustrated in the 1984 newspaper editorial discussed earlier. The claims follow sexual victimological pronouncements, the same ones that previously had targeted the now discredited cases of day care abuse and recovered memories. Just as the Rind et al. (1998) meta-analysis was useful in its day, the current review fits the present vis-à-vis the panic surrounding pederasty by confronting sexual victimology with science. This review's findings of benign or functional pederasty throughout nature are not offered to suggest that this behavior be adopted in our society (the naturalistic fallacy). Its summaries of functional pederasty across numerous other societies are not offered to argue that we instate the practice (the relativistic fallacy). But its findings, summaries, and evolutionary conclusions are offered to expose the moralistic fallacy that pervades the discourse on pederasty, in which moral certitude of its wrongfulness, championed especially by radical feminism and sexual victimology, continually has led to universal claims of its pathological nature and unique harmfulness.

Of the Rind et al. (1998) meta-analysis, it was said that it would open up the floodgates to abuse of children by leading to relaxed laws and vigilance. In the fifteen years since, just the opposite has occurred, in which laws and social attitudes have become increasingly severe (Heller, in this volume; Hubbard, in this volume; *The Economist*, 2009a, 2009b). Scientific reports challenging conventional wisdom generally have little or no effect when faced with powerfully entrenched social structures and cultural ideologies. The same applies to the current review of pederasty. Its potential benefits are in toning down the discursive hyperbole regarding this behavior, as well as illustrating the value of using the broad perspective in analyzing sexual behavior, which has general applications far beyond pederasty. Its potential to alter the relationship between pederasty and society is weak, because this relationship is driven by the dominant social structure and cultural ideologies, which are firmly rooted and unlikely to change significantly in our lifetimes.

Conclusion

2,000 years from now, when the social structure, cultural ideologies, and sexual behavior patterns have significantly altered, as they are bound to do, historians will look back on the sexual patterns of our culture today. When doing so, they will not see our patterns of approved and disapproved sexual behaviors as perfected reference points for judging psychological normality and abnormality, but rather as one manifestation among innumerable others of how cultures construct sexuality, only the totality of which is suggestive of deeper patterns. On the contrary, present-day psychologists, psychiatrists, and other professionals accorded authority to tell us what constitutes normal and abnormal sexual behavior, and what the harms associated with the latter are, do take our patterns as perfected reference points for judgments. This problem has been a recurring one since clinicians supplanted clerics as the "experts" on sex (Foucault, 1978; Szasz, 1990). Kinsey et al. (1948), Ford and Beach (1951), and many others since have complained about this problem, while demonstrating empirically that status-quo theorizing on sexual behavior in many cases is cultural rationalization rather scientific explanation. The present review study on pederasty falls in with this latter tradition in its logic, methods, and conclusions. It offers scientific clarification of this behavioral phenomenon at a time when such clarification is culturally useful, given the constant attention presently surrounding it, yet an attention too often colored by hyperbole and moral panic, rather than one aimed at any kind of objective, dispassionate, and nuanced appraisal.

Notes

1. More precisely, sexual moralities are culturally variable, being constructed from biological foundations in human nature, cultural needs over time, and prevailing cultural ideologies. That is, sexual moral systems are not limitless, even though they are plastic.
2. Drawing inferences from animal, including primate, behavior to human behavior is controversial in many branches of the social sciences. Later in the article, when cross-species data are discussed, due attention will be paid to their controversial nature.
3. Drapetomania was classified as a psychiatric disorder, in which slaves were considered mentally disordered when they ran away from their masters.
4. See Table III in the Historical, Anthropological, and Sociological review later in this article.
5. Subjects were asked how much they enjoyed the event (none, little, some, or much), and "much" was used as "very positive" in this analysis.
6. Unweighted means for reactions were computed, owing to the outlier nature of the Doll et al. (1992) study compared with the other seven studies in terms of its sample type (i.e., quasi-clinical as opposed to purely nonclinical), sample size ($z = 2.22$ above the mean sample size), and reaction pattern (i.e., $z = 1.89$ above the mean negative reaction). The Doll et al. (1992) study also stood apart from the other studies in the way it asked participants about whether they had early age-gap sex. They were asked "whether they were encouraged or forced to have sexual contact before the age of 19 with a person whom they perceived as older or more powerful than themselves" (p. 857), which is a leading question. Its phrase "encouraged or forced" suggests interactions that were mainly passive or unwanted, and its "more powerful" negatively framed the contacts. Compare this question with the completely neutral question in the Stanley et al. (2004) study: "As a child or adolescent, did you have any sexual contact with an adult or older person?"?
7. In these studies, reactions were assessed by direct questions to respondents, as were constructs such as "force." "Abuse" was assessed either by direct questions to respondents or by the researchers' definitional criteria. Importantly, these criteria allowed for non-abusive boy-man sex, in addition to abusive cases. This contrasts with victimological research, where abuse is assumed *a priori*.
8. The studies were, with *n*s followed by positive, neutral, and negative percents in brackets: Fishman (1991) [17—12, 35, 53], Fromuth and Burkhart (1987) [25—n/a, n/a, 52], Okami (1991) [29—72, 17, 10], West and Woodhouse (1993) [29—7, 52, 41], Woods and Dean (1984) [19—16, 32, 52]. Estimated mean percents do not add up to 100 because of missing data in the Fromuth and Burkhart study. Four studies were US samples, and one was British (West & Woodhouse, 1993).
9. "Institutionalized" pederasty, like heterosexual marriage, means a cultural custom, which is organized, socially sanctioned, expected, and ceremonialized—all done because the practice is seen as for the social good. Such cultures are discussed later in detail.
10. Technically speaking, even if the selected societies were unrepresentative, they would still be adequate for testing the dominant assumptions of pathology in the social group, the man, and the youth, assumptions that are *universal* in character. Because pathology is imputed to pederasty per se, regardless of context, contrary examples will serve to challenge this view, and a consistent pattern of contrary examples will negate it.

11. Gat (2006) noted that two views of war have dominated since Hobbes and Rousseau, that of constant war and conflict since the dawn of humankind (Hobbesian), and that of war entering in only with the agricultural revolution ten thousand years ago, when larger societies with their increasing degrees of material possessions encouraged intergroup aggression (Rousseauian). Based on cross-species comparisons and on archeological, historical, and cross-cultural evidence, Gat concluded that Hobbes was much closer to the truth, because the entirety of the evidence indicates that tribe-on-tribe warfare has extended throughout not only the history of our species, but our genus as well. This view is increasingly being espoused among social scientists across many disciplines, as evidence mounts to replace earlier speculation or ideology (e.g., Bowles & Gintis, 2011; Holmes, 2008; Pinker, 2011; Wade, 2008, 2011; Wrangham, 1987). Later in this article, more details are given in the section on humans' "environment of evolutionary adaptedness."
12. In the Greco-Roman world, active partners in homosexual acts between adult men were not stigmatized, only passive partners were. The Sodom myth derogated the active partner as well, with consequence that all forms of homosexual behavior were immoral and then criminal. The Sodom myth thus acted to institutionalize heterosexuality (Rice, manuscript in preparation). Whereas in the classical world, the driving distinction was active-passive, with partner's gender relatively unimportant, in the Christian world, the driving distinction came to heterosexual-homosexual, with the latter always unacceptable (Williams, 1999).
13. In many cases to be examined, age-discrepant homosex parallels human pederasty in relative stages of development of older and younger partners, although age-discrepant homosex has more variability in this regard. In all cases, though, the younger partners are non-adults, and the other partner is significantly older.
14. Bagemihl (1999) featured descriptions of twenty-four primate species (he also included brief references to various other primate species with observed male homosexuality at the ends of some of the featured descriptions). Three of the featured species were omitted from the current review: in two of them, only female homosexuality had been observed (golden monkeys and bushbabies); in the other one (Rufous-naped tamarins), the description was sparse, as was the primary literature. The three species added to Table IV were the mona monkey, patas monkey, and Tibetan macaque.
15. In Vasey's (1995) review, aside from species in the mixed category, mature-immature pairings dominated in 43% of the species, immature-immature in another 43%, and mature-mature in only 14%. In the mixed category, mature-immature pairings were always part of the mix usually along with immature-immature.
16. Spandrels are spaces left in between in architecture—so here, they are functionless side effects of adaptations.
17. *Phylogentic legacy* is another term for vestigial trait, where an adaptation no longer provides any functional purpose but persists through phylogenetic inertia over evolutionary time until it becomes too costly (Thornhill, 1997).
18. Many anthropologists would argue that there is no such thing as "the behavior itself" outside of culture, circumstances, and the individual. And some anthropologists, following this thinking, have argued that gender and sexual relations themselves likewise do not exist outside of culture, circumstances, and the individual. The present article presents a different view, one that clearly endorses cultural and personal effects, but one that also emphasizes a biological component. The fact that mating behavior exists throughout the animal kingdom is proof that human mating behavior has a biological component based on evolutionary heritage. The human form is different from other species: some of that difference is cultural and individual, but some is also biological, as an adaptation to humans' unique evolutionary history. These points apply to homosexual behavior in general and pederasty in particular. Culture, circumstances, and individual factors all matter, but they interact with a biological foundation of evolutionary heritage, as indicated earlier this study.

19. Werner (2006) reviewed pederasty and gender-stratified male homosexuality, but focused on the latter in his hypothesizing. Kirkpatrick (2000) did likewise, presenting a predominance of pederastic cross-cultural evidence, but putting emphasis on androphilia in his hypothesizing, as well as trying to account for female homosexuality. Muscarella (2000) also sought to explain male and female homosexual behavior—a broad task—but focused mostly on pederasty. Neill (2009) similarly sought to explain all of human homosexuality, again with a preponderance of pederastic evidence.
20. The extent to which the study of modern hunter-gatherers provides a basis for inference into the past has been a topic of long-standing debate in anthropology and archaeology. But the fact that the warring pattern is so consistent across extant culturally independent hunter-gatherers of all complexity and primitive agriculturalists is significant. It is suggestive of a long-standing pattern dating back to ancestral humans, when warring became characteristic.
21. Ants are in the class Insecta, which falls in the kingdom Animalia; thus, ants are animals. Group selection in ants is associated with a high degree of relatedness of colony members (importantly, though high degrees of relatedness can contribute to group selection, they are not essential; Wilson & Wilson, 2007). Notably, early human male group members are considered to have generally been related to varying degrees, given current human and African ape evidence indicating that male endogamy and female exogamy (i.e., males stay in their natal group, but females leave at puberty) were most likely the rule in early humans (Wrangham, 1987).
22. Notably, research has repeatedly shown that child sexual abuse in our society is confounded with negative family and peer environments, such that the small association between child sexual abuse and later poorer adjustment cannot be assumed to be causal at the population level. In particular cases, it surely causes severe harm, but so do certain cases of adult-adult sex. The main question is whether harmful outcome is a property of this experience, and the nonclinical empirical research indicates that it is not, but instead is an interaction effect of circumstances and individuals.

References

Adam, B. D. (1985). Age, structure, and sexuality: Reflections on the anthropological evidence on homosexual relations. *Journal of Homosexuality, 11,* 19–33.

Anderson, C. M., & Bielert, C. (1990). Adolescent/adult copulatory behavior in nonhuman primates. In J. R. Feierman (Ed.), *Pedophilia: Biosocial dimensions* (pp. 176–200). New York: Springer-Verlag.

Angelides, S. (2004). Feminism, child sexual abuse, and the erasure of child sexuality. *GLQ, 10,* 141–177.

———. (2005). The emergence of the paedophile in the late twentieth century. *Australian Historical Studies, 126,* 272–295.

Arreola, S., Neilands, T., Pollack, L., Paul, J., & Catania, J. (2008). Childhood sexual experiences and adult health sequelae among gay and bisexual men: Defining childhood sexual abuse. *Journal of Sex Research, 45,* 246–252.

Bagemihl, B. (1999). *Biological exuberance: Animal homosexuality and natural diversity.* New York: St. Martin's Press.

Baldauf, I. (1988). *Die Knabenliebe in Mittelasien: Bacabozlik* [Boylove in Central Asia: Bacabozlik]. Berlin, Germany: Verlag das Arabische Buch.

Baldwin, J. D. (1969). The ontogeny of social behavior of squirrel monkeys (*Saimiri sciureus*) in a semi-natural environment. *Folia Primatologica, 11,* 35–39.

Bartholow, B. N., Doll, L. S., Joy, D., Bolan, G., Harrison, J. S., Moss, P. M., et al. (1994). Emotional, behavioral, and HIV risks associated with sexual abuse among adult homosexual and bisexual men. *Child Abuse & Neglect, 18,* 747–761.

Bartos, L., & Holeckova, J. (2006). Exciting ungulates: Male-male mounting in fallow, white-tailed and red deer. In V. Sommer & P. L. Vasey (Eds.), *Homosexual behavior in animals: An evolutionary perspective* (pp. 154–171). Cambridge, England: Cambridge University Press.

Baurmann, M. C. (1983). *Sexualität, Gewalt und psychische Folgen* [Sexuality, force, and psychological consequences]. Wiesbaden, Germany: Bundeskriminalamt.

Bell, A. P., Weinberg, M. S., & Hammersmith, S. K. (1981). *Sexual preference: Its development in men and women*. Bloomington: Indiana University Press.

Bernard, F. (1981). Pedophilia: Psychological consequences for the child. In L. L. Constantine & F. M. Martinson (Eds.), *Children and sex* (pp. 189–199). Boston, MA: Little, Brown.

Bernstein, I. S. (1975). Activity patterns in a gelada monkey group. *Folia Primatologica, 23*, 50–71.

Blanchard, R., Lykins, A. D., Wherrett, D., Kuban, M. E., Cantor, J. M., Blak, T., et al. (2009). Pedophilia, hebephilia, and the DSM-V. *Archives of Sexual Behavior, 38,* 335–350.

Boag, P. (2003). *Same-sex affairs: Constructing and controlling homosexuality in the Pacific Northwest.* Berkeley: University of California Press.

Boswell, J. (1980). *Christianity, social tolerance, and homosexuality: Gay people in Western Europe from the beginning of the Christian era to the fourteenth century.* Chicago: University of Chicago Press.

Bowles, S., & Gintis, H. (2011). *A cooperative species—human reciprocity and its evolution.* Princeton, NJ: Princeton University Press.

Bullough, V. L. (1976). *Sexual variance in society and history.* New York: Wiley.

_____. (2004). "Pederasty," in *glbtq: An Encyclopedia of Gay, Lesbian, Bisexual, Transgender, and Queer Culture.* Retrieved from: http://www.glbtq.com/social-sciences/pederasty.html

Burg, B. R. (1995). *Sodomy and the pirate tradition.* New York: NYU Press.

Burgess, A. W., & Holmstrom, L. L. (1974). Rape trauma syndrome. *American Journal of Psychiatry, 131,* 981–986.

Buss, D. (2007). *Evolutionary psychology: The new science of the mind* (3d ed.). Boston, MA: Allyn & Bacon.

Buss, D. M., Haselton, M. G., Shackelford, T. K., Bleske, A. L., & Wakefield, J. C. (1998). Adaptations, exaptations, and spandrels. *American Psychologist, 53,* 533–548.

Cantarella, E. (1992). *Bisexuality in the ancient world.* New Haven, CT: Yale University Press.

Carballo-Diéguez, A., Balan, I., Dolezal, C., & Mello, M. (2009). Childhood sexual experiences among men who have sex with men in Brazil. Paper presented at the American Public Health Association (APHA) conference in Philadelphia, November 7 to 11.

Cardoso, F. L., & Werner, D. (2004) Homosexuality. In C. R. Ember and M. Ember (Eds.), *Encyclopedia of sex and gender: Men and women in the world's cultures: Vol. I., Topics and cultures A–K* (pp. 204–215). New York: Kluwer Academic.

Carpenter, C. R. (1942). Sexual behavior of free ranging rhesus monkeys (*Macaca mulatto*). Periodicity of estrus, homosexual, autoerotic and non-conformist behavior. *Journal of Comparative Psychology, 33,* 143–162.

Carrier, J. M. (1980). Homosexual behavior in cross-cultural perspective. In J. Marmor (Ed.), *Homosexual behavior: A modem reappraisal* (pp. 100–122). New York: Basic Books.

Chandos, J. (1984) *Boys together: English public schools, 1800–1864.* New Haven, CT: Yale University Press.

Chevalier-Skolnikoff, S. (1976). Homosexual behavior in a laboratory group of stumptail monkeys (Macaca arrioides): Forms, contexts, and possible social functions. *Archives of Sexual Behavior, 5,* 511–527.

Condy, S., Templer, D., Brown, R., & Veaco, L. (1987). Parameters of sexual contact of boys with women. *Archives of Sexual Behavior, 16,* 379–394.

Constantine, L. L. (1981). The effects of early sexual experiences: A review and synthesis of research. In L. L. Constantine & F. M. Martinson (Eds.), *Children and sex* (pp. 217–244). Boston, MA: Little, Brown.

Coontz, S. (2006). Op-ed [why marriage may not be good for your health]. *New York Times,* November 7, A21.

Cosmides, L., & Tooby, J. (1999). Toward an evolutionary taxonomy of treatable conditions. *Journal of Abnormal Psychology, 108,* 453–464.

Coxell, A., King, M., Mezey, G., & Gordon, D. (1999). Lifetime prevalence, characteristics, and associated problems of non-consensual sex in men: Cross sectional survey. *British Medical Journal, 318,* 846–850.

Crapo, R. H. (1995). Factors in the cross-cultural patterning of male homosexuality: A reappraisal of the literature. *Cross-Cultural Research, 29,* 178–202.

Crompton, L. (2003). *Homosexuality & civilization*. Cambridge, MA: The Belknap Press of Harvard University.
Davenport, W. H. (1965). Sexual patterns and their regulation in a society of the Southwest Pacific. In F. A. Beach (Ed.), *Sex and behavior* (pp. 164–207). New York: Wiley.
de Waal. F. B. M. (1997). *Bonobo: The forgotten ape*. Berkeley: University of California Press.
_____. (1998). *Chimpanzee politics: Power and sex among apes*. Baltimore, MD: Johns Hopkins University Press.
Denniston, R. M. (1980). Ambisexuality in animals. In J. Marmor (Ed.), *Homosexual Behavior. A Modem Reappraisal* (pp. 25–40). New York: Basic Books.
Dickemann, J. M. (2000). Commentary on Kirkpatrick (2000). *Current Anthropology, 41*, 399–400.
Discover Magazine (2006). E. O. Wilson: Biology's chief provocateur explores the evolutionary origins of cooperation, warfare, and the tribal mind, June 25. Retrieved from: http://discovermagazine.com/2006/jun/e-o-wilson
Divale, W. T. (1972). System population control in the Middle and Upper Palaeolithic: Inferences based on contemporary hunter-gatherers. *World Archaeology, 4*, 222–243.
Dixson, A. F. (1977). Observations on the displays, menstrual cycles and sexual behavior of the "Black ape" of Celebes (*Macaca nigru*). *Journal of Zoology, 182*, 63–84.
Dolezal, C., & Carballo-Diéguez, A. (2002). Childhood sexual experiences and the perception of abuse among Latino men who have sex with men. *The Journal of Sex Research, 39*, 165–173.
Doll, L. S., Joy, D., Bartholow, B. N., Harrison, J. S., Bolan, G., Douglas, J. M., et al. (1992). Self-reported childhood and adolescent sexual abuse among adult homosexual and bisexual men. *Child Abuse & Neglect, 16*, 855–864.
Dover, K. J. (1978). *Greek homosexuality*. Cambridge, MA: Harvard University Press.
Edwards, A. M. A. R., and Todd, J. D. (1991). Homosexual behavior in wild white-handed gibbons (*Hylobates tar*). *Primates, 32*, 231–236.
Ember, C. (1978). Myths about hunter-gatherers. *Ethnology, 17*, 439–448.
Evans-Pritchard, E. (1971). *The Azande*. London: Oxford University Press.
Finkelhor, D. (1979). *Sexually victimized children*. New York: The Free Press.
Fishman, J. (1991). Prevalence, impact, and meaning attribution of childhood sexual experiences of undergraduate males. *Dissertation Abstracts International, 52*, 114.
Flynt, J. (1927). Homosexuality among tramps. In H. Ellis (Ed.), *Studies in the psychology of sex*, Volume II, Appendix A.
Fone, B. (2000). *Homophobia: A history*. New York: Picador.
Ford, C., & Beach, F. (1951). *Patterns of sexual behavior*. New York: Harper & Row.
Foucault, M. (1978). *History of sexuality: Vol. 1. An introduction*. New York: Pantheon.
Fromuth, M., & Burkhart, B. (1987). Sexual victimization among college men: Definitional and methodological issues. *Violence and Victims, 2*, 241–253.
_____. (1989). Long-term psychological correlates of childhood sexual abuse in two samples of college men. *Child Abuse & Neglect, 13*, 533–542.
Gat, A. (2006). *War in human civilization*. Oxford, England: Oxford University Press.
Gathorne-Hardy, J. (1978). *The old school tie: The phenomenon of the English public school*. New York: Viking Press.
Gaulin, S. J. C., & McBurney, D. (2004). *Evolutionary psychology*. Upper Saddle River, NJ: Prentice Hall.
Gebhard, P. H., Gagnon, J. H., Pomeroy, W. B., & Christenson, C.V. (1965). *Sex offenders: An analysis of types*. New York: Harper & Row.
Geist, V. (1975). *Mountain sheep and man in the northern wilds*. Ithaca, NY: Cornell University Press.
Gibbs, N. (2010). The pill at 50: Sex, freedom and paradox. *Time magazine*, April 22.
Gilmore, D. (1990). *Mankind in the making: Cultural concepts of masculinity*. New Haven, CT: Yale University Press.
Giovanni's Room press release (1999, March 24). Access to information about pedophilia and the outrages of child abuse.
Glenn, M. E., Ramsier, M., and Benson, K. J. (2006). Homosexual behavior and long-term bonding in wild Mona monkey all-male groups. Paper presented at the International Association of Sex Research conference, Amsterdam, Netherlands, July, 15.

Goodall, J. (1986). *The chimpanzees of Gombe: Patterns of behavior.* Cambridge, MA: Belknap Press of Harvard University Press.
Greenberg, D. (1988). *The construction of homosexuality.* Chicago, IL: University of Chicago Press.
Gregersen, E. (1983). *Sexual practices: The story of human sexuality.* New York: Franklin Watts.
Hamilton, G. V. (1914). A study of sexual tendencies in monkeys and baboons. *Journal of Animal Behavior, 4,* 295–318.
Hanby, J. P., and Brown, C. E. (1974). The development of sociosexual behaviors in Japanese macaques Macaca fuscata. *Behaviour, 49,* 152–196.
Harcourt, A. H. (1979). Social relationships between adult male and female mountain gorillas in the wild. *Animal Behavior, 27,* 325–342.
Hare, E. H. (1962). Masturbatory insanity: The history of an idea. *Journal of Mental Science, 108,* 1–25.
Hashimoto, C. (1997). Content and development of sexual behavior of wild bonobos (*Pan paniscus*) at Wamba, Zaire. *International Journal of Primatology, 18,* 1–21.
Heffernan, V. (2004). What (sex) boys (sex) think (sex) about. *New York Times,* October 7, E7.
Herdt, G. (1984). *Ritualized homosexuality in Melanesia.* Berkeley: University of California Press.
_____. (1987). *The Sambia: Ritual and gender in New Guinea.* New York: Harcourt Brace Jovanovich.
_____. (1991). Representations of homosexuality: An essay on cultural ontology and historical comparison (Part II). *Journal of the History of Sexuality, 1,* 603–632.
_____. (1993). *Ritualized homosexuality in Melanesia.* Berkeley, CA: University of California Press.
_____. (1997). *Same sex, different cultures: Exploring gay and lesbian lives.* Boulder, CO: Westview Press.
Herdt, G. & Boxer, A. B. (1993). *Children of horizons.* New York: Beacon.
Herman, J., & Hirschman, L. (1977). Father-daughter incest. *Signs, 2,* 735–756.
Hinsch, B. (1990). *Passions of the cut sleeve: The male homosexual tradition in China.* Berkeley: University of California Press.
Hirschfeld, M. (1914). *Die Homosexualität des Mannes und des Weibes* (Homosexuality of males and females). Berlin: Louis Marcus Verlagsbuchhandlung.
Hoffman, J. (1994). On lust, liaisons and laws. *New York Times,* October 23, p. 16.
Hohmann, G. (1989). Group fission in Nilgiri langurs (*Presbytis johnii*). *International Journal of Primatology, 10,* 441–454.
Holmes, B. (2008). How warfare shaped human evolution. *New Scientist,* November 12. Retrieved from: http://www.newscientist.com/article/mg20026823.800-how-warfare-shaped-human-evolution.html?full=true
Hooker, E. (1957). The adjustment of the male overt homosexual. *Journal of Projective Techniques, 21,* 18–31.
Hubbard, T. K. (1998). Popular perceptions of elite homosexuality in classical Athens. *Arion,* ser. 3, 6.1, 48–78.
_____. (2000). Pederasty and democracy: The marginalization of a social practice. In T. K. Hubbard (Ed.), *Greek Love Reconsidered* (pp. 1–11). New York: Wallace-New Hampton.
_____. (2002). Pindar, Theoxenus, and the homoerotic eye. *Arethusa, 35,* 255–296.
_____. (2003). *Homosexuality in Greece and Rome: A sourcebook of basic documents.* Berkeley: University of California Press.
Hutchinson, G. E. (1959). A speculative consideration of certain possible forms of sexual selection in man. *American Naturalist, 93,* 81–91.
Ingram, M. (1981). Participating victims: A study of sexual offenses with boys. In L. L. Constantine, and F. M. Martinson (Eds.), *Children and sex* (pp. 177–187). Boston, MA: Little, Brown.
Jay, K. & Young, A. (1977). *The gay report.* New York: Simon and Schuster.
Jay, P. C. (1965). The common langur of North India. In I. DeVore (Ed.), *Primate behavior: Field studies of monkeys and apes* (pp. 197–249). New York: Holt, Rinehart, & Winston.
Jenkins, P. (1998). *Moral panic: Changing concepts of the child-molester in modem America.* New Haven, CT: Yale University Press.
_____. (2006). *The decade of nightmares: The end of the Sixties and the making of eighties America.* London, England: Oxford University Press.
Jones, D. (2000). Commentary on Kirkpatrick (2000). *Current Anthropology, 41,* 400–401.

Kano, T. (1980). Social behavior of wild pygmy chimpanzees (*Pan paniscus*) of Wamba: A preliminary report. *Journal of Human Evolution, 9,* 243–260.

Keesing, R. M. (1982). Prologue: Toward a multidimensional understanding of male initiation. In G. Herdt (Ed.), *Rituals of manhood: Male initiation in Papua New Guinea* (pp. 1–39). Berkeley: University of California Press.

Kempf. E. J. (1917). The social and sexual behavior of infra-human primates with some comparable facts in human behavior. *Psychoanalytic Review, 4,* 127–154.

Kinsey, A., Pomeroy, W. B., & Martin, C. E. (1948). *Sexual behavior in the human male.* Philadelphia, PA: W. B. Saunders.

Kinsey, A., Pomeroy, W. B., Martin, C. E., & Gebhard, P. (1953). *Sexual behavior in the human female.* Philadelphia, PA: W. B. Saunders.

Kirkpatrick, R. C. (2000). The evolution of human homosexual behavior. *Current Anthropology, 41,* 385–413.

Kollar, E. L., Beckwith, W. C., & Edgerton, R. B. (1968). Sexual behavior of the ARL Colony chimpanzees. *Journal of Nervous and Mental Diseases, 147,* 444–459.

Kotrschal, K., Hemetsberger, J., & Weiss, B. M. (2006). Homosociality in male greylag geese (*Anser anser*): Making the best of a bad situation. In V. Sommer and P. L. Vasey (Eds.), *Homosexual behavior in animals: An evolutionary perspective* (pp. 45–76). Cambridge, England: Cambridge University Press.

Kramer, L. (1981). *Reports from the Holocaust.* New York: St. Martin's Press.

Lambert, G. (2000). *Mainly about Lindsay Anderson.* New York: Alfred A. Knopf.

Lambert, R. (1984). *Beloved and god: The story of Hadrian and Antinous.* New York: Carol Publishing Group.

Lambert, R., & Lambert, S. M. (1968). *The hothouse society: An exploration of boarding-school life through the boys' and girls' own writings.* London: Weidenfeld and Nicolson.

Lautmann, R. (1994). *Die Lust am Kind* (Attraction to children). Hamburg: Ingrid Klein Pubs. Inc.

Layard, J. W. (1942). *Stone men of Malekula.* London: Chatto & Windus.

Leahy, T. (1992). Positively experienced man/boy sex: The discourse of seduction and the social construction of masculinity. *Australian and New Zealand Journal of Sociology, 28,* 71–87.

Lear, A. (2004). *Noble eros: The idealization of pederasty from the Greek Dark Ages to the Athens of Socrates.* Unpublished dissertation, University of California, Los Angeles.

Lear, A., & Cantarella, E. (2008). *Images of ancient Greek pederasty: Boys were their gods.* New York: Routledge.

Leupp, G. P. (1995). *Male colors: The construction of homosexuality in Tokugawa Japan.* Berkeley: University of California Press.

Levine, M. P., & Troiden, R. R. (1988). The myth of sexual compulsivity. *The Journal of Sex Research, 25,* 347–363.

Lewis, C. S. (1955). *Surprised by joy: The shape of my early life.* New York: Harcourt.

Mackey, W. C. (1986). A facet of the man-child bond: The teeter-totter effect. *Ethology and Sociobiology, 7,* 117–134.

———. (1990). Adult-male/juvenile association as a species-characteristic human trait: A comparative field approach. In J. R. Feierman (Ed.), *Pedophilia: Biosocial dimensions* (pp. 299–323). New York: Springer-Verlag.

Macklin, W. R. (1997). Drawn to each other: Boys and adult women. *Philadelphia Inquirer,* August 28, C1 and C8.

Malón, A. (2010). Onanism and child sexual abuse: A comparative study of two hypotheses. *Archives of Sexual Behavior, 39,* 637–652.

———. (2011). The "participating victim" in the study of erotic experiences between children and adults: A historical analysis. *Archives of Sexual Behavior, 40,* 169–188. Mann, J. (2006). Establishing trust: Socio-sexual behaviour and the development of male-male bonds among Indian Ocean bottlenose dolphins. In V. Sommer & P. L. Vasey (Eds.), *Homosexual behavior in animals: An evolutionary perspective* (pp. 107–130). Cambridge, England: Cambridge University Press.

Massad, J. A. (2007). *Desiring Arabs.* Chicago, IL: The University of Chicago Press.

Masters, R. E. L. (1962). *Forbidden sexual behavior and morality: An objective re-examination of perverse sex practices in different cultures.* New York: Julian Press.

McBride, A. F., & Hebb, D. O. (1948). Behavior of the captive bottlenose dolphin, Tursiops truncates. *Journal of Comparative & Physiological Psychology, 41,* 111–123.

McClintock, M., & Herdt, G. (1996). Rethinking puberty: The development of sexual attraction. *Current Developments in Psychological Science, 5,* 178–183.

Menasco, D. (2000). Pederasty. In G. E. Haggerty (Ed.), *Gay histories and cultures: An encyclopedia,* pp. 672–675. New York: Garland Publishing.

Money, J. (1979). Sexual dictatorship, dissidence, and democracy. *International Journal of Medicine and Law, 1,* 11–20.

———. (1988). Commentary: Current status of sex research. *Journal of Psychology and Human Sexuality, 1,* 5–15.

Money, J., & Ehrhardt, A. (1972). *Man and woman, boy and girl: The differentiation and dimorphism of gender identity from conception to maturity.* Baltimore, MD: Johns Hopkins University Press.

Money, J. & Weinrich, J. D. (1983). Juvenile, pedophile, heterophile: Hermeneutics of science, medicine and law in two outcome studies. *International Journal of Medicine and Law, 2,* 39–54.

Monroe, J. T. (1997). The striptease that was blamed on Abu Bakr's naughty son: Was father being shamed, or was the poet having fun? In J. W. Wright & E. K. Rowson (Eds.), *Homoeroticism in classical Arabic literature* (pp. 94–139). New York: Columbia University Press.

Moulton, I. (2003). Homoeroticism in *La cazzaria* (1525). *Gay & Lesbian Review,* July-August, 19–21.

Murray, S. O. (1997). Male homosexuality in Ottoman Albania. In S. O. Murray & W. Roscoe (Eds.) *Islamic homosexualities: Culture, history, and literature* (pp. 187–196). New York: New York University Press.

———. (2000). *Homosexualities.* Chicago, IL: University of Chicago Press.

Murray, S. O., & Roscoe, W. (Eds.) (1997). *Islamic homosexualities: Culture, history, and literature.* New York: New York University Press.

———. (1998). *Boy-wives and female husbands: Studies in African homosexualities.* New York: Palgrave.

Muscarella, F. (2000). The evolution of homoerotic behavior in humans. *Journal of Homosexuality, 40,* 51–77.

Nash, P. (1961) Training an elite: The prefect-fagging system in the English public school. *History of Education Quarterly, 1,* 14–21.

Nathan, D., & Snedeker, M. (1995). *Satan's silence: Ritual abuse and the making of a modern American witchhunt.* New York: Basic Books.

Neill, J. (2009). *The origins and role of same-sex relations in human societies.* Jefferson, NC: McFarland & Company.

Nelson, A., & Oliver, P. (1998). Gender and the construction of consent in child-adult sexual contact: Beyond gender neutrality and male monopoly. *Gender & Society, 12,* 554–577.

Oberhelman, S. M. (1997). Hierarchies of gender, ideology, and power in ancient and medieval Greek and Arabic dream literature. In J. W. Wright and E. K. Rowson (Eds.), *Homoeroticism in classical Arabic literature* (pp. 55–93). New York: Columbia University Press.

Ogawa, H. (1995). *Wily monkeys: Social intelligence of Tibetan macaques.* University of Kyoto Press/Trans Pacific Press.

Oi, T. (1990). Patterns of dominance and affiliation in wild pig-tailed macaques (*Macaca nemestrina nemestrina*) in West Sumatra. *International Journal of Primatololgy, 11,* 339–355.

Okami, P. (1991). Self-reports of "positive" childhood and adolescent sexual contacts with older persons: An exploratory study. *Archives of Sexual Behavior, 20,* 437–457.

Otterbein, K. (1991). Comments on "Violence and sociality in human evolution," by B. M. Kauft. *Current Anthropology, 32,* 414.

Paglia, C. (1990). *Sexual personae.* New York: Vintage Press.

———. (1992). *Sex, art, and American culture: Essays.* New York: Vintage Books.

Patanè, V. (2006). Homosexuality in the Middle East and North Africa. In R. Aldrich (Ed.), *Gay life and culture: A world history* (pp. 271–301). New York: Universe Publishing.

Pequigney, J. (2002). Classical mythology. Retrieved from: www.glbtq.com/literature/classical_myth.html

Philadelphia Inquirer (1984). A forceful step forward against child sexual abuse, September 13, 22A.

Pinker, S. (2011). *The better angels of our nature: Why violence has declined.* New York: Viking Penguin.

Poirier, F. E. (1970). The communication matrix of the Nilgiri langur (*Presbytus johnii*) of South India. *Folia Primatologica, 13,* 92–136.

Pratt, D. M., & Anderson, V. H. (1985). Giraffe social behavior. *Journal of Natural History 19*, 771–781.
Prince Peter (1963). *A study of polyandry.* The Hague: Mouton.
Rahman, T. (1989). Boy love in the Urdu ghazal. *Paidika, 2*, 10–27.
Rapp, L. (2005). Lambert, Gavin. Retrieved from: http://www.glbtq.com/arts/lambert_g.html
Redican, W. K., Gomber, J., & Mitchell, G. (1974). Adult male parental behaviour in feral- and isolation-reared monkeys (*Macaca mulatta*). In J. H. Cullen (Ed.), *Experimental behavior: A basis for the study of mental disturbance* (pp. 131–146). John Wiley & Sons: New York.
Reiss, A. J. (1961). The social integration of queers and peers. *Social Problems, 9*, 102–120.
Rice, E. (2005). Greece: Ancient, in *glbtq: An Encyclopedia of Gay, Lesbian, Bisexual, Transgender, and Queer Culture*. Retrieved from: http://www.glbtq.com/social-sciences/greece_ancient.html
_____. (Manuscript in preparation.). *Homosexuality in Western history.*
Rijksen, H. D. (1978). A field study of Sumatran orang-utans (*Pongo pygmaeus abelii* Lesson 1827). *Ecology, Behavior, and Conservation.* Wageningen, The Netherlands: H. Veenman and Zonen.
Rind, B. (2001). Gay and bisexual adolescent boys' sexual experiences with men: An empirical examination of psychological correlates in a nonclinical sample. *Archives of Sexual Behavior, 30*, 345–368.
Rind, B., & Tromovitch, P. (1997). A meta-analytic review of findings from national samples on psychological correlates of child sexual abuse. *Journal of Sex Research, 34*, 237–255.
_____ (Manuscript in preparation.) National samples, sexual abuse in childhood, and adjustment in adulthood: A commentary on Najman, Dunne, Purdie, Boyle, and Coxeter (2005). *Archives of Sexual Behavior, 36*, 101–106.
Rind, B., Tromovitch, P., & Bauserman, R. (1998). A meta-analytic examination of assumed properties of child sexual abuse using college samples. *Psychological Bulletin, 124*, 22–53.
_____. (2001). The validity and appropriateness of methods, analyses, and conclusions in Rind et al. (1998): A rebuttal of victimological critique from Ondersma et al. (2001) and Dallam et al. (2001). *Psychological Bulletin, 127*, 734–758.
Rind, B., & Welter, M. (2012). Enjoyment and emotionally negative reactions in minor-adult versus minor-peer and adult-adult first postpubescent coitus: A secondary analysis of the Kinsey data. Manuscript submitted for publication.
Rocke, M. (1996). *Forbidden friendships: Homosexuality and male culture in Renaissance Florence.* New York: Oxford University Press.
Roheim, G. (1945). *The eternal ones of the dream: A psychoanalytic interpretation of Australian myth and ritual.* New York: International Universities Press.
Ross, M. W. (1991). A taxonomy of global bisexuality. In R. Tielman, M. Carballo, & A. C. Hendriks (Eds.), *Bisexuality and HIV/AIDS: A global perspective.* New York: Prometheus Books.
Rossman, G. P. (1976). *Sexual experience between men and boys.* New York: Association Press.
Rouayheb, K. (2005). *Before homosexuality in the Arab-Islamic world, 1500–1800.* Chicago, IL: The University of Chicago Press.
Rowson, E. K. (1997). Two homoerotic narratives from Mamlūk literature: al-Safadī's *Law'at al-shākī* and Ibn Dāniyāl's *al-Mutayyam*. In J. W. Wright & E. K. Rowson (Eds.), *Homoeroticism in classical Arabic literature* (pp. 158–191). New York: Columbia University Press.
Ruggiero, G. (1985). *The boundaries of eros: Sex crime and sexuality in Renaissance Venice.* New York: Oxford University Press.
Saikaku, I. (1990). *The great mirror of male love.* (P. G. Schalow, Trans.). Stanford, CA: Stanford UP. (Original work published in 1687.)
Sandfort, T. G. M. (1984). Sex in pedophiliac relationships: An empirical investigation among a nonrepresentative group of boys. *Journal of Sex Research, 20*, 123–142.
_____. (1988). *Het belang van de ervaring. Over seksuele contacten in de vroege jeugdaren en seksueel gedrag en beleven op latere leeftijd* [The importance of the experience. Sexual relations in early childhood years and sexual behavior and experience later in life]. Utrecht, Netherlands: Homostudies.
_____. (1992). The argument for adult-child sexual contact: A critical appraisal and new data. In James O'Donohue et al. (Eds.), *The sexual abuse of children (Vol. I): Theory and research* (pp. 38–48). Hillsdale, NJ: Lawrence Erlbaum Associates.
Sandfort, T. G. M., & Everaerd, W. T. A. M. (1990). Male juvenile partners in pedophilia. In M. E. Perry

(Ed.), *Handbook of sexology, Vol. 7: Childhood and adolescent sexology* (pp. 361–380). Amsterdam, Netherlands: Elsevier.
Saslow, J. M. (1986). *Ganymede in the Renaissance: Homosexuality in art and society.* New Haven, CT: Yale University Press.
———. (1989). Homosexuality in the renaissance: Behavior, identity, and artistic expression. In M. B. Duberman, M. Vicinus, & G. Chauncey Jr. (Eds.), *Hidden from history* (pp. 90–105). New York: New American Press.
Savin-Williams, R. C. (1997). *" … And then I became gay": Young men's stories.* New York: Routledge.
Savin-Williams, R. C., & Weisfeld, G. E. (1989). An ethological perspective on adolescence. In G. R. Adams, R. Montemayor, and T. P. Gullotta (Eds.), *Biology of adolescent behavior and development* (pp. 249–274). Newbury Park, CA: Sage.
Schalow, P. G. (1989). Male love in early modern Japan: A literary depiction of the "youth." In M. B. Duberman, M. Vicinus, & G. Chauncey Jr. (Eds.), *Hidden from history* (pp. 118–128). New York: New American Press.
Schieffelin, E. (1982). The *Bau A* ceremonial lodge: An alternative to initiation. In G. Herdt (Ed.), *Rituals of manhood: Male initiation in Papua New Guinea* (pp. 155–200). Berkeley: University of California Press.
Schild, M. (1988). The irresistible beauty of boys: Middle Eastern attitudes about boy-love. *Paidika, 1,* 37–48.
Schulman, S. (2007). What ever happened to complexity? *Gay & Lesbian Review,* November-December, pp. 10–11.
Seligman, C. G., & Seligman, B. Z. (1932). *Pagan tribes of the Nilotic Sudan.* London: George Rutledge and Sons.
Serpenti, L. (1984). The ritual meaning of homosexuality and pedophilia among the Kimam-Papuans of South Irian Jaya. In G. H. Herdt (Ed.), *Ritualized homosexual behavior in Melanesia* (pp. 292–317). Berkeley: University of California Press.
Smuts, B. B., & Watanabe, J. M. (1990). Social relationships and ritualized greetings in adult male baboons (*Papio cynocephalus anubis*). *International Journal of Primatology, 11,* 147–177.
Sommer, V., & Vasey, P. L. (Eds.) (2006). *Homosexual behavior in animals: An evolutionary perspective.* Cambridge, England: Cambridge University Press.
Sommer, V., Schauer, P., & Kyriazis, D. (2006). A wild mixture of motivations: Same-sex mounting in Indian langur monkeys. In V. Sommer & P. L. Vasey (Eds.), *Homosexual behavior in animals: An evolutionary perspective* (pp. 338–372). Cambridge, England: Cambridge University Press.
Sommers, C. H. (1995). *Who stole feminism? How women have betrayed women.* New York: Touchtone.
———. (2000). *The war against boys: How misguided feminism is harming our young men.* New York: Simon & Schuster.
Spada, J. (1979). *The Spada report.* New York: Signet.
Stanley, J. L., Bartholomew, K., & Oram, D. (2004). Gay and bisexual men's age-discrepant childhood sexual experiences. *Journal of Sex Research, 41,* 381–389.
Strehlow, C. (1913–1915) Das soziale Leben der Aranda und Loritja-Stämme in Zentral-Australien [The social life of the Aranda and Loritja tribes in Central Australia]. *Veröffentlichungen aus dem Städtischen Völker-Museum, 1,* 1–108.
Strozier, C. B. (2001). *Heinz Kohut: The making of a psychoanalyst.* New York: Farrar, Straus and Giroux.
Suggs, R. C. (1966). *Marquesan sexual behavior.* New York: Harcourt, Brace, & World.
Szasz, T. S. (1990). *Sex by prescription: The startling truth about today's sex therapy.* New York: Syracuse University Press.
Takenoshita, Y. (1998). Male homosexual behaviour accompanied by ejaculation in a free-ranging troop of Japanese macaques (*Macaca fuscata*). *Folia Primatologica, 69,* 364–367.
Tauxier, L. (1912). *Les Noirs du Soudan: Pays Mossi et Gourounni.* Paris: Émile LaRose.
The Compact Edition of the Oxford English Dictionary (1971). Oxford: Oxford University Press.
The Economist. (2009a). America's unjust sex laws (p. 8), August 8.
———. (2009b). Sex laws: Unjust and ineffective (pp. 21–23), August 8.
The National Lesbian and Gay Survey (1993). *Proust, Cole Porter, Michelangelo, Marc Almond, and me: Writings by gay men on their lives and lifestyles.* London: Routledge.

Thornhill, R. (1997). The concept of an evolved adaptation. In G. R. Bock & G. Cardew (Eds.), *Characterizing human psychological adaptations* (pp. 4–22). West Sussex, England: Wiley.

Thorstad, D. (1998). Pederasty and homosexuality. Speech to the *Semana Cultural Lésbica-Gay*, Mexico City, June 26.

Tindall, R. H. (1978). The male adolescent involved with a pederast becomes an adult. *Journal of Homosexuality, 3,* 373–382.

Tokuda, K, Simons. R. C., & Jensen, G. D. (1968). Sexual behavior in a captive group of pigtailed monkeys (*Macaca nemestrina*). *Primates, 9,* 283–294.

Tooby, J., & Cosmides, L. (2005). Conceptual foundations of evolutionary psychology. In D. M. Buss (Ed.), *The handbook of evolutionary psychology*. Hoboken, NJ: Wiley.

Trachtenberg, R. (2005). *When I knew*. New York: HarperEntertainment.

Trivers, R. L. (1976). Sexual selection and resource-accruing abilities in *Anolis garmani. Evolution, 30,* 253–269.

Tuller, D. (2002). Minor report: Sex between teenage boys and older men is not always coercive- and it can be more ecstatic than traumatic. Retrieved from: http://www.salon.com/mwt/feature/2002/07/22/coming_of_age/print.html

Van Baal, J. (1966). *Dema*. The Hague: Martinus Nijhoff.

Vanggaard, T. (1972). *Phallos: A symbol and its history in the male world*. New York: International Universities Press.

Vasey, P. L. (1995). Homosexual behavior in primates: A review of evidence and theory. *International Journal of Primatology, 16,* 173–203.

_____. (2000). Commentary on Kirkpatrick (2000). *Current Anthropology, 41,* 402–403.

Vasey, P. L., & Sommer, V. (2006). Homosexual behaviour in animals: Topics, hypotheses and research trajectories. In V. Sommer and P. L. Vasey (Eds.), *Homosexual behavior in animals: An evolutionary perspective* (pp. 3–42). Cambridge, England: Cambridge University Press.

Vervaecke, H., & Rodin, C. (2006). Going with the herd: Same-sex interaction and competition in American bison. In V. Sommer and P. L. Vasey (Eds.), *Homosexual behavior in animals: An evolutionary perspective* (pp. 131–153). Cambridge, England: Cambridge University Press.

Wade, N. (2008). Taking a cue from ants on evolution of humans. *New York Times,* July 15.

_____. (2011). Sign of advancing society? An organized war effort. *New York Times,* August 2.

Wakefield, J. C. (1992). The concept of mental disorder: on the boundary between biological facts and social values. *American Psychologist, 47,* 73–88.

_____. (1999). Evolutionary versus prototype analyses of the concept of disorder. *Journal of Abnormal Psychology, 108,* 374–399.

_____. (2007). The concept of mental disorder: Diagnostic implications of the harmful dysfunction analysis. *World Psychiatry, 6,* 149–156.

Wallace, L. (2006). Discovering homosexuality: Cross-cultural comparison and the history of sexuality. In R. Aldrich (Ed.), *Gay life and culture: A world history* (pp. 249–269). New York: Universe Publishing.

Watanabe, T., & Iwata, J. (1989). *The love of the samurai: A thousand years of Japanese homosexuality*. Boston, MA: Alyson.

Weber. I. (1973). Tactile communication among free-ranging langurs. *American Journal of Physical Anthropology, 38,* 481–486.

Weis, J. (1974) *The Gemblakan: Kept boys among the Javanese of Ponorogo*. Paper presented at the American Anthropological Association Meeting, Mexico City.

Weisfeld, G. E. (1979). An ethological view of human adolescence. *Journal of Nervous and Mental Diseases, 167,* 38–55.

Weisfeld, G. E., & Billings, R. L. (1988). Observations on adolescence. In K. MacDonald (Ed.), *Sociobiological perspectives on human development* (pp. 207–233). New York: Springer-Verlag.

Werner, D. (2006). The evolution of male homosexuality and its implications for human psychological and cultural variations. In V. Sommer & P. L. Vasey (Eds.), *Homosexual behavior in animals: An evolutionary perspective* (pp. 316–346). Cambridge, England: Cambridge University Press.

West, D. J. (1998). Boys and sexual abuse: An English opinion. *Archives of Sexual Behavior, 27,* 539–559.

West, D., & Woodhouse, T. (1993). Sexual encounters between boys and adults. In C. Li, D. West, & T. Woodhouse (Eds.), *Children's sexual encounters with adults* (pp. 3–137). New York: Prometheus.

West's Encyclopedia of American Law (2008). Retrieved from: http://www.enotes.com/wests-law-encyclopedia/pederasty
Williams, C. A. (1999). *Roman homosexuality: Ideologies of masculinity in classical antiquity*. New York: Oxford University Press.
Williams, F. E. (1936). *Papuans of the Trans-Fly*. Oxford: Clarendon Press.
Williams, W. L. (1992). *The spirit and the flesh: Sexual diversity in American Indian culture*. Boston, MA: Beacon Press.
_____. (2011). Intergenerational relationships in Java and Thailand. Unpublished manuscript.
Wilson, D. S., & Wilson, E. O. (2007). Rethinking the theoretical foundation of sociobiology. *The Quarterly Review of Biology, 82*, 327–48.
Wilson, E. O. (1978). *On human nature*. Cambridge, MA: Harvard University Press.
Wilson, E.O., & Hölldobler, B. (2008). *The superorganism*. Presentation at the Free Library of Philadelphia, December 2.
Wilson, G. D., & Cox, D. N. (1983). *The child-lovers: A study of paedophiles in society*. London: Peter Owen.
Woods, S. C., & Dean, K. S. (1984). *Sexual abuse of males research project*. Child & Family Services of Knox County, Inc., Knoxville, TN.
Wrangham, R. W. (1987). The significance of African apes for reconstructing human social evolution. In W. G. Kinzey (Ed.), *The evolution of human behavior: Primate models* (pp. 51–70). Albany: State University of New York Press.
Wright, J. W., & Rowson, E. K. (Eds.) (1997). *Homoeroticism in classical Arabic literature*. New York: Columbia University Press.
Yamagiwa, J. (1987). Intra- and inter-group interactions of an all-malt group of Virunga mountain gorillas (Gorilla gorilla beringeni). *Primates, 28*, 1–30.
_____. (2006). Playful encounters: The development of homosexual behaviour in male mountain gorillas. In V. Sommer & P. L. Vasey (Eds.), *Homosexual behavior in animals: An evolutionary perspective* (pp. 273–293). Cambridge, England: Cambridge University Press.
Yamane, A. (2006). Frustrated felines: Male-male mounting in feral cats. In V. Sommer and P. L. Vasey (Eds.), *Homosexual behavior in animals: An evolutionary perspective* (pp. 172–188). Cambridge, England: Cambridge University Press.
Yeager, C. P. (1990). Notes on the sexual behavior of the Proboscis monkey. *American Journal of Primatology, 21*, 223–227.
Zeitzen, M. K. (2008). *Polygamy: A cross-cultural analysis*. New York: Berg.
Zernicke, K. (2005). The siren song of sex with boys. *New York Times*, December 11, wk 3.
Zuckerman. S. (1932). *The Social Life of Monkeys and Apes*. London: Kegan Paul, Trench, Trubner.

Chapter 2

MORE SPEECH OR LESS? CENSORING SOCIAL SCIENCE

Patrick O'Neill and Janice Best

Censorship is an attempt to control the meaning of events. In the long term (and sometimes in the short term) censorship fails because it draws attention to the very facts and opinions that it would suppress.

Here is a classical example showing how censorship defeats itself (Minois, 1995). In the eighteenth century, during the reign of Maria Theresa of Austria, booksellers had to display two lists of books: those for sale and those on the Index of books banned by the established church. There could be no overlap between the lists, of course, but the books on the Index could still be found here and there, if someone took the trouble to look for them.

Maria Theresa's officials became aware that many people were more interested in the list of books on the Index than they were in the list of books for sale. This led the empress to promulgate a law banning the Index itself. With the Index gone, she reasoned, her subjects would not even know that censorship of books was taking place, nor would they know which banned books were worth seeking out.

But the law that banned the Index reinforced public awareness of censorship and took their curiosity about the books on the banned Index to new heights. In order to be truly effective, the empress would have had to ban the act that banned the Index that banned the books—as well as to somehow eradicate all memory of the Index and of the act banning it.

Judith Butler (1997) makes the same point about censorship with a more recent example, the "don't ask, don't tell" policy with regard to homosexuals in the US military. "The regulation *redoubles* the term it seeks to constrain ... the effort to constrain the term culminates in its very proliferation ... the term not only appears in the regulations as that discourse to be regulated, but reappears in public debate over its fairness." (p. 131).

CENSORSHIP SUPPORTING THE POWERFUL

Censorship is traditionally seen as a tool to protect the prerogatives of the powerful. Richard Terdiman has termed the struggle for meaning between those in power and those in opposition as conflict between a dominant discourse and varieties of counter-discourse. In the dominant discourse, social regulation is seen as the natural unfolding of a proper course of events: the king rules by divine right, the person who gets the most votes becomes the leader of the nation, and so on.

The main characteristic of the dominant discourse is that it "goes without saying." Its presence is defined by the apparent social impossibility of its absence. It is like the lines of a script that we all know without knowing that we know them, or how we learned them.

This theory of social control is based on Pierre Bourdieu's (1980, 1982) notion of the *habitus,* which helps explain how people function in stable times. Bourdieu defines the habitus as the regularizing effect produced by the situation in which one finds oneself and that determines the set of "possibles"—what one can say, do, and think. The habitus ensures the continuity of "the way things are."

The dominant discourse seeks to appear monologic, or single voiced. But all forms of speech are cultural practices, reflecting the tensions and inequalities of social life. The fabric of that life includes many strands of discourse, representing the totality of what it is possible to say at any given time. But as Mikhail Bakhtin (1981) has noted, speech is inherently dialogic. Terdiman's counter-discourse is more "noisy" than the dominant discourse. More voices are heard, raising questions about the way things are. The king has impoverished the nation; he has to flee or die. The candidate who lost the election challenges the ballet count, and so on.

Censorship of ideas, however inefficient it has historically proven to be, may be used by the powerful to try to maintain the habitus and support the dominant discourse.

Censorship Protecting the Vulnerable

In our time, censorship has also been promoted on the grounds that it is needed to suppress ideas that would disparage and (thereby) harm vulnerable or marginalized groups. Such ideas, including conclusions based on research findings, are thought to be too outrageous to be entered into the democratic discourse suggested by the ideals of free speech.

Critical race theory, for example, argues that verbal attacks against historically oppressed groups amount to hateful acts that should be outlawed by legislatures and punished by the courts. On the other hand, verbal attacks by the minority against the majority should be permitted to redress the balance of social oppression (Olmstead, 1998). Laws protecting freedom of speech generally allow some exceptions, such as the famous prohibition of shouting "fire!" in a crowded theater. Jurisdictions differ on how narrowly these exceptions to free speech are drawn. Mari Matsuda talks about the deadly violence that accompanies the persistent verbal degradation of subordinated groups. She and her colleagues argue that "words wound," and, therefore, offensive speech should be subject to the same legal restrictions as physical assault (Matsuda, Lawrence, Delgado, & Crenshaw, 1993).

Catharine MacKinnon (1993) used similar reasoning to justify censorship of material offensive to women—particularly pornography. She argues that pornography helps constitute women as an inferior class and, thus, is more appropriately considered a class of sex discrimination rather than a class of protected speech. "Pornography makes the world a pornographic place through its making and use, establishing what women are said to exist as, are seen as, are treated as, constructing the social reality of what a woman is and can be in terms of what is done to her, and what a man is in terms of doing it." (p. 25)

Others warn, however, that involving the state in censorship on behalf of less-powerful groups can backfire. Judith Butler (1997) has pointed out that MacKinnon's arguments can be, and have been, used by conservative organizations and legislators such as Jesse Helms to deny funding to the arts—specifically the National Endowment for the Arts in the United States. Having broadened the definition of obscenity, for example, conservatives can argue that "various lesbian and gay photographers produce work that is obscene and lacking in literary value" (p. 63).

The attempt to protect marginalized groups from offensive comments and conclusions is exemplified by a 1993 policy statement by the Ontario Ministry of Education and Training entitled "Framework Regarding Harassment and Discrimination in Ontario Universities and Colleges" (Horn, 1999). Harassment was defined as anything offensive, hostile, or inappropriate concerning gender, race, ethnicity, religion, sexual preference, or disability. Exclusionary rules were to apply to speech, ranging from jokes and taunts to books in libraries and art exhibitions.

Censoring Science

The arts play a role in constituting reality; so does science. And just as the arts can be threatened by censorship, so can science. A pornographic film may depict women in sexually subservient roles, contributing to their oppression. Similarly, a scientific study in which the author, concluding that working women damage their children, may undercut arguments for equal employment opportunities. Funding for the arts may come under attack on the basis of obscenity; funding for day care may also be attacked on the grounds that mothers should stay home and look after their children.

In this paper we will present and discuss three cases of empirical research that led to cries for censorship on the grounds that marginal groups might be offended or injured by the authors' conclusions.

The traditional response to disputed findings in the research community has been to inspect studies carefully for procedural flaws, and for conclusions that go beyond the data. But sometimes when research results seem to lead to socially unacceptable conclusions, some opponents go beyond methodological critique to demand that the studies not be done or, being done, that the conclusions not be published.

Sequelae of Child Sexual Abuse

The first case is a meta-analysis that purported to show that consensual sex between adults and minors did not necessarily (or always) lead to harmful consequences for the minors.

In 1998, Rind, Tromovitch, and Bauserman published an article in the prestigious *Psychological Bulletin* entitled "A meta-analytic examination of assumed properties of child sexual abuse using college samples." The authors analyzed studies with a combined sample size of 50,000.

They reported that the relationship between being a victim of child abuse and later psychopathology was weak or negligible. The correlations were particularly low when the sexual relationship was between males and was deemed "consensual" by the minors. The authors even reported that some children experienced positive results in "willing" sexual encounters with adults (Rind, Tromovitch, & Bauserman, 1998).

The method came under attack. Critics argued that college samples probably exclude those with severe pathology, biasing the outcome toward finding no effect of early trauma (Dallum, Gleaves, Cepeda-Benito, Silberg, Kraemer, & Spiegel, 2001). The authors replied that their college-student samples were more representative of the general population than the clinical and forensic samples used in research that had shown pathological outcomes (Rind et al., 2001).

Some critics said that because a child cannot legally consent to sexual activity with an adult, the "consent" variable was scientifically meaningless and ethically dubious. The authors replied that the legal status of "consent" and the perception by minors that they were willing participants are two different issues. They noted that whether an event causes psychological damage is a separate question from whether it is "wrong" (Rind et al., 2001). In his chapter in this issue, Rind points out that the original meta-analysis was strictly descriptive and explanatory, yet was vehemently attacked by social conservatives, victimologists, and politicians as being advocatory.

The article was subjected to spin from opposing camps. It was hailed by advocates of "man-boy love," condemned by a group advocating aggressive corrective treatment for homosexuality, and attacked most famously by Dr. Laura Schlessinger, a physiologist with a popular radio talk show. Dr. Laura said, "the point of the article is to allow men to rape male children" (quoted in Lilienfeld, 2002). Her vigorous campaign against the American Psychological Association (APA) as publisher of *Psychological Bulletin* reached an estimated 18 million listeners—and the ears of the US Congress. A precedent-setting resolution condemning the article, the journal, and the APA was introduced in the House of Representatives—the only known instance in which a specific scientific article was singled out for censure in a congressional resolution, or a scientific organization chastised for publishing such an article.

Rep. Matt Salmon (Arizona), introducing House Concurrent Resolution 107, condemned the Rind et al. article as "the emancipation proclamation of pedophiles." According to Resolution 107, "The *Psychological Bulletin* has recently published a severely flawed study ... Congress condemns and denounces all suggestions in the article that indicate that sexual relationships between adults and 'willing' children are less harmful than believed, and condemns any suggestion that sexual relations between children and adults ... are anything but harmful" (Lilienfeld, 2002, p. 181).

During congressional consideration, APA desperately passed internal resolutions condemning child sexual abuse and appealed to sister organizations for help. The organization asked the National Academy of Sciences and the American Association for the Advancement of Science (AAAS) to indicate publicly that APA journals are respected in the scientific community, that their peer review is rigorous, and that the scientific process is self-correcting. Both organizations refused to get involved.

In fact, some scientific organizations took pains to dissociate themselves from APA. The American Psychiatric Association pointed out that they were a different group from the psychologists (both groups are called "APA"). They indicated that one difference between the organizations was that the *psychiatrists* were opposed to pedophilia. This unhelpful clarification was sent, with the psychiatrists' apparent approval, to all members of the House of Representatives (Garrison & Kobor, 2002).

When APA tried to mollify Congress, it created an uproar among its own members. Raymond Fowler, chief executive officer of APA sent a letter to influential congressman Rep. Tom Delay. Fowler said that the Rind et al. piece "included opinions of the authors that are inconsistent with APA's stated and deeply held positions ... sexual activity between children and adults should never be considered or labelled harmless" (Fowler, 1999, p. 1). The letter said that the Rind et al. article should have been evaluated for its potential for misinforming the public policy process. "This is something we failed to do, but will do in the future" (p. 1). It promised that APA would strengthen procedures to address the social policy implications of journal articles. The editor and action editor, who handled the Rind et al. article for *Psychological Bulletin,* refer to this as the "capitulation letter" (Sher & Eisenberg, 2002, p. 209). Angry APA members protested that APA was proposing to censure articles and to interfere with the peer review process.

As Congress prepared to vote on Resolution 107, APA went back to AAAS—one of the influential scientific organizations that had earlier spurned the plea for support. Now, APA asked AAAS to review and evaluate the scientific quality of the article. Again, many APA members were outraged, seeing the request as undermining APA's own journal review process. AAAS declined, commenting that there was "no reason to second guess the process of peer review used by the APA journal in its decision to publish" (quoted in Sher & Eisenberg, 2002, p. 207). The congressional resolution passed 355 to 0 in the House and by a voice vote in the Senate. No member of Congress voted against the resolution.

Even after the public controversy had subsided, the waters continued to roil within the psychological community. Scott Lilienfeld of Emory University submitted an article on the controversy to the *American Psychologist,* the flagship journal of the American Psychological Association. His piece was called: "The bonfires of the vilifiers: Dr. Laura, the U.S. Congress, the American Psychological Association, and the Rind et al. (1998) Sexual Abuse Meta-Analysis."

Professor Lilienfeld analyzed the original article, methodological criticisms of it, the public furor, and what he considered to be APA's backing away from defending its editorial process, including its decision to ask AAAS for a belated external review. Lilienfeld's article was evaluated by four reviewers. Following some requested revisions, in February 2001 the action editor accepted the article for publication. The overall editor, Richard McCarty, was copied on the e-mail and congratulated Professor Lilienfeld. But he then overruled the decision to accept. Without informing either the author or the action editor, he sent the article for "rereview" by five more reviewers. He has said that he knew in advance that at least three of the five would "have concerns with the manuscript" (McCarty, 2002, p. 199).

On the basis of all nine reviews, he informed the author that the original acceptance had been overturned, the article had been rereviewed, and he asked for "changes of a substantive nature." According to Professor Lilienfeld (2002), the changes would have deleted 60 percent of the article, including all material dealing with the Rind et al. controversy, all material critical of the APA and the actions of the APA during the incident, and all material critical of the actions of members of Congress. The author considered this tantamount to a rejection of his previously accepted article.

The wounded author took his story to the Internet. Many prominent psychologists threatened to resign in protest against the perceived "politicizing" of the editorial process. What now became known as the "Lilienfeld controversy" threatened to do as much damage within APA as the Rind et al. controversy had done to the organization from the outside. Summing up the impact of both controversies, Kenneth J. Sher and Nancy Eisenberg, *Psychological Bulletin* editors who handled the original article, called the whole matter "the greatest public relations disaster and threat to its well-being that the APA has ever faced" (Sher & Eisenberg, 2002, p. 209).

Nor did the matter end there. In the current issue, Rind describes the difficulties that have impeded further discussion of the matter, up to the present moment.

Different Country, Different Outcome

Not long after the tumultuous controversy surrounding Rind et al., an article was published in Canada that had the potential to raise the same issues. The piece was entitled "Recension des écrits sur l'impact des contacts sexuels précoces sur les hommes" (Review of studies on the impact of precocious sexual contact among males), by Forouzan and Van Gijseghem (2004). There were many parallels with the Rind et al. controversy. Again, the journal was a respected publication of the national association, in this case *Canadian Psychology,* flagship journal of the Canadian Psychological Association (CPA). The journal received substantial financial support from the Canadian government through one of its funding agencies, making it vulnerable to censure. Again, the work passed rigorous peer review before publication.

The paper by Forouzan and Van Gijseghem, like that of Rind et al., found that in certain cases, early sexual contact between adults and minors did not have later noxious effects. The authors suggested that we need more research to discover which aspects of the sexual relationship predict pathology, the form of that pathology among some, and the reason for the lack of symptoms among others. They presented models that could explain the various results in the literature and suggested variables that might be explored in further work. These included the way the relationship is perceived by the minor, and the possibility that our methods of determining clinical symptoms are not sufficiently subtle to pick up some symptoms that actually do exist.

Editor Thomas Hadjistavropoulos and Associate Editor Simon Grondin were well aware of the problems posed by the Rind et al. article in the United States and decided to provide some context for readers. They asked the first author of this paper, a past president of CPA and former editor of the journal, to write a short commentary to be published with the paper.

The commentary mentioned the Rind et al. case and noted that some scientific articles report facts or draw conclusions that upset many people. Nevertheless, it argued, such papers may contribute to our reflections on subjects of social importance. It also noted that the Rind et al. paper had been misquoted and, hence, flayed, for saying things it had not said. Echoing a comment Rind et al. (2001) made in response to critics, the commentary pointed out that whatever the scientific evidence, there exist legal and moral arguments against pedophilia. The editor published the piece and the commentary (O'Neill, 2004b) and waited for the reaction. There was none.

Perhaps the commentary framed the article so well that readers understood the peer review system, editorial responsibility, and so forth. On the other hand, one difference between the US and Canadian reactions might be the language of publication—the Canadian article was written in French, and so was the commentary. But an earlier comment on the

Rind et al. matter (O'Neill, 2002) was distributed Canada-wide in English with no adverse reaction. In addition, Canada is essentially bilingual at the professional and scientific levels, and CPA has many members who are francophone or who can and do read the literature of their discipline in French. *Canadian Psychology* publishes articles in both languages. It may be that there are simply national differences, with the United States being (at least these days) more subject to distorting, censuring outrage from the moral and political right.

National differences probably do not account for the lack of controversy, because, as we will show, there are several Canadian examples that show an urge to suppress. Instead, it is likely that those who would object do not generally read scientific publications such *Psychological Bulletin* or *Canadian Psychology* but stumble across controversial material in such journals by accident, if at all.

Concomitants of Race

Our second example concerns studies that draw conclusions about race differences. In 1989, J. Philippe Rushton, a psychology professor at the University of Western Ontario, gave a speech to the annual meeting of the American Association for the Advancement of Science (AAAS), entitled "Evolutionary Biology and Heritable Traits." He referred to three broad groupings of human population (in his terms, Mongoloids, Caucasoids, Negroids) as having emerged at different times from the ancestral hominid line. Natural selection, he suggested, had favored the more recently evolved Mongoloids, disadvantaged the Negroids, who were most genetically distant, with Caucasoids falling between the other two.

Professor Rushton presented a variety of findings about racial differences that were unfavorable to blacks with regard to intelligence, morality, aggression, and so forth. After his controversial speech to the AAAS, he continued to present such information in various journals (e.g., 1991), and he drew fire from those who criticized both his methods and his conclusions.

Some thought his use of the concept of race was outmoded. Some questioned his application of evolutionary theory to human racial groups (e.g., Anderson, 1991). And some identified flaws in sources he used in his meta-analyses (e.g., Weizmann, Weiner, Wiesenthal, and Ziegler, 1990, 1991). Professor Rushton admitted that the original studies contained "numerous sources of error," but he said that his analysis relied on the "principle of aggregation" (1991, p. 31) according to which the sum of a set of multiple measurements is a more stable and unbiased estimator than any single measurement from the set. If you have enough studies from enough sources, the flaws in particular studies cancel out.

Such exchanges between Professor Rushton and his critics were typical of the sort of debate that is supposed to ensure that science is self-correcting. But some commentators took the argument to a different level: they called for censorship and suppression—demanding that his papers not be published, that he be denied research funding from public sources, and even that he no longer be permitted to teach.

Biologist David Suzuki said, "By defending Dr. Rushton's right to pronounce and spread his ideas, the academic community is besmirched by shoddy science and stands condemned for a dereliction of its social responsibility." (1989, p. D4).

The University of Western Ontario kept Professor Rushton physically out of theclassroom for a time, showing his lectures to students on videotape. Some thought this did not go far enough. Ontario's premier of the day, David Peterson, joined the chorus of those wanting Western to fire the professor (Horn, 1999).

Nineteen individuals, mainly students, filed a complaint with the Ontario Human Rights Commission. They alleged that Professor Rushton had "poisoned the academic learning environment" at Western. They demanded that he be fired; that any teaching of theories about racial hierarchies be prohibited; that the university be required to examine its entire curriculum to eliminate so-called academic racism, to ensure that the curriculum reflected the province's ethnic diversity, and that "racist research" be prohibited at the University.

The Academic Freedom and Tenure Committee of the Canadian Association of University Teachers (CAUT) voted to seek intervener status if and when the human rights case was heard. The committee was concerned about the breadth of the complaint and the chill that the case might have on free inquiry and scholarship on controversial topics.

The opportunity to intervene never came. The Human Rights Commission was finally ready to proceed in late 1995, more than four years after the complaint had been filed. It attempted to notify the parties, but letters addressed to eleven of the nineteen complainants, all students, were returned "address unknown." The Human Rights Commission considered the case abandoned.

Cheaters' Mothers

In 1990, chemistry professor Gordon Freeman, from the University of Alberta, published a paper in the *Canadian Journal of Physics* entitled "Kinetics of nonhomogeneous processes in human society: Unethical behaviour and social chaos" (Freeman, 1990). He had become concerned about the apparent increase in cheating in his large, first-year courses. He talked to his students in groups as large as 250, and on the basis of these discussions he concluded:

- The tendency to cheat is correlated strongly with the absence of a full-time mother in the home when the child was growing up.
- Mothers entering the workforce show a lack of maternal loyalty to their children, who are "treated as objects both by parents and by caregivers."

- Children of working mothers are at increased risk "for drug abuse, compulsive eating, not telling the truth, and other socially destabilizing behaviour" (pp. 796–797).

As in the previous two cases, there was lively debate with regard to method and conclusions. Sociologist Marlene Mackie said that Professor Freeman's paper ignored decades of social science research, substituted informal chats for rigorous methods, and violated "the scientific canons of empiricism, scepticism, objectivity, and logical reasoning" (quoted in Montagnes, 1993, p. 197).

In his original article, the chemistry professor seemed to present himself as a champion of qualitative methods: "Information gained by surveys and experiments with controls, is likely to be distorted by the artificiality of the gathering situation" (Freeman, 1990, p. 796). To have conclusions such as Professor Freeman's cloaked in the mantle of qualitative research was almost more than some qualitative researchers could bear. Cannie Stark, speaking for the Canadian Psychological Association, said, "Qualitative research, responsibly conducted, is scientific and can be a very rewarding source of rich, meaningful data on important issues." But, she said, Professor Freeman had confounded hypothesis-generation with hypothesis-testing and had attributed causation to potentially spurious correlations. "As they stand, no credence should be given to Freeman's conclusions" (quoted in Montagnes, 1993, p. 197).

Again, over and above this sort of debate, there were complaints about the fact that the original article was published in the first place. It was, after all, an article by a chemist, published in a journal of physics, under the heading "sociology," treating a topic that was arguably psychological. The journal editor was quoted in *Science* as blaming "political correctness" and "vulgar politics of protest" for the strong reaction against publication of the article (Montagnes, 1993, p. 200). The journal published an apology regretting "that this article was published" (Dancik, 1991, p. 1403).

But was it enough to regret publication, or could it be "unpublished"? Some critics wanted all copies recalled and reissued absent of any trace of the physics journal's brief foray into "sociology." One such group was the Women in Physics Committee of the Canadian Association of Physicists, who called on the NRC to require the journal to withdraw the offending issue "in order to have it replaced with a corrected copy" (quoted in Sheinin, 1993, p. 245). The notion of expunging the written record was rejected by the editor in chief, who said, "in addition to being impractical, [this] would be sweeping the article under the carpet and would be an attempt to rewrite history" (Dancik, 1993, p. 271).

In the face of growing pressure to do something, the NRC offered to print a special supplement of the journal with commentaries on the controversy from social scientists. But then, with some invited contributions already in hand, the NRC changed its mind. The editor in chief said that if the physics journal was not an appropriate place to publish the original article, then it was also not the appropriate place to debate it (Dancik, quoted in Dahlin, 1993, p. 9). Stephen Prudhomme, director of research journals at NRC, said the council wanted to give the Freeman article as little media exposure as possible (quoted in Wolfe, 1991, D1). Clive Willis, NRC's vice president (science) said that publication of the supplement would "give Freeman a day in court, and that is the last thing we want" (quoted in Dahlin, 1993, p. 9).

The decision not to publish the critiques drew responses ranging from surprise to outrage. In response, the NRC changed its mind yet again and rescheduled publication of the supplement. Between these two decisions, the embattled NRC held a two-day conference on "The Ethics of Scholarly Publishing." At that meeting, the agency was roundly criticized for its handling of the Freeman affair and for the loose policies that governed the journals it published.

The week after the symposium, the NRC approved a new policy governing authors, editors, and referees. Among other things, the policy directed that, "It is the responsibility of authors to ensure that the language used is inclusive and that gender and racial stereotyping are avoided" (National Research Council of Canada, 1993, p. 275).

As in the Rushton case, students became involved. *The Gateway*, student newspaper at the University of Alberta, reported that students were taking up a petition demanding that Professor Freeman either apologize or resign his academic post (Sheinin, 1993).

Methods and Motives

In the three cases discussed here, controversial material was presented in the form of research findings. Highly respected organizations were involved as publishers or conference sponsors: The National Research Council of Canada, The American Psychological Association, and the American Association for the Advancement of Science. In each case there was debate about method and conclusions of the sort one might expect in the self-correcting nature of scientific inquiry.

Less usual was the focus of some critics on the authors' motivation. In all three cases, the authors were alleged to have biases that compromised their objectivity. Professor Rushton received substantial funding from the Pioneer Fund, an American group dedicated to advancing eugenics. Professor Freeman was said to be driven by an antifeminist agenda. Among the social evils he thought resulted from women at work, he included feminism, which he associated with socialism. Although Professor Freeman said he was "non-judgemental" (1990, p. 795), this posture was somewhat undercut by his circulation, at the height of the controversy, of an unpublished paper arguing against more women in science (Montagnes, 1993.).

Rind et al. were accused of displaying their true colors when they suggested that the term *child sexual abuse* might better be replaced by *adult-child sex*. One of the authors was also attacked for having published in a Dutch journal that had featured articles tolerant of pedophilia (Garrison & Kobor, 2002).

In all three cases, a substantial group of critics argued that the views expressed by the authors were not only in error, but should never have been expressed at all. And, if the authors chose to express them, they should not have been published.

Another issue common to these cases was the fact that the controversial ideas were presented as science—as conclusions based on evidence. Critics argued that presenting one side of the issue as empirical fact gives it a special status in debate, rendering it more credible (e.g., Sheinin, 1993; Zimmerman, cited in Montagnes, 1993). A critic of Professor Freeman's article, Professor Cannie Stark, said, "If Freeman had actually conducted social research in a scientific manner ... if he had examined alternative explanations and weighed them in a dispassionate, scholarly fashion, if he had done all this and yet had been driven, by the force of the carefully gathered data, to similar conclusions, then we ... should be compelled to give his conclusions serious attention" (cited in Montagnes, 1993, p. 197). Science is a powerful trump card.

But if tagging an opinion as "science" gives it a special cachet, it also makes it vulnerable to attack on the grounds that it isn't *real* science. Professor Rushton's work was called "shoddy science"; the Rind et al. paper was called "junk science." Dr. Laura challenged the APA, with regard to the sexual abuse paper, "If it's science, why don't they endorse it? If it isn't science, why do they publish it?" (quoted in Lilienfeld, 2002, p. 181).

Reflecting on events in the Rind et al. case, some social scientists have come up with suggestions for avoiding or mitigating such crises in the future. Scientific organizations, some say, ought to seize every opportunity to educate policymakers, the news media, and the public about research, peer review, and controversies in science.

Deborah Phillips (2002), who worked at the National Academy of Sciences on the implications of social science research for public policy, recommends that authors, editors, and reviewers need to be more aware of, and comment on, the social significance of their findings. "Reviewers, many of whom may not be in a particularly good position to evaluate statements about policy or other broad implications of the results ... need explicit guidance about how to assess these commentaries during the editorial review process" (p. 220).

Censorship vs "More Speech"

Not only does censorship not work, as we said at the outset in our example of the empress and the Index, it is also inimical to debate in a free and democratic society—a principle that neither Maria Theresa nor the church of her day had to worry about.

Current thinking about how to deal with extremely unpopular ideas has focused on the notion of "more speech" rather than censorship. This is especially true in the debate over whether ideas that offend minority groups (as opposed to government) ought to be restricted on grounds of nondiscrimination.

Coleman and Alger (1996) coined the term *more speech* to argue against censoring opinions that offend groups whose rights have been historically challenged or suppressed. The authors promoted the ideal of a society that values *both* free expression and nondiscrimination. Societies, institutions, and individuals can exercise their own free speech rights to disagree with or denounce attitudes or comments perceived to be objectionable. Rather than suppress unpopular opinions, the offended are invited to reply.

We need a climate of discourse that includes all, including the previously marginalized. Feelings will sometimes be hurt, and some opinions will seem outrageous. "If one does not protect the right to be sometimes seen as rude or offensive, no one's academic freedom is safe." (Wilson, 1996, p. 137).

Coleman and Alger (1996), with their concept of *more speech,* said that increasing dialogue rather than employing censorship serves an educational purpose by exposing prejudice and by prompting critical examination of stereotypes. Institutions such as universities, scientific organizations and the like need to ensure that competing voices are heard within the institution's programs, activities, and publications. Former APA president (and former *Psychological Bulletin* editor) Robert J. Sternberg (2002) listed various ways in which editors can balance articles with more speech:

> A controversial article can be published along with one or more companion pieces that represent different perspectives or points of view that put the original piece in one or more alternative contexts. Editors can at least show that they recognize the sensitivity of the particular issue raised, while in no way banning or otherwise interfering with the publication of the original piece.
>
> An editor can choose to write an editorial that provides a larger context for the article. In this way, the editor sets the stage and recognizes the kinds of issues that may arise from the article.
>
> An editor can work with authors of an article to word things very carefully and, in general, to do everything possible to head off possible misinterpretation of what is being said. The goal here is not to change the message but rather to make clear exactly what that message is in the light of misunderstandings that are likely to arise. (p. 195-196)

Professor Sternberg's first two points are consistent with the more-speech notion. The third is aimed at clarifying the message. Professor Rushton, for example, has said that there is more differentiation within human groups than between them and that there is "a great deal of intraracial variability within each broad grouping" (1991, p. 29); in the Rind case, the authors noted that whatever their findings about the pathology resulting from adult-child sex, there are still legal and social reasons to consider such relationships to be wrong. In both cases, the authors did not highlight these qualifications, or only did so when the controversies were already in full bloom (e.g. Rushton, 1991; Rind et al., 2001).

The American Psychological Association eventually found its way out of the morass of the Rind et al. and Lilienfeld controversies by taking a more-speech approach. The flagship journal *American Psychologist*, which earlier had seemed to be opting for suppression with regard to the Lilienfeld article, produced a special issue in March 2002, with multiple perspectives from various sides of the issue. To the extent that this refurbished APA's reputation, the strategy is a testament to the value of the more-speech approach and a lesson in the failure of censorship.

Coleman and Alger (1996) say that speech codes and other restrictions on expression serve only to repress manifestations of ignorance. When offensive opinions are hidden from view, the chance to correct them by astute counterargument is lost. Censorship and suppression give us "less speech." Thus, in the Freeman case, the National Research Council wanted to limit the debate so that Professor Freeman "would not have his day in Court." In the Rind et al. case, the American Psychological Association seemed ready to suppress the Lilienfeld article that would have exposed and commented upon many aspects of the controversy.

Censorship and Its Discontents

We have argued that not only does censorship limit democratic debate, it is also self-defeating. As Georges Minois (1995) says, the permanent paradox of censorship is that it always acts as the strongest publicity agent for banned works. People become curious when they are told that something is bad for them to see, to hear, or to read.

When censorship leaves a blank, or a silence, people learn to "read" the silence. The censor actually creates a more sophisticated interpretative community, which gives meaning back to the words that have been silenced and becomes more adept at searching for unfavorable allusions. On the other hand, just because people learn to read between the lines does not mean they will read the right message. Yet another paradox of censorship is that people's curiosity can lead them to unfounded or even false assumptions.

If we condone censorship, we can never be sure whether the grounds of suppression are what they are purported to be. In social science, can we be sure that criticism of method is not actually masking discontent with the message itself? Often, censorship can be deconstructed so that explicit reasons are found to hide other reasons that are awkward to state (Best, 2001).

The argument for more speech urges us to develop and promulgate as many ideas and opinions as possible about a range of topics and positions, some of which fly in the face of our deeply held beliefs, or even of what we consider to be common sense. (Dr. Laura, in the Rind et al. controversy, said that any scientific findings that conflict with common sense should be regarded as erroneous [quoted in Lilienfeld, 2002]).

At the outset, we noted that censorship has traditionally been thought of as a tool of power, although more recently it has been employed or advocated as a protection for the rights of traditionally less powerful groups. Nevertheless, censorship typically requires action from the powerful, even when it is ostensibly enacted on behalf of disadvantaged groups. MacKinnon's crusade against pornography depended on creation, interpretation, and application of laws by the state. Similarly, to censor social science requires action from the powerful. In the Rind et al. case, Congress was rallied against the publisher of a scientific journal. In the Rushton case, appeals were made to the Human Rights Commission and to the university administration to take action. In the Freeman case, post hoc censorship would have required that a government-funded journal reprint an issue leaving out the offending article.

In sum, we have aligned ourselves with the notion that democratic debate, including debate in the scientific community, must include counterargument rather than censorship. Applying the notion of "more speech" to scientific inquiry, Rauch (1999) noted, "A lot of science is flawed, and most scientists have biases. The answer is for other scientists with other biases to do more science." (p. 2270). Science, like democracy, proceeds only on the basis of free inquiry and open debate.

References

Anderson, J. L. (1991). Rushton's racial comparisons: An ecological critique of theory and method. *Canadian Psychology, 32,* 51–60.

Bakhtin, M. M. (1981). *The dialogic imagination: Four essays.* Austin: University of Texas Press.

Best, J. (2001). *La subversion silencieuse: Censure, autocensure et lutte pour la liberté d'expression.* Montreal: Les Éditions Balzac.

Bourdieu, P. (1980). *Le sens pratique.* Paris: Éditions de Minuit.

———. (1982). Ce que parler veut dire: L'économie des échanges linguistiques. Paris: Fayard.

Butler, J. (1997). *Excitable speech: A politics of the performative.* New York: Routledge.

Coleman, A. L., & Alger, J. R. (1996). Beyond speech codes: Harmonizing rights of free speech and freedom from discrimination on university campuses. *Journal of College and University Law, 23,* 91–132.

Dahlin, K. (1993). An article of little faith, a controversy of grand proportions. *University of Toronto Bulletin,* Monday, Feb. 8, 8–9.

Dallum, S. J., Gleaves, D. H., Cepeda-Benito, A., Silberg, J. L., Kraemer, H., & Spiegel, D. (2001). The effects of child sexual abuse: Comment on Rind, Tromovitch, and Bauserman (1998), *Psychological Bulletin, 127,* 715–733.

Dancik, B. P. (1991). Note to readers. *Canadian Journal of Physics, 69,* 1403.

———. (1993). Learning from error. *Scholarly publishing, 24,* 269–273.

Forouzan E., & Van Gijseghem, H. (2004). Recension des écrits sur l'impact des contacts sexuels précoces sur les hommes. *Canadian Psychology 45,* 59–80.

Fowler, R. D. (1999). *APA letter to the honorable Rep. DeLay (R-Tx).* Cited in Lilienfeld, 2002.

Freeman, G. (1990). Kinetics of nonhomogeneous processes in human society: Unethical behaviour and social chaos. *Canadian Journal of Physics, 68,* 794–798.

Garrison, E. G., & Kobor, P. C. (2002). Weathering a political storm: A contextual perspective on a psychological research controversy. *American Psychologist, 57,* 165–175.Horn, M. (1999). *Academic freedom in Canada: A history.* Toronto: University of Toronto Press.

Lilienfeld, S. (2002). When worlds collide: Social science, politics, and the Rind et al. (1998) child sexual abuse meta-analysis. *American Psychologist, 57,* 176–188.

MacKinnon, C. (1993) *Only words.* Boston, MA: Harvard University Press.

Matsuda, M. J., Lawrence, C. R. III, Delgado, R., & Crenshaw, K. W. (1993). *Words that wound: Critical race theory, assaultive speech, and the First Amendment.* Boulder, CO: Westview Press.

McCarty, R. (2002). Science, politics, and peer review: An editor's dilemma. *American Psychologist, 57,* 198–201.

Minois, G. (1995). *Censure et culture sous l'Ancien Régime.* Paris: Fayard.

Montagnes, I. (1993). Introduction to the issue: The Freeman affair. *Scholarly publishing, 24,* 193–203.

National Research Council of Canada. (1993). A new publications policy for the NRC. *Scholarly publishing, 24,* 274–280

Olmsted, A. P. (1998). Words are acts: critical race theory as a rhetorical construct. *The Howard Journal of Communications, 9,* 323–331.

O'Neill, P. (2002). The perils of publishing. *Psynopsis, 24,* 4.

_____. (2004a). Publishing the unpalatable. In W. Bruneau & James L. Turk (Eds.), *Disciplining dissent: The curbing of free expression in academia and the media* (Chapter 1, pp. 23–37).

_____. (2004b). Étudier l'impact des contacts sexuels précoces: Commentaire sur l'article de Forouzan et Van Gijseghem. *Canadian Psychology, 45,* 93–94.

Phillips, D. (2002). Collisions, logrolls, and psychological science. *American Psychologist, 57,* 219–221.

Rauch, J. (1999). Washington's other sex scandal. *National Journal, 31,* 2269–2270.

Rind, B., Tromovitch, P., & Bauserman, R. (1998). A meta-analytic examination of assumed properties of child sexual abuse using college samples. *Psychological Bulletin, 124,* 22–53.

_____. (2001). The validity and appropriateness of methods, analyses, and conclusions of Rind et al. (1998): A rebuttal of victimological critique from Ondersma et al. (2001) and Dallam et al. (2001). *Psychological Bulletin, 127,* 734–758.

Rushton, J. P. (1989). *Evolutionary biology and heritable traits.* Presented at the Annual Meeting of the American Association for the Advancement of Science, San Francisco, CA. January 19.

_____. (1991). Do r-K strategies underlie human race differences? *Canadian Psychology, 32,* 29–42.

Sher, K. J., & Eisenberg, N. (2002). Publication of Rind et al. (1998): The editors' perspective. *American Psychologist, 57,* 206–210.

Sheinin, R. (1993). Academic freedom and integrity and ethics in publishing. *Scholarly publishing, 24,* 232–247.

Sternberg, R. J. (2002). Everything you need to know to understand the current controversies you learned from psychological research: A comment on the Rind and Lilienfeld controversies. *American Psychologist, 57,* 193–197.

Suzuki, D. (1989). Defence of Rushton "right" is propping up faulty work. *The Globe and Mail,* February 11, page D4.

Terdiman, R. (1985). *Discourse/counter-discourse. The theory and practice of symbolic resistance in nineteenth-century France.* Ithaca, NY: Cornell University Press.

Weizmann, F., Wiener, N. I., Wiesenthal, D. L., & Zigler, M. (1990). Differential K theory and racial hierarchies. *Canadian Psychology, 32,* 1–13.

_____. (1991). Eggs, eggplants and eggheads: A rejoinder to Rushton. *Canadian Psychology, 32,* 43–50.

Wilson, F. (1996). In defence of speech codes. *Interchange, 27,* 125–159.

Wolfe, M. (1991). Important issues unresolved in "Freeman controversy" argues Morris Wolfe. *The Globe and Mail,* September 3, page D1.

Chapter 3

INTERGENERATIONAL SEXUALITIES: A CASE STUDY ON THE COLONIZATION OF LATE MODERN SEXUAL SUBJECTS AND RESEARCHER AGENDAS

RICHARD YUILL

INTRODUCTION

This chapter will argue that the censorship of Bruce Rind's article by Haworth Press (discussed in this volume's introduction and in Rind's own chapter) is far from an isolated example, but is in fact merely one in a series of highly organized attempts to colonize both critical research on child sexual abuse (CSA) and subjective accounts of intergenerational sexualities. In part one it will outline Foucauldian conceptual tools and the potentially rich insights these can provide for understanding child and intergenerational sexual subjectivities. The second part will critically analyze the male survivor literature and contested narratives from my own research on *Male Age-Discrepant Intergenerational Sexualities and Relationships* (Yuill, 2004) to highlight the multiple ways in which victimological discursive formulations have acquired for themselves a dominant and uncontested authorial status. The third part will outline how the very privileging of such discourses has provided the basis for subsequent attacks on critical researchers by Christian fundamentalists, conservatives, CSA professionals, mainstream feminists, and the media. The final part will argue that underpinning many of the recent attempts to colonize both sexual subjects and research agendas on intergenerational sexualities is a system of entrenched power relations, based on a monolithic epistemology underpinned by childhood sexual innocence and powerlessness. However, I will also point to the fragility of this very hegemony, arguing that it will increasingly fracture in the face of future encroaching challenges.

PART ONE: THEORIZING THE EFFECTS OF POWER ON THE SEXUAL SUBJECT

Knowing, Gazing, Colonizing, and Truth Telling

For Foucault (1978), power is constituted in two stages: "in the one who spoke it and in the one who assimilated and recorded it" (p. 66). He identifies four aspects in what he terms an *"analytics of power"*: the localization of power relations through the expansion and encroachment of scientific investigation, increasing specialization in the application of power and appropriated knowledge, strategic alignments within the conjunction of power-knowledge, and resistance to imposed schemas (pp. 98–102). This process constitutes an indissoluble link between power and knowledge, in which power is produced within a "field of interaction" with knowledge, forming an "indissoluble relationship to forms of knowledge" (Nilson, 1998, p. 65).

Foucault identifies multiple "points of implantation ... including institutional devices and discursive strategies," through which modern networks of power have sought to expand their terrain on the body (Foucault, 1978, p. 28). This includes a desire for accumulating knowledge, which is further consolidated and systemized through a process of "epistemologization," which Hakosalo (1991, p. 25) defines as the "rapid institutional centralisation and consolidation of a given discourse, emergence of binding norms and models of how knowledge is to be constructed and checked within the discourse, and a coming into existence of shared conceptions concerning the task of the science in question, its social function, the nature of truth, and the legitimate sources of knowledge."

Foucault sees the scientific professional gaze as a key strategy, through which localized forms of power position themselves and the objects of their concern. It is through such a process that such networks of power achieve their aim of domination, relationally, via their claim to know the human subject's body through medical-psychiatric knowledge.[1] This process effectively constitutes (and reproduces) itself as a technique in anchoring and reinforcing the nexus of power-knowledge. Due to the fact that sexuality acts as a significantly dense transfer point because of its strategic importance as a foundation for knowledge on bodily functions, Foucault (1978) claims that it will inevitably constitute a prime target for the application of a multitude of "anxious gazes" that are exerted on sex (p. 97). He singles out psychoanalysis as a prime example of this, in which confessions about sex can be transmitted and reformulated (p. 112). Foucault likens such practices to the power the confessor had over the confessant in religious approaches to sin, but in modernity he views the attempt by regimes of power-knowledge to gather sexual information on the subject as an instrumental device to achieve dominant truth status.

Foucault (1978) applies the notion of colonization to refer to the way technologies of power effectively "invade" the body and subsequently reclassify individual and collective experiences. A specific corollary of this process, involves the way "sexual irregularity is annexed, and the normalisation of sexual development defined" (p. 36). For Foucault, this is channeled in a systematic way through the production of a binary system, in which normalizing categories and boundaries are created and reinforced (p. 83).

Consequently, "we are dealing less with a discourse on sex than a multiplicity of discourses" (Foucault, 1978, p. 33). Foucault explains this profusion of discourses on sex in modernity through an epistemic, or paradigmatic, transformation in the relationship of the state toward its subjects, reflected in an ever-increasing drive to regulate individual and collective bodies through new forms of "bio-power" (p. 140).

This culminates in a process of subjectivization, defined as the constitution and control of different subjectivities, achieved through "localisation of clinical discourse;" "institutional specialisation"; and "individualisation" (Hakosalo, 1991, pp. 38, 47). This in turn allows for disciplinary practices which formulate "multiple categories of deviancy" through assigning "a certain type of individual" with a "uniform identity," and by doing so, effectively (re)constructs the life-story of the individual (p. 47). For McWhorter, it constitutes a dual process of "simultaneous homogenisation and individualisation," which involves the targeting of specific populations, enabling "technicians to generate norms," and, therefore, constitutes a "powerful means of ordering groups for the purpose of acquiring knowledge about processes" (McWhorter, 1999, p. 156).

As a consequence of the above transformations, Foucault sees the emergence of "a specific type of discourse on sex, in a specific form of extortion of truth" (Foucault, 1978, p. 97). This provides the opportunity for producing "mechanisms and instances which enable one to distinguish true and false statements, the means by which each is sanctioned; the techniques and procedures accorded value in the acquisition of truth; the status of those who are charged with saying what counts as true" (Foucault, 1976, p. 131).

This also implies a close and integral relationship with forms of power, whereby dominant truths on sex can be recognized through their relationship to the most entrenched forms of power and domination. "'[T]ruth' is linked in a circular relation with systems of power which produce and sustain it, and the effects of power which it induces and which extend it. A 'regime' of truth" (Foucault, 1976, p. 133).

Implications for Studying Child and Intergenerational Sexualities

Foucault was well aware of the importance of children's sexuality in enabling modern forms of power to deploy a range of multiple techniques and knowledge—a view strengthened further by the rapid proliferation in different types of interdisciplinary expertise and knowledge (academic and professional) on children's sexuality since Foucault's death.

> What was important in relations between children and adults was that childhood became a common area of interest for: parents, educational institutions and public health. Children's sexuality became both a target and an instrument of power which resulted in the sexual misery of children and adolescents. The object was not to forbid, but to use childhood sexuality

as a network of power over kids. Children consequently became oppressed by the very ones who pretended to liberate them. (Foucault, 1988, p. 113)

Foucault identified the family and medicine-psychiatry of the eighteenth century as crucial emerging sites in generating power relationships and in distributing knowledge on childhood sexuality (Foucault, 1978, p. 104). He also recognized the importance of later disciplinary regimes that were emerging, including social work, psychology, sociology, and child welfare. Each have increasingly coveted and scrutinized knowledge on children's sexuality, which they constitute (through the media and other channels) as problematic, vulnerable, and powerless. However, in relation to tactical productivity, such concerns have been transformed from late-nineteenth century anti-masturbation campaigns, to contemporary fears over problematic sexual behaviors and categories, including child sex offenders and adolescent victims (Okami, 1992). However, this transformation has been most marked in the multiple ways CSA has constituted itself as the sole truth governing child and intergenerational sexualities.

PART TWO: ESTABLISHING CSA HEGEMONY
Building Blocks

The way in which CSA has been able to establish its dominant status with regard to child and intergenerational sexualities fits well with Lemert and Gillan's (1982, p. 17) schema on the key features of a dominant discourse, namely:

1. A type of discourse establishing its own individuality;
2. An episteme establishing a coherent, valid and verified body of knowledge;
3. A body of knowledge developing formal criteria employed as laws for the constructions of propositions; and
4. Formal axioms taken as legitimating and self-evident starting points for knowledge.

The CSA literature has an extensive back catalog of presenting its perspective as an inviolable truth incapable of being contested and minimizing any alternative perspective. For example, Glaser and Frosh (1993) argue that there is no need to specify the power dynamics in CSA, because adult-child sex "always designates an exploitation of power," differentiating it "from other forms of sexual encounter and can never be anything but abuse" (p. 7). Finkelhor (1991) likens positive accounts of intergenerational experiences to slavery and child labor (p. 314). His apparent logic for invoking these dubious analogues is that such accounts do not contradict the "immorality" of these practices (p. 314).

Professional inputs to CSA also adopt such an approach. For example, Hunter (1990) states, "just because some people wouldn't agree that it is abusive doesn't mean that it isn't ... [ ] ....even if the child enjoyed all aspects of the relationship physically and emotionally, abuse still took place' (pp. 4, 62). Other contributors add that adult-child sexual interaction can be defined as abusive, regardless of the intent of the perpetrator or the opinions of the victim (Lew & Bass, 1990).

This literature has been disseminated through professional, popular, academic publishing, where it is presented as the sole reality on intergenerational relationships, with subjective opinions being assigned one voice: the self-identified victims and survivors of child sexual abuse. The assumption, indelibly embedded in late modern storytelling, is that there is only one subjective reality, one story needs to be aired, because that's all there is to it.

Critiquing Male Survivor Literature

Attempts to contextualize or contest survivor accounts of CSA (see Jenkins, 1998) have often been characterized as insensitive, or as disingenuous attempts to superimpose medical-psychiatric schemas or a left libertarian political morality (Scott, 2001, pp. 40–50). However, akin to the way positive experiences of intergenerational sexualities are regularly marginalized, or even dismissed by proponents of CSA, victim-based narratives can also be scrutinized.

A large amount of the male survivor literature relies on inputs from clinical samples and practicing therapists (Rind, Bauserman, & Tromovitch, 1998). This questions not only the representativeness of such accounts, but also why they should be the only ones to speak for all retrospective accounts of intergenerational sexualities. Secondly, much of the language draws on US and UK sources during the 1990s (Hunter, 1990; King, 1995), with most contributors generally adopting mainstream feminist perspectives (Lew & Bass, 1990). Consequently, male sexual abuse (MSA) issues become problematically juxtaposed alongside incest and CSA theories that stress the link between the abuse of children, the patriarchal family structure, and wider patterns of male socialization (Finkelhor, 1984; Jeffreys, 1990).

Furthermore, much of their tone takes a polemical form. For example, it is significant that the vast bulk of male survivor stories cite incestuous, coercive, and violent experiences, while omitting other experiences. Garvey (1999), although adhering to such a "victimisation framework," questions "whether it is always appropriate or wise to talk about all the different forms and occasions of sexual coercion, sexual assault, sexual abuse, and sexual violence as victimisation," because such a strategy could provide "a fertile gap for a backlash discourse to take hold" (p. 77). Although sensitive to their client's experiences, such professional formulations cannot allow non-victimological experiences to be accepted, in order to maintain for themselves an authorial professional gaze and official truth status on CSA (West, 1998). Finally, it is important to examine how CSA has established itself as a central feature in the political and moral landscape. For example, Victor (1998) identifies a series of steps, including defining a person or group as a threat to societal values; the coalescing of social movements around the issues through articulating, reproducing, and reformulating stories (p. 542); and finally, stereotyping the behavior of such sexual deviants through producing typologies of their variations, alongside descriptions of the dangers and harm they cause (p. 544). Clearly, such accounts are not created in isolation, and influential pressure groups (media, legal profession, and support groups) have reinforced this through sensationalist coverage of abuse cases. Consequently, any "revisiting of experience" must be analyzed in the light of the potential for relatively large amounts of compensation and the role played by the police and legal system in encouraging such claims.

Part Three: Two Case Studies

The two case studies set out in what follows were selected from the narrative accounts from respondents to my research to provide contrasting lenses for analyzing male intergenerational sexualities (Yuill, 2004).

(a) A Professional Narrative on CSA

The following account was selected from a total of fifteen face-to-face interviews with professionals working in Scotland in the areas of child protection or sexual offences between 2000 and 2001 (see Yuill, 2004, ch. 7). They were recruited after a series of post, e-mail, and phone calls to local councils and social work departments. I selected Mark's account because he had a specific role in coordinating male child protection measures in a Scottish Local Council. In his account, Mark clearly draws on victimological perspectives that position young people as vulnerable, at risk, and too developmentally immature to consent to sexual relationships with adults. He also stresses the damaging impact of MSA to personal development, and the inability of boys to knowingly consent to sexual relations with adults.

> **Mark:** Depends on how professional construes it.... Boys are trying to mask the fact that they were victims. Being a boy and being a victim are incompatible! Idea is to salvage some of their identities, avoid victim identification, that they instigated it, consented. The socialisation of boys and male sexuality about being in charge, ready to be satiated ... turn abuse around and that they were in control to rescue identities as boys.... Professionals have not learnt boys language very well and miss a lot... Professionals don't know how to change the language and interpret it differently.... The precondition of boy victims is to start to reinforce competence. If boys think that you think they are a victim—simply not going to go there.... Need to recognise his competence, then he can talk about his sexual assault.
>
> **Researcher:** Do boys put other constructs—more positive, that they initiated?

Mark: Constantly, and that's this idea in order to salvage something of their own identities. They're in charge! They were in control! And that they knew what they were doing! ... And they don't! ... Or, so what the literature says, so they can avoid victim identification.

Mark also identifies various strategies that professionals employ to reframe the boy's experience, in line with victimological understandings, including deploying CSA meanings to reinforce competence, reinterpret their experiences, and encourage boys to identify as victims. His account also demonstrates the strategic way professional truths on CSA are superimposed upon their clients, reinforcing the suspicions of some critics of the problematic professional scripting of children's experiences of intergenerational sexualities (West, 1998; Bagley, 1999).

(b) A Non-Victimological Narrative

In order to recruit respondents who had a wide range of intergenerational experiences when they were under eighteen, I made approaches to a number of male survivor, gay and lesbian, and "general population" groups, organizations, and publications throughout Scotland and the UK via post, e-mail, and telephone (see Yuill, 2004, chs. 9–11). I have singled out the following interview with an individual (now in his forties), who, throughout his childhood and adolescence, experienced numerous sexual relationships with adult males. Philip was alerted to the research by another respondent and contacted me by phone, explaining that he wanted to discuss the experiences he had had with adult men when he was a boy.

The sexual attraction of children or young people to an adult has been defined as *gerontophilia* (see Sandfort, 1987, p. 31), however, this term has almost vanished from the contemporary lexicon. Within gay communities, youths have been often categorized as "chickens," and their older partners labeled "chicken hawks." However, more recently the term *chaser* has been used to define boys or youths in the gay community seeking older partners.[2]

Philip's four sexual experiences (as a young boy through to adolescence) with older men are relayed here chronologically. Although differing subjective meanings on intergenerational sexualities are revealed in Philip's account, they are not presented dichotomously as in CSA frameworks: that is, in children bringing an emotional as opposed to an adult's overtly sexualized script (Ferenczi, 1932). Philip relates his first experience as a learning experience, seeing, and being excited by, the somatic changes brought on by the man's subsequent ejaculation. Although he draws a distinction between the psychic and sexual in his recollection of the event, he defines this event as superior to peer sexual experimentation. Philip relays both physical and psychological excitement at the event, substantiating libertarian claims that subjective differences between adults and young people (in terms of understanding and needs in the intimate and

114 • RICHARD YUILL

sexual sphere) do not invalidate a relationship or the possibility for a young person's needs to be fulfilled.

> **Philip:** My first arousal of adult men was when I was in Africa.... It was just my curiosity was piqued and I noticed that he was washing his genitals. He started to get an erection.... I was curious to explore his body further. About three or four days later I crept into his bedroom.... I think he was fast asleep, and I started playing with his penis.... I was just curious what an erection was. I think I'd experienced it a bit as a boy but they would come and go.... and I certainly hadn't seen anything as big as that.... I was most excited by his sexual excitement. There was no sexual excitement for myself, it was just pure curiosity but he was clearly very aroused, and my touching him increased his arousal—that excited me more. I think it was just like childhood curiosity.

In Philip's second experience, there was more of a physical interchange, in which the man carried out particular sexual acts that excited him. Again, the initiative was shown by Philip who viewed it as furtive physical curiosity and playfulness.

> **Philip:** There was a chap who lived in the apartment above ours called Paul.... I got onto the bed with him and he just had his shorts on....He didn't resist me, my advances to touch him and stroke him physically but he was a bit taken aback when I tried to feel his genitals.
>
> **Researcher:** You mentioned the first experimentation, looking at men's erections. Can you recall the first time when you took it further, thinking about sexual activity?
>
> **Philip:** Paul actually on one occasion—when I was playing around with him and he was masturbating—inserted his finger into my backside, which really did excite me!

At various points in the interview, Philip reflected on his childhood experiences. He sums up his sexual experiences with adult men as seduction by him, but firmly embedded within child understandings of sexuality. He lists these as less selfish, playful, pleasure seeking and less fearful of rejection, but also stressing the unavailability of labels to explain the activities he was involved in. This reinforces Dowsett's (2000) claim that man-boy relationships are often exploratory, effectively taking place in "social lacunae," in which a "sexual culture" develops before any formal definition (p. 32).

> **Philip:** Again, with time and sort of seduction, I suppose as a child it's a conscious process but it isn't quite as selfish as the sexuality as you experience as an older person. So there's a genuine interest in making the other person get a response and make them happy or whatever. So I played around with them whenever I could.... They probably weren't gay men

or pedophiles.... I certainly didn't have a name for them at that age.... I think as a child you just learn to take such things in your stride.... You don't take a rejection of a physical advance quite so personally.

Philip characterizes his third experience as a more overtly physically sexual friendship. He contrasts this with a later more mature, intimate, and rounded relationship. He reiterates his assertiveness in initiating the initial encounters, coupled with his careful preplanning of the event.

> **Philip:** We had a next-door neighbour.... and I was probably about nine to ten years old. He was going through a divorce, and I had got to know him quite well.... I asked him if it would be okay if I stopped over for the night.... I got into bed with him and started playing around with him. And at first he objected, but I just persevered and got him fully sexually aroused and was masturbating him and trying to get him to orgasm. Because that was my objective: to get men to achieve orgasm.... I persuaded him that I liked to have my bottom played with.... He loved my arse-hole. Of course that was my dream. And as our friendship—because it wasn't a relationship—developed, we would get more and more bold about inserting things into my backside.

Philip notes significant developmental somatic changes associated with stronger orgasms. Alongside greater excitement, he explains how carrying out sexual acts in public places gave him more power in the exchanges. Philip claims that he had control over his adult partner through the very process of initiation, whereby he could decide whether or not to initiate a sexual exchange. Rather than risk being construed as a negative debarment to adult-child sex, Philip views it as providing the impetus for a greater sexual thrill, in which he was able to appropriate a public space for his own needs.

> **Philip:** Now I was twelve/thirteen, and I was definitely having much stronger sexual responses. I was having orgasms. I wasn't ejaculating as far as I can remember at that time.... I used to get him to do risky things like put his fingers inside me when we were at the swimming baths in the cubicle drying afterwards. That was quite a turn on—the fact that it was in such a public environment, and I think the power I had over him in the sexual department.... I could wrap him round my finger to have sex. It was quite easily done, and it was me that made the advances.... He just identified as a sexual man, and saw me as this curious boy who liked his arse being played with.
>
> **Researcher:** Did he at any time give pleasure to you through masturbation?
>
> **Philip:** I used to masturbate myself. He would occasionally do it but I wasn't really interested in that. My orgasms came through being screwed, the friction of rubbing my body against the sheets. The masturbating element really developed from my playing with him but I could quite easily get orgasms from being buggered.

Philip draws sharp contrasts between the following experience, which he characterizes as more of an emotional and cognitive connection, including a greater symmetry of interests and experiences, and the former, which he views as purely physical. Although alluding to infrequent sexual contact, Philip considers learning from his adult partner, through acquiring knowledge and experience, as more important.

> **Philip:** This was a much older man—in his mid-fifties. Whereas the neighbour was in his thirties—a very virile docker—the older man was much more intelligent, more cultured and the relationship between ourselves was far more cerebral. I'd go round, and we would read and listen to music.... It was a more intelligent, mature relationship than the one I'd had with the docker, which had really been seduction on my part, very physical.... This person didn't have a huge penis unlike the docker, but that didn't bother me. This was a different relationship. We did things together, camping.... The friendship I had with the docker—the physical friendship—there was no sort of mental connection at all. I went round there purely to get my rocks off. But with the older bloke.... I wanted to learn more about music, about literature. It was more of an intellectual side. It was very good and there was equally, if not more, stimulation from the intellectual side than the physical side. Maybe every couple of weeks we would have sex. It was just masturbatory sex.

Throughout, Philip emphasizes the importance of his early familial and cultural context for scripting his early sexual experiences positively. He also positions himself in a libertarian sexual ethic of individual enrichment through empowerment. Philip also challenges dominant notions of age-appropriate interaction, by contending that the central component of his sexuality throughout his life course was a substantial attraction (physical, emotional, and intellectual) to adult men as opposed to his peers.

> **Philip:** I had a couple of friends, but because I was in and out of school my education was a bit all over the place.... It was quite clearly men that interested me not younger boys at all.... Their sexuality was—for want of a better term—now and for then.... just playful and experimental but I wanted to push.... I was pushing things further, but I never thought I was doing anything wrong. My parents—my mother especially—was quite liberated.... I grew up in quite a wholesome and healthy environment, without physical and sexual inhibitions.

Philip alludes to wider social contrasts between his interests and attitudes and those of his peers, leading him to seek adult company and participate in adult activities. Philip's experience is concurrent with respondents in Leahy's (1992) study, who identified a commonality of interests with their adult partner, alongside a conscious minimization of adult-child boundaries, to explain their positive experiences. This was shared by a significant number of respondents in my own study, who describe symmetry of interests with older people at a relatively early age, incommensurate with their chronological age (see Yuill, 2004, ch. 9).

> **Philip:** Because I was quite independent and didn't have many friends.... I had a different social attitude from my peers, different political attitudes through my grandparents. I was a socialist at seven or eight years old.... So I developed a lot of personal interests in music, and I used to like cycling a lot, joining the Youth Hostel Association...... and I joined the Red Cross.

In contrast with CSA formulations, Philip eschews victim status in intergenerational relationships. Although recognizing physical power differences between adults and young people, he maintains that he was always able to distinguish consensual from coercive intergenerational experiences. In all of his encounters and relationships, he saw himself as the active seducer and initiator. He also relates that throughout these experiences, a range of his own needs (physical, educational, emotional, and social) was met. Philip's account criss-crosses the mentor-child empowerment positions referred to in positive discursive presentations of intergenerational sexualities (see Yuill, 2004, ch. 1). Whereas there is a prominent theme of learning from his adult partners (commensurate with mentor-protégé conceptions), Philip also positions himself as an active initiator within such exchanges. Although mindful of physical power differences, he asserts that he was the one who had control throughout such situations, and knew exactly what he was doing.

> **Researcher:** You mentioned that you always had an interest in adult men?
>
> **Philip:** Yeah! I would say that from the age of seven onwards that my focus on sex and men have always been maturer men.... in all the relationships and friendships I was involved in, I knew exactly what I was doing, and knew what I set out to do and was fully in control. And there were times as a boy, I travelled to and from school by train.... and you would occasionally get old men into the apartment.... Sometimes I'd get turned on by that and hope that something happened and I'd engineer a situation. I'd play with my crutch or something to see if they were watching at the corner of their eye but if ever a man made an approach on me that would terrify me.... I had to at all times be the seducer and initiator, and I think that was right and proper because I was a child and I knew my circumstances, I knew I was smaller and they were bigger and stronger men and I knew what rape was, and knew what physical assault was, and I wasn't going to let that happen to me.... It never happened to me!

Despite recognition, even among CSA researchers, of a continuum of experiences in intergenerational sexualities (Coxell, King, Mezey, & Gordon, 1999), this has not been translated into a permitted subjectivity. Instead, non-victimological responses are co-opted by CSA formulations, via a series of strategic and rhetorical techniques, in which their agency status is marginalized or dismissed as a product of either being duped by their abuser, subsumed within structuralist gender norms of hegemonic masculinity, or medical-psychiatric/psychoanalytical paradigms of denial.

Such strategies are curiously identical to those allegedly imposed by "backlash" formulations on CSA (see Scott, 2001). Perhaps not surprisingly (owing to the predominance of victimological sentiments in academic circles), this criticism has rarely been voiced with regard to the way non-victim accounts have been similarly marginalized, medicalized, or insensitively dismissed. However, Leahy (1996) does criticize Finkelhor for deliberately excluding positive accounts from his 1981 summative research findings (p. 32). Okami (1990) also criticizes CSA researchers for employing a moral bias and dubious psychological approach to attribute such responses to victim "denial" (pp. 106, 107). He identifies "intentional, structural and ideological" biases in such research (p. 99), which present for both respondent and reader alike, "a circumscribed universe of experiences—a continuum with a severely truncated positive end—while being told that this universe is inclusive of even the most unusual and unlikely experiences" (p. 103), which lead to the "obvious" "impression that.... catastrophic sequelae are intrinsic to any sexual interaction between an individual under 18 (or 16) and someone five or more years older" (p. 105).

Clearly, there has been a blatant discrepancy in the way victim and non-victim accounts of intergenerational relationships are constructed. The multiple ways in which transgressive subject positions of young people who do not identify themselves as victims have been consciously ignored constitutes not only a biased formulation, whereby "hierarchies of agencies" confer victim-based accounts automatically with a higher status, but also an insensitivity to other accounts of intergenerational sexualities. This point has been well made by Rind et al. (2001a, p. 750) when they argue, "[o]ur critics, and many CSA researchers, have had no difficulty accepting reports of negative experiences at face value, but have selectively denied any validity to reports of positive experiences and seek to discount them as the result of processes such as denial.... To our knowledge, no one has systematically studied the sorts of pressures that might exist on individuals to redefine experiences initially seen as positive."

This final contribution from Philip is a crucial example of the foregoing comment. The way he relays how his account was reformulated by the commentator is also consistent with the way CSA professionals deny access to alternative perspectives. Although Plummer (1995) points out that the pedophile's story is one that cannot be told because there is no willing audience (p. 118), this omits the other component in intergenerational sexualities, namely, how positive accounts from young people have been denied a voice within mainstream discursive channels. In this respect, Philip's experience in attempting to get his story told offers crucial insights into the absence of a public articulation of positive accounts from young people of intergenerational relationships in late modernity.

> **Philip:** There was a radio discussion with an American sex abuse industry commentator Michelle Elliott and there was a.... BBC journalist and she was going on about children's rights.... So I said, fuck this, I'm going to phone up and explain that as a child I was quite happy to have sex and I actively sought sex! ... I got through and I explained to the switchboard and I got on and said my bit in ten seconds, and Michelle Elliott immediately cut in saying, kill the caller, and went on to say this is a perfect example—you can't speak after they've cut you off—of how a child has grown up to believe that what he was doing was his own free will but really he was being manipulated by adults. And I couldn't say a word. Nobody could hear me now. I was pissed off!

Clearly Philip's story, along with other positive accounts of intergenerational sexualities, cannot be analyzed outside available cultural discourses, as Waites (2005) maintains. He refers to Reavey and Warner's (2002) post-structuralist analysis of CSA, in which the authors claim that many children's initial positive experiences will likely be reframed as abuse in later life, owing to the latter's predominance on the cultural landscape (Waites, 2005, p. 27). Waites concludes that such "complexities confound arguments such as those of Rind et al. (1998) which seek to justify sexual behaviour involving a child purely on the basis that it is experienced positively by both parties at the time and has no immediate clear negative psychological consequences" (p. 27).

However, Waites misrepresents Rind et al., because many of the studies they drew on for their 1998 study were based primarily on retrospective self-reporting of respondents, not children at the time of their experience. He also construes the sociocultural framing of CSA tautologically. Victimological perspectives clearly have a hegemonic position in the framing of intergenerational experiences throughout Anglo-American culture; but this fact should neither accredit undue privileging to such positions, nor prevent a critique of that very hegemony, including presenting the considerable variety and number of non-victimological narratives.

PART FOUR: INTERLOPERS BEWARE!
Overview of Contributors

This part examines eight case studies (based on firsthand and secondary accounts) of researchers and commentators who have produced critical analyses of CSA and then faced a series of attacks by professionals, media commentators, and other academics. However, these cases are by no means exhaustive! I could have included the experiences of Theo Sandfort (1987) and Rüdiger Lautmann (1994), who both faced extreme pressure in pursuing their work, and Bill Thompson, whose home was raided by police, despite having been accredited as a long-standing expert defense witness on false abuse accusations.[3]

James Kincaid published *Child-Loving: The Erotic Child and Victorian Culture* in 1992. Li's work in 1990 and 1993 were essentially follow-ups to his Ph.D. thesis, completed in 1987 on pedophiliac sexuality. Matthew Waites conducted his Ph.D. study on "The Age of Consent, Homosexuality and Citizenship in the United Kingdom (1885–1999)" at South Bank University between 1995 and 1999. Rind et al. published their meta-analysis on CSA in the *Psychological Bulletin* in July 1998. In 2002, Judith Levine wrote *Harmful to Minors: The Perils of Protecting Children from Sex*. Harris Mirkin published articles on the subject around moral panics on pedophilia and the politicization of child sexuality in the *Journal of Homosexuality* in 1999 and *Sexuality and Culture* in 2000. The current author conducted Ph.D. research into *Male Age-Discrepant Intergenerational Sexualities and Relationships* between 1999 and 2004. Finally, Pat Sikes conducted life history research on consensual romantic and sexual relationships between teachers and pupils in secondary schools (see Sikes, 2006).

Case Study 1: James Kincaid (1993)

Although based at a US university, the initial attacks on Kincaid came from the UK. These started in 1993 in the *London Times* by an Oxford Don, claiming the book's author championed pedophilia (Kincaid, 2004, p. 14).[4] This was followed up by a Conservative MP, Lord Braine, who attempted to get the home secretary to ban the book, stating, "I simply cannot believe a reputable publisher could consider printing a book with such views. For any rational human being to give currency to what the vast majority of people regard as the vilest crime possible is deeply shocking."[5] *The Daily Mail* headline was "Paedophile Book 'Should Be Banned.'"[6] The article quoted the head of Scotland Yard's Obscene Publication Squad who stated, "[p]eople will be rightly outraged. This book won't offend against the law, but it will give comfort to paedophiles" (quoted in Kincaid, 2004, p. 14). Kincaid also notes that both CSA experts and two Conservative politicians also demanded the book's withdrawal, with one, Jill Knight, stating, "[I]t is crucial for the normal development of children that their innocence be preserved" (p. 14).

Below is James Kincaid's response (January 15, 2006) to my e-mail request for further details on his experience.

> I've been working for some time to analyze why it is our cultures are so dedicated to a single Gothic story on kids, their bodies and sexuality, and what counts as eroticism. It's a form of hysteria that's hardly changed its shrill pitch in the last 30 or so years. With one large exception, my own experience has been pretty tame. There have been a few (very few) nasty reviews of my two books and a couple of anonymous and threatening

phone calls. Very little, really, and my university angrily turned away some calls from alums wanting to protest. The one exception oddly concerned the UK and not the US.

My first book on this subject, published by Routledge (called *Child-Loving: The Erotic Child and Victorian Culture*) was reviewed in the *Sunday Times* (London) by an Oxford Don who said things like, "While Kincaid is coy about his own practices, this is a book which will give comfort to pedophiles." The next day the tabloids picked it up—"American Prof Backs Pedophiles!" Several Tory MPs issued angry statements; Scotland Yard said the book was probably not illegal but very unfortunate.

The House of Lords debated the book and its banning for an entire afternoon. Of course no official action was taken, but almost every single bookstore returned its entire stock to the publishers (a testimony to independent booksellers!!!) and the book was, in effect, unavailable there. Routledge UK issued a very weak statement of support for the book, beginning, "I haven't read it myself, but I would be surprised if it encouraged pedophilia. This is the sort of scholarship which is common in the U.S. and often appears there."

Apart from absolutely killing sales, nothing came of this. It is interesting that this is one area where the business adage—all publicity is good publicity—does not hold.

Case Study 2: Chin-Keung Li (1993)

Li's "troubles" were intimated to me via an informal interview I carried out with his former Ph.D. supervisor, Professor Donald West, at Cambridge University on March 7, 2001. West told me that some years after Li's work was published, he was criticized by CSA professionals in the US for appearing to condone pedophilia. This was followed by a series of media attacks in the local Scottish Press in 1996. For example, Anne Houston, director of ChildLine in Scotland, said, "that there should be no doubt sex with children is wrong and not open for some kind of debate," and a professional working with sex offenders, Ray Wyre, accused Li of giving encouragement to pedophiles.[7] These attacks culminated in an investigation (lasting more than a year) by Li's professional association, the British Psychiatric Association. However, in the end, no career-threatening action was taken.

Case Study 3: Matthew Waites (1997)

In April 1997, Waites delivered a paper at the British Sociological Association (BSA) Conference, during which he discussed the possibility of a reduction in the UK age of consent to fourteen. After delivering his paper, Waites was harangued by a number of journalists and had to be assisted out of the room (Waites, 1999). This was followed up by attacks in the *Daily Mail,* in which Valerie Riches, a spokesperson for "Family and Youth Concern," claimed Waites was advocating pedophilia and that attempts to promote children's sexual rights was an undercover attempt to legalize pedophilia.[8] In the *South London Press*, the National Society for the Protection of Cruelty to Children (NSPCC) stated "Children are emotionally and mentally damaged if they have sex with adults. There are no other arguments."[9] Waites had to explain the study to his funding body, but strong support was given by South Bank University.[10]

Case Study 4: Bruce Rind, Robert Bauserman, and Philip Tromovitch (1998-1999)[11]

Some five months after Rind et al. published their study, there followed a protracted period of criticism and personal attacks on the study and its authors. This was initiated by the National Association for the Research and Therapy of Homosexuality (NARTH) in December 1998, which attacked the study on its website.[12] This was followed in March 1999 by a conservative Catholic newspaper called *The Wanderer,* claiming that Rind et al. were trying to normalize sexual abuse (Rind, 2006).

A Philadelphia talk show host, "Dr. Laura" Schlessinger, then launched an attack against Temple University and Rind, provoking listeners to call the Temple psychology department.[13] She obtained "three renowned, licensed clinical psychologists and a scientist" (two were from NARTH), including information provided by Paul J. Fink, president of a new group called the Leadership Council for Mental Health, Justice and the Media (an organization of professionals advocating the validity of repressed memories and related therapies, i.e., psychopathology centered on CSA)[14] (see Rind et al., 2001b, p. 71). Dr. Laura then dubbed the Rind study "garbage research with a dangerous statement at the end" (Schlessinger, 1999).

By April 1999, the Family Research Council, an ultraconservative Christian lobbying group in Washington, DC, joined Dr. Laura in the attacks.[15] In May it organized a press conference, at which Congressman Tom DeLay demanded that the American Psychological Association (APA) denounce the study. Although initially defending the study, the APA eventually relented in the face of enormous pressure from Congress and agreed to have the paper rereviewed. A month later, the Rind et al. study was condemned by the US Congress as "severely flawed" and censured by votes of 100–0 in the Senate and 435–0, but with 13 abstentions, in the House of Representatives.

However, further reviews by the American Association for the Advancement of Science (AAAS), and a special issue of the *American Psychologist,* published in March 2002, both concluded that the Rind et al. article was scientifically sound and voiced criticism of those in the political arena and in the media for deliberately misrepresenting the study (see Rind, 2006).

Case Study 5: Judith Levine (2002-2003)

Ironically, the ensuing panic over Levine (2002) reinforces her claim that "in America today, it is nearly impossible to publish a book that says children and teenagers can have sexual pleasure and be safe too" (p. xix). Initially, Levine's efforts to get her book published were turned down when a number of publishers rejected the manuscript, with one labeling it "radioactive," because of its argument for providing children with more sexual education and responsibility.[16] When the University of Minnesota Press agreed to publish, it was clear that it would provoke a significant reaction. In order to forestall some of the criticisms and avoid potential embarrassment, the publishers undertook a rigorous scrutiny. The book went through numerous subsequent editorial revisions, resulting in four rewrites.

The media immediately brandished Levine a "pedophile apologist."[17] By May 2002, talk radio hosts and conservative critics reinforced this message across the country, and Tim Pawlenty, the Republican majority leader of the Minnesota House of Representatives, called for the University of Minnesota to cancel the book. After they refused, the state legislature threatened the university's funding because it printed the book. Pawlenty said he believed it endorsed sex between adults and children, adding, "This kind of disgusting victimization of children is intolerable, and the state should have no part in it."[18] The University of Minnesota Press set up a two-month review of the way its press acquires and reviews books. The vice president for research and dean of the graduate school, Christine Maziar, said, "we thought it was important to make sure our processes are in line with those in the rest of the country."

In a telephone interview (conducted with me on February 22, 2006), Levine identifies "professional pedophile hunters," such as "Dr. Laura" Schlessinger, Judith Reisman, and right-wing sensationalist journalists, such as Paul Sahn, in stirring up protest against her book. She believes the attacks themselves are disseminated through right-wing conservative organizations and media, such as "Concerned Women for America" and *Fox News,* as well as "middle-of-the-road" broadcasters, including *MSNBC.* Levine concluded, "these attacks do not need to be organized, but have two main constituents. The first is mobilized through the Christian Right, most notably represented by the Family Research Council, and the second involves a coalition of the child sexual abuse industry, including self-legitimizing professionals, therapists, lawmakers, and certain mainstream feminists."

Case Study 6: Harris Mirkin (2003)

More than three years after Mirkin's published articles, several conservative groups posted online criticisms of his work, claiming that Mirkin was part of an academic conspiracy to legalize pedophilia. He also received phone messages calling him "a pedophile and saying he should die," and another decrying, "why a respected university should not have a monster teaching there."[19] A national news service called Mirkin a "trailblazer" for the view that some sex between children and adults is acceptable.

The article was posted on a conservative website, *WorldNetDaily.com*. The article went on, "his writings have been criticized by groups that fight child molestation, as well as by pro-family organizations. They defend children as immature and vulnerable, no matter what their age, and believe that sexual abuse scars children, no matter what its form."

According to Mirkin, "the media helped create the controversy with less-than-accurate coverage, and most reporters clearly had not read the article, relying on information from an online search."[20] The article went on to say that when the story broke, a radio personality from *KLIK Radio* in Missouri called a Republican state representative, Mark Wright, to tip him off about the allegedly pedophile-supporting professor at the University of Missouri. Republican state Senator John Loudon also weighed in saying, "he's taking molestation and abuse and dumbing them down to intergenerational contact. What we have here is something that I think is absolutely gross."[21]

Missouri's legislature wanted to "fine" the University of Missouri–Kansas City an amount it assumed equal to Mirkin's salary ($100,000). More than three-quarters of the House voted in favor of financially censuring the university. When it reached the state Senate, this was cut to $50,000 from the school's overall budget. Even after the university refused to dismiss Mirkin, Wright said, "we think he's promoting illegal conduct and would like to see him dismissed," and sent a letter signed by thirty or forty representatives, which asked the board of curators to go over the chancellor's head and force the issue.[22]

What follows is Harris Mirkin's account of his experiences, in an e-mail received January 10, 2006.

> They were doing an article on the fuss about the publication of Judith Levine's book, and my name came up. The article was read by the constituent of a very conservative state legislator. The legislator eventually went to the floor of the House in Missouri and asked if they knew that the leader of the movement to legitimize pedophilia was a faculty member at University of Missouri–Kansas City (UMKC).
>
> The legislature's behavior was disgraceful, not because they disagreed with me but because they had no idea what the article said—I don't think any of them bothered to read it. Some media people called me a pedophile. Some people read the article. Surprisingly, to me, I became something of a local hero. Most of the people in the local area where I live regarded me as something of a hero. I was surprised, and still don't have an explanation for that. Some, of course, regarded me as an evil monster.
>
> Most of the national TV media didn't bother to read the story. The print media people were much better. Online stuff from right-wing groups was vicious and stupid. The faculty and the university supported me. No direct pressure once it was clear that the university supported me. The legislature fined the university for having me. Some people were unfriendly. It was a very uncomfortable time for my wife, but that was because of all the

media coverage. The crucial thing that I had was institutional protection. I am still continuing my research and am finishing an article on the legal and political construction of the concept of child pornography.

Case Study 7: Richard Yuill (2001–2005)

The empirical component of my research involved establishing a dialogue with an Internet-based group that seeks to work for a better understanding of child and intergenerational sexualities.[23] Unbeknownst to me, this group had been infiltrated by a Dutch-based conservative group led by Ireen Van Engelen.[24] It was this group that likely passed on information about my research to a freelance tabloid journalist in Scotland, Marcello Mega. Mega then published articles in *The Scottish Daily Mail*[25] and the *Times Higher Education Supplement* (THES).[26]

The content and tone of the articles sought to paint me as a pedophile and suggested that the University of Glasgow should not be supporting such research. This was followed up by further "revelations" by Mega a year later, after sensitive interview transcripts had been stolen from my office and passed on to him. These were printed in the *Scottish Mail on Sunday*,[27] the *Scottish News of the World*,[28] and covered in the *THES*.[29] Throughout this period, I was also subjected to harassment from journalists, offensive phone-calls and e-mails, two lengthy university senate investigations into my work; having to explain my research to officers from the Serious Crime Squad; and experiencing the *News of the World* taking a photo of me inside my house when my father was close to death.

After the completion of the Ph.D., I determined to correct some of the deliberate misinformation that had circulated regarding my research. Throughout this period, the media (both tabloid and broadsheet) presented the research as potentially dangerous. For example, Andrew Durham, an author on MSA (see Durham, 2003) was quoted in the *THES*, saying Dr. Yuill's thesis would "play into the hands of abusers," and "victims of abuse sometimes report positive experiences, but this was often a result of manipulation by their abuser or a coping mechanism."[30] This point was restated in subsequent comments by Chris Harrison (Warwick University social work lecturer) and Anne Houston [again]. Harrison stated, "whatever [Dr Yuill's] intention, one thing we know about sexual offenders is that they seize on this kind of thing and use it to support their position."[31] In similar vein, Houston commented in *Sky News*, "our concern that anything in the public domain which could be used as an 'excuse' by abusers to persuade children that sex between an adult and child is 'normal' is dangerous."[32] Finally, in the *Glasgow Herald*, Rachel O'Connell, director of the cyberspace research unit at the University of Central Lancashire, went further, in stating that such research showed the need for a UK-wide ethics board, suggesting in Orwellian fashion that such a body would scrutinize any future research on what she deemed "sensitive subjects."[33]

As a postscript to these events, during a peer-review process, undertaken from January through April 2005 by *Sociological Research Online* in an article I submitted, one of the peer reviewers made his/her political opposition clear regarding such research, and said that academics such as Harrison and O'Connell were quite justified in criticizing, and even calling for the suppression of, a research study they had not even read![34]

Case Study 8: Pat Sikes (2005)

In late October 2005, a reporter approached Sikes from the *Irish Independent,* for information about research into pupil-teacher relationships, asking for a copy, which was duly sent. Soon after, Sikes was phoned by her university's press office, asking if she would speak to a journalist from the *THES,* who had seen the Irish article and who wanted to follow it up.

In a short unpublished article, Pat Sikes details the unfolding chain of events that then followed.[35]

> On the morning of Thursday November 10, I was surprised to find that my in-box was full of urgent red messages. The first one I opened was from the press office at the university asking me to phone them immediately. I learnt that the office was being inundated with requests from journalists. They wanted to speak with me about my research into pupil teacher relationships that was to be reported in the *TES* [*Times Education Supplement*] the following day.[36]
>
> It turned out that, during the morning, national and local papers and broadcast media organisations and companies had received a press release from an agency about the work of an academic (i.e. me) who had married her teacher, which appeared to champion such relationships, and who advocated an "erotic charge" in the classroom as an aid to teaching. This release also contained condemnatory quotes about me and my work made by representatives from Childline and the NSPCC.
>
> As the day progressed my interrogators kept returning to the same words, phrases and questions. It seemed that references and quotations I had used within my text and which were unequivocally and unambiguously from other people's work, had been attributed to me. With this information a lawyer was engaged on behalf of myself and the university to write to the editor of the *TES* and to put her "on notice that she should not publish an article which contains any of the mistaken quotations."
>
> On Friday, as well as the article in the *TES,* the *Mail, Telegraph, Independent, Yorkshire Post,* and *Sheffield Star* all carried stories reflecting the tenor of the press release. Some had my picture from my University web page, despite me having begged researchers not to show an image of me. During the day I was to find out that, throughout the country, numerous local papers had picked up on the story and that it had also been carried, nationwide and complete with photo, by the free travellers' paper, the *Metro.*
>
> As the phone kept ringing and my email received bleep kept bleeping, I began to feel beleaguered. My 83-year-old mother, who lives some 80 miles

away, phoned to say that reporters from the *Daily Mail* had just been at her door to ask her what she thought about her daughter's work. She was shaken, nonetheless, but was determined not to back out of her numerous social arrangements in order to come and stay with me. I phoned her local police who sent round an officer.

On Saturday the hate emails started to arrive. Most of these were from self-professed Christians in the USA and Canada where, I was to learn, my email address and photograph had been posted on a couple of rightwing "Christian" websites with an invitation to readers to let me know what they thought about me. These people outlined my character (sick, depraved, evil, worse than Joseph Mengele), told me what I deserved (the electric chair would be a waste of good electricity and too quick into the bargain), blamed me for Islamic terrorism, made death threats, described the spots in hell reserved for me, hoped that any children I might have would be taken away to a place of safety, and usually said that they were praying for my soul. They also copied me into emails they sent to my head of department in which they demanded my dismissal on the grounds that I was obviously a pedophile myself and that my employment was untenable in a school of education.

More distressing was the late night call to my sister-in-law's ex-directory number from a journalist asking for "dirt" and the emails I started to receive from people I was at school with 40 years ago saying they had been contacted via "Friends Reunited" and offered a "substantial reward" for information about me when I was a pupil.

Part Five: Reconstituting Subjectivity and Evicting Interlopers

Interrogating Victimology

McWhorter's (1999) description of the way "sexual regimes of truth deny human freedom and punish those of us who seek to exercise our freedom" (p. 188) could have been penned for this topic. Indeed, the very similarities of the experiences of non-victimological subjects, and of researchers critical of CSA, underline the intensity of such regimes of truth. Synthesizing such experiences also reveals a three-stage process in the maintenance and consolidation of a victimological truth regime around child and intergenerational sexualities.

"Owning" Childhood Innocence and Vulnerability

Firstly, CSA, pro-family, conservative, and fundamentalist Christian discourses rely heavily on Enlightenment notions of childhood incapability (Yuill & Evans, 2006). Whereas, this has been presented in moral conservative and fundamentalist Christian discourses as a commitment to, and investment in, childhood sexual innocence, it has been used in CSA discourses to position children and young people as inherently vulnerable, at-risk, and as potential victims, requiring extensive protection. For example, Kincaid (1992) highlights the way both CSA ideology and dominant Anglo-American cultural depictions of children require passive, infantilized, and incapable children (p.70). Kitzinger (1997) argues that "images of frightened children", deployed in CSA literature, rely on a "fetishistic glorification of innocence," which "excludes those who do not conform to an asexual ideal," denying them "access to knowledge and power" (pp. 165, 167). Kincaid (1998) has taken this point further in provocatively arguing that "paedophiles and us aren't much different: both of us really yearn for this empty, incompetent 'child' and if we don't find it, we know ... how to manufacture it" (p. 212).

Childhood incapability and sexual innocence were prominent discursive themes in the attacks waged against the researchers covered in this paper by Christian fundamentalists, conservatives, children's charities and CSA advocates. The representatives of such organizations often portrayed themselves as inheritors of the nineteenth century child savers and defenders of children, to justify their authorial status in speaking for children and victims, and consequently their right to attack the research(ers). See, for example, Spiegel's (2000a) emotively charged title "Suffer the children: Long-term effects of sexual abuse," and his eulogy on the "great beauty in the innocence of childhood" (Spiegel, 2000b, p. 66).

This conception of childhood, what Jenks (1982) calls the "Apollonian conception," is informed by a paternalistic and controlling attitude toward young people. It is also one that has been effectively politicized and co-opted by various groups for their own particular agendas (see Jenkins, 1998). This has been most clearly shown in the multiple ways in which professionals have increased their influence through pastoral monitoring, effectively curtailing young people's autonomy (Kelly, 1999; Furedi, 2001). Such a context has also provided considerable scope for such various power-knowledges to regulate the intimate lives of children and young people (Yuill, 2004), along with setting recent governmental agendas in the US and UK, notably in abstinence-only approaches to sex education (West, 1999; Levine, 2002).

Finally, Evans (1993) sees the above agenda as initiated by a "New Right conservatism," which has used the "pedophile threat" since the 1980s to produce "a crude reification of the sanctity of traditional family life threatened by a range of forces" (p. 233). This produced "a subtle gear change," whereby "childhood sexuality was mainly addressed in utopian essentialist terms, threatened by the legacy of the permissive 1960s which had weakened parental authority," but which also saw, contrary to New Right privatist tenets, a "heightened bureaucratisation and professionalisation of interventionist child care" (p. 233). This latter trend has transformed childhood "from privacy, non-regulation and minimal legal protection into public regulation by a phalanx of specialist agencies" (p. 237).

Othering

Meloy (2000) refers to how late modernity has effectively "othered" the sex offender to distance him/her from the rest of society (p. 13). Others note how the very "unchanging essence" of the pedophile provides the context for the deployment of laws to regulate his behavior and provide him with the lowly status as the "most frequented cultural toilet" (Kincaid, 1998, pp. 88, 94). The epistemologies contributing to CSA's hegemony also require a reified "other": conceived either through governmental and media demonizations of the pedophile as the ultimate immoral "folk devil," a shadowy, pathological individual, an "enemy within," or as an abuser or sex offender, with either an insatiable appetite for power and control or a need to compensate for low self-esteem, a prior history of abuse, or the waning of a series of miscellaneous situational inhibitors (Yuill & Evans, 2006).

This process was also evident in the media and political attacks against the researchers. These were of a two-pronged nature in which the individuals themselves were variously described as irresponsible, unsound, or dangerous, as were the very ideas they were supposedly promulgating, which were characterized as giving succour to pedophiles. Vern Bullough calls this the "Pedophilia Smear,"[37] whereby, "self-appointed guardians of American morality like Laura Schlessinger" target sex researchers, "tarring them with the brush" of their subject matter and accusing them of either being a pedophile or having pedophile sympathies.

Privileging

The third process of the entrenchment of a hegemonic sexual epistemological hierarchy is seen as crucial to the ways in which both non-victimological accounts of intergenerational sexualities, and of critical researchers, have been constituted within mainstream discourses. Its very consolidation has enabled mainstream CSA and conservative perspectives to sign up to a monolithic lexicon, which Kincaid terms "CSA talk" of "sex as power, control, denial" (Kincaid, 1998, p. 218). In this way, terms such as *vulnerability*,[38] *informed consent, immaturity, power, risk,* and *harm* have been effectively inserted into debates on intergenerational sexualities in a relatively uncontested fashion.

As seen in the CSA literature, and both narratives covered earlier, alternative constructions to CSA face an ensemble of counter-explanations from CSA contributors, including denial, collusion with abuser, and problematic characteristics associated with male socialization. The development of such an ever-expanding lexicon has also facilitated the construction of reified, oppositional binaries, such as abuser/abused (denoting an abusive relationship based on power/subjective discrepancies) or predator/victim (reinforcing biolologistic notions of inviolability, immutability, and immorality).

The formulation of such an epistemological hierarchy was also evident in the attacks against the researchers. For example, the opinions of professionals and academics (either in the field of child protection or sex offenders) were used in a "rent-a-quote" manner, to counter (or rubbish) the research(ers). Similarly to the way survivor accounts were constituted as the only permitted voice in mainstream theorizing and research in this area, highlighted in part two of this paper, so theoretical proponents of CSA were also thus positioned. In such presentations, professional discourses were often presented as "higher truths" coming from experts and workers in the field, with "obvious superiority" in the epistemological hierarchy. This was in stark contrast to the opinions of the researchers whose perspectives were formulated through a "discourse of derision" (Ball, 1997) as in some way lesser or irrelevant, or just deliberately misrepresented.

This facilitated various political reactions to the research(ers), ranging along a continuum from mere disapproval or a call for injunctions, to more direct demands for outright censorship and harassment. Often it started with fairly mild comments from local politicians, children's charity representatives, or church leaders, rebuking the researchers, stirring up populist opinion against them, or even questioning whether public monies should be spent on such work. This was often followed by politicians (usually right-wing conservatives—either US Republicans or UK Tories) encouraging, or directly involving themselves in, displays of pique or moral outrage that such researchers should even criticize CSA, question notions of childhood sexual innocence, or discuss pedophilia. Such campaigns often culminated in direct pressure being exerted on a particular funding body, institution, or publisher to cease supporting such work. Finally, these efforts often brought about sustained harassment of critics and their families, through media intrusion, threats to career and future funding applications, and, most sinister of all, personal endangerment, including death threats, both face-to-face and via phone and e-mail.

Resisting

Critics have referred to the "problematic contradiction in combating CSA by questioning the assumption of the passive child" (James & Prout 1997: 30), and how the "top-down model of child abuse derives partly from the dominant image of the vulnerable child," which contrasts with the inclusion of boys under fourteen as sex offenders and the apparent similarity of sex crimes committed by both children and adults (Wyness, 2000, pp. 56, 83, 85).

This contradiction explains why children and young people are constituted as helpless and disempowered dupes in CSA frameworks, and why positive accounts cannot be given any substantive weight. For example, Alcoff (1996) justifies current injunctions on intergenerational sexualities by reference to children's powerless position, rendering them vulnerable to adult sexual attention in intergenerational sexual encounters (p. 122). However, she does want them to be allowed to develop and maintain their own sexual difference "either with themselves or with each other" (p. 126); and proffers a utopian "transformative future ... in which children could be, for the first time ... free from the economy of adult sexual desire and adult sexual demands," and where "the sexuality of children that emerges from it ... will be determined then and only then by children themselves" (p. 133).

Alcoff claims to facilitate the development of young people's sexual difference by protecting them from adult impositions. However, this position itself imposes a politically normative schema on the direction young people's sexuality should take—one that fails to facilitate the very autonomy and self-determination that she asserts should be the central aim in child protection measures.

The earlier contributions by Kincaid (1992, 1998) and Kitzinger (1997) on the key foundations (unknowing and passivity) underpinning victimological ideology provide a more convincing lens for analyzing the construction of CSA accounts than does Waites's position referred to earlier. Rather than simply accepting that researchers or theorists need to understand that individuals in intergenerational relationships will inevitably adopt available cultural discourses, these authors provide a critical interrogation of those very discourses. This includes: critiquing the privileged position held by CSA in the framing of intergenerational experiences, whereby children and young people (including adults who retrospectively reflect on those experiences) must compulsorily assume the status of disempowered victims; and interrogating mainstream perspectives' inability or unwillingness to countenance alternative, empowered notions of children and young peoples' rights.

A Foucauldian resistance strategy to the dominance of such CSA truths needs to address four key points. First, identify "the agents, institutions and discourses which have authority in defining what is to be considered normal, beautiful and desirable in a given society" (Hakosalo, 1991, p. 7). Second, interrogate the power-knowledge regime "that defines and produces each epoch's distinctive subjects and objects of knowledge and power" (Hartsock, 1996, p. 19). Third, recast "subjectivity outside dominant discourses," to transcend forms of power that transfer the subject into a discursive instrument of "truth" (Kritzman, 1988, p. xv). Finally, effect "changes in power relations and the development of subjectivities grounded in the experience of dominated and marginalized" people (Hartsock, 1996, p. 52), through developing "alternative systems of meaning" (McWhorter, 1999, p. 199), and "new forms of subjectivity" (Nilson, 1998, p. 105). A major corollary of such insights could be formulated around an elaborated conception of children and young peoples' empowerment—one that eschews infantilized, disempowered, and unitary notions of childhood, in favor of an active agency status whereby children are central players in the shaping of their social and intimate worlds. This perspective is also informed by existing theoretical approaches that assign subject status to young people, whereby they are conceptualized as active participants in the construction of the social reality of their everyday social contexts (Wyness, 2000; Frosh, Phoenix, & Pattman, 2002). Such perspectives critique developmental approaches, contesting the view that young people should be treated as subjects with participatory status, rather than being processed through an "adult gaze" (James, Jenks, & Prout, 1998), or positioned as "socially out of play" (Bourdieu, 1993, p. 96).

Such an empowerment thesis would seek to effect key practical and institutional transformations in crucial aspects of children and young people's lives, encouraging substantial consultation on decisions affecting them, thereby effecting the realization of a more elaborate conception of rights, and taking the debate beyond limited, tokenistic articulations of rights. This could include drawing on existing policy praxis in which young people are tacitly, and on occasions expressly, assumed capable of giving "informed" consent (see Waites, 2005).[39] It could also identify structural impediments to young people effectively realizing a more agentic subject status. This would not only provide alternative conceptual understandings to mainstream contemporary immutable presentations of young people as "at risk" and "vulnerable" (West, 1999; Kelly, 1999), but would also begin redressing wider concerns over the lack of opportunities given to young people in Western late modernity.

Such a radical, transformative, and empowering conception of children's rights has the potential to challenge dominant CSA notions that children and young people in intergenerational relationships are effectively "cultural dupes," thereby reducing the victimization of children by declassifying them as "as powerless beings" (Federle quoted in Freeman, 1997, p. 11). However, Thorogood (2000) cautions that it is those very empowerment strategies that result in merely reconstituting young people "as objects of disciplinary power" (p. 436). Clearly the full implications of any transformative empowering agenda for children and young people require greater theorizing and research.

Whereas Adams (1997) may be too optimistic in hoping to usher in a situation in which sex is not perceived as something from which young people need to be protected, it is to a position further along such a continuum that future sexual agendas on child and intergenerational sexualities need to traverse. This may also facilitate what Kincaid (1998) identifies as new ways "of imagining new actions and new beings" (p. 290), alongside recognizing in intergenerational sexualities "desiring collectivities," a more agentic subjectivity, and looking "beyond crude categories" (Dowsett, 2000, pp. 41, 44). It may also provide opportunities for research that is not infused with victimological assumptions and that accredit positive experiences of intergenerational relationships given by children and young people with the same agentic status as survivor accounts.

CONCLUSION

This paper provides a wider theoretical and policy-making framework for critically analyzing the original decision by Haworth Press to censor Bruce Rind's article. The eight case studies selected outline the multiple ways critics of CSA in the UK and US have been intimidated through a series of systematic political attacks, punitive legal injunctions, financial penalties, and harassment to stifle debate. One publisher should therefore not be singled out for criticism. Instead, any forthcoming wrath should be directed at mainstream Anglo-American culture, which has produced a victimological hegemony based on lazy reductionist theorizing, fear, and intolerance of iconoclastic contributions to child and intergenerational sexualities.

As Foucault suggests, children's sexuality has been constructed in late modernity as a problematic area, in which truths have been increasingly constituted through a globalized set of power relations, via an ensemble of multidisciplinary professional gazes. This has resulted in the effective colonization of child and intergenerational sexual experiences, through an imposed hegemonic implantation of victimological truths.

I maintain that central to this globalized hegemony is an Enlightenment notion of childhood, which positions children and young people as vulnerable, disempowered beings. Victimological CSA discourses have been able to co-opt this successfully as a foundational cultural ideal, one that they have constituted as a received "sexual truth," providing the basis for an epistemological and ontological "certainty" that intergenerational relationships are immoral.

By co-opting childhood innocence and powerlessness in their literature, victimological professionals and theorists have elevated CSA as the only permitted discourse in theorizing, researching, and speaking about intergenerational sexualities in Anglo-American culture. This is reinforced by victim-advocate and right-wing political groups, who have been able to use such discourses in establishing their respective power bases through academic funding and media access. This also explains why the social and cultural climate in the United States and UK provides such a paucity of social and material resources open to alternative critical approaches, and why such perspectives will likely face continuing injunctions in the near future. It also explains the privileged status of experiential accounts from survivors of CSA as the only subjects "allowed" to speak on intergenerational sexualities and why non-victimological accounts are either marginalized or silenced altogether.

However, the present stranglehold of this monolithic victimological epistemology is encountering increasing resistance. This is because of the fact that its foundations, namely, a narrow, shallow Enlightenment conception of children and young people as cultural dupes, is only partially embedded within Anglo-American culture. Indeed, the severity and concerted attempts of all the various proponents of CSA's dominance to stifle any critical research, theoretical alternative, or non-victimological account suggests a grudging recognition that the current taboos and proscriptions surrounding child and intergenerational sexualities, are, and will in the near future, face overwhelming challenges, most likely when children and young people themselves increasingly contest the dominant truths imposed by others on their sexuality.

NOTES

1. For example, Foucault (1977) refers to the development in late modernity of a clinical gaze, in which physicians can identify the particular problem to diagnose and treat it, subsequently achieving an enhanced status.
2. This term was relayed to me during the course of my research by a worker at a gay and lesbian center in Scotland, who stated that it was frequently used in the contemporary scene to describe a gay youth actively seeking a relationship with older men (see Yuill, 2004, ch. 9).
3. See A. Palmer, "Silent Witness," *Sunday Telegraph*, March 24, 2002, p. 25.
4. Quoted in John Carey, "The Age of Innocents," *Sunday Times* (London), March 7, 1993, "Features," 9–11.
5. Quoted in James Dalrymple, "Anger over US Don's Support for Paedophiles," *Sunday Times* (London), March 7, 1993, n.p.
6. Edward Verity, "Paedophile Book Should Be Banned'," *Daily Mail* (London), March 8, 1993, n.p.
7. Both Houston and Wyre went on to imply that Li's employer, Dykebar Hospital in Paisley, Scotland, should seriously consider his position. Quoted in Fiona Montgomery, "Doctor in Child Sex Fury," *Glasgow Evening Times*, July 3, 1996, n.p.c
8. Quoted in Steve Doughty, "Children's right to sex, by sociologist," *Daily Mail* (London) April 9, 1997, n.p.
9. See Shujaul Azam, "Sociologist slammed as 'sick' report asks ...Should we let kids have sex," *South London Press,* April 22, pp. 1–2.
10. This was confirmed in an e-mail I received from Waites's supervisor at the time, Professor Jeffrey Weeks, March 25, 2006.
11. For a detailed chronology of the attacks, see Rind et al. (2000, 2001) and Ericksen (2000).
12. NARTH consists mainly of therapists who believe that homosexuality is a developmental disorder in need of treatment and prevention. They have also mounted attacks on alleged academic supporters of pedophilia. "Pedophiles Argue Their Case in the Journal of homosexuality," at http://www.narth.com/docs/arguecase.html (Accessed January 31, 2000), and "On the Pedophilia Issue: What the APA Should Have known," at http://www.narth.com/docs/whatapa.html (Accessed August 8, 2000).
13. See "Dr. Laura Blasts APA for Publishing Pro-Pedophilia Propaganda," *CultureFacts,* March 24, 1999, at http://www.frc.org/culture/cu99c4.html (Accessed August 3, 2000).
14. This group is now called the Leadership Council on Child Abuse & Interpersonal Violence (see http://www.leadershipcouncil.org).
15. "Is Pedophilia Really Being Normalized?" *Family Research Report* (April, May 1999), at http://www.familyresearchinst.org/FRR_99_05.html (Accessed August 3, 2000).
16. "Mainstream Book Advocating Adult-Child Sex Draws Howls of Protest," *Fox News,* April 2, 2002.

17. John Leo, "Apologists for pedophilia," *US News & World Report* Cover, *Culture & Ideas*, April 22, 2002, n.p.
18. Robert Worth, "Renegade View on Child Sex Causes a Storm," *The New York Times,* April 13, 2002, n.p.
19. 19 Lynn Franey, "Many criticize professor's writings on pedophilia," *Kansas City Star,* April 1, 2002.
20. Morris Sullivan, (no date) "Trampling the Last Taboo Pedophilia, politicians and academic freedom," at http://www.impactpress.com/articles/junjul02/mirkin6702.html (Accessed July 10, 2006)
21. "Professor's article on pedophilia fans outrage," *CNN News,* April 30, 2002, http://archives.cnn.com/2002/US/04/30/ped.writing.professor (Accessed July 2006)
22. See "Missouri House cuts university budget out of anger" at: http://www.kmovcom/education/education stories/kmov education 020405 mizzoufunding.47a3df34.html (Accessed July 10, 2006)
23. This group can be accessed at www.ipce.info
24. Van Engelen is the chair of a foundation named "Soelaas," which campaigns in the Netherlands on a traditional conservative, pro-family and anti-pedophile platform.
25. Marcello Mega, "Inquiry into researchers' links with paedophiles," *Scottish Mail on Sunday,* September 9, 2001, n.p.
26. Marcello Mega, "If no rules have been broken, perhaps the rulebook requires some attention," *THES,* November 23, 2001, p. 18.
27. Marcello Mega, "Police probe child sex research files," *Scottish Mail on Sunday,* July 28, 2002, n.p.
28. James Mulholland and Marcello Mega, "Paedophiles Confess Sick Crimes But Dodge Arrest," *Scottish News of the World,* August 25, 2002, p. 13.
29. Marcello Mega, "PhD researcher gave anonymity to child abusers," *THES,* August 9, 2002, n.p.
30. Durham quoted in the *THES,* December 3, 2004, p. 3.
31. Chris Harrison, quoted in *THES,* December 3, 2004, p. 3.
32. Anne Houston, quoted in *Sky News,* December 2, 2004 at http://www.sky.com/skynews/article/0,,30000-13258957,00.html (Accessed December, 21, 2004)
33. See Martin Williams, "Thesis on paedophile relationships puts University in middle of controversy," *Glasgow Herald,* December 2, 2004, p. 3. O'Connell's own research could itself have been criticized on ethical standards. See article "One researcher posed as a child online, and deliberately baited paedophiles," at http://www.spiked-online.com/articles/00000006DEAA.htm (Accessed July 10, 2006)
34. This journal can be accessed at www.socresonline.org.uk. The feedback on my article was received by e-mail in April 2005.
35. These events will formed the basis of an article by Pat Sikes in 2006 entitled "A Cautionary Tale Concerning Journalists and Moral Panic," *Research Intelligence* 95, pp. 4–6
36. The *TES* followed this up with Sophie Kirkham's article entitled, "Dangerous liaisons in class," November 11, 2005, p. 3.
37. See V. Bullough, (no date) "The Pedophilia Smear," http://theposition.com/takingpositions/provocateur/00/06/05/pedophilia/default.htm (Accessed October 10, 2002).
38. Indeed, for Foucault the very notion of "vulnerability" as a construct in such relationships, has developed a whole body of psychological knowledge, "imbibed from psychoanalysis, where the psychologist is the one who is able to say: I can predict that a trauma of this degree of importance will occur as a result of this or that type of relationship" (Foucault, 1988, p. 277).
39. There have been some embryonic attempts where young people have been instrumental in attempts to increase their participation in decisions affecting them, notably through campaign groups such as Article 12 (www.article12.org.), who run regional

organizations where young people formulate policies and decisions on a range of issues.

References

Adams, M. (1997). *The trouble with normal: Post-war youth and the making of heterosexuality.* Toronto: University of Toronto.
Alcoff, L. (1996). Dangerous sexualities: Pedophilia. In S. Hekman (Ed.), *Feminist interpretations of Michael Foucault* (pp. 99–136). University Park: Pennsylvania State University Press.
Bagley, C. (1999). Children first: Challenges and dilemmas for social workers investigating and treating child sexual abuse. In C. Bagley and K. Mallick (Eds.), *Child sexual abuse and adult offenders: New theory and research* (pp. 27–47). Aldershot, UK: Ashgate.
Ball, S. (1997). Policy sociology and critical social research: A personal review of recent policy and policy research. *British Educational Research Journal, 23,* 257–274.
Bourdieu, P. (1993). *Sociology in question.* London: Sage Publications.
Coxell, A., King, M., Mezey, G. & Gordon, D. (1999). Lifetime prevalence, characteristics, and associated problems of non-consensual sex in men: Cross-sectional survey. *British Medical Journal, 318,* 846–850.
Dowsett, G. (2000). Bodyplay: Corporeality in a discursive silence. In R. Parker, R. Barbosa and P. Aggleton (Eds.), *Framing the sexual subject: The politics of gender, sexuality and power* (pp. 29–45). Berkeley: University of California Press.
Durham, A. (2003). *Young men surviving child sexual abuse: Research stories and lessons for therapeutic practice.* Bognor Regis: Wiley and Sons.
Ericksen, J. (2000). Sexual liberation's last frontier, *Society, 37,* 21–25.
Evans, D. (1993). *Sexual citizenship. The material construction of sexualities.* London: Routledge.
Ferenczi, S. (1932). The Confusion of tongues between the adult and the child. In J. Masson (1992). *The assault on truth: Freud's suppression of the seduction theory.* New York: Harper Collins Publishers.
Finkelhor, D. (1981). *Sexually victimized children.* New York: Free Press.
_____. (1984). *Child sexual abuse: New theories and research.* New York: Free Press.
_____. (1991). Response to the Bauserman critique. In T. Sandfort et al. (Eds.), *Male intergenerational intimacy: Historical, socio-psychological, and legal perspectives* (pp. 313–315). New York: Harrington Park Press.
Foucault, M. (1980). *Power/Knowledge: Selected interviews and other writings 1972–1977.* New York: The Harvester Press.
_____. (1977). *Discipline and punish: The birth of the prison.* London: Penguin.
_____. (1978). *The history of sexuality, volume one: An introduction.* New York: Pantheon.
_____. (1977). Power and Sex. In L. Kritzman (Ed.) (1988). *Michel Foucault: Politics, philosophy, culture: Interviews and other writings* (pp. 110–124). New York: Routledge.
Foucault, M., Hocquenghem, G. & Danet, J. (1978). Sexual morality and the law. In L. Kritzman (Ed.) (1988). *Michel Foucault: Politics, philosophy, culture: Interviews and other writings* (pp. 271–285). New York: Routledge.
Freeman, M. (1997). *The moral status of children: Essays on the rights of the child.* The Hague: Martinus Nijhoff Publishers.
Frosh, S., Phoenix, A., & Pattman, R. (2002). *Young masculinities: Understanding boys in contemporary society.* New York: Palgrave.
Furedi, F. (2001). *Paranoid parenting: Abandon your anxieties and be a good parent.* London: Allen Lane.
Garvey, N. (1999). "I wasn't raped, but...": Revisiting definitional problems in sexual victimization. In S. Lamb (Ed.), *New versions of victims: Feminists struggle with the concept* (pp. 57–81). New York: New York University Press.
Glaser, D., & Frosh, S. (1993). *Child sexual abuse: Practical social work.* London: MacMillian Press.
Hakosalo, H. (1991). *Bio-power and pathology: Science and power in the Foucauldian histories of medicine, psychiatry and sexuality.* Oulu, Finland: Ouluensis Universitas.
Hartsock, N. (1989). Postmodernism and political change: Issue for feminist theory. In S. Hekman (Ed.). (1996). *Feminist interpretations of Michael Foucault* (pp. 39–58). University Park, PA: Pennsylvania State University Press.
Hunter, M. (1990). *Abused boys: The neglected victims of sexual abuse.* Lexington, MA: Lexington Books.

James, A., & Prout A. (Eds.). (1997). *Constructions and reconstructions of childhood: Contemporary issues in the sociological study of childhood.* London: Falmer Press.
James, A., Jenks, C., & Prout, A. (1998). *Theorising childhood.* Cambridge: Polity Press.
Jeffreys, S. (1990). *Anticlimax: A feminist perspective on the sexual revolution.* London: The Women's Press.
Jenkins (1998). *Moral panic: Changing concepts of the child molester in modern America.* New Haven, CT: Yale University Press.
Jenks, C. (Ed.). (1982). *The Sociology of childhood: Essential readings.* Aldershot: Gregg Revivals.
Kelly, P. (1999). "Wild and tame zones": Regulating the transitions of youth-at-risk. *Journal of Youth Studies, 2,* 193–211.
Kincaid, J. (1992). *Child-loving: The erotic child and victorian culture.* London: Routledge.
_____. (1998). *Erotic innocence: The culture of child molesting.* London: Duke University Press.
_____. (2004). Producing erotic children. In Steven Bruhm and Natasha Hurley (Eds.), *Curiouser: On the queerness of children* (pp. 3–16). Minneapolis: University of Minnesota Press.
King, N. (1995). *Speaking our truth: Voices of courage and healing for male survivors of childhood sexual abuse.* New York: Harper-Perennial.
Kitzinger, J. (1997). Who are you kidding? Children, power and the struggle against sexual abuse. In A. James, and A. Prout (Eds.), *Constructions and reconstructions of childhood: Contemporary issues in the sociological study of childhood* (pp. 157–183). London: Falmer Press.
Kritzman, L. Introduction: Foucault and the Politics of Experience. In Kritzman, L. (Ed.) (1988). *Michel Foucault: Politics, philosophy, culture: Interviews and other writings* (pp. IX–XXV). New York: Routledge.
_____. (Ed.) (1988). *Michel Foucault: Politics, philosophy, culture: Interviews and other writings.* New York: Routledge.
Lautmann, R. (1994). *The sexual attraction to children (Die Lust am Kind).* Hamburg: Ingrid Klein Pubs. Inc.
Leahy, T. (1992). Positively experienced man/boy sex: The discourse of seduction and the social construction of masculinity. *Australian and New Zealand Journal of Sociology, 28,* 71–88.
_____. (1996). Sex and the age of consent: The ethical Issues. *Social Analysis, 39,* 27–55.
Lemert, C., & Gillan, G. (1982). *Michael Foucault: Social theory and transgression.* New York: Columbia University Press.
Leo, J. (2002). "Apologists for pedophilia," *US News & World Report* Cover, *Culture & Ideas,* April 22, 2002, n.p.
Levine, J. (2002). *Harmful to minors: The perils of protecting children from sex.* Minneapolis: University of Minnesota Press.
Lew, M., & Bass, E. (1990). *Victims no longer: Men recovering from incest and other sexual child abuse.* New York: Harper Collins.
Li, C-K. (1987). *Sexual experiences of adults with children: An analysis of personal accounts.* Unpublished Ph.D. thesis. Cambridge: Cambridge University.
_____. (1990). "The main thing is being wanted": Some case studies on adult sexual experiences with children. *Journal of Homosexuality, 20,* 129–143.
_____. (1993). Adult sexual experiences with children. In C. Li, D. West, and T. Woodhouse (Eds.), *Children's sexual encounters with adults* (pp. 139–316). Buffalo, NY: Prometheus.
McWhorter, L. (1999). *Bodies and pleasures: Foucault and the politics of sexual normalisation.* Indianapolis: Indiana University Press.
Meloy, M. (2000). "Stranger danger": Some problems with community notification. In K. Buckley and P. Head (Eds.), *Myths, risks and sexuality: The role of sexuality in working with people.* Lyme Regis, UK: Russell House.
Mirkin, H. (1999). The pattern of sexual politics: Feminism, homosexuality and pedophilia. *Journal of Homosexuality, 37,* 1–24.
_____. (2000). Sex, science, and sin: The Rind Report, sexual politics and American scholarship. *Sexuality and Culture, 4,* 82–100.
Nilson, H. (1998). *Michael Foucault and the games of truth.* London: Macmillan Press.
Okami, P. (1990). Sociopolitical biases in the contemporary scientific literature on adult human sexual behavior with children and adolescents. In J. Feierman (Ed.), *Pedophilia: Biosocial dimensions* (pp. 91–121). New York: Springer-Verlag.

_____. (1992). Child perpetrators of sexual abuse: The emergence of a problematic deviant category. *The Journal of Sex Research, 29,* 109–130.
Plummer, K. (1995). 1995 *Telling sexual stories: Power, change and social worlds.* London: Routledge.
Reavey, P., & Warner, S. (Eds.).. (2002). *New feminist stories of child sexual abuse: Sexual scripts and dangerous dialogue.* London: Routledge.
_____. (2006). *Research findings and controversies in child sexual abuse and pederasty.* Talk presented at Cornell University, February 16.
Rind, B., Bauserman, R., & Tromovitch, P. (1998). A meta-analytic examination of assumed properties of child sexual abuse using college samples. *Psychological Bulletin, 124,* 22–53.
_____. (2000). Condemnation of a scientific article: A chronology and refutation of the attacks and a discussion of threats to the integrity of science. *Sexuality and Culture, 4,* 1–62.
_____. (2001a). The validity and appropriateness of methods, analyses, and conclusions in Rind et al. (1998): A rebuttal of victimological critique from Ondersma et al. (2001) and Dallam et al. (2001). *Psychological Bulletin, 127,* 734–758.
_____. (2001b). The condemned meta-analysis on child sexual abuse: Good science and long-overdue skepticism. *Skeptical Inquirer,* 68–72
Sandfort, T. (1987). *Boys on their contacts with men.* New York: Global Academic Publishers.
Schlessinger, L. (1999). Article on pedophilia is just "junk science." *Times-Picayune,* April 18, E6.
Scott, S. (2001). *The politics and experience of ritual abuse: Beyond disbelief.* Buckingham, UK: Open University Press.
Sikes, P. (2006). Scandalous stories and dangerous liaisons: When male teachers and female pupils fall in love. *Sex Education.* 6, 3, 265–280.
Spiegel, D. (2000a). Suffer the children: Long-term effects of sexual abuse. *Society, 37,* 18–20.
_____. (2000b). The price of abusing children and numbers. *Sexuality & Culture, 4(2),* 63–66.
Thorogood, N. (2000). Sex education as disciplinary technique: Policy and practice in England and Wales, *Sexualities, 3,* 425–438.
Victor, J. (1998). Moral panics and the social construction of deviant behavior: A theory and application to the case of ritual child abuse. *Sociological Perspectives, 41,* 541–565.
Waites, M. (1999). The age of consent, homosexuality and citizenship in the United Kingdom (1885–1999): A history. In J. Seymour and P. Bagguley (Eds.), *Relating intimacies: Power and resistance* (pp. 91–117). London: Macmillan.
_____. (2005). *The age of consent: Young people, sexuality and citizenship.* Basingstoke, UK: Palgrave Macmillan.
West, D. (1998). Boys and sexual abuse, *Archives of Sexual Behavior, 27,* 539–559.
West, J. (1999). (Not) talking about sex: Youth, identity and sexuality, *The Sociological Review, 47,* 525–547.
Wyness, G. (2000). *Contested Childhood.* London: Falmer Press.
Yuill, R. (2004). *Male age-discrepant intergenerational sexualities and relationships.* Unpublished Ph.D. thesis. Department of Sociology, University of Glasgow.
Yuill, R, and D. Evans (2007). "Pedophilia." In G. Ritzer (Ed.), *The Blackwell Encyclopedia of Sociology, 7,* 3385–3387. Oxford: Blackwell Publishing.

Chapter 4

BLINDED BY SCIENCE: A CRITIQUE OF RIND'S VIEWS ON PEDERASTY

RICHARD D. MCANULTY & LESTER W. WRIGHT JR.

[Editors' Note: Some details of this essay respond to an earlier, more detailed version of Rind's chapter. Rind has included the omitted section as an Appendix to his response in Chapter 12.]

In the current article, Rind offers an overview of the scientific data on pederasty, with special emphasis on the question of harmfulness. Like his previous work (Rind, 2001; 2003; Rind & Bauserman, 1993; Rind & Tromovitch, 1997; Rind, Bauserman, & Tromovitch, 1999; Rind, Tromovitch, & Bauserman, 1998; 2001), the current review proposes to advance the scientific understanding of pederasty by focusing on relevant and representative research while excluding nonrepresentative studies (i.e., clinical-forensic samples). The current review also attempts the ambitious task of offering historical, cross-cultural, and cross-species perspectives on pederasty. Rind concludes his review by suggesting that pederasty has been common, widespread, and potentially adaptive in some contexts.

Rind's summary of contemporary popular and professional views of pederasty is that such relations are universally and inherently harmful to minors. Furthermore, such harm will be evident in several areas of functioning, including school, career, and social relationships. Treating these views as the "null hypothesis," Rind argues that although confirming anecdotes or cases cannot be used to verify these claims (after all, one can never accept the null hypothesis, only reject it), consistent disconfirming anecdotes can be used to reject the null hypothesis. He assures the reader that such disconfirming anecdotes are indeed "abundant," particularly in the gay population.

The abundance of evidence from the gay population reviewed by Rind essentially entails six cases and five "nonrandom" surveys. Rind concludes his review of these sources by stating that pederasty is commonly a positive experience for minors. He decisively discards the null hypothesis by asserting that the "inadequacies of these hypotheses, which dominate popular and professional discourse, with respect to empirical reality are huge." The views of his critics, he alleges, have not been subjected to scientific scrutiny despite obvious shortcomings. In our view, Rind's analysis is subject to the very criticisms that he levels at his critics. Specifically, we hope to show that several of the cases and surveys that Rind cites as evidence are in fact flawed and potentially biased. By relying on such questionable sources, we argue that Rind is guilty of using the very double standard that he identifies in his critics.

Case Studies or Autobiographies?

Rind complained that critics have relied on biased and nonrepresentative anecdotes to argue that the practice of pederasty is harmful. He argued that disconfirming anecdotes abound, especially in the gay population. He proposed to use case studies to support his argument. However, his case studies are mostly brief summaries of autobiographies. This implies that case studies and autobiographies are equivalent, which is debatable.

The case study is an accepted research method, consisting of an intensive description or study of an individual (Trull, 2005). It is viewed as particularly useful for studying unique and uncommon cases and also as a prelude to investigation using other scientific methods. Autobiographies, or memoirs, are a literary genre. Case studies are intended to be informative and descriptive. Autobiographies are supposed to be entertaining and mostly accurate. However, several recent controversial memoirs show that a certain creative license is tolerated, if not expected.

Writing under the pseudonym of Margaret B. Jones, author Margaret Seltzer recently admitted that she fabricated an "autobiography" entitled *Love and Consequences*. The story of her alleged childhood as a "gangbanger" and drug dealer in Los Angeles received rave reviews before the deception was revealed (Rich, 2008). This is certainly not the first time that a sensational autobiography was proven to be a ruse. Misha Defonseca's memoir of surviving the Holocaust years in Europe was exposed as a hoax (Shields, 2008). James Frey's (2003) best-selling account of his struggle to recover from drug addiction in *A Million Little Pieces* was proven to contain significant fabrications and embellishments (Peretz, 2008). After being confronted with inconsistencies, Frey eventually admitted that he made up critical segments of his story, and his publisher added a disclaimer in subsequent printings of the book. They also offered a refund to buyers of the book who felt duped by the deception.

According to former book review editor for the *New York Times*, Charles McGrath, fabrications frequently occur in autobiographies (Sterling, 2003). Shocking and sensational stories offer the prospect of fortune and fame (Bissinger, 2007). Naturally, memoirs should be as accurate as possible, and readers should be informed of any exception. However, this is often not the case. It is, therefore, questionable, if not irresponsible, to conclude that a literary genre that is often sensational, subjective, and impervious to verification, can be used to draw scientific conclusions.

One case summary offered by Rind is that of Augusten Burroughs, a best-selling author of several memoirs. This case is important, because it allegedly involves a sexual encounter between 14-year-old Burroughs and a member of the clergy, culminating in what was described as his first "excellent" experience with fellatio by a priest (Burroughs, 2002b). This case is sensational on several accounts. Not only does it cast a negative light on the priesthood, the memoir was also the subject of tremendous controversy and litigation. In his summary of the case, Rind failed to mention any of the controversy surrounding Burroughs's memoir entitled *Running with Scissors*. If Rind is to be objective, impartial, and thorough in his review, he owes it to his audience to present both sides of the story rather than only the portions that appear consistent with his views.

In addition to his alleged sexual encounters with priests, Burroughs (2002a) claimed that his mother effectively abandoned him to be reared by her psychiatrist and his dysfunctional family. The memoir is replete with fantastic accounts, such the children administering electroconvulsive shock to each other, using an ECT machine kept under the stairway, the mother regularly consuming dry dog food, and the psychiatrist's designation of a room next to his office as his "masturbatorium" (Bissinger, 2007). Perhaps more doubtful is Burroughs's insistence that he vividly remembers learning to walk and being fed nicotine gum between bites of omelet as an 8-month-old! (Anderson, 2008). After the publication of the memoir, members of Burroughs's surrogate family filed a lawsuit against him and his publisher, alleging that the account was inaccurate, defamatory, and exaggerated for the sole purpose of promoting sales (Beggy & Shananan, 2006). Burroughs and his publisher settled the lawsuit out of court, and Burroughs later reportedly admitted that the book was only loosely based on a period of his life (Ngowi, 2007). It is worth noting that Burroughs's follow-up memoir, *Dry* (2003), has been described as fiction (Yardley, 2003). The author himself confessed that some parts of the latter memoir were "imaginative re-creation" and that it included fabrications (Sterling, 2003).

If Rind is to offer case examples to contradict "universalistic claims or views" of the harmfulness of pederasty, these should be objective, unbiased, and informative. In our view, autobiographies would not usually meet these criteria, therefore, they cannot be treated as equivalent to scientific case studies. Similarly, the case of Harry Hay is not likely to be viewed as an unbiased account. As an outspoken advocate of the North American Man-Boy Love Association (NAMBLA), Hay's views on pederasty are probably just as "heavily invested with ideology" as those of the sexual victimology movement.

"Representative" Research Studies

One of Rind's key points is that findings from studies using clinical samples cannot be generalized to the entire population. To correct this problem, he reviewed several studies that he viewed as more relevant and presumably unbiased. Two in particular are worthy of mention: *The Gay Report* by Jay and Young (1979) and *The Spada Report* (Spada, 1979).

According to Rind, both reports include "representative examples" of adult-minor sex that is a positive experience for the younger person. However, Rind failed to mention any of the profound methodological problems with both surveys.

English professor Karla Jay and journalist Allan Young (1979) conducted the pioneering survey known as *The Gay Report*. At the time, their study was described as the first comprehensive survey of the gay and lesbian community. It was, however, severely criticized on methodological grounds (Burroway, 2006). By the authors' own estimate, as many as 400,000 gay men and women were exposed to the survey, yet only 4,239 completed it, which represents a response rate of approximately 1 percent. Such a response rate would invalidate virtually any survey (Lauritsen, 1979). The likelihood of sampling bias is quite high: 2,462 of the questionnaires, or 58 percent, were obtained from the readership of *Blueboy*, a gay pornographic magazine. Additionally, some questionnaires were distributed to patrons of "all-male movie theaters in Boston and Los Angeles" (Jay & Young, p. 9) and even to men cruising a rest area near Holyoke, Massachusetts. Unless one assumes that the gay community is unusually homogeneous, any serious researcher would have to conclude that the survey suffers from sampling bias. Indeed, some critics have described it as "statistically worthless" (Burroway, 2006) and "hopelessly inept" (Lauritsen, 1979). In fact, the very authors of *The Gay Report* admitted that they "do not claim to have a scientific or representative sample of lesbians and gay men" (Jay & Young, p. 9). We find it curious that Rind nevertheless concluded that it provides "representative examples of childhood and adolescent male homosexual experiences with both peers and older males."

Similar methodological problems exist with *The Spada Report* (Spada, 1979). It relied completely on an open-ended questionnaire that is not even reproduced in the report. The qualitative report essentially includes verbatim responses selected from several of 1,038 gay men. Most participants were Caucasian, college-educated, and Protestant. The scientific value of the project was seriously compromised by the data tables, which have been described as "shockingly bad" and meaningless (Lauritsen, 1979). Rind did not mention any of these methodological limitations, contending instead that these surveys were devised in order to correct the misconceptions about pederasty derived from "anomalous clinical samples." The assumption that these survey results are valid and representative is an empirical question.

Conclusions

As he has done in his previous articles (Rind et al., 1998; 2001; 2003), Rind discounted all studies based on clinical and forensic samples as unrepresentative. The problem with relying solely on community samples is that it may result in the exclusion of individuals who are most negatively affected by pederasty (Dallam et al., 2001; Haugaard & Emery, 1989). This is akin to deciding that any person who is so severely impacted by a sexual experience with an older person that he requires professional help will systematically be excluded, which could result in a significant underestimation of the harmfulness of pederasty. This problem is compounded by Rind's reliance on questionable "case studies" and surveys to disconfirm the "null hypothesis" that pederasty is invariably and universally harmful to underage persons.

We agree with Rind that scientists must be more "scientific in their treatment of this topic." To that end, scientists must be objective, skeptical, and unbiased in reviewing and reporting research results. These criteria require researchers to report not only the research findings that support their views and assumptions, but also the methodological limitations of the same studies. Anything less gives the impression that the scientist in question is clinging to "firmly entrenched and facilely reached opinion" regarding the subject under study, pederasty in this case. Like other critics of Rind's conclusions have noted, "Our deeper concerns—like those of many—lie less with the data than with their presentation (Ondersma et al., 2001, p. 708). As a result, critics will continue to question the motives of scientists like Rind, leading to more accusations of advocacy (see Dallam, 2001, for example). The topic of pederasty is extremely socially and politically sensitive. Therefore, discussions of the topic will be subjected to unusual scrutiny. Any responsible and prudent discussion of such a sensitive topic requires balanced coverage.

References

Anderson, S. (2008). The memory addict. *New York Books,* April 27. Retrieved from http://nymag.com/arts/books/features/46475/

Beggy, C., & Shanahan, M. (2006). "Scissors" author accused as a fraud. *The Boston Globe,* December 5. Retrieved from http://www.boston.com/ae/celebrity/articles/2006/12/05/scissors_author_accused_as_a_fraud/

Bissinger, B. (2007). Ruthless with scissors. *Vanity Fair,* January 1. Retrieved from http://www.vanityfair.com/fame/features/2007/01/burroughs200701

Burroughs, A. (2003). *Dry: A memoir.* New York: St. Martin's Press.

_____. (2002a) *Running with scissors.* New York: St. Martin's Press.

_____. (2002b). A priest on his knees. *Salon.com.* Retrieved from: http://www.salon.com/sex/feature/2002/05/15/holy/index1.html

Burroway, J. (2006). The gay report. *Box Turtle Bulletin.* Retrieved from http://www.boxturtlebulletin.com/Articles/000,005.htm

Dallam, S. J. (2001). Science or propaganda? An examination of Rind, Tromovitch, and Bauserman (1998). *Journal of Child Sexual Abuse, 9,* 109–134.

Dallam, S. J., Gleaves, D. H., Cepeda-Benito, A., Silberg, J. L., Kraemer, H. C, & Spiegel, D. (2001). The effects of child sexual abuse: Comment on Rind, Tromovitch, and Bauserman (1998). *Psychological Bulletin, 127,* 715–733.

Defonseca, M. (1997). *Misha: A mémoire of the Holocaust years.* Mt. Ivy, NY: Mt. Ivy Press.

Frey, J. (2003). *A million little pieces.* Broadway, NY: Doubleday Books.

Haugaard, J. J., & Emery, R. E. (1989). Methodological issues in child sexual abuse research. *Child Abuse & Neglect, 13,* 89–100.

Jay, K., & Young, A. (1979). *The gay report.* New York: Simon & Schuster.

Lauritsen, J. (1979). Reviews: The gay report by Karla Jay and Allen Young & The Spada report by James Spada. Retrieved from http://www.williamapercy.com/wiki/index.php/Reviews:The_Gay_ Report_by_Karla_Jay_and_Allen_Young_&_The_Spada_Report_by_James_Spada

Ngowi, R. (2007). Burroughs settles lawsuit with "Scissors" family. *USA Today*, August 30. Retrieved from http://www.usatoday.com/life/books/news/2007-08-30-scissors-settlement_N.htm?POE=click-refer

Ondersma, S. J., Chaffin, M., Berliner, L., Cordon, I., Goodman, G., & Barnett, D. (2001). Sex with children is abuse: The Rind et al. meta-analysis controversy. *Psychological Bulletin, 27*, 707–714.

Peretz, E. (2008). James Frey's morning after. *Vanity Fair*, June. Retrieved from http://www.vanityfair.com/culture/features/2008/06/frey200806

Rich, M. (2008). Author admits acclaimed memoir is fantasy. *International Herald Tribune*, March 4. Retrieved from http://www.iht.com/articles/2008/03/04/arts/04fake.php?page=1

Rind, B. (2001). Gay and bisexual adolescent boys' sexual experiences with men: An empirical examination of psychological correlates in a nonclinical sample. *Archives of Sexual Behavior, 30*, 345–368.

_____. (2003). Adolescent sexual experiences with adults: Pathological or functional? *Journal of Psychology & Human Sexuality, 15*, 5–22.

Rind, B., & Bauserman, R. (1993). Biased terminology effects and biased information processing in research in adult-nonadult sexual interactions: An empirical investigation. *Journal of Sex Research, 30*, 260–269.

Rind, B., & Tromovitch, P. (1997). A meta-analytic review of findings from national samples on psychological correlates of child sexual abuse. *The Journal of Sex Research, 34*, 237–255.

Rind, B., Bauserman, R., & Tromovitch, P. (1999). Interpretation of research on sexual abuse of boys. *Journal of the American Medical Association, 281*, 2185.

Rind, B., Tromovitch, P., & Bauserman, R. (1998). A meta-analytic examination of assumed properties of child sexual abuse using college samples. *Psychological Bulletin, 124*, 22–53.

_____. (2001). The validity and appropriateness of methods, analyses, and conclusions in Rind et al. (1998): A rebuttal of victimological critique from Ondersma et al. (2001) and Dallam et al. (2001). *Psychological Bulletin, 127*, 734–758.

Shields, R. (2008). Adopted by wolves? Bestselling memoir was a pack of lies. *The Independent*, March 1. Retrieved from http://www.independent.co.uk/news/world/europe/adopted-by-wolves-bestselling-memoir-was-a-pack-of-lies-790000.html

Spada, J. (1979). *The Spada Report*. New York: Signet.

Sterling, T. G. (2003). Confessions of a memoirist. *Salon.com*, August 1. Retrieved from http://dir.salon.com/story/books/feature/archives/2003/08/01/gornick/index.html

Trull, T. J. (2005). *Clinical psychology* (7th ed.). Belmont, CA: Thomson Wadsworth.

Yardley, J. (2003). Belly up to the bore: An addict's memoir. *Washington Post*, July 3, C 01–05.

Chapter 5

A Critique of the Academic Process and Application of Evolutionary Theory in Pederasty: An Integration of Empirical, Historical, Sociological, Cross-Cultural, Cross-Species, and Evolutionary Perspectives by Dr. Bruce Rind

L. Eric Alcorn

Introduction

Dr. Rind introduces his manuscript, Pederasty: An Integration of Empirical, Historical, Sociological, Cross-Cultural, Cross-Species, and Evolutionary Perspectives, by explaining this iteration of the paper is the latest of several. An earlier version was to be published in a special edition of the *Journal of Homosexuality,* along with some ten reviews such as this. He also explains that the publisher, Taylor & Francis, decided to pull the publication. I was one of the ten reviewers for that publication. When Left Coast Press agreed to publish a shortened version of Dr. Rind's manuscript, I was asked by the editors to let my review stand. I rewrote my review with a couple stipulations, including commentary on the process of this publication as well as the science in the paper. This review critiques the terminology, use of sources, the application of evolutionary theory, and the Mentoring-Bonding / Enculturation-Alliance (MB/EA) Hypothesis and ends with a discussion concerning advocacy in academia.

Terminology

The precise use of terms is a hallmark of academia. Academics must be careful not to confuse or misinform a reader by using terms out of context, or by mixing multiple meanings. For example, a term like *adaptation* can mean very different things in different contexts. It could be a physical manifestation, such as a welt forming in response to an injury, a behavioral response, such as a bear entering a cave to stay warm, a societal response, such as a town digging a well to ensure a constant supply of clean water, or a moral adaptation, such as a society developing taboos to prevent murder. In each case, the event is an adaptation, but in no two cases are they the same kind of adaptation. Thus, it is incumbent on academics to clearly reveal the context, and what meaning, we are invoking when we use such terms. Throughout the manuscript, Dr. Rind uses these polyseme terms as though the meanings were interchangeable, which is not only inaccurate, but can easily confuse the reader. As revealed in the example just mentioned, the term *adaptation* is one such case. *Adaptation,* when used in the context of culture (anthropology), or sociology, or biology, has different meanings. The term *evolutionary adaptation* has a very specific meaning that involves genetics, inheritance, and natural selection. The term, in this specific biological sense, should not be applied to culture or sociology. Evolutionary adaptation does not equal adaptation in general. Yet, Dr. Rind applies the term *adaptation* to passages concerning culture, social environments, and evolution, without ever distinguishing its contextual meanings. *Evolution* is another such term. Like adaptation, evolution, when used in different disciplines or by the lay public, has different meanings. For example, in the section Manhood Ideologies, Dr. Rind talks of manhood as an evolved capacity, in a social sense, not a biological one. Besides the non-contextual use of terms, he uses other terms that are functionally ambiguous to imply connection where none exists. The most obvious example of this is the term *pederastic-like behavior.* This term is new to this version of the manuscript, and I suspect it is in response to my earlier criticism concerning the un-contextualized use of animal data in interpreting human behavior. At no point does Dr. Rind define the term, and more importantly, he makes no attempt to distinguish pederastic-like behavior from pederasty. Terms such as this may appear scientific but are ill-defined at best, and meaningless at worst, because they do not explain to what degree they are like, but yet not the same as the object term. As with adaptation and evolution, terms such as *pederasty-like* provide the reader no distinction between meanings or context. Whether or not this is the desired effect, this fluid use of terms can make apparent connections and equivalents where there are none.

Sources: *Cherry Picking and Misrepresentation*

In the earlier version of the manuscript, Dr. Rind relied heavily on Bagemihl (1999), and de Waal (1997) as main sources of animal behavior evidence for his enculturation (evolution) model. After a careful reading of these sources, it became apparent that Dr. Rind was "cherry picking" the information, meaning he only mentioned points from these authors that specifically supported his theory and, more importantly, actively ignored evidence in the same sources that contradicted his theory. (See *Animal Behavior as Evidence of Inheritance* in this review.) The current version of the manuscript continues to show evidence of cherry picking sources. In one case, Adaptations, Exaptations, and Spandrels (Buss et al., 1998), Dr. Rind uses the paper to support the idea that pederasty is an evolved behavior, while at the same time ignoring the authors' clearly spelled out criteria for developing theories within evolutionary psychology, particularly, conforming to biological evolutionary theory, predictive power, parsimony, and standards concerning exaptations and spandrels. (See The Mentorship-Bonding / Enculturation-Alliance Hypothesis (MD/EA) in this review.) As well, he ignores their conclusion with respect to the total lack of evidence for exaptations or spandrels in evolutionary psychology theorizing. However, one of the most alarming cases is the use of Wade Mackey's paper, Adult-Male/Juvenile Association as a Species-Characteristic Human Trait: A Comparative Field Approach (1990). As he did with Bagemihl and de Waal in the previous edition, Dr. Rind relies heavily on Mackey's paper for support of his MD/EA Hypothesis. In fact, he cites this paper at least a half dozen times with respect to pederasty functioning to facilitate recruitment of boys into the adult male group. So, it was a surprise to discover that the paper has very little, if nothing at all, to do with pederasty. Mackey's paper is a survey of contemporary cultures documenting adult/juvenile associations. The purpose of the paper is to examine father-like behavior in an effort to explain it as a social human trait, because it does not occur in animals (Mackey, 1990). Among other things, Mackey discusses two central tendencies: 1) That once with juveniles, adult males interacted with them in much the same way as adult females, and 2) The sex of the juvenile had little relevance to the way adult males interacted with them (Mackey, 1990). Sexual relations are barely mentioned, and not discussed. He does mention sex in the context of adult males gaining access to adult females through the association with juveniles (likely the offspring of the adult female), and in the context of pedophilia:

> As a variant of this strategy [access to adult females] adult males who are pedophiles or hebephiles (in the sexual or erotic sense) could use the socially acceptable adult-male/adult-female relationship to gain intimate access to the adult female's offspring: a less acceptable relationship. (p. 315)

As well, Mackey mentions, but does not examine, sexual relationships in the context of pederasty. He reports elevated interactions between adult-males/juvenile-males in hunting and scavenging groups compared with other groups:

> This latter finding may be an important determinant in science's understanding of the biosocial roots of sexual behaviour that occasionally occurs between adult-male and prepubescent-male humans. (p. 316)

These are the only statements concerning pederasty in the paper, not the definitive or conclusive statements concerning pederasty's role in facilitating boys into the male group, as Dr. Rind presents it. Mackey does discuss recruiting juveniles males into the adult group, but there is no mention of pederasty facilitating the recruitment. Not only does Dr. Rind grossly exaggerate Mackey's statements concerning pederasty, he also ignores Mackey's position concerning the evolution of adult-male/juvenile interaction. Mackey very clearly states that adult-male/juvenile interaction, in the absence of adult females and outside of the home-range, is a uniquely human trait, not found in any nonhuman primate. These associations evolved within the hominid line. (Mackey, 1990). Mackey's position contradicts Dr. Rind's assertion that we inherited pederasty (an adult-male/juvenile interaction) from our primate ancestors. Thus, seriously undermining the plausibility of Dr. Rind's evolutionary enculturation model. There are other examples of exaggerated claims, but because an exhaustive account is beyond the scope of this review, I encourage the reader to let the sources speak for themselves.

EVOLUTION

The vast majority of evolutionary support that Dr. Rind appeals to comes from evolutionary psychology. For the benefit of readers who may not be familiar with evolutionary psychology and its relationship to biology, I will say this: Evolutionary psychology attempts to explain modern human behavioral characteristics by elucidating, through psychological methods, the evolutionary conditions in which they were originally formed. Evolutionary psychology is not accepted in main-stream biology for numerous reasons, such as misuse or misunderstanding of evolutionary theory, reliance on just-so stories, and an inability to create testable hypotheses, to name a few. For a primer on the arguments against evolutionary psychology, I suggest the reader turn to *Alas Poor Darwin: Arguments Against Evolutionary Psychology* (2001) edited by Hilary Rose and Steven Rose. However, in an attempt not to get side-tracked, I will limit my comments on the relationship between biology and psychology by saying the two are often in disagreement, including, as I mentioned earlier, the context in which they use the term *evolution*.

A modern biological definition of evolution is: A change in allele frequency over time. This rather simple statement assumes some important caveats: 1) Evolution involves the changing and inheritance of genes, 2) that new phenotypes, alleles (variants of a gene), are brought about by mutation, 3) the persistence of alleles in a population over time (through generations) depends on natural selection (or other mechanisms, such as drift), which is the differential survival of individuals based on the phenotypes they exhibit. It is from this position I critique Dr. Rind's hypothesis.

Phylogeny

Dr. Rind claims, in the Evolutionary Synthesis section of his paper, that the animal behavior studies he presents conclusively show that human pederasty has phylogenetic roots in our primate relatives. Phylogenies are testable hypotheses about the evolutionary history of a taxon, or groups of taxa, based on apomorphies.[1] They show relatedness among taxa, called phylogenies, are often visualized using phylogenetic trees, and can be used to calculate taxonomic distance and other such measures of relatedness. Advances in molecular techniques (gene sequencing) have greatly increased our ability to create these phylogenies, based on comparisons of sequences of DNA or RNA that represent enzymes, proteins, and so forth. The point is that a phylogeny is a hypothesis concerning the evolutionary history of taxa based on many traits or synapomorphies (shared, derived traits). It is not a hypothesis about a *single* trait. A phylogenetic tree is established using many traits. Generally speaking, more traits equate to stronger evidence of the relatedness among organisms. Traits that can be used to develop phylogenetic trees are determined by taxonomic rules, and these traits are not constricted to genetics. Several types of evidence can be used in concert to create phylogenies, such as genetics, paleontology, anatomy, embryology/development, and even ecological niche. The important point is that a group of traits is used to establish a phylogenetic tree (an hypothesis), not vise versa. Phylogenies do not establish traits. Herein is the main problem with Dr. Rind's use of phylogeny; he attempts to use phylogeny as evidence for the genetic (thus evolutionary) foundations of a trait (pederasty). He has, in fact, inverted the process. It should be noted that evolutionary biologists do talk of phylogenetic legacy, which refers to specific traits or groups of traits in a descendant evolutionary line, as Dr. Rind mentions in the section Evolutionary Considerations and Previous Hypotheses. Phylogenetic legacy refers to vestigial traits, for example, the human appendix, that persists functionless in descendants. The term *phylogenetic legacy* is only applied to traits after the homology and phylogeny have been established. It is not used to determine homology. Dr. Rind's misuse of *phylogenetic legacy* is another example of term fluidity, and demonstrates a lack of understanding of biological evolutionary methods.

Homology and Analogy

That humans and primates are related can be conclusively shown using phylogeny. However, that we are related does not necessitate that all traits we have in common, or seem to have in common, are homologous. The crux of Dr. Rind's argument is that because primates (and other animals) demonstrate pederastic-like behavior (a non term), then pederasty in humans (though different) must have evolved from it. That two taxa share a common trait is *not* evidence of evolutionary relatedness. Common traits can be homologous (same origin) and/or analogous (same function). Traits that are homologous share an evolutionary ancestor. For example, the embryonic notochord (which becomes the back bone in humans) can be traced back to the earliest chordates, and all descendant chordate taxa have one. Thus, the notochord in humans and turtles is a homologous trait. However, human compound eyes and squid compound eyes did not come from a common ancestor. They have the same function, so they are analogous traits, but our closest ancestor did not have a compound eye, so the trait is not homologous. It is very common for two taxa to display similar traits, especially if they evolved in similar environments, subject to the same selective pressures. This is called convergent, or parallel, evolution, the development of analogous traits in unrelated taxa. The torpedo-shaped body of the shark (fish), dolphin (mammal), and ichthyosaur (reptile) is an example of convergent evolution. Each evolutionary line independently solved an adaptive problem (moving quickly through water to hunt) in the same way (a streamlined body). Even if animals and humans displayed a similar pederastic-like behavior (a point I will address next), Dr. Rind is wrong to conclude the traits are homologous without further evidence. Analogy does not imply homology.

Animal Behavior as Evidence of Inheritance

The final points concerning phylogeny are the use of animal behavior evidence in Dr. Rind's paper, and the validity of suggesting an analogy between human pederasty and animal pederastic-like behavior. As I mentioned in the introduction, this is my second review of Dr. Rind's manuscript. In the first, I critiqued him for relying on un-contextualized animal behavior data as evidence of the genetic (evolutionary) basis for pederasty (see below). In this version, he has backed away somewhat from his original contention that pederasty in animals is the same as pederasty in humans and, therefore, is evolved. By introducing terms like *pederastic-like behavior,* it appears he is no longer equating human and animal pederasty, and he can claim that he is not using un-contextualized animal behavior data. However, as I pointed out, there is no difference in his use of the terms *pederastic-like* and *pederastic,* and this sort of pseudo-science terminology does not mask the connection he appears to be assuming.

In this latest version of the manuscript, Dr. Rind still relies heavily on the evolutionary connection between animals and humans, as indicated by his many references to phylogenetic evidence. In my first review of the earlier version of the manuscript, I cautioned him that interpretation of animal behavior data relies on understanding the context of the behavior for the animals being studied. It is all too easy to observe behavior in animals and then equate it to a seemingly similar behavior in humans. However, there is a huge contextual gulf that must be overcome. Animal behavior data can only show that a certain behavior takes place under certain conditions a certain amount of time. It cannot explain the motive behind the behavior. Both Bagemihl (1999) and de Waal (1997) warn against making such an error. Bagemihl (1999, p. 44), warns us not to "jump to broad conclusions" when comparing animal homosexuality and human homosexuality. Homosexuality in animals or humans is a "blend" of many factors, and comparisons between humans and animals must recognize these complexities in order to be valid. In reporting results from other studies, Rind does not sufficiently recognize those complexities. As an example, in the earlier version, Dr. Rind presented several cases citing de Waal (1997), involving bonobos of both sexes, where there was sexual contact between adults, adolescents, and even juveniles, and used these observations to support his evolutionary argument. Bonobos, or pigmy chimps, are particularly relevant to this debate, because they are our closest hominid relative. Therefore, it is important to note that, according to de Waal (1997, p. 100) "sexual" behavior in bonobos is not necessarily for sex. De Waal suggests that some of these seemingly sexual behaviors are, in fact, not sexual, because people tend to think of "sex" as a discrete category, where the cause is sexual desire, goal is orgasm, and purpose is reproduction; for bonobos, sexual climax and reproduction are but two of the many functions served by "sexual" behavior. De Waal (1997) cites many occasions of "sexual" behavior between adult male/adolescent male, adolescent male/adolescent male, and infant female/ adult male, and in all of these observations, there was no penetration or ejaculation (pp. 103, 104, 105, 109). Bonobos use what may appear to be sexual interaction for many social purposes, for example, to mitigate rivalries, reduce competition over food, reconcile after conflict, ease tension, and show affection. This, according to de Waal, explains the many different partner combinations. Though Dr. Rind has removed that particular source, he is still using animal behavior data to establish analogies with human behavior. However, we simply cannot know what the animal(s) are thinking or if the behavior is a conscious choice versus instinctive reaction. By equating pederastic-like behavior in humans and primates without further behavioral parallel explanations, Rind is making a contextual error.

Natural Selection

In my original review, I pointed out several deficiencies concerning Dr. Rind's application of evolutionary theory, particularly his understanding of natural selection. Dr. Rind made the erroneous statement that selection pressure created, or modified, adaptations. This is simply wrong. I had hoped that he would have corrected this in the current version, but that is not the case. In multiple sections, for example, Evolutionary Considerations and Previous Hypotheses, Environment of Evolutionary Adaptedness (EEA), Current Hypothesis (*Design Features*), Dr. Rind continues to claim that adaptations are produced and shaped by natural selection. Selective pressure may influence the frequency of a trait in a population (by differential survival), but selective pressure does not create or modify traits. The process of modification occurs at the subcellular level, for example, mutation, and is a chance event. Selection acts on genetic variants that already exist in the population, but does not create genetic entities. The need for hunting and warring did not create the adaptation of pederasty.[2] Considering this is one of his main tenants, he has failed to incorporate biological evolutionary theory into his hypothesis.

Genes and Evolution

As mentioned earlier, genes are a necessary component of evolution. Evolution is more than simple change; it is a change in allele frequency. Any claim of evolution must involve genes, inheritance (of those genes), and natural selection acting on those genes. Throughout the manuscript, such as in the Evolutionary Synthesis and EEA sections, Dr. Rind claims several times that human pederasty is evolved, yet at no time does he ever discuss the genetics of pederasty except to say that it must be genetic. He states that pederasty in humans evolved and is therefore genetic. The circular nature of Dr. Rind's argument does not support the claim that pederasty has a genetic component. There is no genetic evidence in the manuscript, that is, no gene sequencing or other experimental data. Nor is there any evidence that it is heritable. Therefore, to imply a genetic foundation, he must show evidence of pederasty in our ancestors and the line by which it descended to modern humans. There can be no fossil evidence, and the previous discussion indicted that the connection from humans to primates is doubtful at best, and impossible at worst (Mackey, 1990). This leaves only one avenue for Dr. Rind to pursue: show that pederasty evolved in the genus *Homo*. For that he needs to show the adaptive problem, the evolutionary solution, and a parsimonious explanation.

The Mentorship-Bonding/Enculturation-Alliance Hypothesis (MD/EA)

Buss et al. (1998) clearly spell out the methods used in evolutionary psychology for establishing a theory concerning the evolution of behavior. There needs to be a recurring adaptive problem that is being solved by the adaption in question. The theory must coordinate with known processes in biological evolution, that is, show that the adaptation, or trait, came from a genetic mutation (variation of previous form), is heritable, and increases fitness (differential survival). New specific empirical predications must be possible from the theory. The theory must be falsifiable, and parsimonious compared with competing theories. In the case of an exaptation or spandrel, the theory must describe the original adaption or function that is being co-opted (exaptation), or from which the by-product came (spandrel), demonstrate a new biological function, and must explain, in terms of selection, the maintenance of the original function, how the co-opted functioned/by-product came about, and how the co-opted function/by-product is maintained in the population. Applying these criteria to Dr. Rind's hypothesis reveals many gaps.

To paraphrase Dr. Rind, the MB/EA hypothesis claims that pederasty "evolved" to facilitate the recruitment of para-pubescent boys into the adult male group for the purposes of big-game hunting and warring. Dr. Rind claims that the recurring problem, in the EEA, were the dangers and hardships involved in big-game hunting and warfare. Facilitative methods such as pederasty evolved to prepare the boys for these hardships by instilling emotions of loyalty, courage, and self-sacrifice in the boys toward the group. In this way, the male group was replenished and maintained.

The first problem with the theory is that there is no problem that needs an adaption. One can easily argue that big-game hunting and warfare are actually the adaptations to the recurring problem of food shortages and encroachment from other clans. Recruitment into the male group comes by way of necessity; the need to learn to hunt and fight, there is no *need* for a facilitative method that does not directly involve the skills of hunting and fighting. Thus, the MB/EA hypothesis fails to meet the first and most important criterion, being adaptive. Because the facilitation of hunting and warring skills can be achieved without an erotic component, it fails a second test; it is not parsimonious. It also does not conform to processes in biological evolution, that is, there is no explanation of the genetics. There is an explanation of fitness, increased survival from successful hunting and combat, but that applies to the skills of hunting and warring and not necessarily to pederasty[3]. Given that the theory is an explanation of current behavior and there are no predictions arising from it, it is not testable and therefore not falsifiable. Dr. Rind does suggest that pederasty may be an exaptation or spandrel, but his theory fails the evidentiary burden of explaining the original adaption from which it was co-opted or of which it is a by-product. Thus, in terms of both biological evolutionary theory, and evolutionary psychology methods (Buss et al., 1998), the hypothesis is left wanting.

Fundamentally, the issue with the MB/EA Hypothesis is that it is a solution looking for a problem to solve. Dr. Rind starts with the observation of pederasty through cultures and time and then tries to explain how it came about, instead of starting with an adaptive problem that needed a solution. The latter approach would have encouraged multiple hypotheses and predictions. In short, Dr. Rind has created an elaborate just-so story, despite Gould's cautioning (Gould and Lewontin, 1979). To demonstrate, using the same cultural observation data, I can postulate that pederasty is a cultural meme that has developed independently in many societies. Some studies suggest that cultures at the extreme protector end of the plowman protector index, a measure of societies' reliance on adult male brute strength to perform certain tasks (Mackey, 1990), tend to have severe initiation rites for juvenile males (Gilmore, 1990; Weisfeld and Billings, 1988). This, coupled with the increased adult male/juvenile male interaction and less female/male (juvenile or adult) interaction in those societies (Mackey, 1990), may lead to sexual substitution/mimicry (Bagemihl, 1999). Sexual substitution is a situation where a heterosexual will engage in sex with a member of his or her own sex because members of the opposite sex are not available, and sexual mimicry is when a member of one sex, often juvenile, appears phenotypically the opposite sex (Bagemihl, 1999). The cultural recurring problem is isolation from preferred sexual partners, and the adaptation is taking what you can get from feminine juveniles who are subservient. Thus, pederasty is a convergent social meme that develops independently in societies that have the necessary similar conditions. I am not suggesting that this hypothetical theory is by any means correct, but it is a story that fits the same evidence used by Dr. Rind. It is equal in its explanatory power in that it creates a cultural problem that the theory can solve, and further, does not need to meet the burdens of evolutionary evidence, because it is a meme. However, it is also a just-so story.

Homosexuality and Pederasty

In his earlier version of the manuscript, Dr. Rind defined pederasty as a subset of homosexuality. By doing so, he could use evolutionary and social arguments supporting homosexuality as an evolved trait to support his theory that pederasty is an evolved trait. I critiqued his argument, pointing out that the two are not related. Even by his own admission, pederasty is defined in terms of a functional role and not a life partnership role. Further, different types of homosexuality have different evolutionary origins. Even though Dr. Rind has backed away from the argument that pederasty is a subset of homosexuality, he still connects and equates them throughout the manuscript, citing Bagemihl (1999), Kirkpatrick (2000), and Muscarella (2000), and arguing that much of the evidence used in these works on homosexuality was actually age-discrepant data. As well, in the section Current Hypothesis: Individual and Group Selection, he describes pederasty in humans as exapted from animals and in the section Previous Evolutionary Hypotheses for Pederasty, he discusses pederasty as exapted homosexual behavior in animals (contrary to Buss et al., 1998). Thus, it is necessary for me to address his continued conflation of homosexuality and pederasty.

The homoerotic relationships in the MB/EA Hypothesis cannot be lifetime obligate. Bagemihl supports the notion that some animals who are homosexual also engage in some heterosexual activity at some point in their lives. Dr. Rind further confirms this, saying that at the same age that the men lose erotic interest in the boys, the boys lose erotic interest in the men to pursue girls. Thus, Dr. Rind's model assumes that the men and adolescents involved in pederastic relations are bisexual in a Kinseyian sense (Kinsey et al., 1948), meaning they may not be erotically attracted to both sexes at the same time, but will engage in both homosexuality and heterosexuality at some point in their lives. Bisexuality is a necessity for the MB/EA Hypothesis to work, otherwise these widespread lifetime-exclusive homosexual relationships would threaten the stability of the group as a whole by lowering the fitness of many, perhaps most, of the male individuals. This functional bisexuality is not at all the same as lifetime homosexual sexual orientation. Bagemihl (1999), Vasey (1994), Kirkpatrick (2000), and Muscarella (2000) argue that female and male homosexualities are different in origin, and Rind himself, in the Mentorship-Bonding/Enculturation-Alliance Hypothesis section, argues that pederasty is different from both in origin. Thus, homosexuality and pederasty are not synonymous in terms of origin or function. As with the animal behavior observations, without analogy or homology, there can be no link between pederasty and adult homosexuality.

Clearly, pederasty and adult homosexuality are not the same, so why does he attempt to link them? First, he wants to use evolutionary evidence for homosexuality as evidence for the genetic nature of pederasty. Second, the direct connection of pederasty and adult homosexuality is necessary for his contention that pederastic relationships are not pathological and do not intrinsically cause psychological harm. His apology for pederasty rests, in part, on the argument that all the pathological explanations and vilifications of adult homosexuality were wrong, and, therefore, the pathological explanations and vilifications of pederasty must also be wrong. However, without an evolutionary or culturally functional connection to homosexuality, Dr. Rind's defense of pederasty is without support from research concerning homosexuality.

ACADEMIC PROCESS AND ADVOCACY

This is my second review of Dr. Rind's manuscript. That there needed to be a second review is a subject of some concern. In 2007, the special editors of the *Journal of Homosexuality* asked me to write a review of the earlier version of the manuscript. At that time I was told by the editors that Dr. Rind's peer-reviewed manuscript would form the centerpiece of a special edition of the *Journal of Homosexuality* and would be accompanied by ten reviews, of which mine was one. The reviewers where drawn from the disciplines of anthropology, classics, psychology, sociology, languages, communications, gender studies, and biology (as represented by me). The special journal would consist of the manuscript, the ten reviews, and a final rebuttal by Dr. Rind, giving him an opportunity to address any critiques and the final word. I began my critique operating under the assumption that normal academic protocols would be followed. This was not the case. As Dr. Rind received the reviews, he was allowed by the editors to rewrite his manuscript in response to the reviewer's comments. In fact, in at least one case, there was considerable communication between Dr. Rind and one of the reviewers, which resulted in substantive changes during the review process. I was taken aback by this breach of protocol and lack of objectivity. After receiving a third edition of the manuscript, I informed the editors that I would no longer continue with the project if Dr. Rind continued to rewrite his paper with each review. After all, it was much like trying to hit a moving target. The editors assured me that no further revision would be allowed, and I completed my critique. However, before the special edition could be published, the publisher of the journal pulled the edition.

In 2010, I was informed by one of the editors that a new publisher had been found. However, the manuscript had to be abridged, and I was asked if I would like to contribute my review. Given my previous experience, I gave conditional permission, contingent on reading the abridged version of the manuscript. As I suspected, the new version of the manuscript, the one currently under review, was not an abridgment, but rather a complete reworking of the hypothesis concerning pederasty. The current version is different enough from the one originally reviewed that it rendered my first review obsolete. I informed the editors of such and suggested that Dr. Rind abridge the original manuscript, so they could use the reviews already completed. The editors did not approve of the suggestion and still pressed for permission to use my original review. I declined and withdrew from the project. After some back-and-forth with the editors, I agreed to rewrite my review with some provisos: 1) that Dr. Rind not revise the manuscript, and 2) that I would comment on the academic process leading to this publication.

In my opinion, the academic process has been undermined. Dr. Rind should never have been allowed to revise his manuscript on a go forward basis as each review came in. It is unfair and disrespectful to the reviewers. Further, in the second round, Dr. Rind should not have been allowed to substantially change his original thesis, because it was the one that was peer-reviewed and critiqued. (Though I asked the editor, he did not tell me if this new version of the manuscript has been peer-reviewed.)

From the outset, I have assumed the academic integrity of the process and wrote at length, in my first review, about the need to allow the objective pursuit of knowledge. I wrote about how wrong it was for his detractors (see Dallam et al., 2001, Dallam 2002, and Ondersma et al., 2001) to use ad hominem attacks on Dr. Rind, and how it is the role of science to inform the debate, not frame it. I believe these things are still true. However, the process leading to this publication has been, in my opinion, tarnished, and leaves me doubtful as to its integrity. In my opinion, this academic process has been manipulated and agenda driven. For evidence, turn to the section Evolutionary Mismatch, where Dr. Rind describes the modern-day pederast as the proverbial white moth in a postindustrial society. Where the "light-coloring mechanism" (pederasty) is operating as designed, but that functioning puts the pederast in peril in the "sooted" postindustrial environment, which is modern Western culture. The description of the pederast as white and pure and society as dark and dirty is hyperbole. This sort of advocacy does not belong in a manuscript that claims to be objective and scientific. To be fair, though, everyone has a horse in this race. The subject matter is unlike most academic studies, in that most studies do not invoke a strong emotional response in the reader. I do not recall an outcry over the last paper I read concerning taxonomy. My point is, where most academics can be dispassionate about other people's research (we are always passionate about our own), the subject of pedophilia is never dispassionate. Regardless of discipline, background, or level of expertise, everyone (in modern Western culture) holds a strong opinion about men having erotic relationships with boys. This may adversely affect the objectivity of anyone; no matter how well trained they may be in research. So, I have examined my own conclusions concerning the manuscript, in an attempt to rout out any bias. It is because of the risk of bias that I have kept my review to those parts of the manuscript that relate to biology, evolutionary theory, and academic process. I believe I have been honest and as objective as possible. I wish I could say I felt the same about the rest of the process.

CONCLUSION

At the heart of his manuscript, Dr. Rind makes the case for the genetic nature of pederasty. He bases his argument on a genetic determinism that would make Richard Dawkins blush (c.f. Dawkins, 1976). His argument can be broken down as such: A trait (pederasty) is observed in animals and humans. All traits that are multigenerational are genetically inherited. Therefore, pederasty is genetically inherited. The rest of his manuscript is simply observations of inheritance and a description of function (adaptation) to explain why it survived the process of natural selection. Like many people, Dr. Rind has conflated adaptation with evolution. Not all adaptations are evolved, not all traits are genetic, and not all behaviors are inherited. For an account of the misuse of the concept of a gene and the dangers of genetic determinism, read *The Century of the Gene* (Keller, 2000).

As for the specifics, Dr. Rind relies heavily on the connection between pederastic-like behavior in animals and humans to support his evolutionary model. I have shown that this support is suspect at best and nonexistent at worst. Nor can he turn to a connection between homosexuality and pederasty for support. Despite his claims, there is no direct genetic evidence either. In terms of pederasty being an evolutionary trait, he has not established homology or analogy. Given the criteria set out in Buss et al. (1998) for hypotheses in evolutionary psychology, Dr. Rind fails to demonstrate a necessary recurring adaptive problem and does not conform to biological evolutionary theory. As for the possibility of pederasty being an exaptation or spandrel, he has not met the evidentiary burden of showing the development or maintenance of the original adaptation, or of the exaptation/spandrel. His argument is further weakened by his selective use of source information and suspect terminology. Behavior can be influenced by many environmental, epigenetic, and genetic factors, and Dr. Rind does not present a case for a genetic basis. He has confused memetics with genetics and presents an elaborate just-so story that fabricates a past evolutionary environment to explain a current human behavior.

As for the process and advocacy, I will defend anyone's right to conduct honest and objective research, including Dr. Rind, and including subjects that may be uncomfortable or unfashionable to discuss. However, with respect to this project, I am left with doubts concerning its academic objectivity. This is a shame for all concerned, for Dr. Rind does present a substantial amount of data concerning pederasty through human history and culture, which the victimologists do not seem to account for. These observations are deserving of further objective research. For even though I conclude that Dr. Rind's MB/EA Hypothesis is deficient, there is nothing in my review that precludes the notion that pederasty *could* be a human evolutionary trait. However, if true, Dr. Rind's hypothesis brings us no closer to its realization.

NOTES

1. An apomorphy is a derived trait, one that is found in descendant taxa but not in the ancestor.
2. That is, the need for hunting and warring does not create phenotypes that are advantageous for hunting and warring. The concept of "vital needs" facilitating the creation of traits was proposed by J. B. de Lemark and debunked by Gregor Mendel in the nineteenth century.
3. Not to mention that the selection mechanism relies on a tenuous appeal to a newly redefined group selection (Wilson and Wilson, 2007), which itself is controversial, where Rind does not distinguish between the concepts of inter- and intragroup selection.

REFERENCES

Bagemihl, B. (1999). *Biological exuberance: animal homosexuality and natural diversity.* New York: St. Martin's Press.

Buss, D. M., Haselton, M. G., Shackelford, T. K., Bleske, A. L., & Wakefield, J. C. (1998). Adaptations, exaptations, and spandrels. *American Psychologist, 53,* 533–548.

Dallam, S. J. (2002). Science or propaganda? An examination of Rind, Tromovitch &
Bauserman (1988). *Journal of Child Sexual Abuse, 9* (3/4), 109–134.

Dallam, S. J., Cepeda-Benito, A., Kraemer, H. C., Gleaves, D. H., Silberg, J. L., & Spiegel, D. (2001). The effects of child sexual abuse: Comment on Rind, Tromovitch, and Bauserman (1988). *Psychological Bulletin, 127,* 6, 715–733.

Dawkins, R., (1976). *The selfish gene.* Oxford: Oxford University Press.

De Waal, F. B. M. (1997). *Bonobo: The forgotten ape.* Berkeley: University of California Press.

Gilmore, D. (1990). *Mankind in the making: Cultural concepts of masculinity.* New Haven, CT: Yale University Press.

Gould, S. J., & Lewontin, R. C. (1979). The Spandrels of San Marco and the Panglossin paradigm: A critique of the adaptionist programme. *Proceedings of the Royal Society of London B, 205,* 581–598.

Keller, E. F. (2000). *The century of the gene.* Cambridge, MA: Harvard University Press.

Kinsey, A., Pomeroy, W.B., & Martin, C. E. (1948). *Sexual behavior in the human male.* Philadelphia, PA: W. B. Saunders.

Kirkpatrick, R. C. (2000). The evolution of human homosexual behavior. *Current Anthropology, 41,* 3, 385.

Mackey, W. C. (1990). Adult-male/juvenile association as a species-characteristic human trait: A comparative field approach. In J. R. Feierman (Ed.), *Pedophilia: Biosocial dimensions* (pp. 299–323). New York: Springer-Verlag.

Muscarella, F. (2000). The evolution of homoerotic behavior in humans. *Journal of Homosexuality, 40,* 51–77.

Ondersma, S. J., Berliner, L., Chaffin, M., Cordon, I., Goodman, S., & Barnett, B. (2001). Sex with children is abuse: Comment on Rind, Tromovitch, and Bauserman (1988). *Psychological Bulletin, 127,* 6, 707–714.

Rose, H., & Rose, S. (Eds.). (2001). *Alas poor Darwin: Arguments against evolutionary psychology.* London: Vintage Press.

Vasey, P. L. (1994). Homosexual behavior in primates: A review of evidence and theory. *International Journal of Primatology, 16,* 173–203.

Weisfeld, G. E., & Billings, R. L. (1988). Observations on adolescence. In K. MacDonald (Ed.), *Sociobiological perspectives on human development* (pp. 207–233). New York: Springer-Verlag.

Wilson, D. S., & Wilson, E. O. (2007). Rethinking the theoretical foundation of sociobiology. *The Quarterly Review of Biology, 82,* 327–348.

Chapter 6

SAME SEX, DIFFERENT AGES:
ON PEDERASTY IN GAY HISTORY

D. H. MADER AND GERT HEKMA

On Monday, March 3, 2008, as one of the earlier drafts of this paper was being written, the British House of Lords debated an amendment to the Criminal Justice and Immigration Bill moved by Lord Thomas of Gresford, a Liberal Democrat, which would have made it a criminal offense to "assert" or "imply," orally or in written form, that there is "an association" between homosexuality and sexual offenses against minors.[1] Lord Gresford argued that to make such an assertion or implication was "threatening" to homosexuals, and thus a hate crime which should come under the law.

That association is precisely what Dr. Rind is asserting in this study, when, on his way to asserting the "normality" of pederasty and demonstrating the invalidity of the victimologists' assertions that sexual relations between adult males and boys are always and intrinsically productive of extreme invariable harm, he argues from various disciplines that homosexuality in human cultures and the animal kingdom has often taken the form of exactly those age-stratified sexual relations that our present culture has chosen to term *sexual offenses*. It is precisely because of this, and the penchant toward historical forgetfulness on the part of the LGBT or gay establishment, for which liberal politicians such as Lord Gresford act as spokespersons, and are now even attempting to make discussions of the historical data itself, such as Dr. Rind's a crime, that we wish to respond to Dr. Rind's work.

In the course of his historical and cross-cultural analysis, Rind states, "pederastic and gender-stratified forms [of male homosexual behavior] have both frequently occurred cross-culturally and historically, with the former often being practiced society-wide but the latter being restricted to much smaller numbers of individuals. Notably, the gay pattern (i.e., exclusively same-sex relation between relatively equal adults), a subtype of the egalitarian form, has been restricted to the modern West and is exceptional from a cross-cultural and historical perspective." (pg. 37, this volume)

Accordingly, for his purposes, he bases his arguments regarding the normality of age-stratified homosexuality primarily on non-Western and non-modern societies. (For a quick review of these societies, see his Table III; the exceptions to this non-Western, non-modern rule are Renaissance Italy, Albania, English boarding schools, pirates, and hobos.) In our response, we propose to expand the scope of his sources and examine the evidence for the frequency (if not "normality") of age-stratified relations within Western homosexuality itself and to determine whether the same factors he finds operative in the non-Western, non-modern societies also apply there. Our method—both as a corrective to the amnesia of the LGBT movement in general, and as a bit of an homage to Dr. Rind's previous meta-analytical work—will involve first a "meta-analysis" of historical sources—the sources of "gay history" itself. We will then look briefly at theoretical writing and ego documents and at material culture. In the course of our discussion we will question Rind's assertion that pederasty lessened as a pattern in the West with the Industrial Revolution; the sources we will be enumerating suggest this took longer and had other causes. We will also discuss some of the other issues our survey raises.

Reflecting the multiplicity of sources we will be examining, in this text the term *minor* will necessarily be defined flexibly, because different authors, and the various countries in which or about which they are writing, have used different definitions. This notwithstanding, *minor* is generally here to be understood as applying to an individual in or approaching adolescence, which most often comes down to someone below the age of 16 to 18 years, but does not include infants or younger children.

In our survey we will be looking only at the Western world, and the pre- or early modern and modern eras. We are aware that there are constructionist arguments that question whether cross-cultural and diachronic comparisons can be made, or whether the "homosexualities" of the ancient world, or of Islamic, or Oriental, or other non-Western societies are not too differently constructed to permit comparison. Obviously, Rind, following Crompton (2003) and others who have written "universal" histories of homosexuality, has accepted that such comparisons can be made and has done so. Whatever the arguments may be, this is not an issue which we can address within the scope of this article, so we will content ourselves with a review of male same-sexual historical material from Western societies, in which there is wide agreement among the researchers themselves that we are dealing with a phenomenon recognizably similar to our own "homosexuality" today.

A caveat at the outset, for those readers, either from the gay community, or among their enemies, who may be inclined to misread or misrepresent our conclusions: Although we will be affirming that age-structured relations have played a prominent and persistent role in Western, modern homosexuality, we are NOT suggesting that homosexuals are in any way to be specifically associated with child sexual abuse. Quite on the contrary, and entirely in line with Dr. Rind's argument, it is our contention that the very prominence of age-differentiated relations in the tradition should be read as evidence that these relations are not necessarily abuse, except as individual circumstances may make them so.

HISTORICAL SOURCES

Almost since Foucault dated the birth of the new "identity" of homosexuality to 1870 (Foucault, 1978), and with it, the birth of the culture that was the key to understanding the concept of homosexuality, scholars have been busy discovering evidence from earlier dates for such a culture, sociability and identity, which for historical reasons has most often been termed *sodomitical*. The author who takes this farthest back, to what he regards as its "invention" in the eleventh century, is Mark Jordan (Jordan, 1997). In the earliest example he adduces for a sodomitic identity, the legends of the martyrdom of St. Pelagius, even before the word *sodomy* had been invented to describe it, we find that age-differentiated sexual relations are at the heart of this "new" concept. As Jordan points out, the 13-year-old Pelagius knows precisely what the Moorish "king" has in mind. Granted, there is also in his rebuke to the king another category besides age: "Do you think me like one of yours, an effeminate?" The young male is desirable among these Moors, at the birth of distinctively European, Christian civilization, because in his immaturity he is still non-male, while also being male.[2] Although Jordan makes it clear that there is an immense amount more going on, theologically and culturally, in these first discourses around sodomy and sodomites, for our purposes it is enough to note that the age-structured paradigm is already there as a part of them.

Moving forward to the high Renaissance we have the study of Florence by Rocke which Rind cites, with its assertion in the title itself, with its reference to a male *culture* rather than *subculture*, that "the evidence shows beyond much doubt that in Florence, and probably elsewhere as well, sodomy between males normally assumed a hierarchical form that would now be called 'pederasty'" (Rocke, 1996, p. 12). This same picture is generally borne out by the sixth chapter of Guido Ruggiero's study of sexuality in Venice, though he does not go so far as to suggest this was more than a distinct and active subculture there (Ruggiero, 1985). *Fallen Order,* Karen Liebreich's history of the scandal-ridden Piarist teaching order prior to their suppression in 1646, is written entirely from a victimological/child abuse/priestly abuse perspective and fits all its evidence into that mold, but is nonetheless suggestive of the intertwining of homoeroticism and education in the initial success of that order's novitiate and schools—and its capacity for abuse—in the scandals (Liebreich, 2005). Proceeding still farther forward in Italy, there is Enrico Oliari's study of homosexual scandals in Italy from the Unification (1861) to World War I (Oliari, 2006). Of the nineteen cases discussed, seven appear to have involved minors—frequently students in church-run boarding schools, although youths modeling for two German photographers, Pluschow and von Gloeden (both in 1908) were involved in others.

The Netherlands is a country where the historiography of homosexuality is reasonably thorough. D. J. Noordam's study of five centuries of homosexuality in The Netherlands covers the years 1233 to 1733, including at its end the great persecution of sodomites in 1730 (Noordam, 1995). Drawn largely from examination of court records, it makes clear that the present-day hegemonic concept of "childhood innocence" extending far into adolescence is still a thing of the future. One of the earliest cases recorded, in 1321, involves an adult man and a 16-year-old boy being burned to death for sodomy, memorable for the fact that the boy staggered out of the fire several times and had to be thrown back in. Indeed, a number of the cases prior to 1570 involve punishments for both adult and minor partners. Contrary to what one might be tempted to argue from our current perspectives, these were not instances where a court punished a "child victim" along with the "perpetrator." The presence of other cases where the courts recognized that coercion, force or violence on the part of the man toward a younger victim (or, for that matter, a peer) was involved, and only the adult was burned, make it clear that judges were prepared to, and did, distinguish between homosexual rape and consenting sexual relations, where both persons were condemned. Over the next two and a half centuries, between the 1320 case and around 1680, gradations in the culpability assigned to the younger partner in these cases which the legal system clearly saw as consensual were introduced: under the age of 13 the boy was regarded as ignorant of the gravity of his acts, and punishment was waived; between 13 and 17 the punishment for the minor was generally reduced to whipping or penal servitude.[3] Similar gradations in regard to the acts involved can be observed in a 1676 case involving a former burgomaster of Utrecht and two of his servants, one of whom had permitted his master to engage in anal intercourse with him over a fifteen year period, between the ages of 10 and 25, while the other, from the age of 15, had allowed himself to be whipped in the nude. The burgomaster escaped from custody while awaiting trial and fled; the only sanction the court could impose in his absence was lifelong banishment. The young man who had permitted anal intercourse was strangled, and the other younger man was ordered transported to the East Indies as an indentured servant. It is about this same time that Noordam can begin using other forms of evidence besides court records, introducing biographical material and political gossip regarding the relations between nobles and other prominent citizens and their young servants, similar to those of the former burgomaster, though without the tragic ending. These in turn furnish background for the most famous of these relations, the "silver friendship" between William III and Hans Willem Bentinck, son of a lesser noble family who had become Willem's page and attendant at the age of 14, when Willem was 13. More parallel to the age structured relations of the other nobles and regents was Willem's second great relation, with Arnold Joost van Keppel, who had become his page as a young teenager and was still only 19 when he crossed over to England with his royal master in 1688.

Open public knowledge of these relations, and a decline in the number of sodomy prosecutions in general, suggest some increase in tolerance toward such relations in The Netherlands during its years of prosperity. (And of course in the case of William III, he was a person of the highest nobility, a status that also included sexual privileges.) With the country's political decline in the beginning of the eighteenth century, things changed rapidly, and in 1730–31 The Netherlands witnessed one of the most concerted persecutions of sodomites in history, which figures at the end of Noordam's study and the beginning of the histories by Theo van der Meer (Van der Meer, 1995) and Gert Hekma (Hekma, 2004). In his study of sodomy in The Netherlands Van der Meer is at pains to protest Crompton's characterization of these events as a "gay holocaust" (Crompton, 1978) as inflated language; be that as it may, 355 indictments leading to 82 executions (figures according to Noordam, 1995) within about a year was an event of such unprecedented ferocity that it was remarked upon unfavorably even in England, and as far away as Japan.[4] It began with the arrest of two men in Utrecht, one of whom appears to have been particularly well traveled and named no less than 140 fellow sodomites who had been his contacts in a number of Dutch cities. As more and more arrests followed and ever more names were named, well-organized social circles of sodomites were revealed in Dutch cities and towns, including males ranging from diplomats, sheriffs and law court officials, through merchants, shopkeepers and common tradesmen and apprentices, servants and orphan boys, meeting each other in taverns and various public places. Again, the boys and youth cannot be written off as "victims;" testimony includes information that some of them were active in recruiting and procuring others of their own background for voluntary and remunerative relations with men—in short, willing and active participants in these circles. As the differences in the figures between the total numbers indicted and the number executed indicate, large numbers of the suspects, the gentlemen, but also many tradesmen and servants, managed to flee and in their absence were merely banned for life. Of the younger boys who did not manage to evade arrest, a number were transported to the East Indies. The exception to this was in a particularly vicious outburst in the village of Faan, in the province of Groningen, where of the 23 sodomites sentenced to be strangled and burned, seven were between the ages of 16 and 18; two further boys of 14 were sentenced to life long detention in the house of correction (from which, once the hysteria died down, they were permitted to "escape"). For the rest, in this case, which involved a judge who had political grudges to repay[5] and a radical clergyman, torture of the suspects, and accusations by the boys which bear an uncanny resemblance to those of the girls in the Salem witchcraft case in Massachusetts some forty years before, it is difficult to say what had taken place in Faan, but historians have argued that probably many of the men and boys had been involved in same-sexual practices (Boon, 1989).

To return to the world of statistics: It is worth noting, from Van der Meer's table of the sodomy cases in the Province of Holland, 1352-1838, that of those accused of sodomy who from their professions can be tentatively identified as youths, most appear to have been apprentices or servants, with a few beggar or orphan boys. It is interesting to compare this with Noordam's discussion of cases, where the victims of forced or coerced acts of sodomy are frequently identified as either beggars or orphans. This might suggest that in fact adolescents who were no longer financially dependent on their families but part of the working population—in short, independent economic players—were also independent moral players, and willing (perhaps in part for financial reasons—but none the less voluntary) participants in age-stratified sexual relations within larger circles of sodomites. It was perhaps the younger boys, or at any rate those without any place in the financial or social structure, who were at risk of victimization.

British histories of homosexuality largely pick up from the seventeenth century onward. Alan Bray's short (and comparatively early) survey *Homosexuality in Renaissance England* (1982) is singularly silent on the issue of pederasty, instead concentrating on the emergence of gender-structured homosexuality and the figure of the "molly." Randy Trumbach, who further develops this perspective in his "Gender and the Homosexual Role in Modern Western Culture" (Trumbach, 1989), states that pederasty was the standard in same-sexual relations from 1200 to 1700, but remains silent about how widespread it was after that date. It is unfortunate to have to note, however, that sometimes these silences appear disingenuous. For instance, in his posthumous volume *The Friend* (Bray, 2003), an otherwise very important work in tracing the presence of religiously based friendship pacts in England which permitted same-sex unions in popular religion, if not officially, Bray fails to inform us that one of his key male pairs, around whom he shapes his third chapter, Dr. John Gostlin (1565/6–1626) and Dr. Thomas Legge (1535–1607), were an age-discrepant pair. We are told they began their friendship in 1582, but nowhere does Bray give us their dates. These are easily found on the Internet, however, and permit one to work out that they began their relation when Gostlin was 16 and Legge was 47. One is left wondering how many other age-discrepant wedded brothers and friends there are out there, still to be discovered.[6]

B. R. Burg is more clear-cut in his *Sodomy and the Pirate Tradition: English Sea Rovers in the Seventeenth-Century Caribbean*. He points out that the one thing that appears certain is that the pirates were exclusively homosexual while aboard ship, and goes on to portray the pirate community as almost exclusively pederast, comparing it for instance to the vagabond community on the road, where men also paired off with boys (Burg, 1984). Another study of a British seafaring community by Burg focuses on the early years of the nineteenth century, with his re-evaluation of the HMS *Africane* affair. In his discussion of it, Burg notes that one feature that distinguishes this affair from other naval sodomy and indecency trials of the eighteenth and nineteenth centuries was the nature of the interaction among the men and boys involved. Here, unlike the other cases which generally involved officers coercing shipboard boys, the testimony indicates the boys "were for the most part willing and in some cases enthusiastic partners in the ship's homoerotic society." Testimony at the courts martial revealed that one of the six boys charged was so "notorious and flagrant" in his participation that he was hung, along with three of the most culpable adults (Burg, 2009).

Ashore, at about the same time, as background for the two figures who are central to his discussion, Byron and Jeremy Bentham, Crompton's *Byron and Greek Love* gives a picture of homosexuality in England in the first decades of the nineteenth century, and not unexpectedly, with Byron's own interests, age-discrepant sexual relations play a large role in that picture (Crompton, 1985). The notes to the pseudo-Byronic *Don Leon* (to our knowledge first published in 1866 but clearly annotated in the period between 1825 and 1856) cite a fair number of contemporary legal cases, at least a third of which involve alleged offenses against, or with, boys (most of the remainder being between adults, though usually with a difference in social status and sometimes with a considerable age difference as well) (*Don Leon,* 1934).

H. G. Cocks's "revisionist" study of the configuration of homosexual desire in nineteenth century Britain, in which he demonstrates the influence of earlier popular ideas about sodomy on the public discourse on homosexuality at the end of the century, focuses largely on issues of masculinity and effeminacy, and thus on the gender-differentiated aspects of homosexuality. However, the first section of his book, reviewing the legal development and policing of homosexuality, contains statistical material regarding the ages of offenders and "victim/partners" which is relevant here. Whwreas adult males made up the largest group among both offenders—no surprise there—and victim/partners (the largest single cohort within that being ages 20 to 30), the second largest group of victims/partners were composed of the categories aged 10 to 20 and those identified not by age but by the terms *boys, lads, youths, apprentices* and *young men* (which together were larger than the 20 to 30 cohort). Cocks's use of the term *victim/partner* is also telling. He notes that the majority of the committals were for indecent assault (which included all homosexual acts short of sodomy, such as fellatio and mutual masturbation and even touching and kissing, which might result in surprising situations where the two offenders were charged with "indecently assaulting each other") and assault with the intention to commit sodomy (which Cocks notes was largely synonymous with indecent assault, the assumption being that these acts were preludes to sodomy), and thus terms which were also used to describe consenting acts (Cocks, 2010, pp. 22ff.).

Moving into the late nineteenth century, the case histories published with Havelock Ellis's *Sexual Inversion* (first published 1895) provide insight into the proportion of age-discrepant sexual relations in the homosexual population—at least among those who wrote life histories. The number and arrangement of these case histories varies from edition to edition; the copy the authors used is the third, revised and enlarged edition of 1915. Of the cases Ellis prints here that specify the age of the object of desire, nineteen involve attraction to adults, and nine to adolescent boys; two further men report attraction to both men and boys—and two to effeminate males, one of these cases involving professional teenage prostitutes who cross-dress (Ellis, 1915). All the respondents who identify themselves as "womanly" indicate a preference for masculine adult males as partners. It should be noted that Ellis regards all of these individuals equally as *inverts*. He does not define those whose preference focuses on minors as *pedophiles,* although he had used that term since 1906 for persons attracted exclusively to children (in a narrow sense of the word) without regard to whether the children were male or female. In Ellis's classification, the sex of the object trumps the age.

Two recent studies of homosexuality in London, one dealing with the fifteen years on each side of the turn of the twentieth century, from the Labouchere amendment to World War I, the other with the forty years from the end of World War I to the Wolfenden report, require our notice. Although age-discrepant sexual relations are rarely specifically discussed, except in the case of the Cleveland Street scandal and the adolescent telegraph boys available there, the former is pervaded by the cross-class and age-differentiated sexuality of the circle surrounding George Cecil Ives—penal reformer, friend of Oscar Wilde, and founder of the first organization for homosexual liberation, the Order of Chaeronea—whose person and papers provide a focus for the book (Cook, 2003). We will encounter Ives and his circle again in the cultural section. The latter study addresses the subject more directly, twice discussing at some length the prevalence of intergenerational relations during this period, particularly among the working class, where boys could be found as "trade" or for longer-term relations which might see the boy ultimately rise out of his class (Houlbrook, 2005). (There are numerous autobiographical accounts of these early twentieth century age-discrepant, cross-class relations; a random mention of three will suffice here: from the adult's perspective, Davidson, 1971, pp. 125–139; from the boy's perspective, Robinson, 1986, Chapter 4; and for a unique photographic documentation of such a relation, see Gardner, 1993.) As part of his discussion of the reasons why such age-discrepant relations became more marginal as the period under examination went on, Houlbrook mentions not only the shifts in educational and work practices as the twentieth century advanced, which removed boys from contact with men in in shops and on the job and entrusted their vocational training to the state and schools rather than the workplace, but also a change in the whole geography of homosexuality and its privatization, reducing the number of public places where men and boys encountered one another.

Because the British were among the major colonial powers, we might include Robert Aldrich's history of *Colonialism and Homosexuality* at this point as well. The evidence Aldrich presents makes it clear that the European empires were sites not only of intercultural and interracial encounters between adults, but that there were often age-discrepant relations as well. Exemplary for this is the photograph he prints (one of a number of similar pictures which exist) of the explorer Henry Morton Stanley and his Black bearer Kalulu—not the robust adult warrior depicted in the engravings used to illustrate Stanley's publications, but a young adolescent. (Whether the warrior image is more erotic than the "real" Kalulu, as the captions for these two pictures suggest, is a matter of erotic taste.) In the final section of the book Aldrich also performs the service of underscoring the fact that these relations cannot always be read as a powerful European colonialist exploiting the African or Asian colonial victim, but that on occasion the "man of empire," at the same time that he benefited from his colonial status, could also as a result of his erotic encounters come to adopt an anticolonialist stance critical of European colonial expansion and its accompanying economic exploitation. One clear example is the French-Algerian poet and boy-lover Jean Senac, who sided with the Algerians against the French occupation and stayed in Algeria after its independence (Aldrich, 2003). Since his survey was published, a separate study has appeared devoted to one of the minor figures Aldrich mentions, the British writer and palm oil trader J. M. Stuart-Young, in which the author seeks to answer how a white, colonialist "paedophile"— someone who by all standards—both Igbo and European—should have been a candidate for infamy, became an honored and revered figure in his African community (Newell, 2006). What she discovers is precisely the sort of intercultural negotiation of sexualities and critical stance rooted in erotic experience that Aldrich suggests is possible.

The first two chapters of Chris Brickell's *Mates and Lovers,* a recent, comprehensive history of homosexuality in New Zealand establishes the presence not only of egalitarian relations between adult men in its early, disproportionately male rural society, but of relations between adults and minors, the latter both Maori and European. He sees a shift toward gender-stratified and egalitarian relations in the first three decades of the twentieth century, which he attributes to forces such as urbanization and changing definitions of childhood and youth (Brickell, 2008).

One of the strongest arguments for the continuing importance of intergenerational relations through the nineteenth and into the twentieth century comes from Magnus Hirschfeld (1914, p. 281), who claimed half of his respondents had pederast and the other half adult homosexual relations, specifying that 45 percent of the pederasts preferred adolescents (14-21 years) and 5 percent prepuberal youngsters. His homosexual rights movement, the Scientific-Humanitarian Committee, sometimes worked together with and sometimes had disagreements with the other more culturally oriented homosexual movement of those times, *Der Eigene*, which had a strong pederastic outlook (Oosterhuis & Kennedy, 1991). In the case of The Netherlands, the situation was rather similar. Research on public indecency cases in the Dutch court districts of Amsterdam and The Hague for the period 1830 through 1909 shows that about a third were intergenerational (Hekma, 1987). The leader of the Dutch gay rights movement, J. A. Schorer, was himself a pederast (Van der Meer, 2007). Only in the 1960s did the Dutch homosexual movement start to differentiate itself from what then becomes the pedophile movement (Sandfort, 1983). The biggest modern Dutch homosexual scandal took place in 1938/1939 in the Dutch East Indies, now Indonesia, and targeted some 200 men suspected of having sex with minors (meaning under 21 years) ("Koloniale zedenschandalen, 1936-1939," in Staal, 2004).

According to Penniston (2004, p. 113) a third of the public indecency cases in Paris in the 1870s involved contacts between youth under 20 and men over 20 years of age. Only six of the 23 men over 50 were accused of contacts with men over 40, so many sexual relations among adults also involved major age discrepancies. Penniston sees a development from a pederast to an adult homosexual model that continues into the twentieth century. Revenin (2005) studied male prostitution in Paris around the turn of the twentieth century, and found abundant evidence of pecuniary pederast relations in that period. His more recent work on criminal institutions for youth underlines that this culture of adults and young men having sex together continued on a widespread basis in France into the 1950s (Revenin, 2007).

Information on sexual practices between boys and men is sparser for other parts of Europe. Dan Healey (2001) describes the homosexual subculture in late czarist and early Soviet Russia as being a mix of boys, soldiers, servants and gentlemen, with male prostitution playing an important role. Jens Rydström (2003) discusses Sweden between 1880 and 1950 and shows a subculture where men and youth sexually interact. Only boys under the age of 12 were considered innocent, whereas adolescents received punishments as harsh as those of adult males. With the modernization of sexual discourses the old religious perspective of sodomy was replaced with medical theories that stressed the dangers of homosexual predators for adolescents. This led to efforts to control homosexuality and restrain its visibility, and also to a differentiation between men who have age equivalent relations with other adults and pedophiles who "abuse" boys. The material on the Grand Tour that Robert Aldrich addresses in his book on *The Seduction of the Mediterranean. Writing, Art and Homosexual Fantasy* (1993) contains accounts of many Northern-European men from the period after 1700 who traveled southward for homosexual pleasures, often with adolescents. This tradition has continued unabated to the present day, but is now designated by a more pejorative term, *sex tourism*. Boy-lovers continue to travel to ever-changing destinations in North Africa, Eastern Europe and Southeast Asia.

Crossing the Atlantic, William Benemann's study of *Male-Male Intimacy in Early America* includes information on age-discrepant sexual relations in pre-revolutionary America and the early republic which generally parallels that found in the European histories. He coins the terms *romantic mentorships* for such age-differentiated relations, and *chickenships* for shipboard relations on merchant vessels that paralleled those discussed by Burg for his pirates and sailors, and discusses diaries that reveal erotic master-apprentice relations (Benemann, 2006). The material Burg provides in *An American Seafarer in the Age of Sail: The Erotic Diaries of Philip C. Van Buskirk 1851–1870* (Burg, 1994) makes it clear that *chickenship* was also widespread in the US Navy. The expression refers to non-exploitative relations between men and boys, the "chickens," who greatly profited from the relations and willingly engaged in them. Jonathan Ned Katz's *Love Stories: Sex Between Men Before Homosexuality* picks up the thread from there, as the subtitle indicates dealing with the mid-nineteenth century, before the widespread use of the term *homosexuality* and the acceptance of the identity it implied. The subtitle also says "between men," but this should more properly be "between males," because the collection includes discussions of Whitman's 1841 "Child's Companion," the story of a relation between a 12-year-old boy and an adult, and accounts of similar relations between soldiers and boys during the Civil War which serve as background for Whitman's experience as a war nurse to his "boys"—some of whom, given the age for military service, not to mention the presence of flag-bearers and drummer boys, were very literally boys (Katz, 2001). Whitman's own relations as revealed in his correspondence, and their background in the composition of the Union army, are documented and discussed in Charley Shively's *Drum Beats* (Shively, 1989). Much of the documentation of the sexological (and pederastic) history of the American Civil War remains buried in widely dispersed and unpublished correspondence from its soldiers; one rare example which has reached print is found in T. P. Lowry's sexual history of the Civil War, excerpted from a letter from a Massachusetts soldier to his wife, describing a nearly all-male "ball" in camp: "We had some little Drummer boys dressed up and I'll bet you could not tell them from girls if you did not know them.... Some of them looked almost good enough to lay with and I guess some of them did get laid with.... I know I slept with mine." (Lowry, 1994, pp. 112–113).

Katz ends with a discussion of sexual encounters in working-class New York saloons in the 1890s; George Chauncey's *Gay New York* then picks up the thread. What is striking there is that, with no intent of deliberately making a case for the prevalence of age-discrepant relations, it is our estimate after reading his book that approximately a third of the sodomy or homosexuality cases he reports or discusses, from newspaper reports, reports of public morals groups and personal accounts, involve precisely such relations (Chauncey, 1994). He also underlines the role of social class and ethnicity in the differing conceptions of (homo)sexuality, the role of xenophobia and racism in public morality campaigns, and the changing geography of male-male (including man-boy) encounters in the half century he covers. Moving outside urban areas, one has Peter Boag's *Same-Sex Affairs: Constructing and Controlling Homosexuality in the Pacific Northwest* (2003). In his first two chapters Boag discusses the relations between men and boys on the road among hoboes, in logging camps and saw mills, and among the migratory working class in the nearby cities. The evidence he presents indicates that among transient agricultural and industrial laborers around 1900 sex between men and male youths was common, and part and parcel of male homosocial culture. Notwithstanding the ambiguous terminology, which could be understood as either censorious or playful—the men were called "wolves" and the boys "lambs"—the relations were generally mutually chosen and often mutually beneficial for the individuals' survival on the road. A similar picture is provided by an eyewitness, in the report on "Homosexuality Among Tramps" by "Josiah Flynt" (Josiah Flynt Willard, 1869–1907), printed as Appendix I to *Sexual Inversion* (Ellis, 1915; it first appeared in the 1897 edition). The few cases of prosecution for sodomy in the same period that Gary L. Atkins discusses in *Gay Seattle* (2003) also include man-boy examples. As Margot Canaday found in her *The Straight State: Sexuality and Citizenship in Twentieth-Century America,* the tradition of transient men having sexual relations with younger males was still present in the 1930s, when social workers were concerned about "wolves" and "pansies," and discussed the dangers of "hobohemia" (Canaday, 2009).

There are also studies or discussions which bring the presence of age-discrepant male sexual relations in American urban working-class neighborhoods up well beyond the 1940 cut off date of Chauncey's book, for instance with reference to Nashville, Tennessee (Reiss, 1967), Baltimore/Highlandtown ("Neighborhood Man/Boy Scenes in the United States," in Reeves, 1992), and Boston/Revere (Mitzel, 1980). Ralph Tindall's pioneering longitudinal studies of the outcomes for nine cases where adolescent boys were sexually involved with adult men provides a picture of the phenomenon in the American Midwest in the mid-twentieth century (Tindall, 1978). In his autobiographical *Puppies,* the underground journalist Chester Anderson, writing under the pseudonym John Valentine, sketches a picture of his sexual involvements involving teenage boys in the countercultural scene of the late 1960s and early 1970s, principally in Los Angeles, with some excursions to New York and other smaller cities (Valentine, 1979). Mack Friedman's rather sensationalistic history of homosexual hustling in America includes male and trans sex workers of all kinds, ages and degrees of professionalism, including teenage boys, and not only collects material from previous surveys, but carries the story forward into the 1970s for cities like New York, Boston, Chicago, San Francisco and Los Angeles (Friedman, 2003).

William Eskridge's history of sodomy laws in America (2008) approaches the issue from a unique perspective. He begins with the presumption that "Most of the Americans actually charged with committing the crime against nature did so with minors, and the records in these cases reveal a broad range of sexually stimulating or abusive activities, including touching and fondling erogenous zones;" he immediately goes on to identify one of the major driving forces behind the development of American sodomy law as a fear of "*predation,* especially as regards our children" (p. 3; italics his). The statistical basis for his "most" is never stated. He returns to this theme of the putative "predation" against boys when examining the child protection laws, spin-offs from sodomy laws that were enacted between 1880 and the 1920s (pp. 53–55), and traces how, between the 1930s and 1960s, it takes on a new life as the fear of corruption and recruiting of boys by homosexuals (pp. 83–84). He finally notes its afterlife in the twenty-first century: although few Americans today, he says, believe that gay men (and the occasional lesbian) actually assault children or are involved in "recruiting" for homosexuality, there is a lingering fear that the "public celebration of homosexuality—sex for pleasure alone—is predatory in its supposed effect—namely to lure naive and innocent children into hedonistic lifestyles and away from traditional marriage" (p. 5). Although at no point does Eskridge present any hard statistical evidence—as opposed to alarmist figures from legislators and those lobbying for broader morals legislation—it is obvious from what our other sources have shown that age-stratified relations did exist, and that the waves of moral panic were not being created from the whole cloth. Whether these relations were necessarily "predatory" or "abusive" as Eskridge appears to accept, is another matter.

Two final studies should be noted in closing, which do not deal with individual instances of age-discrepant relations, but rather with the place of such relations in the intellectual discourse on homosexuality. Graham Robb's *Strangers* gives those who advocated erotic man-boy relations their proper place in the discourses on homosexuality going on in England, France and Germany, although he is rather disparaging to them (Robb, 2003). The collection of writings from *Der Eigene* allows some of that group to speak for themselves, as they contest the forensic medical view and Hirschfeld's "third sex" theories and promote their view of male bonding and pedagogical Eros (Oosterhuis & Kennedy, 1991).

Theory

There are a number of texts and their authors that the GLBTQ websites like to claim as their own, but which are frankly pederast discourses. Adolf Brand and his *Der Eigene* get that treatment, without any serious discussion of the ideas that the magazine and its authors advocated; so does John Henry Mackay, whose work has also been brought into English by Hubert Kennedy (Mackay 1985 and 1988; see also Kennedy 2007 and 2002 and Kennedy's notes and introductions in his two Mackay translations). The standard article about Mackay on these websites—a text provided by Kennedy[7]—notes that he was most attracted to boys who were between 14 and 17. Another group around the poet Stefan George took its distance from the more pederast *Der Eigene,* but they were just as inspired by boys, the ancient Greeks, the Renaissance, and the German tradition of *Bildung*—that ideal of an all-male educational culture with close bonds between teachers and pupils. George's poetry addressed boys, and his followers continued his tradition after the Second World War in Amsterdam with the journal *Castrum Peregrini* (1951–2008; Keilson-Lauritz, 2006).

Some texts don't even get that far: for instance Antonio Rocco's *Alcibiade fanciullo a scola.* In his afterword to the first English translation of this 1652 work, Mader makes the case that the book could be considered the first homosexual novel: the existence of a document like *Alcibiade,* and an audience for it, is evidence for the existence of a sodomitic identity and culture in Venice in 1650 (Afterword, in Rocco, 2000). One might think this would be welcome in LGBT circles, but alas, the book is pederastic. Yes, it does rate a mention in a note on Antonio Rocco on the GLBTQ site[8]—again written by the indefatigable Hubert Kennedy—but no entry of its own. The publisher tells us that in 2000, when he approached the then leading American gay book distributor about handling it, he was informed that "our book stores do not deal in books on this subject" (letter from Alamo Square distributors to the publisher, Entimos Press). "This subject" being gay history, we presume?

A third example might be the Uranians, a loosely knit group of British and American poets and writers who were active from around 1890 to 1930. They were first chronicled by Timothy d'Arch Smith in 1970, as including both a number of admittedly minor poets, and early homosexual activists and theorists such as George Cecil Ives, Leonard Green, Kenneth Ingram and the American art dealer resident in England, Edward Perry Warren. In addition, d'Arch Smith attached the poet and homosexual socialist campaigner Edward Carpenter and John Addington Symonds, who had died too early to participate but exercised an enormous influence on them, as "godfathers" of a sort (d'Arch Smith, 1970). Further research over the years turned up connections with an American circle who shared their outlook and in 1924 produced the first anthology of homosexual poetry published in America, *Men and Boys* (Mader, 2006). This information reinforced the understanding of the bidirectional nature of the influences of Walter Pater on some of the Americans and of Whitman (via Carpenter and Symonds) on the British, and also clarified the purpose of the group in making an artistic argument for asymmetrical male relations—both age-structured and cross-class—and ultimately for homosexual liberation through the organizations they created and the publishing they did. In short, they constituted one of the first "gay liberation" movements in the English-speaking world—and it had age-discrepant sexual relations at its heart. Such news is not welcome. Robb is honest enough to note the existence of the Uranians, but cuttingly remarks, "The recurring characteristics of English 'boy-worship' are self-deception, trickery and bad poetry" (Robb, 2003, p. 218). A new introduction for a new edition of *Men and Boys* has been prepared, but can't find a publisher.[9] A recent doctoral dissertation on the Uranians (Kaylor, 2006) which attempts to commend them by nominating Oscar Wilde, Gerald Manley Hopkins and Walter Pater as members, is not likely to improve the situation.[10]

Another example is the network of writers and poets in France, in particular surrounding André Gide: Roger Martin du Gard, Pierre Louys, Maurice Sachs, François Paul Alibert and Jean Cocteau. It was inspired not only by Oscar Wilde but also by Verlaine and Rimbaud and J. K. Huysmans. Gide wrote a defense of homosexuality, *Corydon* (1924), which blends the androphile and pederast. Count Jacques d'Adelswärd-Fersen, who was persecuted for his relations with young males, wrote novels and poetry mainly figuring young men, and with like-minded artists created the journal *Akademos*. He retreated to Capri, an island well-known for its pederast exiles and visitors (Money, 1986).

Theories and theorists about age-discrepant sexual relations have played a significant role in the history of homosexuality, but one would never know it. As Foucault also observed, silences are an integral part of the strategies that underlie and permeate discourses (Foucault, 1978).

Ego Documents

A brief word should be said about biographical, autobiographical or literary sources that are reworkings of autobiographical fact, particularly by members of the gay community, which have become largely taboo, excluded from discussion because of their positive or mixed accounts of the writers' boyhood sexual experiences with adults. For instance, there are no less than six which readily come to mind in Dutch. Three are by men born around 1930. Two of these—*Operatie Montycoat*, by the writer Jaap Harten (b. 1930) and *Voor een Verloren Soldaat* (translated into English as *For a Lost Soldier*), by the dancer/choreographer Rudi van Dantzig (1932–2012)—involve their authors' sexual experiences with soldiers during World War II, the former at age 14, the latter at age 11 to

12 (Harten, 1970; Van Dantzig, 1986/1996); the third involves the account by the dancer, choreographer and photographer Hans van Manen (b. 1932) of how he took the initiative in his first contacts with men in public toilets at just over the age of 11 (Schaik, 1997). Two more involve The Netherlands in the 1950s. *Een jongen met vier benen,* the basically autobiographical *Bildungsroman* by Kees Verheul (b. 1940), includes an account of the sexual relation he had at the age of 14 with the father of one of his female friends. In a new afterward to the 2010 edition, Verheul laments that the situation regarding boy love has only deteriorated since the novel was published in 1982, and that his contribution to the debate had no positive influence on social attitudes (Verheul, 1982). In his autobiography, which appeared shortly before his assassination, the Dutch professor and politician Pim Fortuyn (1948-2002) recounts his sexual experiences with men from the age of five—experiences he characterizes not as abusive, but as tremendously exciting (Fortuyn, 2002). He himself was later a defender of non-abusive pedophile relations. In his book *Zeer kleine liefde* the poet and writer Ted van Lieshout (b. 1955) reflects on his relation with a man at the age of 12; the theme is somewhat of a replay of Van Dantzig's wartime experience, where the hurt left by the relation was not a result of its sexual nature, but of the man's sudden disappearance, experienced by the boy as a crushing betrayal (Van Lieshout, 1999). In Van Lieshout's case, the book arose when years later he discovered that the disappearance had been occasioned by threats—of which he had not previously known—made to the man by Van Lieshout's mother, when she discovered his relation with her son.

There are two similar documents in English that could also be mentioned. The first is *Memories That Smell Like Gasoline,* by the gay artist David Wojnarowicz (1954-1992), and the second, the *Diary of a Dirty Boy* by Luis Miguel Fuentes (b. 1977). Both are accounts of their authors' experiences as boys in the New York sex scene, the first in the 1960s, the second in the 1980s. Both are also united by their generally unflattering portrayal of the johns—the customers—their authors encountered there, but at the same time, by the authors' clear statements of their intention to willingly participate in that scene (Wojnarowicz, 1992; Fuentes, 1998). We are certain that this list could be expanded by other memoirs, from other countries and in other languages.

Material Culture: Von Gloeden to *Grecian Guild*

When it comes to some forms of material culture—in this case visual culture—which provide evidence of age-discrepant relations in Western, European society, the political filtration system has not been so thorough. Histories of homosexual art, for instance the recent, quite comprehensive compilation by Dominique Fernandez, are replete with erotic adolescents and even younger boys—Cupids, Narcissi, Ganymedes ("Modern Uses for Greek Myths"), Arcadian shepherd boys, young Davids and St. Johns,

Neapolitan fisherboys, and boy bathers: the list seems endless (Fernandez, 2002). However, apart from confirming that these materials do exist (one would be hard-put to argue for the prevalence of age-structured relations through the centuries if *no* visual evidence existed!), they are of limited value for our survey. First, they represent elite culture, whether from an era when the patrons were cardinals and nobles, or later when they were wealthy merchant-princes, or patrons of pricey Soho galleries today. At best they speak of the erotic interests of those who were wealthy enough to patronize artists (or, in the case of neoclassical public art, such as the warrior and his adolescent companion who gives a whole new meaning to *sans-culotte,* front and center in Rude's "Marseillaise" on the Arc de Triomphe, those who were powerful enough to commission it). In addition, however, such collections are necessarily defined by the tastes of the compiler and the market for which they are intended. Néret's *HomoArt,* in the Taschen series, with its Cocteaus, Quaintances, Tom of Finlands and Pierre and Gilleses, clearly caters to the LGBT market. That there are as many erotic images of boys and adolescents in it as there are tells us not as much about the society in which they were first created as about the compiler's and publisher's judgment about the persistence of a fascination with age-discrepant eroticism today. Nonetheless, one further recent collection must be mentioned here too, Germaine Greer's *The Boy,* of interest not only for the images it presents but for her analysis of, and defense of erotic interest in young males (Greer, 2003). Although her announced purpose was "to reclaim for women the right to appreciate the short-lived beauty of boys," her responses to those who accused her of pandering to pedophiles made it clear that the persistence of the male gaze and appreciation, which after all had created most of these images in the first place, was not something which upset her.

For evidential value we are perhaps on firmer ground with photography. It is, after all, the "democratic" medium par excellence, affordable to the masses, after a certain point in its history wholly accessible to the masses for them to create their own images, and (again after a certain point in its history) easily reproducible in printed form, in particular in magazines. There are still the problems of selection: If one is to believe the lavish French history of gay photography (Borhan, 2007) no homosexual ever looked at anyone under 21; the only image there of someone under that age is by Larry Clark—who strenuously rejects the suggestion he is a gay photographer! Thankfully, one does not have to rely on such surveys; there are also less filtered collections such as the latest and largest study of the work of Baron Wilhelm von Gloeden, *Auch ich in Arkadien,* which prints more than eight hundred photographs by him and his contemporaries and competitors (Kiermeier-Debre&Vogel, 2007). It is the largest and probably most representative sample of Von Gloeden's oeuvre yet presented. Browsing through it one finds that some 30 to 40 percent of the images involve boys under 18, the bulk of the remainder being of males in their late teens or early 20s. About 5 percent of the total involve prepubescent boys, sometimes as young as seven or eight, normally as part of groups with older boys and/or men, but occasionally, particularly for boys approaching puberty, in nude studies alone. About 5 to 10 percent of the total involve fully mature men. Because Von Gloeden was a commercial photographer, presumably working with his market in mind, and because he was engaged in mass marketing (many of his more popular images were available in postcard form, either at his studio in Taormina or from agents in Rome [his Roman agent, located on the Via Sistina, was curiously named G. Pedo], Munich, Berlin and Paris, from whom one could also order larger prints), it is safe to assume that this can inform us about the proportion of his homosexual clientele who were interested in age-discrepant relations—if not precise percentages, at least to say that it was a substantial slice of the market.

A half century later one can similarly make use of the small homosexual magazines that flourished in America from the late 1950s to the early 1970s (*Fizeek, Grecian Guild Pictorial, Manorama, Trim, 101 Boys*) for similar purposes. Often termed *beefcake* magazines, the majority of the models found there were over 18 (indeed, many over 21), but there was also enough "chicken" on the menu to make it clear that age-discrepant sexual interests were alive and well among their readership. Two of the most outstanding examples were the wildly popular models Ernie Niemi, photographed by both Anthony Guyther of Capital Studio and by Don Wight, and Bobby Pell, another of Capital Studio's models. Ernie debuted in *Trim* in November 1960, at the age of 14, was "cover man" on *Grecian Guild Pictorial* two months later, and photo sets of him were still selling in mid-1964; Bobby first appears in *Trim* in February 1962—a "cover man" on his first appearance, no less—at the age of 10, and is still returning in subsequent photo sets as late as 1967, when he was 14. These were only two of the longer-running instances. It should also be noted that in the collections of drawings, amateur and professional, issued by these magazines as their "art quarterlies," there were an even higher percentage of drawings of young subjects. Once again, though, one cannot use the percentage of younger models or subjects here to determine the proportion of the buyers in the homosexual community with age-discrepant interests; it is only indicative of the fact that right up to the eve of Stonewall, they were there as an integral part of that community—and in substantial enough numbers to warrant putting models like Ernie Niemi and Bobby Pell on the front cover.

The sort of evidence we have just discussed will soon no longer be available—indeed, may no longer exist at all. More than a decade ago, in the introduction to *Hard to Imagine*, Thomas Waugh's history of male eroticism in photography (in Chapter 2 of which he also discusses the question of why there was such a proliferation of "ephebophile" images during the late Victorian era and how that reflects the homosexual community of the day) Waugh already remarks, "Other restraints have led regrettably to some unavoidable distortions, especially the slant that today's fanatical legal prohibition of the erotic representation of models under the age of eighteen has had on the historical representativeness of this book's selection of illustrations. Earlier eras were—and other cultures are—much less timorous than our own about adolescent bodies and desires" (Waugh, 1996, p. xv). The day had already passed when he could run photographs of a 16-year-old and a 25-year-old together as illustrations for his arguments about age dynamics in male erotic photographs (Waugh, 1984). Alas, by 2004, in his *Lust Unearthed,* an examination of homosexual erotic *drawings* from "Tijuana Bibles" and the art quarterlies mentioned previously, he is forced to explain.

> This image [a drawing] of a gentle scoutmaster swarmed by his teenage charges (probably U.S.A., c. 1960) has been cropped in deference to the dangers of doing historical research in an atmosphere of contradictory, anti-erotic and anti-child paranoia, both legal and commercial. Ephebophilia has been accepted in other cultures, and the erotic dimensions of mentorship have been forthrightly explored by scholars within earlier, more open-minded regimes, from Weimar Germany to the pre-1975 U.S. (Waugh, 2004, p. 45)

Unfortunately, in the years since that was written things have only gotten worse. The wave of censorship that was originally justified as necessary to protect children from sexual abuse in the production of photographic or cinematic images involving sexual activities and/or the exploitation of their sexuality in the commercial distribution thereof, has now spread to where there is no longer any demonstrable connection with child protection at all. Justified by the argument that if you allow pedophiles to have images in any medium, they will want photographic or video images, an expansion from photographic images, which did involve living/real models, to drawings and virtual images, which do not, occurred between Waugh's two comments. A further expansion that had already largely taken place by then was from penalizing not just the production and sale of such images, but their *possession,* with the excuse (despite the knowledge that such a policy has been a total failure with regard to drugs) that attacking demand would accomplish the control of the supply that previous laws had not been able to effect. A third expansion has been the ever-broadening range of images deemed pornographic, going beyond those involving sexual acts to include all nudity, provocative poses and emphasis on the genital area (even if the minor depicted is clothed), and most recently, in The Netherlands (in prosecutorial guidelines issued by the Ministry of Justice in September 2007) to "placing a minor in a sexual context." At the same time, the definition of *child* has become inflated. For instance, in The Netherlands the definition of *child* has moved from

16—the age of consent—to "persons under the age of 18"—the age of consent for prostitution, on the grounds that all "child pornography" is a form of prostitution—to persons "not *obviously over* the age of 18" (our emphasis; the Dutch September 2007 guidelines). In light of the Dutch age of consent being 16 for consensual sexual activities, this creates the legal absurdity of criminalizing the possession of an image of a person engaged in an act which is legal.

With the inclusion of virtual children and subjects over the age of consent, and the extension to cover images that are—in the minds of the police and judges, at least—merely sexually suggestive, it is hard not to conclude that the purpose of the "child pornography" law has shifted, leaving behind all concern for the protection of real children from actual abuse, to become a tool for the persecution of a demonized sexual minority. At a personal level, it provides grounds for their arrest and incarceration as individuals, simply for their sexual desires, quite apart from whether they have committed any act involving a person. But it is also a manner of eliminating material culture that could be evidence that "pederasts" or "pedophiles" had a culture and history (whether or not that is part of the history of homosexuality) and were never more than isolated, deviant "sexual predators." That is to say, it is precisely the tactic that was used against colonial peoples in the nineteenth and early twentieth centuries, when their cultural artifacts were carted off to European ethnological collections, stripping them of their identity and reinforcing their status as "primitive"—or the tactic of Nazi Germany in its effort to destroy all remnants of Jewish culture to justify their destruction of the Jewish people themselves.

The impact of this on scholarship should be obvious. Most of the visual material involved here still remains in private hands; institutions have never been very active in collecting such material. Its possession is now criminalized, and if seized it will be destroyed (or, more likely now, turned over to the police to be digitized for use in identifying "victims" and "perpetrators"—even if we are talking about seventy-five-year-old images—and *then* destroyed). Institutions that do hold material of this sort refuse to allow anyone to use it; even between the time of Waugh's 1984 article, which had been based on images in the Kinsey Institute, and his 1996 book, most of their collection was closed to him (Waugh, 1996). Nor does this impact only on material specifically involving pederasty or "pedophilia;" because of the presence of any images of minors, magazines like *Grecian Guild* are now qualified as child pornography in their entirety, and not only do they become inaccessible as evidence of the role and presence of age-discrepant relations and desires among homosexuals, but the gay community loses access to them as documents of its own history. Indeed, when the age for "child pornography" rises to 21, a very significant part of the visual history that the LGBT community now celebrates becomes off limits. If today we cannot imagine

LGBT history without Von Gloeden, we'd better start trying, because tomorrow we will have to.

Discussion

The evidence reviewed above is highly varied. All of it is limited in one way or another. There are unresolved questions about the representativeness of evidence gained from legal records. In this case there is particularly the question of whether age-discrepant relations might be overrepresented there, either because they came to the notice of the authorities more easily, or because pederasts were more likely to abuse their power in relation to the boys. (For the record, we believe the former is an anachronistic reading; unlike contemporary society, with its segregation of boys, the presence of men and boys together would have been as common in Renaissance Florence or in Amsterdam in the Golden Age as the presence of men together; in regard to the latter, there are enough cases involving forced sex with adult male servants to indicate that abuse of authority was no more uncommon with adults.) Still, there remains the question of how representative the incidents that did come to the attention of authorities were of those that did not. Other evidence is from elite culture, or from particular male subcultures (maritime situations, transients, colonial situations) which are inherently not representative of the rest of society. However, in a sense these various failings cancel one another out: although legal records, including commoners, in some respects tell a different story from that of the elite culture, they all tell the same story: age-discrepant sexual desires, and relations, and their cultural representations have been a constant in homosexuality in Western culture and society.

The evidence reviewed is strongest from those countries and language groups where research into modern, Western homosexuality has been strongest: England, the United States, The Netherlands, France and Italy. On the other hand, there are enough other sources involving Scandinavia, Germany and Russia to suggest that the picture from the countries with the greatest depth of research would also apply for other areas not yet researched in such depth. Although the different eras are represented by different sorts of or combinations of documents, in the countries for which the documentation is most thorough all periods from at least the sixteenth and seventeenth centuries to the mid-twentieth century are covered.

Although there are some exceptions, the age ranges of the boys involved in these age-stratified relations in modern Western homosexuality is generally in line with the ages discussed in Rind's definitions (pp. 7–9, this volume), namely, the second decade of life.

More important, the evidence would also suggest that the age-stratified relations in modern Western homosexuality largely conform to Rind's picture of relations that are consensual. With the advent of anecdotal accounts the evidence explicitly testifies to the voluntary, consensual, sometimes long-term, and presumably not damaging or unpleasant nature of these relations, and this is entirely clear from the ego documents. Prior to that, with the legal records, we can only infer this from the length of the relation recorded in the court papers (for instance, the fifteen years that the Utrecht burgomaster and his servant were involved in their relation) or the court's finding that both parties were equally guilty of sodomy, whereas cases which did involve force or coercion were handled as rape. We would emphasize again here that the legal evidence from the sixteenth and seventeenth century Dutch examples through early nineteenth century examples, such as the HMS *Africaine* affair, makes it plain that courts were quite able to distinguish rape or other coerced sexual acts from consensual pairings—whether between adults and minors or between two adults of varying degrees of power or authority—and charged and sentenced accordingly.

Based on the present evidence, the degree to which these consensual relations can be characterized as *mentoring* is somewhat less clear. In the context of a teacher-student or master-apprentice relation, the word might be entirely appropriate. Without further knowledge of the particular circumstances which an ego document might provide, in situations where there was no specific body of knowledge or skills to be passed on it is difficult to know to what degree the relation might have been mentoring in the generalized sense of providing the younger partner with life skills, or whether, particularly in military or maritime situations, or among transients, these relations were perhaps more on the order of alliances for mutual support in difficult circumstances. Many of these relations may have been entered into simply for the sexual pleasure they provided. And of course, there could have been a mixture of several of these reasons.

All this does however suggest that these age-stratified relations—even if not romantic or even pedagogical, but merely strategic alliances (for instance, between men and boys or youths on shipboard or among hobos), or even entirely pecuniary relations in the late nineteenth and twentieth century urban settings (working-class "trade")—were experienced by the younger partner as in some way beneficial—or at any rate, as not harmful. This historical evidence is thus in line with the conclusions of the literature reviews and meta-analyses of contemporary surveys done by Rind and others, that young people generally do not suffer serious or long-lasting damage as a result of age-discrepant relations unless either incest, or force, threat or coercion are involved, and that a significant percentage—two-thirds—of the boys involved found them positive or neutral (Bauserman & Rind, 1997; Rind & Tromovitch, 1997; Rind, Tromovitch, & Bauserman, 1998a; Rind, Tromovitch & Bauserman, 1998b).[11] It at least in no way contradicts the arguments of the various theorists who have written about the pedagogical potential of age-structured erotic relations, from "erotic socialists" like William Paine (Paine 1912, 1920) and advocates of Hellenic ideals like Edward Perry Warren among the Uranians (Mader, 2006), through the group surrounding *Der Eigene*, including Adolf Brand, Elisar von Kupffer, Benedict Friedländer and Hans Blüher, or Gustav Wyneken and the German pedagogical Eros theorists (Oosterhuis & Kennedy, 1991; for Wyneken himself, see Wyneken, 1921 and Maasen, 1988; Wyneken's theories and his Wickersdorf school were a source of inspiration for A. S. Neill and other Free School proponents), and ultimately even arguments made for the value of man-boy relations by the much-maligned Walter Breen ("J. Z. Eglinton") in his *Greek Love* (Eglinton, 1964; for a summary and discussion, see Mader, 2002).

By the same token, the evidence makes it clear that the simple persistence of age-differentiated sexual relations, or even evidence of their potential positive or neutral outcomes, is not a reason for their uncritical acceptance. All of the evidence points to these relations often being not only age-discrepant, but also frequently unequal in terms of social class (and/or in some cases race as well). The legal evidence particularly is replete with accounts of abuse of power by the older partner, not only the power granted simply by age in our society, but also that which accrues from social or economic status. Once it is recognized that not all age-discrepant relations are, by definition, abusive, research is necessary to determine what the circumstances are in which some are experienced as abusive, when others are not. The parameters for this suggested previously—incest, force, violence, threat, coercion, deceit—would seem fairly obvious, but research could tell us more.[12] That some of these behaviors are a possibility for either partner—for instance, threats in the form of blackmail by the younger or "weaker" partner—should also be kept in mind. In addition to this sociological research, we would also welcome further thought from the proponents of age-discrepant relations in regard to the ethics operative in them.

Rind asserts that age-stratified relations were the norm for homosexual behavior in the societies he considers in his historical and cross-cultural examination. (There were, of course, other societies, such as the Shamanistic societies of Siberia and North America, where gender-structured homosexuality was the norm for a very small minority, but those are neither here nor there with regard to his argument. He also notes—correctly—that the "gay" pattern [i.e., exclusively same-sex relations between relatively equal adults] is exceptional from a cross-cultural and historical perspective.) Based on our review of historical evidence, can the same be said for Western homosexuality?

As has frequently been argued, homosexuality would appear to be a ternary phenomenon, with age-structured, gender-structured and egalitarian strands. Regrettably, we do not have as clear a picture of the extent of the presence of gender-structured relations throughout the period and across all the territory our question involves, as we do for age structured relations, although evidence from the beginning of the eighteenth century onward—for instance, the rise of the "molly house" in England (Bray, 1982), Parisian police records of behavior in taverns there (Rey, 1987), the Vere Street and Boulton and Park scandals (1810 and 1870, respectively) in London (Cook, 2003), Cocks's discussion of the continuity of earlier effeminate expressions of homosexuality in nineteenth century Britain (Cocks, 2010), records of cross-dressing prostitutes and taverns they frequented, from the archives of the police and societies for the suppression of vice in New York (Katz, 2001; Chauncey, 1994)—through the drag balls of Paris's Magic City (shut down by French authorities in 1932) and in New York's Harlem and Weimar Berlin's transvestite clubs, all indicate that it was a not inconsiderable presence in major urban centers through that period, along with (and as we have seen, occasionally overlapping with) age-discrepant relations. On the other hand, *urban* may be the operative word here. Plausibly in Classical times, and most probably for locations such as Renaissance Florence (Rocke, 1996), or indeed Renaissance Italy in general, pederasty apparently trumps both gender-structured and egalitarian forms of homoeroticism combined. In other places and periods examined it may well have remained the most frequent expression of the three. Certainly looking at the visual artifacts of the elite culture, the eroticized image of the boy always retains a certain dominance in its discourse. But we must also recognize that the discourse in elite culture is not the only contesting voice here; the way that working-class communities appear to have had different outlooks on age-discrepant relations (Houlbrook, 2005; Chauncey, 1994; but also for instance Reeves, 1992), along with the long history of age-differentiated relations in those communities revealed by the legal records, should also alert us the fact that such relations may have been more prominent in one segment of a particular community than in another. On the whole, for the homosexual subculture of premodern and modern Europe, although one might rightly be reluctant to say that age-structured relations were the *norm,* unquestionably they were persistent, always prominent, and never negligible.

Further, on the basis of our evidence, we would go beyond Rind's assertion that this prominence declined with the Industrial Revolution (pg. 38, this volume), and argue that age-structured relations remained a prominent component—though perhaps increasingly challenged—right up to the 1970s, and in a sense remain so to this day. Although the American Civil War was perhaps the last conflict in which very young boys participated, World War I still saw the participation of boys in their mid-teens both aboard warships and in the trenches, where they interacted with older men. While this had become exceptional by World War II (Britain's youngest WW II casualty was recently established to have been only 14[13]), two of the three Dutch ego-documents pertaining to World War II suggest that by then the interaction between men and boys in wartime had moved to outside the military services themselves. Nineteenth century industrialization merely provided a new site for their interaction—the shop floor—and Boag's study of the Pacific Northwest and Montague Glover's rural photographs in interwar England, in Gardner's collection (Boag, 2003; Gardner, 1993) suggest that the mechanization of agriculture and lumbering by no means eliminated the participation of men and boys together in these sectors, although now perhaps working with steam equipment rather than animals. The "living-in system" for boys working in London's burgeoning commercial establishments, against which Paine inveighs, provided opportunities for both close emotional relations among the boys and opportunities for sexual exploitation of the boys by the more vicious of their overseers (Paine, 1912). As the twentieth century went on there were a whole series of changes in the geography of homosexuality in general (specifically the increased privatization of homosexuality cited by Houlbrook, 2005), and likewise changes in the geography of the interaction of men and boys, as boys were increasingly segregated and ghettoized by being removed from the workplace as workers, and their vocational training being entrusted to the state rather than taking place in employment situations. The period of childhood was extended and on the one hand was increasingly restricted to the nuclear family, which itself was becoming more insulated in a complex world, and on the other, to an educational system that strongly invested in "preserving" the "innocence" of the young. These were the changes which ultimately reduced the opportunities for interaction between men and boys, both with regard to informal mentoring relations and for more commercial intercourse. The number of places of public entertainment (cinemas and swim baths) where men and boys had interacted also declined during the same period, or shortly thereafter, with changes in recreation patterns and the development of a specific commercial youth culture where boys mixed with their age-mates, male or female, rather than with men. Although a smaller circle of men continued to seek out contact with boys in the remaining formal situations (the "continuum" effect Rind cites (pg. 30, this volume) as teachers, coaches, and scout leaders, age-disparate contacts were less common—and in time these remaining opportunities too came increasingly under scrutiny as a result of efforts by homophobes like Anita Bryant, who saw the persistence of age-disparate relations as an opportunity to attack the emerging gay movement. Once under attack, a gay movement, increasingly concerned with holding on to its gains, joined the child protection clamor Rind describes and finally supported the legal marginalization seen today—and in the course of this, also marginalizing young queers under the age of consent, who were surrendered to straight institutions like family, schoolyard or sport club. Even its criminalization and organizational marginalization has not eliminated the persistence of age-structured eroticism, however: both the demand for (and supply of) illegal visual material of under-age subjects and the valorization of youth among gay males are indicative of its survival. This valorization is revealed, for example, in the constant use of the word *boy* for anyone under 40, efforts to retain boyish appearance even to the extent of shaving and body-waxing (although of course there is also the backlash to that, the "bear cult"), legal gay visual imagery that skates as close as possible to the line with "boys" who look under age but are provably 18, and the "my first time" and autobiographical literature which often focuses on experiences of boys before the age of consent. Even ideas about protecting gay youth can be linked to broader cultural ideas about youthfulness (Marshall, 2004).

It is true that age-structured homosexual relations today no longer have the same clear social potential in mentoring that they did before formal, mass education was the rule, and before relations between pupils and teachers even in the schools became impersonal and professionalized toward the end of the nineteenth century and then desexualized in the aftermath of the "harassment" debates toward the end of the twentieth. The settings for these age-discrepant relations have also changed as boys and youth have been removed from the workplace—and from work in general—over the past century, shifting to other settings such as sports clubs, youth clubs or scout troops. In a structure where the nuclear family is more insulated and autonomous and parental responsibility has been enlarged while education is the tightly controlled prerogative (indeed monopoly) of the state (and increasingly its commercial partners, as the state privatizes its prerogative), a pedagogical Eros is today a "misfit." Yet it also "misfits" that structure in the same way that it has always "misfit" authoritarian structures, since Socrates was condemned for corrupting his pupils into questioning official verities. An education, in the broadest sense, that is based on a personal, erotic relation (sexualized or not) is unpredictable; it potentially undermines, subverts and challenges the structures by which a state shapes its future citizens. In light of the increasingly totalitarian claims of the state to the control of pedagogy—clad in velvet gloves, as they may be—pedagogical Eros, perhaps, fits precisely as a response, or at any rate as a compensation for or supplement to educational systems today. Perhaps we should be critically rereading "erotic socialists" such as Edward Carpenter and William Paine (Paine, 1912, 1920), and pedagogical Eros advocates.

A Concluding Recommendation

Finally, the evidence we have seen leads to a recommendation for the LGBT movement. Almost precisely a century after the putative birth of the "homosexual," with Stonewall a new identity was born: the gay. It was not long before it ran into problems: although gays insisted they were welcome, lesbians did not feel at home without their name on the door; so institutions that had been Gay became Gay & Lesbian. At the same time, other groups who had formerly been homosexuals went by the boards. Borrowing from the wisdom of evolving feminism, sexual desire, which had formerly been constructed largely around differences in gender, age, class or race, must now be founded (according to the Gay & Lesbian *bien-pensants,* following the example of straight mainstream feminists and left-wingers) on equality and symmetry. Power relations became unacceptable, and that was especially true for intergenerational contacts (Hekma, 2006; 2008; see also Kulick, 2005 for prostitution in Sweden). There was briefly a movement based on the umbrella of all "transgressive" sexualities: queer. Quite quickly it became clear however that the most transgressive of sexualities—the pedophiles and pederasts (the latter by now having been merged into the former by media and public opinion)—were not welcome under this umbrella either, and anyway queers soon lost their way in a thicket of academic jargon. Eventually the need to be a bit more inclusive reemerged: a B for Bisexuals was added, and a T for Trans (except that to be *truly* inclusive one must have Transvestites, Transgenders *and* Transsexuals), and the anti-identitarian Queers found a place under the broadening eaves. Those Questioning the identity received another Q, and most recently the Intersexuals joined the lengthening list of initials. We still await the lovers of each of these species, their supportive parents, children from same-sex couples, and new additions like Androgynes or Polyamorists. Meanwhile, the perverts of the past remain conspicuously absent from this list—not only men and women who engage in age-discrepant sex, but also sadomasochists, men who like public sex or bestiality, and the johns who find sex for money easier than nightlong, desperate searches for Mr. Right, are all excluded from the list that now comprises LGBTTTQQI.

So: Nowhere in this alphabet soup is there a P for Pederasts—who, on the basis of our survey, have as much right if not more to be part of it. We are well aware that discourses create realities—or rather, rearrange them, making them comprehensible—and that it is the perfect prerogative of the LGBTTTQQI to define (homo)sexuality in terms of equal and symmetrical relations only. But there is a certain dialectic here: discourses can change realities by reshaping their dynamics, but they cannot create them out of the whole cloth. The history of pederasty is to a large extent the history of homosexuality, and vice versa; one cuts off a part of their history only at a risk to themselves. Moreover, as Marshall has pointed out, desire that transcends age differences remains stubbornly alive in the LGBT community. Perhaps most seriously, denying the erotics of difference needlessly impoverishes experience. On a less grand scale, it also creates problems in dealing with and incorporating youngsters into gay society (Hekma, 2006). No, the suggestion here is not to add a P to the alphabet soup. It is not even to give pederasty "its rightful place." Confirming the prominence of age-structured sexual relations in the history of homosexuality confirms the need for a new round of sexual liberation, open to the erotics of difference—including age difference—that were closed off in the aftermath of the first round. We're pretty certain the name problem will resolve itself when we cross that rainbow.

Notes

1. For the text, Amendment No. 136B to the Criminal Justice and Immigration Bill, Schedule 26, page 268, at line 38: http://www.publications.parliament.uk/pa/ld200708/ldhansrd/text/80303-0009.htm The debate can also be found at http://www.TheyWorkForYou.com/lords/>id=2008-03-03a873.8 The amendment was ultimately withdrawn for revision of the language.
2. This introduces the second form of homoeroticism cited by Rind, namely gender-structured. It would be interesting for someone to trace the fluctuations and interferences among age-structured, gender-structured and egalitarian male homosexualities in European culture, as historians working from anthropological sources have done for Africa (Murray and Roscoe, 1998). The Pelagius legends are also an early source for the pernicious influence discourses on sodomy and homosexuality have had in Christian/Muslim relations—and continue to have to this day.
3. Parallel instances of judicial discretion in dealing with punishment of minors who were nonetheless regarded as culpable for sodomitical offenses are recorded in sixteenth and seventeenth century Switzerland (Naphy, 2007).
4. For example, in Morishima Chūryō's compendium of information about the West, *Kōmō zatsuwa* (Red-fur Miscellany; 1778). See pp. 17–18, and 21 of Timon Screech, *The Lens Within the Heart: The Western Scientific Gaze and Popular Imagery in Later Edo Japan.* Honolulu: University of Hawaii Press, 2002. Our thanks to the American scholar Mark McHarry for drawing our attention to this.
5. A suspiciously large number of the adult men executed seem to have been supporters of the judge's opponent in the previous election. We apparently have here another constant in the history of sodomy and homosexuality: the use of accusations of these practices to eliminate, or at least disqualify one's political enemies.
6. We certainly should not be surprised at the presence of age-discrepant relations among Bray's British wedded brothers and Eucharistic friends, given that these forms of same-sex alliances are self-evidently related to (if not direct continuations of) the same-sex unions that John Boswell uncovered in premodern Europe (including in the Celtic and Irish church, which preserved early practices that diverged from the those evolving in the main Western/Latin church, after it was cut off from the main stem of the European church by Danish-Norse invaders), and which, like Bray's religiously blessed friendships, lent themselves to multiple purposes, from cementing family alliances and preserving property inheritance, to providing a form of same-sex "marriage." Although in *Same-Sex Unions in Premodern Europe* Boswell is no more forthcoming on the matter than Bray is in *The Friend*, Boswell's own translations betray that these unions were sometimes *intended* to be age-discrepant: for instance, the rubrics given on page 305, "the priest shall take the *elder* of them that have been joined together and the latter of them in turn takes the *younger* by the hand", or page 335, "the priest shall place the right hand of the *elder* upon the holy Gospel and upon that of the *younger*" (Boswell, 1995; our italics in both cases). See also Randolph Trumbach's review of Boswell's *Unions* in the *Journal of Homosexuality*, affirming his belief that these were unions between an adult and an adolescent (Trumbach, 1995).
7. http://www.glbtq.com/literature/mackay_jh.html
8. http://www.glbtq.com/literature/rocco_a.html
9. It is presently available on the Web at http://williamapercy.com/wiki/index.php/On_Men_and_Boys
10. If for no other reason, because it is from an obscure Eastern European university, too far outside the academic and commercial "loop" to attract much notice at all. However, in terms of its content, it must be regarded cautiously. In the course of pushing the Uranians forward by a quarter century to include Hopkins, Pater and Wilde, and focusing on what he terms *Greek ideals* (i.e., age-discrepant sexual

relations), Kaylor redefines them again as a purely literary movement and amputates not only the Americans (and with them the influence of Whitman, both directly and to and through Edward Carpenter's poetry) but the later Uranians, now "minor" figures in his concept—and the group's overt political activism. This also largely eliminates the theme of cross-class as well as cross-generational relations, which bound together the androphile and pederast wings of the Uranians. Despite the new "major" names, the end result of Kaylor's effort is to once again domesticate the Uranians and reduce them to a footnote or dead-end street in gay history—where LGBT historians like Robb want them—rather than a group who still have something to say in the ongoing discussion about the definition of homosexual identity.

11. For the contentions regarding harm being related to incest or force, see Table 6 in Rind, Tromovitch, & Bauserman, 1998a, and Table 8 in Rind, Tromovitch & Bauserman, 1998b, and the discussion of these tables. The same tables indicate that there is no significant statistical correlation to factors such as the duration of the sexual relation, the frequency with which sexual acts occurred within it, or whether these acts were penetrative. For the contention regarding percentages of males evaluating sexual experiences they had with adults when they were minors as positive or neutral, see Tables 7 and 8 of Rind, Tromovitch & Bauserman, 1998a, repeated as Tables 9 and 10 in Rind, Tromovitch & Bauserman, 1998b, with a less technical discussion. Their conclusion is worth citing here: "Of the 606 male experiences, 37% were positive, 29% were neutral, and 33% were negative. The results for males strongly contradict the popular image.... The majority of boys (two-thirds) did not react negatively" (Rind, Tromovitch & Bauserman, 1998b, page 12 of the English text).

   These low levels of harm were previously reported in Theo Sandfort's Dutch research on consensual intergenerational relations, most easily accessible to international readers in the English summary (Sandfort, 1987).

12. In addition to the examination of factors which invariably cause negative reactions or harm, discussed in note 11, a further discussion that is not present in their earlier papers is to be found in Rind, Tromovitch & Bauserman, 1998b, regarding sources of negative effects of agediscrepant sexual encounters such as anxiety or guilt. The situation, summarized in Table 14 of Rind, Tromovitch & Bauserman, 1998b, indicates that the best outcomes, for low anxiety and low guilt, were found among young persons who were "sexually knowledgeable" and who had not absorbed "conventional moral negatives", whereas the worst, for high anxiety and high guilt, were among those sexually ignorant and with deeply inculcated sexual taboos. The implications of this for preventing negative effects through adequate sexual education deserve further study and development.

13. See http://news.bbc.co.uk/2/hi/uk_news/8498113.stm

References

Aldrich, R. (1993). *The seduction of the Mediterranean: Writing, art and homosexual fantasy.* London: Routledge.

———. (2003). *Colonialism and homosexuality.* London: Routledge.

Atkins, G. L. (2003). *Gay Seattle: Stories of exile and belonging.* Seattle: University of Washington Press.

Bauserman, R., & Rind, B. (1997). Psychological correlates of male child and adolescent sexual experiences with adults: A review of the nonclinical literature. *Archives of Sexual Behavior,* 26:2, 105–142.

Benemann, W. (2006). *Male-male intimacy in early America: Beyond romantic friendships.* New York: Harrington Park.

Boag, P. (2003). *Same sex affairs: Constructing and controlling homosexuality in the Pacific Northwest.* Berkeley: University of California Press.

Boon, L. J. (1989) Those damned sodomites: Public images of sodomy in eighteenth century Netherlands. In K. Gerard & G. Hekma (Eds.), *The pursuit of sodomy in Renaissance and Enlightenment Europe* (pp. 237-248). New York: Harrington Park.

Borhan, P. (2007). *Man to man: A history of gay photography.* New York: Vendome.
Boswell, J. (1995). *Same-sex unions in premodern Europe.* New York: Vintage.
Bray, A. (1982). *Homosexuality in Renaissance England.* London: Gay Men's Press.
———. (2003). *The friend.* Chicago, IL: University of Chicago Press.
Brickell, C. (2008). *Mates and lovers: A history of gay New Zealand.* Auckland: Random House New Zealand.
Burg, B. R. (1984). *Sodomy and the pirate tradition: English sea rovers in the seventeenth-century Caribbean.* New York: New York University Press.
———. (1994). *An American seafarer in the age of sail. The erotic diaries of Philip C. Van Buskirk 1851–1870.* New Haven, CT: Yale University Press.
———. (2009). The HMS *African* revisited: The Royal Navy and the homosexual community. *Journal of Homosexuality, 56:*2, 173–189.
Canaday, M. (2009). *The straight state: Sexuality and citizenship in twentieth-century America.* Princeton, NJ: Princeton University Press.
Chauncey, G. (1994). *Gay New York: Gender, urban culture, and the making of the gay male world 1890–1940.* New York: Basic Books.
Cocks, H. G. (2010). *Nameless offences: Homosexual desire in the 19th Century.* London: Tauris.
Cook, M. (2003). *London and the culture of homosexuality, 1885–1914.* Cambridge: Cambridge University Press.
Crompton, L. (1978). Gay genocide from Leviticus to Hitler. In L. Crew (Ed.), *The gay academic* (pp. 67–69). Palm Springs, CA: ETC Publications.
———. (1985). *Byron and Greek love: Homophobia in 19th-century England.* Berkeley: University of California Press.
———. (2003). *Homosexuality and civilization.* Cambridge, MA: Belknap.D'Arch Smith, T. (1970). *Love in earnest: Some notes on the lives and writings of English 'Uranian' poets from 1889 to 1930.* London: Routledge & Kegan Paul.
Davidson, M. (1971). *Some boys.* Kingston, NY: Oliver Layton.
Don Leon: A poem by Lord Byron ... Forming part of the private journal of his lordship ... to which is added Leon to Annabella. London: Fortune Press, n.d. [1934].
Eglinton, J. Z. [pseudonym of Walter Breen]. (1964). *Greek love.* New York: Oliver Layton.
Ellis, H. (1915). *Studies in the psychology of sex. Volume II: Sexual inversion* 3d Ed. Philadelphia, PA: Davis.
Eskridge, W. N., Jr. (2008). *Dishonorable passions: Sodomy laws in America, 1861–2003.* New York: Viking.
Fernandez, D. (2002). *A hidden love: Art and homosexuality.* Munich: Prestel.
Fortuyn, P. (2002). *Autobiografie van een babyboomer.* Rotterdam: Karakter.
Foucault, M. (1978). *The history of sexuality. Volume I: An introduction.* New York: Pantheon.
Friedman, M. (2003). *Strapped for cash: A history of American hustler culture.* Los Angeles, CA: Alyson.
Fuentes, L. M. (1998). *Diary of a dirty boy.* New York: Wallace Hamilton Press.
Gardner, J. (1993). *A class apart: The private pictures of Montague Glover.* New York: Serpent's Tail.
Greer, G. (2003). *The boy.* London: Thames and Hudson.
Harten, J. (1970). *Operatie montycoat.* Amsterdam: Bezige Bij.
Healey, D. (2001). *Homosexual desire in revolutionary Russia.* Chicago, IL: University of Chicago Press.
Hekma, G. (1987). *Homoseksualiteit, een medische reputatie.* Amsterdam: SUA.
———. (2004). *Homoseksualiteit in Nederland van 1730 tot de moderne tijd.* Amsterdam: Meulenhoff.
———. (2006). The gay world: 1980 to the present. In R. Aldrich (Ed.), *Gay life and culture: A world history* (pp. 333-363). London: Thames and Hudson.
———. (2008). The drive for sexual equality. *Sexualities* 11:1, 51–55.
Hirschfeld, M. (1914). *Die homosexualität des Mannes und des Weibes.* Berlin: Marcus.
Houlbrook, M. (2005). *Queer London: Perils and pleasures in the sexual metropolis, 1918–1957,* Chicago, IL: University of Chicago Press.
Jordan, M. D. (1997). *The invention of sodomy in Christian theology.* Chicago, IL: University of Chicago Press.
Katz, J. N. (2001). *Love stories: Sex between men before homosexuality.* Chicago, IL: University of Chicago Press.
Kaylor, M. M. (2006). *Secreted desires. The major Uranians: Hopkins, Pater and Wilde.* Brno, Czech Republic: Masaryk University.

Keilson-Lauritz, M. (2006). Centaurenliefde. Duits verzet in Nederland rondom de schuilplaats Castrum Peregrini. In K. Müller & J. Schuyf (Eds.), *Het begint met nee zeggen. Biografieën rond verzet en homoseksualiteit 1940–1945* (pp. 191–213). Amsterdam: Schorer.

Kennedy, H. (2002). *Anarchist of love: The secret life of John Henry Mackay.* Revised and enlarged edition: San Francisco, CA: Peremptory.

_____. (2007). *John Henry Mackay (Sagitta). Anarchist der Liebe.* Hamburg: Männerschwarm.

Kiermeier-Debre, J., & F. F. Vogel (eds.). (2007). *Wilhelm von Gloeden—auch ich in Arkadien.* Cologne: Böhlau.

Kulick, D. (2005). Four hundred thousand Swedish perverts. *GLQ* 11:2, 205–235.

Liebreich, K. (2005). *Fallen order: Intrigue, heresy and scandal in the Rome of Galileo and Caravaggio.* London: Atlantic Books.

Lowry, T. P. (1994). *The story the soldiers wouldn't tell: Sex in the Civil War.* Mechanicsburg, PA: Stackpole.

Maasen, T. (1988). *De pedagogische Eros in het geding. Gustav Wyneken en de pedagogische vriendschap in de Freie Schulgemeinde Wickersdorf tussen 1906–1931.* Utrecht: Interfacultaire Werkgroep Homostudies, Rijksuniversiteit Utrecht.

Mackay, J. H. (1985). *The hustler: The story of a nameless love from Friedrich Street.* Translated by H. Kennedy. Boston: Alyson.

_____. (1988). *Fenny Skaller and other prose writings from the books of the nameless love.* Translated by H. Kennedy. Amsterdam: Southernwood.

Mader, D. H. (2002). Walter H. Breen (J. Z. Eglinton) (1928–1993). In V. L. Bullough (Ed.), *Before Stonewall: Activists for gay and lesbian rights in historical context* (pp. 312–321). New York: Harrington Park.

_____. (2006). The Greek mirror: The Uranians and their use of Greece. In B. Verstraete & V. Provencal (Eds.), *Same-sex desire and love in Greco-Roman antiquity and in the classical tradition of the West* (pp. 377–420). New York: Harrington Park.

Marshall, D. (2004). Brongersma, *Paidika* and anti-paedophile groups. (Notes taken during his Mosse Lecture, November 24, 2004, at the University of Amsterdam).

Mitzel, (1980). *The Boston sex scandal.* Boston, MA: Glad Day Books.

Money, J. (1986). *Capri. Island of pleasure.* London: Hamish Hamilton.

Murray, S. O. & W. Roscoe (eds.). (1998). *Boy wives and female husbands: Studies of African homosexualities.* New York: St. Martin's Press.

Naphy, W. G. (2007). "Under-age" sexual activity in reformation Geneva. In G. Rousseau (Ed.), *Children and sexuality from the Greeks to the Great War* (pp. 108–127). Basingstoke: Palgrave Macmillan.

Néret, G. (2004). *HomoArt.* Cologne: Taschen.

Newell, S. (2006). *The forger's tale: The search for Odeziaku.* Athens: Ohio University Press.

Noordam, D. J. (1995). *Riskante relaties. Vijf eeuwen homoseksualiteit in Nederland, 1233–1733.* Hilversum: Verloren.

Oliari, E. (2006). *L'omo delinquente: Scandali e delitti gay dall'Unità a Giolitti.* Rome: Prospettiva.

Oosterhuis, H., & Kennedy, H. (eds.). (1991). *Homosexuality and male bonding in Pre-Nazi Germany: The youth movement, the gay movement and male bonding before Hitler's rise.* New York: Harrington Park.

Paine, W. (1912). *Shop slavery and emancipation.* London: King.

_____. (1920). *A new aristocracy of comradeship.* London: Parsons.

Penniston, W. A. (2004). *Pederasts and others. Urban culture and sexual identity in nineteenth-century Paris.* New York: Harrington Park.

Reeves, T. (1992). Reviving and redefining pederasty. In M. Pascal (Ed.), *Varieties of man/boy love: Modern Western contexts* (pp. 45–84). New York: Wallace Hamilton Press.

Reiss, A. J. (1967). The social integration of queers and peers. In H. S. Becker (Ed.), *The other side: Perspectives on deviance* (pp. 181–210). New York: Free Press.

Revenin, R. (2005). *Homosexualité et prostitution masculines à Paris 1870–1918.* Paris: L'Harmattan.

_____. (2007). "Deviant" male sexuality in France: The case of male homosexuality and male prostitution among minors (under 21 years old) in Paris, 1945–1962. Paper delivered at the Postwar Homosexual Politics 1945–1970 conference in Amsterdam, August 2–3.

Rey, M. (1987). Parisian homosexuals create a lifestyle, 1700–1750: The police archives. In R. P. Maccubbin (Ed.), *Tis nature's fault: Unauthorized sexuality during the Enlightenment* (pp. 179–191). New York. Cambridge University Press.

Rind, B., & Tromovitch, P. (1997). A meta-analytic review of findings from national samples on psychological correlates of child sexual abuse. *The Journal of Sex Research, 34*:3, 237–255.

Rind, B., Tromovitch, P., & Bauserman, R. (1998a). A meta-analytic examination of assumed properties of child sexual abuse using college samples. *Psychological Bulletin, 124*:1, 22–53.

———. (1998b) An examination of assumed properties of child sexual abuse based on nonclinical samples. In the conference report *De andere kant van de medaille: Veronderstellingen omtrent de gevolgen van seksueel misbruik van kinderen in niet-klinische populaties, Pauluskerk, 18 december 1998*. Rottterdam: Stichting KSA.

Robb, G. (2003). *Strangers: Homosexual love in the nineteenth century*. London: Picador.

Robinson, J. (1986). *Teardrops on my drum*. London: GMP.

Rocco, A. (2000). *Alcibiades the schoolboy*. Translated by J. C. Rawnsley. Amsterdam: Entimos.

Rocke, M. (1996). *Forbidden friendships: Homosexuality and male culture in Renaissance Florence*. New York: Oxford University Press.

Ruggiero, G. (1985). *The boundaries of Eros: Sex crime and sexuality in Renaissance Venice*. New York: Oxford University Press.

Rydström, J. (2003). *Sinners and citizens. Bestiality and homosexuality in Sweden, 1880–1950*. Chicago, IL: Universotu of Chicago Press.

Sandfort, T. (1983). Homosexual identity and the experience of attraction towards boys. In M. Aerts, et al. (Eds.), *Among men, among women* (pp. 176–180). Conference papers, Amsterdam: University of Amsterdam.

———. (1987). *Boys on their contacts with men: A study of sexually expressed friendships*. Amsterdam: Global Academic.

Shively, C. (ed.). (1989). *Drum beats: Walt Whitman's Civil War boy lovers* San Francisco, CA: Gay Sunshine Press.

Staal, F. (2004). *Drie bergen en zeven rivieren*. Amsterdam: Meulenhoff.

Tindall, R. (1978). The male adolescent involved with a pederast becomes an adult. *Journal of Homosexuality 3*:4, 373–382.

Trumbach, R. (1989). Gender and the homosexual role in modern Western culture. In D. Altman, et al. (Eds.), *Homosexuality, which homosexuality?* pp. 149-169. London: GMP.

———. (1995). Review of John Boswell, *Same sex unions in premodern Europe*. *Journal of Homosexuality 30*:2, 111–117.

Valentine, J. [pseudonym of Chester Anderson]. (1979). *Puppies*. Glen Ellen, CA: Entwhistle.

Van Dantzig, R. (1986). *Voor een verloren soldaat*. Amsterdam: Arbeiders Pers; English: (1996). *For a lost soldier*, translated by A. J. Pomerans. London: Gay Men's Press.

Van der Meer, T. (1995). *Sodoms zaad in Nederland. Het ontstaan van homoseksualiteit in de vroegmoderne tijd*. Nijmegen: SUN.

———. (2007). *Jonkheer Mr. Jacob Anton Schorer. Een biografie van homoseksualiteit*. Amsterdam: Schorer Boeken.

Van Lieshout, T. (1999). *Zeer kleine liefde*. Amsterdam: Leopold.

Van Schaik, E. (1997). *Hans van Manen, leven en werken*. Amsterdam: Arena.

Verheul, K. (1982). *Een jongen met vier benen*. Amsterdam: Van Oorschot. Eighth edition, 2010, with a new afterword by the author.

Waugh, T. (1984). Pornography, passion & power. *Body Politic: A Magazine for Gay Liberation* (Toronto), No. 101, March, 29–33.

———. (1996). *Hard to imagine: Gay male eroticism in photography and film from their beginnings to Stonewall*. New York: Columbia University Press.

———. (2004). *Lust unearthed: Vintage gay graphics from the DuBek collection*. Vancouver: Arsenal Pulp Press.

Wojnarowicz, D. (1992). *Memories that smell like gasoline*. San Francisco, CA: Artspace.

Wyneken, G. (1921). *Eros*. Lauenberg: Saal.

Chapter 7

"HERE'S TO YOU, MR. ROBINSON": MEN WHO HAVE SEXUAL RELATIONS WITH MALE MINORS[1]

DAVID F. GREENBERG

Historical and comparative studies of sexual relations between same-sex partners in different times and places first appeared more than a hundred years ago (Symonds, 1883, 1891; Carpenter, 1904). The genre continues to attract research and readers (Greenberg, 1988; Murray, 2000; Crompton, 2003; Neill, 2009). This body of work has found that the extent of participation in homosexual relations has been much greater in some societies than others and that the opprobrium visited on participants in the Christian world is not a transhistorical or transcultural universal. Attitudes and social responses have been highly variable.

Bruce Rind's (Chapter 1, this volume) provocative study draws on this literature to focus specifically on one particular form of same-sex sexual relationship—those in which there is a socially meaningful discrepancy between the ages of the two partners, one of whom is no longer a child, but is not yet a full-fledged adult. Rind is particularly interested in those relationships in which one of the parties is roughly at the age of puberty or slightly older and according to contemporary American law, a minor—someone who is physiologically no longer a child, yet too young to consent lawfully to sexual activity. These are the relationships now designated as *pederasty*, to distinguish them from *pedophilia*, a term applicable when the youthful partner is prepubescent. In American law and in virtually all other countries throughout the world, an adult who has sexual relations with someone who is below the age of consent is guilty of statutory rape, even though no force or coercion was used. Rind's study and the circumstances under which it was written raise a number of issues regarding the sociology of scientific knowledge, the history and explanation of legal change, and social policy—particularly legal policy. I offer my reflections on these issues here.

KNOWLEDGE

One of the earliest sociological studies of science noted the potential for conflict between the ethos of science, in which claims regarding knowledge are supposed to be evaluated on the basis of logic and empirical evidence, and popular beliefs, which some people may hold immune from logical scrutiny or empirical testing (Merton, 1957, pp. 537–549). Conflicts between the scientific mode of inquiry and the teachings of religious authority date back at least to Galileo, whose ideas about the structure of the solar system clashed with those handed down from ancient writers and endorsed by the leadership of the Roman Catholic Church. Such conflicts have persisted down to the present day and have focused on a variety of issues surrounding the production and distribution of scientific knowledge, for example, stem cell research and the teaching of evolution and "creation science" in high school biology classes (Hunt, 1999).

Interest groups also mobilize when scientific research, theory, or speculation threatens to damage their reputations. For example, a conference on the genetics of crime, to be held at the University of Maryland in 1995, was canceled in response to protests that it was racist (Angier, 1995). A federal research program on the biological causes of violence drew objections on the same grounds (Horgan, 1993). Feminist protests over Lawrence Summers's speculative remarks about the reasons women are underrepresented in science are widely thought to have contributed to his resignation as president of Harvard University (Bombardieri & Sacchetti, 2006).

The attempts made to discredit the research by Rind and his collaborators (Rind & Tromovich, 1997; Rind, Tromovich, & Bauserman, 1998) on the effects of intergenerational sex between males, and to block its publication, are another instance, one in which the attacks were not launched by members of a historically subordinated group seeking to prevent the reinforcement of damaging stereotypes or the adoption of harmful policies, but rather by those who want to control the dissemination of knowledge claims that challenge hegemonic beliefs, and that they believe threaten the well-being of children, a group that is not well-positioned to defend itself.[2]

It is important, in this connection, to note that those attempting to prevent the publication of Rind et al.'s work and to discredit their findings did not limit themselves to the usual steps taken when critics believe that scientific work is flawed— writing letters to the editor or publishing critiques. Although some of the critics did pursue these conventional tactics,[3] the critics—demagogic radio talk show hosts, conservative newspapers, advocacy groups who take an unfavorable view of homosexuality or whose mission includes the protection of children, and some Republican congressmen—also held press conferences, pressured the American Psychological Association to repudiate the publication, sought (and obtained) congressional condemnation, and pressured publishers not to publish Rind's work. These attacks had extra-scientific roots.

A few decades ago it might have seemed plausible that increases in the number of years students spend in school and the gradual dissemination of scientific thinking to a wide public would reduce lay efforts to curb or censor science. Yet opponents of the scientific worldview have not disappeared. Lay acceptance of science as a way to know reality is quite uneven. Substantial segments of the population are threatened by scientific modes of inquiry. They may be fighting a losing battle, but they have not given up.[4] In a society characterized by multiple group identities, values, and meaning systems, a profusion of lifestyles, political philosophies, and religious beliefs and affiliations, public conflicts over science seem to be occurring more often than they did in the early twentieth century, when the Scopes trial (over the teaching about evolution in Tennessee public schools) took place. Previously silent groups now organize politically to challenge unpalatable ideas and can more easily do so on a national basis. The personal costs of challenging dominant views have also fallen. The Internet facilitates the mobilization of supporters. The protection of vulnerable, powerless populations, such as children, can be an effective way of attracting support and of neutralizing opposition based on defense of free speech or freedom of scientific inquiry. In recent years, this strategy has worked well in gaining support for legislation banning the distribution of child pornography (Stanley, 1987; Schuijer & Rossen, 1992), as it did a hundred years ago in the creation of the juvenile court (Platt, 1969).

Because those opposed to science believe the stakes to be large, they will not be stopped by mockery or defenses of free inquiry—two common strategies that have been widely deployed against the antiscience forces. Though Rind refrains from recommending acceptance of intergenerational sex, those who have tried to discredit his work undoubtedly know that historical studies such as those he uses have been used in the past to advocate the normalization of same-sex relationships. His findings are likely to be cited by those seeking to liberalize law and social policy toward adults who have sexual relations with minors. The findings may provide adults who seek such relations with the mental "techniques of neutralization" (Sykes & Matza, 1957) that permit them to engage in such relations free from the moral reservations that might otherwise restrain them.

The scientific enterprise has a strong interest in preventing research efforts from being obstructed and in preventing censorship of research findings. The adoption of codes of research ethics by many professional associations indicates a widespread consensus that research is not always innocuous and at times calls for restrictions. However, the protection of human subjects from risks occasioned by participation in research poses quite different issues from those associated with the dissemination of research that has already been completed. Where to draw the line in regulating research is an issue that merits deliberation and discussion. Lay censorship, for extra-scientific reasons, is quite a different matter, and the scientific societies must be prepared to speak loudly and clearly when it occurs.[5]

Dr. Rind's study also identifies issues regarding the knowledge base on which therapeutic practice is based. Unavoidably, therapy is not merely descriptive or explanatory, the way pure science aims to be. Designed and undertaken to bring about change in patients or clients, it cannot be value-neutral; it must be able to specify some conditions as pathological or undesirable, and others as normal or desirable. One way of doing this is to let a patient or client determine whether a particular condition is wanted or unwanted. Though therapists sometimes take the goals of treatment from their patients, historically, therapists have also interjected their own notions of normalcy and pathology, bringing with them lay beliefs about normalcy and pathology. This is also true of theoretical writings and textbooks in psychology and psychiatry. The history of explanations for homosexuality and therapeutic interventions to "cure" it is a case in point (Bayer, 1981; Minton, 2002).

These notions are communicated in professional training; they are incorporated in standard references works like the *Diagnostic and Statistical Manual* for the classification of psychiatric disorders; and they may be reinforced by contact with a population of patients or clients selected by authorities, or self-selected for psychological and social problems. When told by a colleague that all his homosexual patients were quite sick, psychoanalyst Ernest van den Haag remarked that this was also true of all of his heterosexual patients (Havemann, 1964). That is why people go to therapists—because they are troubled and need help. A study of subjects who experienced any phenomenon whatsoever based on a clinical sample selects on the dependent variable, a procedure known to bias research results. Any study based on such a research design will almost inevitably lead to the misleading conclusion that the phenomenon being studied is harmful, but would actually tell us little about its effects.

It is not surprising that these generalizations are valid in relation to psychological and psychiatric discussions on the effects of intergenerational intimacy, and on the adults who seek them. Even if therapists approached the subject entirely free from stereotypes and prejudices (which is unlikely), the nature of the populations from which they draw their patients or clients would tend to produce them. Conclusions that sexual relations between adults and minors tend to be harmful based on clinical populations are likely to exaggerate the prevalence of harmful outcomes if extrapolated to nonclinical populations.[6]

In recent decades, the therapeutic enterprise has largely abandoned invidious stereotypes of homosexuality—a development that received important impetus from data generated by non-patient populations, including the psychometric research conducted by Evelyn Hooker (1957), the "coming out" of large numbers of gay people, and gay activism directed at the psychiatric establishment (Bayer, 1981; Schmiecher et al., 1992; Minton, 2002). Minors are not well-positioned to carry out comparable campaigns for the de-deviantization of intergenerational sexual expression, and their adult partners would risk a great deal by undertaking them. Membership of advocacy organizations like the North American Man-Boy Love Association (NAMBLA) appears always to have been quite small, and they have won few victories. Its British counterpart, the Paedophile Information Exchange (PIE) ceased operations in 1985.[7] Some gay rights advocacy organizations have repudiated NAMBLA and sex with minors, possibly to avoid the political costs associated with "child molesting." For this reason, and perhaps for others as well, the shift that has taken place in the way psychologists and psychiatrists think about and deal with homosexuality has not occurred in relation to patients who seek sexual relations with minors (both male and female). Little change is likely to occur in the near future.

History

Rind's reliance on a small number of historical surveys, some of them now more than twenty years old, inevitably results in a somewhat simplified historical narrative that does not fully reflect the most up-to-date scholarship and that may benefit from comment. Rind emphasizes the high esteem in which the ancient Greeks held pederasty, regarding it as a lofty, pedagogical institution. In any complex civilization, one is likely to find a range of views about many issues, and that was true of Greek views of pederasty. Ancient Greece was distinctive for its large number of enthusiasts for pederasty (Percy, 1996), but their views were not universally shared, and shifts occurred over time long before the appearance of Christianity (Cohen, 1991; Hubbard, 1998, 2000, 2006; Allen, 2006; Davidson, 2007; Jennings, 2009). Greek sources tell us that different city-states dealt with pederasty in different ways (Plato (1998), *Symposium* 182A). According to Xenophon (1968), the Spartan law-giver Lycurgus approved of pedagogical pederasty only when it was chaste; carnal relations between the boy and his adult lover were as much an abomination as incest (*Constitution of the Lacedaemonians* 3–14). Some writers warned of the efforts tutors made to seduce their students by introducing them to the lives of the great philosophers.[8] Concerns were expressed that a youth's experience of pederastic sex would lead to an adoption of a receptive role with men in adulthood—which would be shameful (Thornton, 1998, pp. 103–109). In Plato's (1926) last work, *Laws,* a speaker argued (636D, 836E) that pederasty generated so much social conflict that it should be banned from the polis.[9] Aristotle (1944) advocated steps to prevent boys from being subjected to it (*Politics* 1331a36–43, 1336b3–23). Writing much later, Plutarch (1961) put some anti-pederastic arguments in the mouths of Daphnaeus, one of the interlocutors in his *Dialogue on Love.*

In ancient Rome, though it was generally considered normal for an adult man to be sexually attracted to boys as well as to women, free youthful citizens were supposed to be off-limits. Slaves and male prostitutes (who were often slaves) were considered fair game (C. Williams, 2010). Had Romans accepted the notion that sex with an older male was good for youths, they would not have discouraged it in this way. Moreover, the pedagogic model of pederasty, highlighted by its advocates in antiquity and in modern times, presumably did not apply to sexual relations with male prostitutes or with slaves. They would not have been free to say no to overtures from customers or their owners and would surely have been vulnerable to exploitation.

To be sure, the negative consequences ancient writers associated with pederasty were not those claimed by contemporary opponents of sex between adults and youths. They never contended that it leads to nightmares, anxiety, or depression. People of antiquity were not as psychologically minded as we are and did not think in those terms. It cannot be ruled out that some youth in antiquity did experience these adverse psychological consequences, but there is nothing to suggest that many did. Youths often sought these relationships and wrote positively about them when they were older. It is hard to believe that if psychological problems were commonly being caused by pederasty, this would not have been realized by some Greeks and Romans, given the extent of participation.[10]

Feminist Campaigns and Age-of-Consent Laws

Rind attributes the modern American moral panic concerning sexual relations between men and male youths to feminists. They did contribute, but they were not alone. Boise, Idaho, saw a wave of men prosecuted for sexual relations with male teenagers (some of them above the age of consent) and given sentences as long as ten years, in 1955–1956, before the rise of second-wave feminism (Gerassi, 1966). The Cleveland Street scandal that erupted in England in 1869, involved aristocratic men visiting a male brothel and engaging in sex with seventeen- and eighteen-year-old youths (Hyde, 1976; Simpson, Chester, & Witch, 1976; Aronson, 1994). The public reaction to the scandal does not suggest public indifference to intergenerational intimacy between males, even at a time when they were tolerated between men and girls.

Apart from the Boise case, same-sex intimacy attracted very little attention in mid–twentieth-century America, possibly because there was not much sexual contact between men and boys, or at least not much that was known to law enforcement agencies or the mass media. Consequently there were few campaigns over sex between men and male youths.[11]

Feminist writings gave these relations relatively little attention by comparison with rape, pornography, incest, and sexual harassment on the street and in the workplace. Feminists were drawn to the issue by a few women who spoke publicly about their own experiences of abuse in childhood. Soon self-help therapy groups, consisting of former victims, almost all of them women who had been abused by men, drew attention to the issue and analyzed it in feminist terms.

With their attention turned to child sexual abuse in this way, some feminists conducted surveys and wrote books analogizing sex between adults and minors to rape and incest, even when the relations were consensual, extra-familial, and regarded positively by the youths involved (Okami, 1990; Jenkins, 1998; Whittier, 2009). The feminist moral entrepreneurs drew on interviews and surveys for evidence of its damaging psychological consequences (focusing primarily on female victims) and campaigned for the revision of state laws so as to criminalize sexual relations between adults with minors, regardless of the sex of the adult or the minor.

At the time they were writing (early and mid-seventies), only relations between men and girls were prohibited in statutory rape laws. Until 1963, when Illinois decriminalized sexual relationships between consenting same-sex adults, all sexual transactions between males were criminal and typically carried very long prison sentences, regardless of the age of the parties, so there was no need for age-of-consent laws to prosecute same-sex intimacy. Statutory law, then, was hardly indifferent to sexual relations between men and boys. Little is known about prosecutions, because no one has done the archival work to determine their extent, or the penalties typically imposed. Intergenerational sex figured in the discussions surrounding the adoption of sexual psychopath laws in mid-twentieth century America, but most of the advocacy had to do with violent crimes, not with consensual relationships. Attention to intergenerational sex swelled in the last few decades, when prosecutions of nursery school staff, along with the widely watched television program *To Catch a Predator* (in which adults were enticed to solicit adolescent minors online for sexual purposes in order to set them up for arrest), broadcast by NBC, and the Roman Catholic priest scandal gave wide publicity to the topic. A fair amount of this attention focused on incest, which was little discussed before feminist efforts in the 1970s drew attention to its prevalence and harm. The weakening of taboos against discussion of sexual matters in the mass media has enabled campaigners to publicize their perspectives on these issues.

In discussions about possible changes in the age of consent, some feminists expressed reservations about the adoption of gender-neutral language in age-of-consent legislation, fearing that this would obscure the greater victimization of girls (W. W. Williams, 1982; Olsen, 1984; MacKinnon, 1991; for Canada, see Dauda, 2010), and the US Supreme Court ruled that because only girls could get pregnant, there was a legitimate rationale to laws that singled out girls for special protection.[12] Those who favored equalization were not so much hostile to male-youth sexual contact as they were eager to avoid reinforcing the image of women as invariably victims and men as invariably victimizers in sexual matters. By advocating that sexual relations between an adult and a minor be a crime, regardless of the sex of either party, feminists were implicitly taking a stand in favor of decriminalizing homosexual relations among adults (Cocca, 2002, 2004). They were also making it easier to prosecute adults for sexual relations with minors where coercion was involved. Because of widely held understandings as to what constitutes a rape (e.g., it must entail force, be committed by a stranger, involve penetration, and be resisted), it would in many instances have been difficult to prosecute many adults for obtaining consent from minors coercively. The statutory rape laws made the minor's consent irrelevant and thus allowed for the prosecution of cases that technically constituted forcible rape, but could not be prosecuted effectively as such.

The feminists were not alone in these campaigns. In some, they were joined by law enforcement officials. The crusade against child pornography was led by a Los Angeles Police Department sergeant and Judianne Densen-Gerber, a psychologist who was prominent in drug rehabilitation and not especially known for feminist activism (Stanley, 1987; Whittier, 2009). Campaigns conducted by the anti-gay crusader Anita Bryant ("Save Our Children"), *The Moral Majority,* and other conservative Christian organizations gave enormous publicity to the stereotype of gay men as child molesters. Though much of the feminist initiative was not punitive toward adults who sought or had sexual contact with minors, law enforcement agencies and conservative advocates of punitive criminal justice policies developed alliances with those feminist elements who shared their outlook and agendas (Whittier, 2009). In some states, feminists appear not to have been involved in legislative change at all (Cocca, 2004). In addition, some feminists were reluctant to seek protection from a state that had historically sustained a patriarchal social order and male domination of women. A few feminists even defended adult-child sexual interaction (Millet, 1984; Rubin, 1984). In Canada, too, the campaign for the most recent legislation raising the age of consent, although reflecting a feminist sensibility in treating boys and girls equally, was carried out by social and cultural conservatives. Feminists were not involved at all (Dauda, 2010).

During the sexual liberalization of the 1960s and 1970s, a number of states reduced the age of consent, or they reduced or eliminated penalties where the age differences between partners were small (Cocca, 2004, p. 29). This reform was intended to diminish presumed power differentials between the partners,[13] evidently a more important issue than the prevention of pregnancy or disease, which are potential outcomes even when a partner is close in age to the minor.

Although feminists promoted the ideal of egalitarianism in marriage and intimate relationships more generally, the ideal resonated with broader cultural developments associated with the rise of "companionate marriage" based on romantic love, psychological intimacy, shared interests, and mutuality, rather than the building of political alliances, acquiescence to parental agendas, or a functional division of labor, all important to premodern marriage. It is a trend that had been in the making long before the rise of modern feminism (Lindsey and Evans, 1927; Stone, 1977; Trumbach, 1978; Hanawalt, 1986; Macfarlane, 1986; Corbin, 1990). This mutuality, it is widely thought, is enhanced by a period of courtship, through which two people can assess one another's compatibility and build affection and confidence, and through the choice of a partner who is not too different in age (MacDonald, 2002).

This ideological shift occurred at a time when increased access to contraception and abortion associated with sexual liberalization promoted teenage sexual activity. The rising rate of births to unwed teenage mothers requiring welfare support alarmed conservatives and stimulated campaigns to reduce teenage pregnancy. The prosecution of adult men responsible for these pregnancies was one component of this campaign (Oliveri, 2000; Levine, 2007). These efforts, needless to say, focused on age-discrepant *heterosexual* relationships (Hollenberg, 1999; Oliveri, 2000), not on those between men and boys.

Even with gender-neutral language in a statute, this new legislation need not have led to a large growth in numbers of men prosecuted for having sexual relations with male youths. Prosecutorial discretion permits prosecutors to ignore cases that they consider socially unimportant. Cases of consensual sexual relations between minors and adults, where the youth is not pregnant and does not consider himself to have been a victim, might easily fall into this category. No systematic study of the process by which statutory rape cases involving boys or girls are selected for prosecution has been done, and it would be reasonable to worry that the criteria used would disadvantage same-sex contacts.

Levine (2006) notes that in California, prosecutions are, in fact, rare, and reserved largely for cases that entail coercion or clear exploitation. It was prosecutors who, adopting a new rationale of protecting immature adolescents from manipulation, and who, in an atmosphere shaped by the scandal over sexual relations between Roman Catholic priests and youths under their care (Wills, 2002), launched a more energetic program of prosecution targeting a much wider range of sexual contacts, including those that did not involve penetration. Still, the great majority of prosecutions are of adults accused of sexual relations with girls[14] (Frost et al., 2001 p., 20), with decisions regarding the choice of cases to prosecute heavily influenced by the circumstances of the case. There is likely to be a good deal of variation across jurisdictions. Where the capacity to prosecute is present, individual prosecutors have wide latitude to make decisions based on idiosyncratic considerations, or to take local factors into account. It would be desirable to know more about the patterns of prosecution in different jurisdictions.

Natural Selection

Rind supplements his historical analysis with documentation of same-sex relations among nonhuman animals. From antiquity to the present, one of the arguments presented against homosexual relations has been that nonhuman animals do not do it; consequently it is "unnatural."[15] Evidence that this is untrue of many species throughout the animal kingdom effectively undercuts this argument. Rind uses the high frequency of intergenerational sexual activity between males in societies scattered around the globe and the animal evidence to argue that this particular form of sexual relationship cannot be considered unnatural or abnormal.[16] He takes the variation among human societies in this form of sexual expression to be strong evidence that cultural and social arrangements have a powerful impact on sexual interests and expression.[17] That a number of geographically dispersed societies, both ancient and fairly contemporary, have encouraged or accepted such relationships also tells us that disgust or revulsion at this type of intimate contact is not an inherent part of the human psychological makeup.

Scientific ideas about evolution (often poorly understood) have led to new natural law perspectives about homosexuality. One commonly hears that from the point of view of natural selection, homosexual activity is puzzling, because it would result in reduced fertility and so should die out. Psychologist J. Michael Bailey (2003: 115) opined that "homosexuality might be the most striking unresolved paradox of human evolution," and called it "maladaptive" from an evolutionary point of view (Bailey, 2003: 116). In a radio interview given to an Austin, Texas, radio station in May 2003, he said that "evolutionarily, homosexuality is a big mistake."[18] We do not have good data on the incidence of homosexuality over a long stretch of time, but there is no evidence that it is disappearing. It seems to be too common nowadays to have been strongly selected against for an extended period of time.

For half a century, proposals have been made to resolve the seeming puzzle. These efforts begin with the premise that, notwithstanding Bailey's language, natural selection does not make mistakes. Mistakes occur when someone intends an outcome, tries to achieve it, but something else results. Natural selection does not work by intentions. It is an impersonal process. Apart from a degree of randomness associated with survival and reproduction (genetic drift), a trait becomes established only if it (or something associated with it) contributes to reproductive fitness, or at least fails to impair it (S. H. Rice, 2004). Maladaptive traits are selected against, and should gradually disappear. If homosexuality (especially the form that involves a mature male and a younger male, not yet fully mature) is inherited and occurs commonly in many species, it is a reasonable conclusion that it does not impair reproduction. It, or a trait associated with it, must contribute to reproductive fitness. A number of suggestions have been made as to how these relationships might do so.[19]

Rind, focusing particularly on male-male intergenerational relationships, not on homosexuality in general, bases his suggestion on the observation that something can contribute to reproductive fitness by enhancing the likelihood of survival, rather than by directly affecting the number of offspring who are born and themselves survive to reproduce. By recruiting a young male into a group and securing the youth's attachment and support libidinally, a band could replenish losses of males in warfare, and thus enhance its strength in future combat. In this way, sexual relations between youths and adults could further their later reproduction by enabling them to defend themselves against attacks from other bands and to expand their access to resources such as food.

This benefit would extend to the entire band, not just to the participants in the intimate relationship. Rind's argument, then, invokes group selection. Biologists have argued against group selection, pointing out that if a trait damages an individual's reproductive fitness, it will tend to die out, regardless of the benefit to the group. However, it can be demonstrated mathematically that this is not always the case, especially where members of the group are genetically related (Traulsen & Nowak, 2006; Lehmann, Keller, West, & Roze, 2007). The operative principle is that the benefit accruing to the group can enhance the reproductive fitness of a gene carried by an individual who carries a gene responsible for a trait. Moreover, the gene carriers themselves may benefit from the enhanced prospects of the group. If a practice makes for stronger social solidarity, and in this way enables its fighters to wage war or defend themselves more effectively, the benefits may accrue to everyone in the group, including the carriers of the gene in question. It is probable that in our evolutionary past, early humans lived in small groups that were closely related, making this possibility directly relevant to our evolutionary past.

Furthermore, if the junior partner's participation ended around the time of puberty, he would not be sacrificing any reproductive potential. Nor would the adult partner, whose survival was enhanced. He may have been having sexual relationships with women while also involved in relationships with younger males, as well as after the relationship with a youth ended. These patterns have been extensively documented in modern anthropological studies of pederastic relations, as well as in many societies in earlier historical periods.

Because it is difficult to learn about selection processes among humans experimentally, it is important to make full use of the nonexperimental evidence in evaluating hypotheses like this. One important piece of evidence has to do with intergenerational sex in nonhuman species. If sexual contact between adults and juveniles of both sexes is as prevalent in the animal kingdom, as Rind (Chapter 1, this volume) contends, and is found in numerous species that do not recruit the juvenile male partner into the role of a warrior on behalf of a band, one might wonder whether we need postulate such a mechanism as critical when it comes to the human species. Parsimony would take the capacity for intergenerational sex and an interest in engaging in it to be a legacy of humans' evolutionary past and would not require a special explanation. This preexisting practice might well be institutionalized in settings where it benefitted the group, even if no selection on the basis of this trait took place at this stage of human history.

Another question we might ask about Rind's argument is whether the numbers of people killed in violent intergroup conflict in small-scale societies have been large enough to have created substantial evolutionary pressures. The answer seems to be in the affirmative. Where estimates have been made for deaths in human raids in contemporary primitive societies, they are substantial (Keeley, 1986). The archaeological record suggests that they were also high in earlier times (Knauft, 1987; Walker, 2001).

Are the patterns of sexual behavior in the animal kingdom those we would expect from Rind's theory? Among the primates, intergenerational sexual relations between males are found among chimpanzees and bonobos (our two closest living relatives among the primates). Bonobos get along fairly amicably with their neighbors. Though one encounters claims that chimpanzee bands tend to have conflictual relationships with nearby bands, sometimes taking the form of organized raids, the claims are contested (Goodall, 1986; Manson & Wrangham, 1991).[20] Thus, the presence of warfare does not seem to have been necessary for the development of a propensity for same-sex sexual relationships. Moreover, young male chimpanzees and bonobos both stay with their natal band as they mature. It is females who leave. Consequently, recruitment of juvenile males from other groups does not appear to have been necessary for the development of age-differentiated relationships among these two primate species.

In some of the human societies where adult-juvenile sexual relations are most strongly institutionalized, such as those in Papua New Guinea that practice ritualized homosexual initiation, boys also remain with the group into which they were born; it is girls who are exchanged in marriages (Herdt, 1984; Lindenbaum, 1984). The relationships established between initiators and initiated do help to cement alliances within a group (as does marriage in many societies), while at the same time, facilitating warfare by providing a basis for mobilization and collective action of the males against other peoples (Otterbein, 2004). But they are not used to recruit males from other neighboring groups. Indeed, doing so would threaten the security of the group, because neighboring groups are precisely the ones with whom a given group is episodically at war. Recruiting youths from a hostile group would entail the risk that they would side with their natal group when hostilities broke out.

Anthropological research about the origins of human warfare (Kelly, 2000; Otterbein, 2004) suggests that it is a relatively late development in our history as a species. Clear physical evidence of organized human conflict (as distinct from violence associated with individual encounters) dates to around 20,000 years ago, in the Sudan. If it existed before then, it left no trace, at least none that has been detected to date. Primitive armed conflict is thought to have arisen from disputes between men over access to women and food. So long as hominids and humans were sparsely distributed over the earth, there should have been few occasions for conflict over food, except, perhaps, in times of severe scarcity, or when *homo sapiens* were first entering Europe and had to deal with Neanderthals, who were already there. It is generally characteristic of contemporary foraging and hunting bands that they prefer to avoid violent conflict if possible. If this was true in the past, there might have been little need to recruit outside male youths to replace men killed in wars—though fatalities inflicted by animal predators or from accidents and illness might have created shortages.

That warfare is common among contemporary hunter-gatherers does not refute this conclusion, because most modern hunter-gatherers are now living in conditions quite different from hunter-gatherers in the remote past. Many have been pushed into inhospitable and difficult environments by the incursion of the more advanced civilizations. This did not occur in the highlands of Papua New Guinea, where white contact with the indigenous population occurred only in the mid-twentieth century, but the population density is nevertheless high relative to the carrying capacity of the land, promoting conflict between peoples. This overcrowding may stem from gradual population growth, leading to densities much higher than prevailed thousands of years ago. Because ritualized pederasty is restricted to certain language groups in Papua New Guinea, it is thought that it was carried to Papua New Guinea by immigrants who came there many thousands of years ago, at a time when warfare between groups may not have been important. That a majority of indigenous Papua New Guinea groups lack institutionalized ritual pederasty is a further challenge to explanations based on generalizations about ancient warfare and masculinity.

Another potentially relevant factor concerns residence rules in relation to marriage. Matrilocality tends to disperse males. The males living in a given group are not necessarily kin and tend not to form strong alliances. Their dispersion promotes peaceful forms of intergroup interaction. Patrilocality, on the other hand, concentrates males, thereby lending itself to the formation of fraternal interest groups, notions of collective responsibility, and armed conflict (Ember & Ember, 1971).

When different residence rules developed, and when fraternal interest groups were first established, is of course, hard to ascertain. The simplest foraging societies known to modern anthropology tend to lack both matrilineal and patrilineal descent groups, and, as a result, conflicts are treated as personal matters rather than collective ones (Kelly, 2000 pp. 46–47). Homicide rates are typically high in these societies, but war is not. If, as Kelly thinks, this was the prevalent pattern until fairly recently in human history, then too little time may have elapsed to explain the adaptive advantage of age-discrepant, same-sex sexual relations. But we do not know. It would, however, be possible to use standard ethnographic data sets, such as the Human Relations Area Files, to see whether there is a relationship between same-sex pederastic relationships and warfare. From my quick examination of the evidence, none of the peoples for which institutionalized man-youth sexual relations is attested are simple foragers without fraternal interest groups.

Once simple societies established states, governments tended to suppress private feuds in order to create a more peaceful and orderly society. Success in these efforts was imperfect, of course, but in some regions of the world, very substantial. In these locations, the selection processes on which Rind focuses would not have operated. One thinks, for example, of China, which for most of the last two thousand years has been domestically pacified. China is one of the civilizations that Rind identifies as having traditionally had high levels of pederasty. If Rind's evolutionary argument is valid, it means that, once established, mentoring forms of pederasty flourished for a very long time after the circumstances that made pederasty functional for the group had disappeared. Perhaps the material and social advantages to the family of a Chinese boy taken up by an affluent adult were sufficient to allow the practice to thrive even in the absence of cultural support of the kind found in ancient Greece or in the Arab world, until suppressed in modern times.

An additional issue has to do with the sex specificity of Rind's argument. It is intended to explain relationships between men and boys at the point of puberty. What about men and girls? In many societies, men marry girls at what the modern Western world would consider an exceptionally young age (Westermarck, 1922). This was true in ancient Greece[21] (Lacey, 1968; Pomeroy, 1995, pp. 42, 64, 85; Sallares, 1991 pp. 149–150; Percy, 1996) and in Rome (Balsdon, 1962; Hopkins, 1965; Eyben, 1985; Lelis, Percy, & Verstraete, 2003; Scheidel, 2007), among medieval European Jewry (Goldberg, 2003, Ch. 4), and in some social strata, among premodern European Christians. A conventional evolutionary psychology explanation might be that the husband maximizes his reproductive potential by marrying someone who is just at the start of her reproductive career (Symons, 1979; Buss, 2003). Feminists would argue that men could more easily dominate wives who were much younger than they were. It might be easier for men to maintain a sexual monopoly on female sex partners if they were small and slightly built. By limiting their sexual access to other men—something more easily accomplished when the females were smaller and weaker—a dominant man could more easily ensure that he fathered any children his wives bore (Feierman, 1990). If this is so, a male propensity to prefer young girls over fully mature women might well have been selected for. For this reason, there is no inconsistency between the feminist argument and the argument from evolutionary psychology. Neither argument depends on speculations about bands recruiting replacement for members killed in combat. If this is so, one may wonder whether we need a special explanation for male same-sex, age-discrepant sexual relations.

An argument can be made that we do not. If men are attracted to girls at the age of puberty, then it may be that the same process will explain their attraction to boys around the same age. The problem is that boys at that age are not starting a reproductive career by having sexual relations with an adult male. Yet this is not necessarily a fatal objection to the argument. Consider imprinting, in which a newly hatched gosling takes the first moving object it sees to be its mother. In the wild, this helps to ensure the survival of a newly hatched gosling, by keeping it close to its mother, who will protect and feed it. Were a gosling to imprint on a moving object that was not its mother in nonexperimental settings in the wild, the gosling would most likely die. One wonders why an inherited response that would appear to damage the likelihood of survival and reproduction has not disappeared. The answer is presumably that a newly hatched gosling would need a larger brain capacity to enable it to make finer cognitive distinctions between the species. This might mean a larger egg and greater food requirements after birth. These would be costly.[22] Given that it would be rare in nature for the first object seen not to be its mother, the gosling's reproductive fitness might be better enhanced with a more general, less discriminating cognitive response.

The same may be true of other responses, including erotic ones. Animals may be better off with a sexual response that is broader than needed for narrowly reproductive purposes, because of the costs in brain size that finer distinctions would require. This might be especially true of young brains, which are still growing in adolescence, and of species like *homo sapiens,* in which the transition from childhood to a sexually mature adult is gradual (Feierman, 1990). Forcible rapes of postmenopausal women, which could confer no reproductive benefit, might have a similar explanation.

This less-discriminating response could, in some circumstances, promote reproductive fitness. In some small-scale bands, marriage sometimes takes place through the exchange of sisters. This is, in fact, an ideal in the Melanesian groups that have institutionalized rituals involving man-boy sexual contact (Herdt, 1984; Lindenbaum, 1984). To obtain a wife from another band, a man supplies someone in that band with his own sister. In the absence of a sister of marriageable age, a younger brother may serve as a substitute. Later on, when the man has a sister to exchange, she replaces the boy. This system rests on the acceptability of the substitution; if the male participants did not have the capacity to respond to a same-sex partner, marriage between men and females would be significantly more difficult. In numerically small bands, one supposes that there would often be a shortage of marriageable females, so that the circumstance described here could well have occurred often in the distant past of the human species. This kind of substitution would be harder to manage with an older boy, both because older boys would look less like girls, and because they would be looking for wives of their own.[23]

For a trait to contribute to the evolution of a species, it is necessary that it be hereditary. A trait that is not transmitted genetically, because, for example, it is learned, will not be passed on to the next generation. Currently, we have no evidence that male attraction to youthful boys or girls is inherited, but it may be. We do not know the distribution of this propensity to be attracted or aroused in the general population, though we do know that a substantial minority of male subjects in experiments are aroused by images of bodies that are not yet fully mature sexually (Quinsey et al., 1975; Briere & Runtz, 1989; Freund & Watson, 1991; Hall, Hirschman, & Oliver, 1995; Smiljanich & Briere, 1996). The distribution could be approximately normal, as Rind suggests, but it could equally well be skewed. An empirical determination of the shape of the genetic contribution to this distribution would be hard to obtain, because it can only be assessed empirically by studying subjects who have already had a number of years of life experience that could potentially contribute to their erotic responses. This would make it hard to separate the effects of learning and acculturation from genetically transmitted traits.

Policy

Unlike many who address policy issues relating to sexuality or other matters, Rind understands that policies do not exist in a vacuum. Social scientists commonly ignore this elementary observation by formulating recommendations for policies that do not have a ghost of a chance of being adopted, because they are radically at odds with a society's culture and institutionalized social arrangements, or because there is no powerful constituency willing or able to mobilize on their behalf. If imposed by an idiosyncratic power-holder on an unaccepting society, or where existing institutions will not mesh well with the new policy, a policy is not likely to perform as hoped. It follows that an examination of the possibilities for change, and the limitations to those possibilities, is a critical part of a policy analysis.

In conducting such an analysis, it is important to avoid an overly rigid social determinism. It has been common, in trying to explain the existence of certain laws or policies, to argue that they are functionally necessary for a society of a particular type, and, for that reason, could not be otherwise. Some of these explanations are simplistic and can be refuted by evidence that the law or policy is absent in other societies of the same type. Fernbach (1976), for example, proposed that the Labouchère Amendment to the Criminal Law Amendment Act of 1885 (48 & 49 Vict. C. 69), which criminalized oral sex for the first time in English history, was adopted because it was needed to preserve the heterosexual nuclear family at a time when middle-class men were delaying marriage so that they could earn and save enough capital to open a business. Not only is there no evidence in the Parliamentary debates over the bill, or in newspaper stories covering the debates on the bill, that anyone involved in the Act had this in mind, no such law was adopted in France, making clear that capital accumulation could proceed satisfactorily without criminal bans on oral sex. (Indeed, if this form of sexual stimulation were really a major impediment to the functioning of capitalism, capitalism would have collapsed long ago).

In the case of masturbation fears, it is tempting to see them as closely related to capitalism, because the language of the anti-masturbation texts written in the eighteenth and nineteenth centuries employs metaphors clearly derived from a market economy, for example, when they warn against the dangers of boys or men "spending" their semen (Spitz, 1952; Hare, 1962; Neuman, 1975, 1978; Greenberg, 1988; Laqueur, 2003). In an age when budding entrepreneurs began living in cities, emancipated from familial and community social controls, they had to avoid depleting their financial assets by wasting them on unproductive indulgences, making the control of urges to indulge in pleasure imperative. But the prohibition of masturbation long antedates capitalism. The Talmud states that a hand reaching below the navel should be cut off (*Babylonian Talmud, Tractate Niddah* 13a, b.[24])! The influential medieval Jewish philosopher Maimonides condemned masturbation in his *Mishneh Torah (Hilkhot Issurei Biah* 21:18), and Christian Penitentials from the first millennium AD imposed penances for masturbation (Brundage, 1987). A new wave of anti-masturbation literature, beginning with the publication of *Onania* early in the eighteenth century, took over the old prejudices, but voiced them in a medical vocabulary that was alien to the earlier Jewish and Christian writings.

It is difficult to imagine that the rise and growth of capitalism actually depended on the repression of masturbation. The most one can reasonably say is that the capitalist economy facilitated distribution of anti-masturbation tracts and provided metaphors for thinking about masturbation. In doing that, capitalism's work was ideological. Even here, however, one must not claim too much; *Tractate Shabbath* I.2 of the *Babylonian Talmud* attributes dropsy to masturbation (Rodkinson, 1903, p. 56), and Maimonides claimed that coitus could be bad for men's health.[25] Weston La Barre (1985) presents evidence that the ideology of semen as a carrier of the life force and which provides conceptual underpinnings for both masturbation phobia and insemination of boys as part of their initiation rituals, dates back to the Paleolithic Era.

A relationship can be seen between the prohibition of intergenerational intimacy, especially for same-sex partners, and a particular stage in economic and social development, but the relationship is not simple or direct. A hundred years ago, psychologists began to argue that a distinct stage of human development intervened between childhood (a time when children were sexually innocent and physically unprepared for sex) and adulthood (when people were physically and psychologically ready) (Hall, 1904). This development was closely associated with legal changes designed to remove youths from the paid labor force by enacting child labor laws in order to create jobs for adult men unable to support their families in times of high unemployment. To keep unemployed young people off the streets and to prepare them for jobs requiring formal education, mandatory school attendance laws were adopted (Ariès, 1962; Gillis, 1974; Greenberg, 1977). Juvenile courts were established so that youthful offenders could be handled differently from adults charged with crimes (Platt, 1969; Feld, 1999, pp. 17–35). Comparable legislation was adopted in other countries. In a general sense, it can be seen as a response to the changed labor force needs of an advanced industrial society (Greenberg, 1977).

These changes were also accompanied by new forms of governance within economic institutions and in the state. The changes can be summarized by the word *bureaucracy*. As limned by sociologist Max Weber, bureaucracies ideally govern through rules that are enforced impartially, without regard to personal identities, preferences, or allegiances of individuals. Although this ideal is imperfectly realized in existing businesses and government agencies, it roughly describes the ways schools, large corporations, and government should operate. With dominant institutions operating bureaucratically, the personal ties that are generated and maintained libidinally in premodern societies through sexual contact between adults and juveniles are not necessary or functional to the group (Greenberg, 1988). The technical demands of a modern economy call for a protracted education administered by a school bureaucracy and carried out on a large-scale collective basis by teachers in classrooms, for an extended period, not through individualized mentoring reinforced sexually. These needs underlie the historical shift in the age at which a youth can marry.

A hundred years ago, most US states allowed children to consent to sexual relations at age 10, in accord with a provision in English law dating to 1577 (before that it had been 12). In at least one state, it was 9. The minimum age for marriage was typically 12 for girls, 14 for boys, the same as in Roman law, common law, and the canon law of the Roman Catholic Church (Bullough, 2004; Cocca, 2004). Several developments contributed to legislative change raising the lawful age of consent and marriage. Evolving understandings of sexual development suggested the desirability of protecting children's developing minds and bodies from sexual stimulation, especially stimulus that would overexcite or fix development. This belief figured prominently in anti-masturbation campaigns, which were concerned with both boys and girls. The wide dissemination of Sigmund Freud's ideas about stages of psychosexual development in the early twentieth century made this seem more important than it might have seemed in an earlier age. In addition, feminists sought to weaken the "double standard" that stigmatized young unmarried girls for premarital sex by establishing criminal penalties for men who took girls as partners.

The growth of cities, mass immigration, and changing gender norms made the existing legal age standards seem inadequate to social reformers of the Progressive Era. Higher ages were proposed to preserve a childish asexual innocence and to protect girls' marriageability in cities where girls could meet strange men on the streets, in the workplace, and at recreation centers. In a small town in Europe or the United States, a man who impregnated a single girl might be pressured to marry her, but in an urban environment, where informal social pressures were weak, this could not be counted on. Higher ages would also deter the recruitment of young girls into prostitution and protect them from venereal disease. Middle- and upper-class social purity reformers, temperance organizations, such as the Woman's Christian Temperance Union, and child welfare advocates, like the Society for the Prevention of Cruelty to Children, working-class men's organizations, such as the Knights of Labor, and religious conservatives campaigned to raise the age of consent so that criminal penalties could be assessed against adult seducers (Denno, 1998; Jackson, 2000; Cocca, 2004, p. 12; Leonard, 2004; Levine, 2007). They also helped in the prosecution of child rapists. In England, antiprostitution crusaders, child welfare advocates, and feminists sought the same objectives and enjoyed mass support, as evidenced by huge attendance at meetings and outdoor rallies (Simpson, 2007).

Around a hundred years ago, in response to these campaigns, state legislatures raised the age at which it was possible to marry or to consent to sexual relations (Cocca, 2004; Robertson, 2005). Even so, there was much variation among the states; in some states, for example, young boys were still allowed to marry without parental consent. They were generally not given "protection" from adult men analogous to what girls were receiving, because all same-sex sexual relations were already criminal, with high penalties. This history makes clear that laws specifying a high age of consent did not merely formalize long-standing social norms.

That English law also raised its age of consent in 1885—from 13 to 16—in the Criminal Law Amendment Act[26] (Stafford, 1964; Pearson, 1972; Simpson, 2007), and that now most Western countries have adopted age of consent laws, with cutoffs not too different from those in the United States,[27] demonstrates that the change was not a result of anything distinctly American, such as Puritanism. It was part of a change in the age structuration of society that fundamentally transformed the social roles and norms regulating young people and those who interacted with them. The change encompassed many social contexts, including work, education, criminal law, marriage, and sexuality.

These changes had implications for the kinds of same-sex relationships men sought when looking for male partners. As recently as the late nineteenth century, a substantial fraction of men arrested in New York for homosexual relations had partners who were minors (Chauncey, 1996). Half a century later, the proportion would have been quite a bit smaller, though the exact numbers are not known. In New York, the Progressive-era arrests were usually brought on the initiative of the Society for the Prevention of Cruelty to Children, or had its support. Their interest was to protect helpless children in a world where familiar and neighborhood ties were losing their ability to do so.

When it came to be realized that adolescents were, in fact, sexual, some thinkers argued for tolerance of sexual exploration with peers short of intercourse (e.g. "necking" or "petting"). This toleration continued to rule out sexual contact with older adults, possibly from the belief that older men would not be satisfied with anything short of intercourse. The decade of the 1950s brought greater uniformity among the states. The general liberalization of sexual attitudes in the 1960s (Petersen & Donnenwerth, 1997) and acceptance of the notion that young people should have some rights, led legislatures to reduce the minimum age for marriage and for sexual activity, but not by very much. In recent years, the trend has reversed, so that in most American states it is now 16 or higher. Hawaii used to have the lowest age (14), but it was recently raised to 16. In many states, such as Virginia, the age of consent is 18 (Phipps, 1997–1998. 2002–2003; Drobac, 2004). The trend in Canada has been similar: it was raised from 12 to 14 in 1890, and then to 16 in 2008 (Dauda, 2010). That it remained at 14 for more than a century and was then raised without any clear evidence that the younger age was responsible for social harms, demonstrates that a high age of consent is not a necessary correlate of "modernity."

Are there barriers to further reductions? Is there an inherent tension between existing social arrangements and the mentoring sexual relations between adults and youths? The abandonment of all barriers to sex, even when the child is very young, is so far removed from broad acceptability as to stand no chance at all of adoption. Moreover, for the reasons that Rind points out, modern industrial societies are not going to institutionalize the ritual mandatory sexual relations between men and boys practiced by some groups in Papua New Guinea or the pedagogical pederasty found in classical Greece. This may mean that we cannot expect to see such relationships embraced with enthusiasm or occurring in a high percentage of the population. But that does not necessarily mean that they have to be heavily repressed either. Consider sadomasochistic practices. They appear to be a minority taste in the contemporary United States, and they do not promise important social benefits to the society. Yet they are not banned by law, and little is done to stop them. Clubs and societies focused on sadomasochistic practices flourish.

That there is a mismatch between pederasty and contemporary social arrangements does not mean that some change is inconceivable. That the age of consent differs somewhat from one modern Western society to another tells us that the conditions of modern life do not completely specify the precise age of consent. Contemporary American society is now more sexually tolerant than it was half a century ago. Thanks to many state legislatures and to the US Supreme Court,[28] homosexual relations between consenting adults are no longer criminal, and public opinion polls show reduced intolerance (Yang, 1997; Frost et al., 2001; Loftus, 2001; Pew Research Center, 2007). Support for gay marriage has been rising. A number of jurisdictions now allow same-sex civil unions or marriage. Americans' sexual repertoires are now wider than they used to be. More people engage in oral stimulation,[29] use sex toys, watch pornographic films, and adopt bondage-domination or sadomasochistic practices. References to these activities appear in popular music and television programs, so that knowledge of them is widely diffused throughout society. Familiarity helps to normalize them. Many who do not engage in these activities themselves tolerate them in others. A live-and-let-live atmosphere characteristic of large cities, freedom of the press (permitting publication of magazines oriented toward minority sexual tastes), a market economy that encourages entrepreneurs to meet consumer demand by producing and selling commodities designed for specialized tastes (e.g., fetish clothing and equipment), constitutional protections securing freedom of speech and of the press, freedom of assembly, and the rise of the Internet (which provides new modes of communication) all foster the proliferation of sexual subcultures in which only minorities of the population participate actively. The percentage of the American people who describe themselves as strongly religious has been dropping, which means that an important source of opposition to liberalization has diminished. Support for traditional gender norms has weakened, and fewer people endorse "old-fashioned values about family and marriage" (Pew Research Center, 2007). A federal judge has ruled unconstitutional the US military's "Don't Ask, Don't Tell" policy, which required invisibility of US armed forces personnel regarding their homosexuality; in December, 2010, Congress repealed it. These developments should facilitate greater acceptance of intergenerational sex, even if relatively few adults or juveniles want it.

A second favorable factor is the earlier sexual maturation of children—generally attributed to better nutrition and weight gain (Ducros & Pasquet, 1978; Wyshak & Frisch, 1982; Eveleth & Tanner, 1990; Keizer-Schrama & Mul, 2001). Because the age at which people typically marry has been rising[30] (Simmons & Dye, 2004), youths are experiencing a much longer period in which they are physiologically ready for sex and want it, but do not have a spouse. In this period, which arrives before the age of sexual consent, most youths seek, or respond affirmatively to sexual invitations from non-spousal partners, usually, but not always, close in age to themselves (Darroch et al., 1999; Weiss & Bullough, 2004), and they commonly have a number of partners before they marry (if they ever do). A national probability sample of men and women taken in 2002 found that 26 percent of females had had vaginal intercourse by age 15, and another 8 percent had oral sex but not vaginal intercourse. At age 16, the corresponding figures were 40 percent and 15 percent. At 17, the percentages were 49 percent and 15 percent. These are large increases over previous generations (Mosher, Chandra, and Jones, 2005; see also Chilman, 1979, 108–135).[31]

These shifts are reflected in popular culture. Popular films, television programs, commercials, and magazine advertisements depict teenagers as sexually active and glamorize their sexual activities. The mass media publicize every sexual escapade of popular entertainers. Clothing for children is designed to call attention to their sexuality. It is no longer possible to argue that an adult who has sexual relations with a teenager steals that child's "innocence" or that children of that age are ignorant about sex. Though some adults greet these trends with dismay—sometimes for moral and religious reasons, sometimes because of unwanted pregnancies, welfare costs, and sexually transmitted diseases—they are widely accepted as part of a reality that cannot easily be changed. Sex education to promote sexual abstinence and virginity-pledge campaigns directed to high school students can make a difference, but only at the margin (Bearman & Brücker, 2001; Smoyer & Blankenship, 2006).

It is also true, it must be noted, that these trends have not—at least as yet—led to greater acceptance of sexual relations between adults and minors under the age of consent. Although disapproval of premarital sex has declined, 69 percent said in 1996 that it was always wrong for adolescents between the ages of 14 and 16 to have sex.[32] Despite these beliefs, the age-of-consent laws are not being enforced vigorously. The ratio of prosecutions to violations of the law must be tiny. Yet there is little public pressure for energetic prosecution, and law enforcement officers do not learn about most cases. Where they do, the underage partners may not want to identify their adult partners or testify against them (Frost et al., 2001, p. 18), making prosecution difficult.

A certain contradiction in the way American law deals with adolescents also points to a possible source of pressure for change. As part of the broad "toughening" of criminal justice policies in the United States during the past quarter-century, manifested in higher prison populations and the restoration of the death penalty, juveniles charged with some crimes are now prosecuted in adult criminal courts alongside adult defendants, instead of in the juvenile court, where a youth's reduced responsibility supposedly leads to a less punitive, more rehabilitative orientation (Feld, 1999; Fagan & Zimring, 2000; Kupchik, 2007).[33] If a 15-year-old can be tried as an adult for robbery, it is not clear why that same 15-year-old is too immature to consent to sexual relations, or to pose for a pornographic photograph or film, or why adults should be prosecuted for consensual sexual relations with that juvenile or for photographing or filming that juvenile.³⁴ Arguably, many of the large number of young people who grow up in broken homes, with limited financial resources, could benefit from attention, nurturing, emotional support and guidance, and material assistance from adults (Brunoz, 1995). If adults are willing to provide that, and receive sexual gratification from the juveniles who are being helped, what harm could come of this?

The legal academy has identified another seemingly irrational feature of contemporary penal law—its failure to protect adults who honestly believe that their underage partners are old enough to give consent, perhaps because the youths fraudulently misrepresented their ages (Carpenter, 2003; Christopher & Christopher, 2007). It is difficult to see what legitimate law enforcement purpose could be served by prosecuting men for mistakes of fact when they have been brought about by fraud on the part of the so-called victim of their actions. This suggests that one important constituency might be supportive of change. Yet other legal academicians support the status quo or want to raise the age of consent or see statutory rape case prosecutions stepped up or have other restrictions placed on girls' ability to consent, to protect them from harm (Oberman, 1994-1995, 2000; Phipps, 2002–2003; Drobac, 2006).

There is also much that mitigates against quick abandonment of present policies and attitudes. The research that Rind and his colleagues analyzed finds a modest relationship between intergenerational intimacy and undesirable psychological states. It also demonstrates that substantial numbers of young people are not harmed by sexual relations with adults and that they sometimes welcome it, are grateful for it, and initiate it. Kilpatrick's (1992) study of women corroborates this conclusion. Interpreting correlations as causal, this research is consistent with the claim that some youths suffer detrimental psychological and social consequences from this type of sexual contact. In some of the research, the relationships are not trivial (we look at some numbers in what follows).

These findings provoke a question as to whether the position Rind successfully refutes (that intergenerational sex is always, or almost always, harmful) is the appropriate target in discussions of public policy. Certainly, one does encounter empirically unsupported dogmatic assertions of this sort, even in writings that appear to be sympathetic to adults who are sexually attracted to children (e.g., Goode, 2010, 178), and it can be valuable to refute them. Yet, for purposes of policy assessment, this is hardly the right standard. Most of the time, driving while intoxicated and over the speed limit harm no one. Yet no one argues that laws prohibiting driving while intoxicated and speeding should be repealed. Driving in this manner raises the chances of an accident resulting in serious injury or death. Even if this happens infrequently, the consequences are grave enough to warrant efforts to reduce the frequency of these behaviors. If intergenerational sex poses a significant threat of harm even to a substantial minority of youths, most people would desire to discourage it.

Some have maintained that the ban on intergenerational sex should be maintained, if anyone would be harmed by it. This principle, however, would lead to a ban on virtually all human activities, including all sexual contacts between consenting adults, because these sometimes lead to undesirable outcomes, including unhappiness and disease. Some balancing of harms and benefits is needed if we are not to prohibit all sexual contact. If harm is indeed a rare outcome, then one might well be willing to put up with intergenerational sex, given the evidence that Rind (Chapter 1, this volume) provides that it is frequently experienced positively by minors.[35] The numbers Rind quotes regarding these adverse effects (that if two of one hundred persons in the general population have clinically significant problems, only three of one hundred persons having had child sexual abuse do) seem small.[36] It is not clear exactly how these figures were obtained. Presumably they are based on the studies Rind cites. A number of these studies have fairly small samples that are not nationally representative. However, the problems with this figure go beyond the sample size and the representativeness of the data.

Consider first the study by Nelson et al. (2002) using Australian data. This study is of particular interest because it is based on a comparison of twins, one of whom experienced childhood sexual abuse (CSA), whereas the other did not. This research design controls for family background better than previous research. In this study, CSA is defined as being forced into sexual activity prior to age 18, having any sexual contact before age 16 with someone who was not a family member and who was five or more years older, having any sexual contact before age 16 with a family member, or being raped or molested. If any of these were present, CSA was considered to have taken place.[37]

Of the eight outcomes considered in this study, consider, for illustrative purposes, just one—major depression. The frequencies and percentages of males and females who experienced depression are shown in Table 9.1. Of the females who experienced CSA, 50.9 percent had major depression, almost twice as high as the 27.7 percent of females who did not. For males, the relevant percentages were 35.6 percent compared with 19.8 percent, an increase of about 80 percent.

Table 9.1. Major Depression by Child Sexual Abuse (CSA) and Sex

| | Child Sexual Abuse (CSA) | | | |
| | Males | | Females | |
Depression	No CSA	CSA	No CSA	CSA
None	1262	58	1396	190
	80.2%	64.4%	72.3%	49.1%
Some	312	32	535	197
	19.8%	35.6%	27.7%	50.9%
Total	1574	90	1931	387
	100.0%	100.0%	100.0%	100%

Source: Nelson et al. (2002)

In a separate study, Molnar, Buka, and Kessler (2001) examined the prevalence of 17 different psychiatric outcomes in the nationally representative National Comorbidity Survey. This study found that 19.2 percent of the females who did not report CSA experienced depression, compared with 39.3 percent who did. For males, the comparable figures were 11.4 percent and 30.3 percent. When the outcome measure was any psychiatric disorder, the percentages were 48.9 percent and 78.0 percent for females, and 51.1 percent and 82.2 percent, respectively, for males.

These figures point to the possibility that child sexual abuse can cause later psychological problems in a substantial proportion of cases. This is a very different impression than Rind's numbers convey. The explanation for the seeming discrepancy is that the percentages quoted by Nelson et al. (2002) and by Molnar, Buka, and Kessler (2001) are conditional on abuse having taken place. Rind's are unconditional. The less common the conditioning status, the smaller the percentages would be. This difference can expressed in a simple mathematical formula. If A represents an adverse psychological output, and p(A) is its probability, we can express this probability as the product of the probabilities p(A|B) and p(B). Here, p(A|B) represents the probability that A occurs conditional on B occurring. For us, B is the probability that someone experiences child sexual abuse.

With this in mind, consider the figures shown in Table 9.1 for boys. In this data set, 344 boys, or 20.67 percent of the 1664 boys in the sample, became depressed, and 90 experienced CSA. This is 5.41 percent. Of these 90 boys, 32 experienced major depression—just over a third. The proportion of all the boys in the sample who experienced major depression as a result of sexual abuse is thus (90/1664)(32/90) = 0.0192, or 1.92 percent. This can be compared with the outcomes for the boys, making up 94.6 percent of the sample, who did not experience CSA. For them, 312/1574 became depressed. Thus, (1574/1664)(312/1574) = .1875, or 18.75 percent of the boys became depressed without having been sexually abused. Assuming that the higher rate of depression for the boys exposed to CSA was due to the abuse, approximately 18 of the abused boys would have become depressed in the absence of abuse. Consequently, only 14 cases of depression in the sample of 1664 boys can be attributed to the abuse. This is a little less than 1 percent of the population, or 4.1 percent of the boys who experienced depression. This may seem trivial.

Another way of measuring the strength of the relationship between CSA and depression is to compute the correlation coefficient between these two variables. For the males it is .088. The percentage of the variance in depression explained by CSA is the square of the correlation coefficient, which in this case is .0077. In other words, less than 1 percent of the variation in depression is due to child sexual abuse.

If we were interested in what percentage of the male population at large becomes depressed owing to child sexual abuse, these numbers would be relevant. Assuming the relationship to be causal, CSA makes just a tiny contribution to the amount of depression found among males in American society. This is because it occurs to boys infrequently, and because most cases of depression have other causes. By the same reasoning, drunken driving and speeding on the highway make only a very small contribution to overall mortality rates. Indeed, one could make this argument about shooting people in the head, because so few people are shot in the head. This would be so, even though shooting people in the head will often kill them. But if we are interested in whether shooting people puts them at serious risk, the answer would be quite different. If we are interested not in the impact child sexual abuse makes to overall levels of depression and other adverse psychological conditions, but in the likelihood that these activities will be damaging to the children who experience them, the answer, again assuming the relationships found by Molnar, Buka, and Kessler (2003) and by Nelson et al. (2002) are causal, is that this likelihood is not trivial. In the Nelson et al. (2002) study, child sexual abuse raised the percentage of subjects experiencing major depression from 19.8 percent to 35.6 percent, This is a substantial increase.[38]

In various writings, Rind and his collaborators have rightly noted that correlation does not always imply causality. It could be, for example, that unhappy, troubled youths are more likely to respond favorably to overtures from adults or to seek adult partners. The research that would help us to tease apart the different contributions to the correlation has not been done. Until it has been done, many are likely to think that it would be best to discourage possibly damaging relations. The situation is similar to the one that prevailed after a link was established between smoking cigarettes and lung cancer. The tobacco companies argued that the relationship might not be causal: perhaps cancer-prone individuals were especially likely to take up smoking. In this instance, subsequent research confirmed that smoking does enhance the likelihood of getting lung cancer. At least some of the association between CSA and undesirable outcomes found in these studies may well be causal.

In the National Comorbidity Survey, 13.5 percent of the girls and 2.5 percent of the boys experienced either molestation or rape. The infrequency of these episodes (to which legal bans have probably contributed) and the fact that many of them are not reported, will make them seem weird to many people, so that those who seek intergenerational relations with children will have little broad support or sympathy. It is not necessarily relevant that a good deal of the negative reactions youths experience in the aftermath of sexual activity with an older partner are a result of the strong reactions other people display when a case comes to light. In the short run, social responses are beyond the control of policy makers and constitute the environment for which policies must be made. Prosecutorial discretion could easily be brought to bear in de facto policies of benign neglect, where a juvenile initiated a sexual interaction or where it appears that no harm has been done. Dutch law used to formalize such a principle by allowing prosecutions in cases involving a juvenile between ages 12 and 16 only when the juvenile, its guardian, or a child protection agency seeks prosecution (Schuijer, 1993).

The argument that it is inconsistent to treat juveniles as too immature to be able to make sound judgments about sex, while treating them as adults in criminal court, is a knife that cuts both ways. The treatment of juvenile law violators as adults has elicited much opposition, on the grounds that adolescents' brains are still developing. Though youths may understand risks attached to various behaviors cognitively (Drobac, 2006; Reyna & Farley, 2006), they are more prone to impulsivity. This may explain why involvement in many kinds of crime and other risky activities is higher for juveniles than adults (Greenberg, 1977, 2008; Hirschi & Gottfredson, 1983; Cauffman & Steinberg, 2000; Scott, 2000b; Drobac, 2006). The United States Supreme Court accepted this reasoning in *Roper* v. *Simmons*,[39] probably reflecting a widely held understanding that adolescence is a distinct stage of life, often characterized by poor judgment.

In addition to the considerations raised by developmental psychologists, adolescents have less experience to draw on in sizing up prospective partners and consequently are likely to misjudge their character more often. They are probably easier to manipulate or to pressure and more likely than older people to give in when solicited for sex, even when they would prefer to say no. Indeed, in a number of studies, a fair number of teenage girls indicated that they did not really want their first sexual experience, even though, for various reasons, they consented to it (Moore et al., 1995; Oberman, 1994, 2000) or regretted it afterward and wished that it had come later (Wellings et al., 2001). The dividing line between consent and non-consent is not always clear when partners are adults; it is probably even more blurred when one or more of the participants is young.

In recent decades, juveniles' rights have been cut back in a number of areas—perhaps as a backlash against what conservatives consider to have been the over-permissiveness of the 1960s. In a number of states, minors have lost the right to obtain abortions without parental permission (National Abortion and Reproductive Action Rights League, 2008). The National Minimum Drinking Age of 1984 provides for the withholding of federal funds from states whose minimum age for purchasing alcoholic beverages is under 21. The states have complied, giving the United States one of the highest minimum drinking ages in the world.[40] This trend suggests that the times are not auspicious for lowering the age of consent to sex.

Growing up in a society whose mass media tacitly promote teenage sex, it is not surprising that substantial numbers of minors will see themselves as ready for it, want it, have the opportunity to get it, and act accordingly. One supposes that many adults who might think minors desirable now refrain from acting on their desires to avoid legal sanctions and in response to informal social pressures that stem from the associated stigma. If the legal sanctions are removed, then it is at least plausible that more adults will act on their desires. For them, and for some juveniles, this may be to the good; however, it would also mean more minors exposed to unwanted and unpleasant overtures, more adults responding favorably to minors' solicitations, and a larger number of unhappy outcomes for the minors. The extent to which this is actually true is not known, but the argument is likely to be persuasive to many.[41]

Today, the main institutional settings where adults interact with minors are schools, the workplace, and religious institutions. Schools and workplaces are primarily bureaucracies in which there are social expectations that students and employees will be evaluated, hired, promoted, and fired on the basis of impersonal, meritocratic standards. Intimate relationships, including sexual ones, potentially threaten the impartiality of evaluation and decision making that is widely considered desirable in these institutions. The potential for superiors to offer inducements to sex (promotions, pay raises, high grades), as well as tacit or explicit threats (of demotions, loss of job, low grades) conflict with the voluntarism that many people think should characterize sexual relations. Antidiscrimination laws, bans on sexual harassment, and rules against dating and affairs between teachers or supervisors and those under their authority have been introduced to ensure that this impartiality is not jeopardized by illegitimate discrimination and favoritism. These protections are undoubtedly imperfect, but they testify to the existence of a commitment to an ideal. If sex with minors is accepted, students and adults in positions of authority will predictably seek it more than they do now. The result will be more incidents where students either seek favors by initiating affairs with a teacher or fear retaliation for saying no or for breaking off an affair. Most people will regard these outcomes as undesirable.

Some of the studies of the effects of age-discrepant sexual relations suggest that boys are less likely than girls to experience harm. This raises the possibility that law reform could restrict statutory rape laws to underage girls or could introduce a lower age of consent for boys than for girls (Rind, 2004). Though this would be constitutionally permissible under current case law, the norm that the law should not discriminate on the basis of sex is now so strongly incorporated in American legal culture that all fifty states have incorporated equal treatment of boys and girls into their statutory rape laws. These changes are not likely to be repealed anytime soon. They would be seen as an endorsement of man-boy sex, while treating man-girl sex as a crime. American culture would have to change radically for anything like that to happen.

A continued ban need not mean that the line has to be drawn where it is now, or that responses need to be highly punitive. The age limits in other developed countries are lower than those in the United States. A recent listing shows the age of consent as being 13 in Spain, 14 in Austria,

China, Colombia, Hungary, Iceland, Italy, Peru, and Romania, and 15 in Denmark, France, Poland, and Sweden (Aggrawal, 2009, pp. 249–253). Among the US states, it ranges from 16 to 18, but in some, it is 14 or 15 when the difference in ages between the partners is small. Some states (Alabama, California, Kansas, Texas) exempt homosexual relationships from this leniency. This exemption has no obvious rational justification and may be a violation of the Equal Protection clause (Shvartsman, 2004; Higdon, 2008).

The terminology we now use constitutes a major obstacle to reform. By calling all minors "children," we fail to distinguish 5-year-olds from 15-year-olds. Many people will recognize that there is a difference between a sex partner who is 15 and one who is 5. All but a few will think that a 5-year-old is too young to be able to give meaningful consent to sex, whereas a 15-year-old may well be old enough. When sexual contact between adolescents and adults is called "child sexual abuse," it is difficult to defend it without appearing to defend the sexual abuse of a toddler. The term *abuse* itself can be misleading when applied to cases in which the minor takes the initiative or gladly responds to an adult's solicitation and experiences no short-term or long-term harm. This is often the case (Kilpatrick, 2012).

The sensationalist mass media contribute to our linguistic difficulties by publishing headlines referring to high school teachers or priests who seek or have affairs with their students as *pervs, monsters,* or *predators*. The term *pervert* is normative and judgmental. Technically, it has been used in sexology to refer to modes of sexual contact that are not potentially procreative. By this standard, intercourse between an adolescent and an adult of a different sex does not qualify. *Monster* does not even purport to be a scientific term. But the derogatory connotations of the term interfere with dispassionate discourse. The social work literature sometimes refers to minors who have had sexual relations with adults as *survivors,* implying that intergenerational sexual intimacy typically entails the use of violence and that injury and death are normal outcomes; in fact, these outcomes are extremely rare. *Predator* also suggests violence, not seduction or consent. The previously mentioned television program, *To Catch a Predator,* uses this language to refer to men who use the Internet to find underage consensual sex partners who are generally above the age of puberty and who seek sex with older men.

Distinctive features of US politics also mitigate against major relaxation of standards. Criminologists writing about the "punitive turn" in American criminal justice policy in the past thirty years have argued that distinct features of US electoral politics and the judicial system have contributed to the harshening of law enforcement (Savelsberg, 1994; Steiker, 2002; Zimring, 2003; Garland, 2005). Primaries are open, giving the public a larger voice in setting public policy than in countries where candidates are picked by political party leaders. In coalition governments such as are common in parliamentary democracies, party leaders cannot easily deploy inflammatory rhetoric against other parties' initiatives without jeopardizing the government of which they are a part. By contrast, the winner-take-all character of elections for executive positions in US government encourages demagogic attacks on opponents. Ever since Massachusetts Governor George Dukakis was denounced by his rival for the presidency, George H. Bush, for permitting convicted murderer Willie Horton to participate in a prison work furlough program (during which he committed a grave crime of violence), politicians have been wary of being denounced as "soft on crime." The same political considerations create an obstacle to liberalization of statutory rape laws. A legislator who called for the lowering of the age of consent would be attacked for promoting child molestation. One who attempted to do so just for relationships between males would also be accused of trying to bestow "special privileges" on gay men, a rhetorical ploy that has been used effectively in various states to block legislation banning discrimination on the basis of sexual orientation.

In most US states, judges are elected, rendering them vulnerable to defeat if they step too far ahead of public opinion. Federal court judges are appointed, an arrangement that in principle provides for greater independence. Thus protected, some judges have protected minorities, including sexual minorities, though only up to a point. Currently a majority of the judges on the federal bench have been appointed by conservative Republican presidents and were chosen only after being screened for their views on social and moral issues. They are not likely to strike down age-of-consent laws. Even with the broadening of the right to sexual autonomy established in *Lawrence v. Texas*,[42] it would be far too much of a stretch beyond existing case law for any judge to rule that adults have a constitutional right to engage in sexual relations with minors, or that minors have a right to do so with anyone. In *Carey v. Population Services International,* the US Supreme Court's majority opinion held that "in the area of sexual mores, the scope of permissible state regulation is broader as to minors than as to adults."[43] This is a precedent federal judges are not likely to ignore.

For all these reasons, it is unlikely that statutory rape laws will be eliminated or even much liberalized in the foreseeable future, notwithstanding the existence of some auspicious factors.

Notes

1. I am grateful to Stephanie Budin, Carolyn Cocca, Wayne Dynes, Judith Gibber, Adam Isaiah Green, Gert Hekma, Thomas Hubbard, Theo van der Meer, Michael Peachin, and Lawrence Schiffman for helpful comments and suggestions on an earlier draft.
2. Detailed accounts of the suppression efforts can be found in Rind, Tromovitch, and Bauserman (2000b), Lilienfeld (2002) at www.mhamic.org/rind/ and www.ipce. info/ipceweb/Library/rbt_files.htm. The March 2002 issue of *American Psychologist*

(vol. 57 no. 3) was devoted to the controversy. These sources do not deal with the attempts to prevent the publication of Rind's most recent work, which are recounted in Hubbard (Chapter 11, this volume).
3. Rind, Tromovich, & Bauserman (2000a, 2001) have responded to the distortions and misrepresentations in these allegations in several publications.
4. I do not want to leave the impression that it is always lay persons opposed to science who try to block the publication of objectionable ideas. When Immanuel Velikovsky tried to publish heterodox ideas about astronomy that mainstream scientists considered ludicrous, a number of them tried to stop publication (Greenberg & Sizemore, 1977; De Grazia, 1978).
5. I refer to external censorship based on extra-scientific considerations, because the peer review system widely used by journals is, of course, also a form of censorship—one that is mitigated by the existence of large numbers of journals in most scientific fields. Meritorious work that is rejected by one journal can almost always be published in others. There are circumstances where extra-scientific reasons may justify censorship—bans on the publication of classified state and military secrets might be an example. The collective enterprise of advancing scientific knowledge has an interest in minimizing such limits on censorship. Where research bears on matters of public policy, the public also benefits from the availability of information. Nothing in the Rind et al. controversy suggests that national interests were threatened in a manner that might justify suppression of their research.
6. Most studies of the effects of sexual contact with an adult on minors have been carried out on clinical patients or subjects caught up in the criminal justice system (Kilpatrick, 1992: 27-30). It should be kept in mind that the population under treatment is also part of the total picture, and should not be forgotten in a study of the effects of intergenerational sexual contact. How large a fraction of the total it is, is another question. It is also worth noting that some studies of the general population have also found evidence of harm to some of the youthful participants; see, for example, Kilpatrick's (1992) and Browning & Laumann's (1997) studies of sexual contact between girls and men, Nelson et al.'s (2002) twin study, and Molnar, Buka, & Kessler's (2001) analysis of data from the National Comorbidity Survey.
7. See http://en.wikipedia.org/wiki/Pro-pedophile_activism (Accessed February 22, 2008).
8. See the lines given to Dosis in Lucian's (1928) *Mimes of the Courtesans: The Philosopher.*
9. That pederastic relationships sometimes culminated in violence was well known to the ancients. That this was so raises questions about the potential contribution of mentoring-type pederasty to group cohesion, although, admittedly, the popular account of the Theban Sacred Army of Lovers lends support to the idea.
10. To be sure, we have no firm information as to the percentage of adults or of male youths who participated. In antiquity there were no survey researchers asking people questions about their sexual practices. In Renaissance Florence, we know from the court records for prosecutions that pederasty was very common—close to universal (Rocke, 1996). However, the continuity that Rind sees Florence as having with ancient Rome cannot be demonstrated from the extant historical record, which does not point to exceptionally high levels of pederasty in pre-Renaissance Italy. One gets the impression from many ancient texts that the percentage of the male population experiencing intergenerational sex as a youth or as a mature adult was higher than it is today, but we have no way to quantify this difference.
11. In one of the few episodes, a number of men in Revere, Massachusetts, were arrested, but the charges were eventually dropped, and the state attorney-general announced that in the future men would not be prosecuted unless they used force. It was this episode that led to the founding of NAMBLA. Surveys of the general population seeming to show growing rates of unwanted sexual attention paid by men to boys

were probably a further stimulus (Russell, 1984). According to Finkelhor (1984, p. 200), professionals (presumably referring to social workers, psychologists, and physicians) saw few cases of child sexual abuse before the mid-1970s. They increased a great deal from that time on. The reasons for this increase are unclear. It may be that gay liberation led to greater public awareness of homosexuality, or that gay liberation led to more frequent sexual contacts between adults and adolescents.

12. *Michael M. v. Superior Court of Sonoma County,* 450 U.S. 464, 101 S. Ct. 1200, 67 L. Ed. 2d. 437.
13. There was then, and there remains today, relatively little research as to whether age-discrepant sexual relations involving small disparities in age are less likely to lead to undesirable outcomes than those where the differences in age are larger. Rind (2001) concludes that the magnitude of the difference in ages between boys and their adult male partners has no significant effect on self-esteem, but an analysis of a sample with just twenty-six cases has very low statistical power and consequently is limited in its capacity to identify all but very large effects. Moreover, it did not include heterosexual boys, who might be expected to experience more adverse outcomes than homosexual boys to sexual contact with a male adult. A larger study of women reached the same conclusion—the age of the partner relative to that of the subject had no significant effect on any of five measures of the subject's adult functioning (Kilpatrick, 1992: 103).
14. This may reflect the smaller number of same-sex cases known to prosecutors.
15. The first known appearance of this argument is in Plato, *Laws* (636a–c).
16. Much ink has been spilled in discussions of what ancient writers meant when they referred to same-sex relations as "natural" or "unnatural " (Boswell, 1980). In modern scientific thinking, all events occur according to the laws of nature and cannot, therefore, be considered unnatural. (Events that are supernatural, if there are any, lie outside the domain of scientific understanding). The frequency of an event is irrelevant to its being natural.
17. Rapid temporal variation provides further support for this position. When Gilbert Herdt conducted fieldwork among the Sambia (1984), extensive ritual sexual practices between men and boys were universal and mandatory. Now, on his return visits to the field, he finds, two generations later, that these practices are unknown. Boys are astonished at learning what their grandfathers did regularly. This rapid change could hardly have taken place were a propensity to engage in pederasty obligatory, but would be consistent with a facultative trait.
18. Available at www.donnarose.com/JMBInterview.html
19. Twin research finds a low concordance for homosexuality between identical twins (Whitehead & Whitehead, 2010; W. R. Rice, Friberg & Gavrilets, 2012), suggesting that emphasis on inheritance in theorizing about the determinants of sexual orientation may be misplaced.
20. An argument has been made that bonobos are actually no more peaceful than chimpanzees (Parker, 2007) but the weight of the evidence is that they are (De Waal, 1989, 1997, pp. 81, 84, 1998, 2007; Idani, 1990; Kano, 1992).
21. In Athens, the ideal marriage was of a 14-year-old girl to a 30-year-old man (Xenophon, *Oeconomicus* 7.5). In Sparta, women married somewhat later, at about 18 (Plutarch, *Pericles* 34.5–6).
22. The human brain consumes energy at a rate highly disproportionate to its share of body weight (Kandel & Schwarz, 1985; Magistretti, Pellerin, & Martin, n.d.).
23. The importance of secondary sexual characteristics on object choice can be relevant in some settings, even when the submissive partner is an adult. The late Steven Donaldson, a victim of prison rape, told me that when he was serving a prison sentence, his cell mate forced him to let the hair on his head grow long and to shave his body hair. He had to sleep on his stomach, so that his cell mate in the bunker bed above him could look down at him and see the image of a woman.

24. The statement was surely not intended to be taken literally, but it does display a strong aversion to masturbation.
25. See Maimonides's (1964) *Fī Tadbir al-Ṣiḥḥah*, Ch. 4. Interestingly, he does not speak of masturbation here and sees the greatest danger from coitus being for elderly men, not boys.
26. The bill was to protect girls from prostitution and exploitation, particularly at the hands of wealthy men.
27. See Graupner (2004) and www.ageofconsent.com/ageofconsent.htm (Accessed Feb. 20, 2008).
28. *Lawrence v. Texas,* 123 S. Ct. 2472 (2003).
29. In 2002, 83.0 percent of males and 82.0 percent of females between the ages of 15 and 44 had engaged in oral sex with a partner of a different sex. These figures are larger than those reported in the Kinsey surveys for males (Kinsey, Pomeroy, & Martin, 1948, p. 370) and females (Kinsey, Pomeroy, Martin, & Gebhard, 1953, pp. 257–258), The corresponding figures for anal intercourse in 2002 were 34.0 percent and 30.0 percent; 11 percent of males and females in the 15- to 19-year-old age bracket had had anal intercourse with someone of a different sex, whereas 3.7 percent of males had had anal intercourse with another male, and 5.7 percent had had oral sex with a male partner (Mosher, Chandra, & Jones, 2005, pp. 21–26). The figures for male homosexual experience are much lower than those reported in the Kinsey study, suggesting either major historical change or that Kinsey and his collaborators greatly over-sampled males with homosexual experience. A reanalysis of the Kinsey data with institutionalized subjects eliminated from the sample reduces, but does not eliminate, the discrepancy between the Kinsey data and more recent surveys (Gebhard, 1972; Gebhard & Johnson, 1979; Gagnon & Simon, 1973).
30. According to the US Bureau of the Census, the median age at first marriage in 1950 was 22.8 for males and 20.3 for females. In 2012 the figures had risen to 28.6 and 26.6 (http://marriage.about.com/od/statistics/a/medianage.htm) (Accessed May 28, 2013).
31. In the Kinsey survey, 3 percent of the females had experienced first coitus by age 15, 20 percent between ages 16 and 20, and 35 percent between 21 and 25. Over the next 20 years, the percentages rose to higher than 40 (Kinsey, Pomeroy, Martin, & Gebhard, 1953, 288).
32. In 1972, 37 percent of American adults said that premarital sex was always wrong, compared with 24 percent in 1996. By comparison, a survey conducted in Great Britain in 2001 among people aged 17 to 25 found that 64 percent of men and 54 percent of women thought it acceptable for someone to have more than ten partners before marriage. See www.ageofconsent.com/comments/partners.htm (Accessed February 12, 2008).
33. The age at which this is possible varies from state to state. In Kansas and Vermont, it is as low as 10. Information about each state's provisions as of the end of the 2006 legislative session can be found at www.ncjj.org/stateprofiles/overviews/transfer_state_table.org.
34. There are many spheres of activity where juveniles are denied rights that adults have, e.g., to drive a car, to purchase alcoholic beverages, to vote, to serve on a jury, to hold full-time jobs, to exercise free speech rights, and to refrain from attending school; and where they are granted special rights, e.g., not to be executed or drafted into the armed services (Scott, 2000a). There may be sensible reasons for drawing the line at different ages in relation to different rights, but the matter seems to have had little systematic attention.
35. An earlier study, of women who had sexual contacts with adults when they were girls or adolescents, came to the same conclusion (Kilpatrick, 1992).
36. Clinically significant psychological problems are only some of the potentially adverse outcomes associated with children having coercive sexual contact with adults. Seto

et al. (2010) have studied the contribution that this type of contact makes to the adoption of sexually coercive behavior by its Swedish and Norwegian male victims and conclude that 18 to 25 percent of the sexually coercive behavior in the population can be traced to this sort of experience. If the estimate is correct, it is not trivial.
37. Some of these events may have taken place when the subject was prepubescent. Some may not have involved an adult partner or perpetrator. Where there was an adult, that adult could have been female, and the episode(s) may have occurred when the subject was no longer below the age of consent, i.e., at age 17. Consequently the study is not well designed to answer the question pertinent to Rind's work—how much harm is done to male youths by uncoerced consensual sexual relations with adults who are not members of his immediate family. However, these events are reasonably classified as child sexual abuse (CSA), making them relevant to his claim about the frequency of adverse outcomes associated with CSA.
38. A parallel analysis between CSA and depression for the female subjects shows the correlation to be .185, implying that CSA explains about 3.4 percent of the variation in depression, seemingly a small amount, though higher than for the males. Yet, if the figures in Table 1 are interpreted causally, CSA raises the percentage experiencing depression from 27.7 to 50.9, which is a substantial amount.
39. 543 U.S. 551 (2005), declaring that it was unconstitutional to execute children under the age of 18.
40. According to Wikipedia, a few countries, including Egypt, Malaysia, Oman, Pakistan, Sri Lanka, Ukraine, the United Arab Emirates, match the United States. In parts of India it is 25 (http://en.wikipedia.org/wiki/Legal_drinking_age).
41. Relatively little research has exploited state variation in the age of consent to examine the effectiveness of statutory rape laws in preventing age-discrepant sexual relations. One study concludes that the presence of statutory rape laws reduces nonmarital births for white females and that the enforcement of these laws does so for blacks and Hispanics (Jepsen and Jepsen, 2006). A limitation of this study is that it includes all births to unmarried women aged 15 to 18, even though many of these births would have been to women too old to have been "protected" by their state's age-of-consent laws.
42. 123 S. Ct. 2472 (2003).
43. 431 U.S. 678, 694 (1977).

References

Aggrawal, A. (2009). *Forensic and medico-legal aspects of sexual crimes and unusual sexual practices.* Boca Raton, FL: CRC. Raton, FL: CRC Press.
Allen, R. H. (2006). *The classical origins of modern homophobia.* Jefferson, NC: McFarland.
Angier, N. (1995). Disputed meeting to ask if crime has genetic roots. *The New York Times,* September 19, C1.
Ariès, P. (1962). *Centuries of childhood; a social history of family life.* Tr. R. Baldick. New York: Knopf.
Aristotle (1944). *Politics.* Tr. H. Rackham. London: W. Heinemann.
Aronson, T. (1994). *Prince Eddy and the homosexual underworld.* London: John Murray.
Bailey, J. M. (2003). *The man who would be queen: The science of gender-bending and transsexualism.* Washington, DC: Joseph Henry Press.
Balsdon, J. P. V. D. (1962). *Roman women: Their history and habits.* London: The Bodley Head.
Bayer, R. (1981). *Homosexuality and American psychiatry.* New York: Basic Books.
Bearman, P. S., & Brücker, H. (2001). Promising the future: Virginity pledges and first intercourse. *American Journal of Sociology, 106,* 859–912.
Bombardieri, M. & Sacchetti, M. (2006). Summers to step down, ending tumult at Harvard. *Boston Globe,* February 22, A1.
Boswell, J. (1980). *Christianity, social tolerance, and homosexuality: Gay people in Western Europe from the beginning of the Christian Era to the Fourteenth Century.* Chicago, IL: University of Chicago Press.

Briere, J., & Runtz, M. (1989). University males' sexual interest in children: Predicting potential indices of "Pedophilia" in a nonforensic sample. *Child Abuse and Neglect, 13*, 65–75.
Browning, C. R., & Laumann, E. O. (1997). Sexual contact between children and adults: A life course perspective. *American Sociological Review, 62* (August), 540–560.
Brundage, J. A. (1987). *Law, sex, and Christian society in Medieval Europe*. Chicago, IL: University of Chicago Press.
Brunoz, O. (1995). On boy-love paedophilia: Historical and scientific perspectives. *Paidika, 3.4* (Winter), 27–63.
Bullough, V. (2004). Age of consent: A historical overview. In H. Graupner & V. L. Bullough (Eds.), *Adolescence, sexuality, and the criminal law: Multidisciplinary perspectives* (pp. 25–42). Binghamton, NY: Haworth.
Buss, D. M. (2003). *The evolution of desire: Strategies of human mating*. New York: Basic Books.
Carpenter, C. (2003). On statutory rape, strict liability, and the public welfare offense model. *American University Law Review, 53*, 313–391.
Carpenter, E. (1904). *Intermediate types among primitive folk: A study in social evolution*. London: G. Allen.
Cauffman, E. & Steinberg, L. (2000). (Im)maturity of judgment in adolescence: Why adolescents may be less culpable than adults. *Behavioral Science and the Law, 18*, 741–760.
Chauncey, G. (1996). *Gay New York: Gender, urban culture, and the making of the gay male world*. New York: Basic Books.
Chilman, C. S. (1979). *Adolescent sexuality in a changing American society: Social and psychological perspectives*. Bethesda, MD: US Department of Health, Education and Welfare.
Christopher, R. L. & Christopher, K. H. (2007). Adult impersonation: Rape by fraud as a defense to statutory rape. *Northwestern University Law Review, 101*, 75–123.
Cocca, C. E. (2002). The politics of statutory rape laws: Adoption and reinvention of morality policy in the American states, 1969–1999. *Polity, 35*, 51–72.
_____. (2004). *Jailbait: The politics of statutory rape laws in the United States*. Albany: State University of New York Press.
Cohen, D. (1991). *Law, sexuality and society: The enforcement of morals in classical Athens*. New York: Cambridge University Press.
Corbin, A. (1990). Intimate relations. In Michelle Perrot (Ed.), *A history of private life, vol. 4. From the fires of the revolution to the Great War* (pp. 549–612). Cambridge, MA: Harvard University Press.
Crompton, L. (2003). *Sex and civilization*. Cambridge, MA: Harvard University Press.
Darroch, J., Landy, D. J., & Oslak, S. (1999). Age difference between sexual partners in the United States. *Family Planning Perspectives, 31*, 160–167.
Dauda, C. L. (2010). Childhood, age of consent, and moral regulation in Canada and the UK. *Contemporary Politics, 16*: 227–247.
Davidson, J. (2007). *The Greeks and Greek love: A radical reappraisal of homosexuality in ancient Greece*. London: Weidenfeld & Nicolson.
De Grazia, A. (Ed.). (1978). *The Velikovsky affair: Scientism versus science*. Rev. ed. London: Sphere.
Denno, D. W. (1998). Life before the modern sex offender statutes. *Northwestern University Law Review, 92*, 1317–1413.
De Waal, F. B. M. (1989). *Peacemaking among primates*. Cambridge, MA: Harvard University Press.
_____. (1997). *Bonobo: The forgotten ape*. Berkeley: University of California Press.
_____. (1998). *Chimpanzee politics: Power and sex among apes*. Rev. Ed. Baltimore, MD: Johns Hopkins University.
Drobac, J. A. (2004). Sex and the workplace: "Consenting" adolescents and a conflict of laws. *Washington Law Review, 79*, 471–573.
_____. (2006). "Developing capacity": Adolescent "consent" at work, at law, and in the sciences of the mind. *UC Davis Journal of Juvenile Law & Policy, 10* (Winter), 1–38.
Ducros, A., & Pasquet, P. (1978). Évolution de l'âge d'apparition des premières règles (ménarche) en France. *Biométrie Humaine, 13*, 35–43.
Ember, M., & Ember, C. R. (1971). The conditions favoring matrilocal versus patrilocal residence. *American Anthropologist, n.s. 73*, 571–594.

Eveleth, P. B., & Tanner, J. M. (1990). *Worldwide variation in human growth*. 2d. ed. New York: Cambridge University Press.
Eyben, E. (1985). Geschlechtsreife und Ehe in greichisch-römisch Altertum und im frühen Christentum. In E. W. Müller (Ed.), *Geschlechtsreife und Legislation zur Zeugung* (pp. 403–478). München: K. A. Freiburg.
Fagan, J., & Zimring, F. E. (Eds.). (2000). *The changing borders of juvenile justice*. Chicago, IL: University of Chicago Press.
Feierman, J. (1990). Human erotic age orientation: A conclusion. In J. Feierman (Ed.), *Pedophilia: Biosocial dimensions* (pp. 552–566). New York: Springer-Verlag.
Feierman, J. (Ed.). (1990). *Pedophilia: Biosocial dimensions*. New York: Springer-Verlag.
Feld, B. C. (1999). *Bad kids and the transformation of the juvenile court*. New York: Oxford University Press.
Fernbach, D. (1976). Toward a Marxist explanation of gay liberation. *Socialist Review, 28,* 29–41.
Finkelhor, D. (1984). *Child sexual abuse: New theory and research*. New York: Macmillan.
Freund, K., & Watson, R. J. (1991). Assessment of the sensitivity and specificity of a phallometric test: An update of phallometric diagnosis of paedophilia. *Journal of Consulting and Clinical Psychology,* 3: 254–260.
Frost, J. J., Jones, R. K., Woog, V., Singh, S., & Darroch, J. E. (2001). *Teenage sex and reproductive behavior in developed countries. Country report for the United States*. New York: Alan Guttmacher Institute.
Gagnon, J., & Simon, W. (1973). *Sexual conduct: The social sources of human sexuality*. Chicago, IL: Aldine.
Garland, D. (2005). Capital punishment and American society. *Punishment and Society, 7,* 347–376.
Gebhard, P. H. (1972). Incidence of overt homosexuality in the United States and Western Europe. In J. M. Livingood (Ed.), *National Institute of Mental Health Task Force on Homosexuality: Final report and background papers* (pp. 22–29). Rockville, MD: National Institute of Mental Health.
Gebhard, P., & Johnson, A. B. (1979). *The Kinsey data: Marginal tabulations of 1938–1963. Interviews conducted by the Institute for Sex Research*. Philadelphia, PA: W. B. Saunders.
Gerassi, J. (1966). *The boys of Boise: Furor, vice, and folly in an American city*. New York: Macmillan.
Gillis, J. R. (1974). *Youth and history: Tradition and change in European age relations, 1770–present*. New York: Academic Press.
Goldberg, H. E. (2003). *Jewish passages: Cycles of Jewish life*. Berkeley: University of California Press.
Goodall, J. (1986). *The chimpanzees of Gombe: Patterns of behavior*. Cambridge, MA: Harvard University Press.
Goode, S. D. (2010). *Understanding and addressing adult sexual attraction to children: A study of paedophiles in contemporary society*. New York: Routledge.
Graupner, H. (2004). Sexual consent: The criminal law in Europe and outside of Europe. In H. Graupner & V. L. Bullough (Eds.), *Adolescence, sexuality, and the criminal law: Multidisciplinary perspectives* (pp. 111–171). Binghamton, NY: Haworth.
Greenberg, D. F. (1977). Delinquency and the age structure of society. *Contemporary Crises: Crime, Law and Social Policy, 1,* 643–651.
———. (1988). *The construction of homosexuality*. Chicago, IL: University of Chicago Press.
———. (2008). Age, sex and racial distributions of crime. In Erich Goode (Ed.), *Out of control: Assessing the general theory of crime* (pp. 38-48). Stanford, CA: Stanford University Press.
Greenberg, L. M., & W. B. Sizemore (Eds.). (1977). *Velikovsky and establishment science*. Glassboro, NJ: Kronos Press.
Hall, G. S. (1904). *Adolescence: Its psychology and its relations to physiology, anthropology, sociology, sex, crime, religion and education,* 2 vols. New York: D. Appleton.
Hall, G. C. N., Hirschman, R. & Oliver, L. L. (1995). Sexual arousal and arousability to pedophilic stimuli in a community sample of normal men. *Behavior Therapy, 26:* 681–694.
Hanawalt, B. (1986). *The ties that bound: Peasant families in Medieval England*. New York: Oxford University Press.
Hare, E. H. (1962). Masturbatory insanity: The history of an idea. *Journal of Mental Science, 108,* 1–25.
Havemann, E. (1964). Why? *Life,* (July 27), 76–80.
Herdt, G. H. (1984). *The Sambia: Ritual and gender in New Guinea*. New York: Holt, Rinehart and Winston.

———. (1984). Semen transactions in Sambia culture. In G. Herdt (Ed.), *Ritualized homosexuality in Melanesia* (pp. 167–210). Berkeley: University of California Press.
Higdon, M. J. (2008). Queer teens and legislative bullies: The cruel and invidious discrimination behind heterosexist statutory rape laws. *UC-Davis Law Review, 42*, 195-253.
Hirschi, T., & Gottfredson, M. (1983). Age and the explanation of crime. *American Journal of Sociology, 89*, 552–584.
Hollenberg, E. (1999).The criminalization of teenage sex statutory rape and the politics of teenage motherhood. *Stanford Law and Policy Review, 10*, 267–286.
Hooker, E. (1957). The adjustment of the male overt homosexual. *Journal of Projective Techniques, 21*, 18–31.
Hopkins, M. K. (1965). The age of Roman girls at marriage. *Population Studies, 18*, 309–327.
Horgan, J. (1993, February 20). Genes and crime: A US plan to reduce violence rekindles an old controversy. *Scientific American, 268*, 24.
Hubbard, T. K. (1998). Popular perceptions of elite homosexuality in Classical Athens. *Arion, Ser. 3, 6*, 48–78.
———. (2000). Pederasty and democracy: The marginalization of a social practice. In T. K. Hubbard (Ed.), *Greek love reconsidered* (pp. 1–11). New York. Wallace Hamilton Press.
———. (2006). History's first child molester: Euripides *Chrysippus* and the marginalization in Athenian democratic discourse. In J. Davidson, F. Muecke, & P. Wilson (Eds.), *Greek drama III: Essays in honour of Kevin Lee* (pp. 223–244). BICS Supplement 87. London: Institute of Classical Studies.
Hunt, M. (1999). *The new know-nothings: The political foes of the scientific study of human nature.* New Brunswick, NJ: Transaction.
Hyde, H. M. (1976). *The Cleveland Street scandal.* London: W. H. Allen.
Idani, G. (1990). Relations between unit-groups of bonobos at Wamba: Encounters and temporary fusions. *African Study Monographs, 11*, 153–186.
Jackson, L. A. (2000). *Child sexual abuse in Victorian England.* London: Routledge.
Jenkins, P. (1998). *Moral panic: Changing concepts of the child molester in modern America.* New Haven, CT: Yale University Press.
Jennings, T. W. (2009). *Plato or Paul? The origins of Western homophobia.* Cleveland, OH: Pilgrim Press.
Jepsen, C. A., & Jepsen, L. K. (2006). The effects of statutory rape laws on nonmarital teenage childbearing. *Contemporary Economic Policy, 24* (Jan.), 35–51.
Kandel, E. R., & Schwarz, J. H. (1985). *Principles of neural science,* 2d. ed. New York: Elsevier.
Kano, T. (1992). *The last ape: Pygmy chimpanzee behavior and ecology.* Stanford, CA: Stanford University Press.
Keeley, L. H. (1986). *War before civilization.* New York: Oxford University Press.
Keizer-Schrama, S. M. P. F. D. M., & Mul, D. (2001). Trends in pubertal development in Europe. *Human Reproduction Update, 7*, 287–291.
Kelly, R. C. (2000). *Warless societies and the origin of war.* Ann Arbor: University of Michigan Press.
Kilpatrick, A. C. (1992). *Long-range effects of child and adolescent sexual experiences: Myths, mores, and menaces.* Hillsdale, NJ: Lawrence Erlbaum.
Kinsey, A. C., Pomeroy, W. B.,& Martin, C. E. (1948). *Sexual behavior in the human male.* Philadelphia, PA: W. B. Saunders.
Kinsey, A. C., Pomeroy, W. B., Martin, C. E., & Gebhard, P. H. (1953). *Sexual behavior in the human female.* Philadelphia, PA: W. B. Saunders.
Knauft, B. M. (1987). Reconsidering violence in simple human societies. *Current Anthropology, 28*, 457–498.
Kupchik, A. (2007). *Judging juveniles: Prosecuting adolescents in adult and juvenile courts.* New York: New York University Press.
La Barre, W. (1985). *Muelos: A Stone-Age superstition about sexuality.* New York: Columbia University Press.
Lacey, W. K. (1968). *The family in Classical Greece.* Ithaca, NY: Cornell University Press.
Laqueur, T. (2003). *Solitary sex: A cultural history of masturbation.* New York: Zone.
Lehmann, L., Laurent, K., West, S.,& Roze, D. (2007). Group selection and kin selection: Two concepts but one process. *Proceedings of the National Academy of Science,* 104.16 (April 17), 6736–6739.

Lelis, A., Percy, W. A., & Verstraete, B. C. (2003). *The age of marriage in ancient Rome*. New York: Edwin Mellen.
Leonard, G. (2004). Towards a legal history of American criminal theory: Culture and doctrine from Blackstone to the Model Penal Code. *Buffalo Criminal Law Review, 6*, 691–776.
Levine, K. L. (2006). The intimacy discount: Prosecutorial discretion, privacy, and equality in the statutory rape caseload. *Emory Law Journal, 55*, 691–750.
_____. (2007). The external evolution of criminal law. Public law & legal theory research paper series. Research Paper No. 07–17.
Lilienfeld, S. O. (2002). When worlds collide: Social science, politics, and the Rind et al. (1998) child sexual abuse meta-analysis. *American Psychologist 57*: 1776–1788.
Lindenbaum, S. (1984). Variations on a sociosexual theme in Melanesia. In G. H. Herdt (Ed.), *Ritualized homosexuality in Melanesia* (pp. 337–361}. Berkeley: University of California Press.
Lindsey, B. B., & Evans, W. (1927). *Companionate marriage*. New York: Boni and Liveright.
Loftus, J. (2001). America's liberalization in attitudes toward homosexuality, 1973–1998. *American Sociological Review, 66*, 762–782.
Lucian (1928). *Mimes of the courtesans: The philosopher*. Translated by A. L. Hillman. New York: Rarity Press. Available at www.sacred-texts.com/cla/luc/motc/index.htm (Accessed December 27, 2007).
MacDonald, K. (2002). What makes western culture unique. *The Occidental Quarterly, 2* (Summer). Available at www.theoccidentalquarterly.com (Accessed February 26, 2008).
Macfarlane, A. (1986). *Marriage and love in England: Modes of reproduction 1300–1840*. Boston, MA: Basil Blackwell.
MacKinnon, C. A. (1991). Reflections on sex equality under the law. *Yale Law Journal, 100*, 11287–11328.
Magistretti, P. J., Pellerin, L., & Martin, J-L. (n.d.). Brain energy metabolism: An integrated cellular perspective. Available at www.acnp.org/g4/GN01000064/CH064.html (Accessed February 27, 2008).
Maimonides, M. (1964). Two treatises on the regimen of health. *Transactions of the American Philosophical Society*, n.s. 54, pt. 4, 3–50. Translated by A. bar-Sea, H. E. Hoff, & E. Faris.
Manson, J. H., & Wrangham, R. W. (1991). Intergroup aggression in chimpanzees and humans. *Current Anthropology, 32*, 369–390.
Merton, R. K. (1957). *Social theory and social structure*. Revised and Enlarged Edition. Glencoe, IL: Free Press.
Millet, K. (1984). Beyond politics? Children and sexuality. In C. S. Vance (Ed.), *Pleasure and danger: Exploring female sexuality* (pp. 217–224). Boston, MA: Routledge and Kegan Paul.
Minton, H. L. (2002). *Departing from deviance*. Chicago, IL: University of Chicago Press.
Molnar, B. E., Buka, S. L., & Kessler, R. C. (2001). Child sexual abuse and subsequent psychopathology: Results from the National Comorbidity Survey. *American Journal of Public Health 91*, 753–759.
Moore, K. A., Miller, B. C., Sugland, B. W., Morrison, D. R., Glei, D., & Blumenthal, C.(1995). *Beginning too soon: Adolescent sexual behavior, pregnancy and parenthood*. Washington, DC: US Department of Health and Human Services. Available at http://aspe/hhs.gov/HSP/cyp/xsteesex.htm (Accessed February 27, 2008).
Mosher, W., Chandra, A., & Jones, J. (2005). *Sexual behavior and selected health measures: Men and women 15–44 years of age, United States, 2002*. Advance data from vital and health statistics (Sept. 25). Number 362. Atlanta, GA: US Department of Health and Human Services. Centers for Disease Control and Prevention. National Center for Health Statistics. Available at www.cdc.gov/nchs/data/ad/ad362.pdf (Accessed May 25, 2013).
Murray, S. O. (2000). *Homosexualities*. Chicago, IL: University of Chicago Press.
National Abortion and Reproductive Action Rights League. (2008). *Who decides? The status of women's reproductive rights in the United States*. 17th ed. Washington, DC: NARAL Foundation. (Available at www.naral.org). (Accessed March 8, 2008).
Neill, J. (2009). *The origins and role of same-sex relations in human societies*. Jefferson, NC: McFarland.
Nelson, E. C., Heath, A. C., Madden, P. A. F., Cooper, M. L., Dinwiddie, S. H., Buchholz, K. K., Glowinski, A., McLaughlin, T., Dunne, M. P., Statham, D. J., & Martin, N. G. (2002). Association between self-reported childhood sexual abuse and adverse psychosocial outcomes. *Archives of General Psychiatry, 59*, 139–145.

Neuman, R. P. (1975). Masturbatory madness and the modern concepts of childhood and adolescence. *Journal of Social History, 8,* 1–27.

———. (1978). The priests of the body and masturbatory insanity of the late nineteenth century. *Psychohistory Review, 6,* 21–32.

Oberman, M. (1994). Turning girls into women: Re-evaluating modern statutory rape law. *Journal of Criminal Law & Criminology, 85,* 15–79.

———. (2000). Regulating consensual sex with minors: Defining a role for statutory rape. *Buffalo Law Review, 48,* 703–784.

Okami, P. (1990). Sociopolitical biases in the contemporary scientific literature on adult human sexual behavior with children and adolescents. In J. Feierman (Ed.), *Pedophilia: Biosocial dimensions* (pp. 91–121). New York: Springer-Verlag.

Oliveri, R. C. (2000). Statutory rape law and enforcement in the wake of welfare reform. *Stanford Law Review, 52,* 463–508.

Olsen, F. (1984). Statutory rape: A feminist critique. *Texas Law Review, 63,* 387–432.

Otterbein, K. F. (2004). *How war began.* College Station: Texas A & M University Anthropology Series.

Parker, I. (2007, July 30). Swingers. *The New Yorker, 48*–61.

Pearson, M. (1972). *The age of consent: Victorian prostitution and its enemies.* Newton Abbot, UK: David and Charles.

Percy, W. A., III. (1996). *Pederasty and ancient pedagogy in archaic Greece.* Urbana: University of Illinois Press.

Petersen, L. R., & Donnenwerth, G. V. (1997). Secularization and the influence of religion on beliefs about premarital sex. *Social Forces, 75* (3), 1071–1089.

Pew Research Center. (2007). Political landscape more favorable to democrats: Trends in political values and core attitudes: 1987–2007. (March 22). Available (1997-1998) at http://pewresearch.org/pubs/434 (Accessed February 12, 2008).

Phipps, C. A. (1997–1998). Children, adults, sex and the criminal law: In search of reason. *Seton Hall Legislative Journal, 22,* 1–141.

———. (2002–2003). Misdirected reform: On regulating consensual sexual activity between teenagers. *Cornell Journal of Law and Public Policy, 12,* 373–445.

Plato (1926). *Laws.* Tr. Robert Gregg Bury. London: W. Heinemann.

——— (1998). *Symposium.* Tr. Robin Wakefield. New York: Oxford Universit Press,

Platt, A. M. (1969). *The child savers: The invention of delinquency.* Chicago, IL: University of Chicago Press.

Plutarch (1961). *Moralia,* vol. 9 (Table talk), Books 7–9. Tr. Edwin L. Minar, Jr., F. H. Sandbach, and W. C. Helmbold. Cambridge, MA: Loeb Classical Library.

Pomeroy, S. B. (1995). *Goddesses, whores, wives, and slaves: Women in classical antiquity.* New York: Schocken.

Quinsey, V. L., Steinman, C. M., Bergersen, S. G., & Holmes, T. F. (1975). Penile circumference, skin conductance and ranking responses of child molesters and "Normals" to sexual and nonsexual visual stimuli. *Behavior Therapy, 6,* 213–219.

Reyna, V. F., & Farley, F. (2006). Risk and rationality in adolescent decision making: Implications for theory, practice, and public policy. *Psychological Science in the Public Interest, 7,* 1–44.

Rice, S. H. (2004). *Evolutionary theory: Mathematical and conceptual foundations.* Sunderland, MA: Sinauer Associates.

Rice, W. R., Friberg, U., & Gavrilets, S. (2012). Homosexuality as a consequence of epigenetically canalized sexual development. *The Quarterly Review of Biology, 87,* 343–368.

Rind, B. (2001). Gay and bisexual adolescent boys' sexual experiences with men: An empirical examination of psychological correlates in a nonclinical sample. *Archives of Sexual Behavior, 30,* 245–268.

———. (2004). An empirical examination of sexual relations between adolescents and adults: They differ from those between children and adults and should be treated separately. In H. Graupner & V. L. Bullough (Eds.), *Adolescence, sexuality, and the criminal law: Multidisciplinary perspectives* (pp. 55–67). Binghamton, NY: Haworth.

Rind, B., & Tromovich, P. (1997). A Meta-analytic review of findings from national samples on psychological correlates of child sexual abuse. *Journal of Sex Research 34:* 237–255.

Rind, B., Tromovich, P., & Bauserman, R. (1998). A meta-analytic examination of assumed properties of child sexual abuse using college samples. *Psychological Bulletin, 124,* 22–53.

_____. (2000a). Debunking the false allegation of "statistical abuse": A reply to Spiegel. *Sexuality & Culture 4:* 101–111.

_____. (2000b). Condemnation of a scientific article: A chronology and refutation of the attacks and a discussion of threats to the integrity of science. *Sexuality & Culture, 4:* 1–62.

_____. (2001). The validity of methods, analyses, and conclusions in Rind et al. (1998): A rebuttal of victimological critique from Ondersma et al. (2001) and Dallam et al. (2001). *Psychological Bulletin, 127:* 734–758.

Robertson, S. (2005). *Crimes against children: Sexual violence and legal culture in New York City, 1880–1960.* Chapel Hill: University of North Carolina Press.

Rocke, M. (1996). *Forbidden friendships: Homosexuality and male culture in Renaissance Florence.* New York: Oxford University Press.

Rodkinson, M. L. (Trans.) (1903). *The Babylonian Talmud. Tract Sabbath.* Boylston, MA: New Talmud Publishing Co. Available at www.sacred-texts.com/jud/t01/t0110.htm (Accessed May 24, 2013).

Rubin, G. (1984). Thinking sex: Notes for a radical theory of the politics of sexuality. In C. S. Vance (Ed.), *Pleasure and danger: Exploring female sexuality* (pp. 267–319. London: Routledge and Kegan Paul.

Russell, D. E. H. (1984). *Sexual exploitation: Rape, child sexual abuse and workplace harassment.* Beverly Hills, CA (Sage).

Sallares, R. (1991). *The ecology of the ancient Greek world.* Ithaca, NY: Cornell University Press.

Savelsberg, J. (1994). Knowledge, domination, and criminal punishment. *American Journal of Sociology, 99,* 911–943.

Scheidel, W. (2007). Roman funerary commemoration and the age at first marriage. *Classical Philology, 102,* 389–402.

Schmiecher, R., Harrison, J., Haugland, J., & Hooker, E. C. (1992). *Changing our minds: The story of Evelyn Hooker.* San Francisco, CA: Frameline.

Schuijer, J. (1993). The Netherlands changes its age of consent law. *Paidika, III (1),* 13–17.

Schuijer, J., & Rossen, B. (1992). The trade in child pornography. *IPT Journal 4,* available at www.ipt-forenics.com/journal/volume4/j4_2_1.htm (Accessed January 4, 2008).

Scott, E. S. (2000a). The legal construction of adolescence. *Hofstra Law Review, 29,* 547–598.

_____. (2000b). Criminal responsibility in adolescence: Lessons from developmental psychology. In T. Grisso & R. G. Schwartz (Eds.), *Youth on trial: A developmental perspective on juvenile justice* (pp. 291–324). Chicago, IL: University of Chicago Press.

Seto, M. C., Kjellgren, C., Preibe, G., Mossige, S., Svedin, C. G., & Långström, N. (2010). Sexual coercion experience and sexually coercive behavior: A population study of Swedish and Norwegian male youth. *Child Maltreatment, 15,* 219–228.

Shvartsman, S. H. (2004). "Romeo and Juliet": An examination of *Limon* v. *Kansas* in light of *Lawrence v. Texas. Seton Hall Law Review, 35:* 359-401.

Simmons, T., & Dye, J. L. (2004). What has happened to median age at first marriage data? Paper presented to the American Sociological Association. Available at www.census.gov/acs/www/Downloads/MedAge_revised_final.ppt (Accessed February 15, 2007).

Simpson, A. E. (2007). Organized prostitution in 19th century England: Legal campaigns & the origins of the Criminal Law Amendment Act of 1885. Pp. 9-49 In W. T. Stead, *The maiden tribute of modern Babylon* (pp. 9–49). Edited by A. E. Simpson. Lambertville, NJ: The True Bill Press.

Simpson, C., Chester, L., & Witch, D. (1976). *The Cleveland Street affair.* Boston, MA: Little, Brown.

Smiljanich, K., & Briere, J. (1996) Self reported sexual interest in children: Sex differences and psychosocial correlates in a university sample. *Violence and Victims, 11,* 39–50.

Smoyer, A., & Blankenship, K. (2006). *The effectiveness of abstinence-only sex education: A review of the evidence.* New Haven, CT: Yale University Center for Interdisciplinary Research on AIDS. Available at http://cira.med.yale.edu/law_policy_ethics/pu_abstinence_06.pdf (Accessed February 27, 2008).

Spitz, R. (1952). Authority and masturbation: Some remarks on a bibliographical investigation. *Psychoanalytic Quarterly, 21,* 490–527.

Stafford, A. (1964). *The age of consent.* London: Hodder and Stoughton.

Stanley, L. A. (1987). The hysteria over child pornography and paedophilia. *Paidika, 1.2* (Autumn), 13–34.

Steiker, C. S. (2002). Capital punishment and American exceptionalism. *Oregon Law Review, 81,* 97–130.
Stone, L. (1977). *The family, sex, and marriage in England: 1500–1800.* New York: Harper and Row.
Sykes, G., & Matza, D. (1957). Techniques of neutralization. *American Sociological Review, 22,* 664–670.
Symonds, J. A. (1883). *A problem in modern ethics, being an inquiry into the phenomenon of sexual inversion.* London: distributed privately.
_____. (1891). *Studies in sexual inversion.* London: distributed privately.
Symons, D. (1979). *The evolution of human sexuality.* New York: Oxford University Press.
Thornton, B. (1998). *Eros: The myth of ancient Greek sexuality.* Boulder, CO: Westview.
Traulsen, A., & Nowak, M. A. (2006). Evolution of cooperation by multilevel selection. *PNAS, 103(29),* 10952–10955.
Trumbach, R. (1978). *The rise of the egalitarian family: Aristocratic kinship and domestic relations in eighteenth-century England.* New York: Academic Press.
Walker, P. L. (2001). A bioarchaeological perspective on the history of violence. *Annual Reviews of Anthropology, 30,* 573–596.
Weiss, D., & Bullough, V. L. (2004). Adolescent American sex. *Journal of Psychology & Human Sexuality, 16,* 45–53.
Wellings, K. K. et al. (2001, December 1). Sexual behavior in Britain: Early heterosexual experience. *The Lancet, 358* (9296), 1843–1850.
Westermarck, E. (1922). *The history of human marriage.* 3 vols. 5th ed. New York: Alberton.
Whitehead, N. E., & Whitehead, B. (2010). *My genes made me do it!—homosexuality and the scientific evidence.* Available at http://www.mygenes.co.nz/index.html (Accessed May 2, 2013).
Whittier, N. (2009). *The politics of child sexual abuse: Emotions, social movements, and the state.* New York: Oxford University Press.
Williams, C. A. (2010). *Roman homosexuality.* 2d. ed. New York: Oxford University Press.
Williams, W. W. (1982). The equality crisis: Reflections on culture, courts, and feminism. *Women's Rights Law Reporter, 7,* 175–200.
Wills, G. (2002, June 13). Priests and boys. *New York Review of Books, 49(10).*
Wyshak, G., & Frisch, R. (1982). Evidence for a secular trend in age at menarche. *New England Journal of Medicine, 306,* 1033–1035.
Xenophon (1968). *Scripta Minora.* Cambridge, MA: Harvard University Press.
Yang, A. S. (1997). Trends: Attitudes toward homosexuality. *Public Opinion Quarterly, 61,* 477–507.
Zimring, F. (2003). *The contradictions of American capital punishment.* New York: Oxford University Press

Chapter 8

HARMING CHILDREN IN THE NAME OF "CHILD PROTECTION": HOW MINORS WHO HAVE SEX WITH OTHER MINORS ARE ABUSED BY THE LAW AND THERAPY

ANDREW HELLER

Although the current heightened concern about sexual abuse is undoubtedly motivated in part by concern for the well-being of minors, there are numerous indications that other motives lie behind current policies. In a special issue of the journal *Feminist Review* on the topic of child sexual abuse, appearing during the early years of heightened scholarly and popular concern about the topic, Jenny Kitzinger speculated that parental anxiety about sexual abuse might have more to do with a desire to control minors' own expressions of sexuality rather than to protect them from harm per se (Kitzinger, 1988). More than twenty years later, we are now in a position to document that the reactions in the 1980s to the perceived crisis of child sexual abuse have resulted in laws and treatment methods that can be as or more harmful to the minors involved than actual sexual abuse when the sexual events under examination involve minors having sex with other minors. That is, although the laws and treatments have been offered up as means of protecting minors, they have too often been seriously harming minors in the process.

Each year, approximately 20,000 juveniles are arrested for sex offenses other than forcible rape and prostitution. About half of these juveniles are under age 15, more than for any other crime except arson (Office of Juvenile Justice and Delinquency Prevention, 2004). Although some of these offenses are violent and very harmful to their victims, others are illegal not because they are coercive or harmful, but because the participants are under the age of consent. Unfortunately, the proportion of sex offenses that are in fact non-abusive is unknown, because laws and police records do not make a distinction between coercive and mutually desired sexual behavior when it is illegal.

The fact that minors frequently engage in non-abusive but illegal sexual behavior may surprise those who are not aware of the empirical research on child and adolescent sexual behavior. For example, in the

United States, in the late 1940s and early 1950s, Kinsey found that 40 percent of prepubescent boys had engaged in heterosexual play and 60 percent had engaged in homosexual play, with such behavior beginning at age 9 on average. A study by the University of California at Los Angeles found that 46 percent of children had engaged in interactive sex play by age six. One study of eighth graders in rural Maryland found that 61 percent of the boys and 47 percent of the girls had had sexual intercourse (Garfinkle, 2003).

Although researchers believe that such childhood sex play is not normally harmful and may even be developmentally valuable, such behavior is illegal in many jurisdictions. In about half of all states, mutual sexual interaction among similarly aged children under the age of consent constitutes a sex offense. In 60 percent of states, all sexual activity under the age of 14 is illegal (Garfinkle, 2003). Thus, the majority of children could be guilty of sexual offenses.

Sex laws define sexual behavior under certain ages as "assault," "rape," and "sodomy," and classify these legal violations as "violent," simply because of the ages (or age differences) of the participants in the absence of actual violence or coercion. Although the normal but illegal sexual behavior of many minors is often not discovered and therefore not prosecuted, sometimes it is, and the consequences can be disastrous for the accused minors. Kentucky juvenile defense attorney Gail Robinson (2003) writes:

> Even children under age 12 are prosecuted for rape first degree and sodomy first degree for sexual conduct with each other. Furthermore, it is not uncommon for a 13 year old who has sexual contact with an 11 year old to be prosecuted for a class A felony.... A youthful offender convicted of rape or sodomy in the first degree is a "violent offender" who must serve at least 85% of his sentence before he can be paroled.... Youthful offenders are subject to "Megan's Law" requirements. (p. 62)

Much more common are cases of teenagers arrested for sexual relationships with younger teenagers, and their sex acts are again labeled as "violent," "assault," "rape," "molestation," or "abuse," not because any violence, force, unwillingness, or harm was involved, but based only on the age difference. A series of reports on this phenomenon in the *Texas Examiner* resulted in a deluge of letters from parents whose teenage children were prosecuted and imprisoned for consensual sex (*Texas Examiner*, 2005). The ABC-TV news magazine *20/20* aired a series on the increase in prosecution of such cases (ABC News, 2008; Stossel et al., 2008a; Stossel et al., 2008b). In Wisconsin, a 17-year-old was charged with felony sexual assault for having consensual sex with two underage girls, and faced up to fifty years in prison and fines of up to $200,000 (*Sheboygan Press*, 2007).

Fairly common are cases where teenage boys are arrested for consensual sex with girls who lie about their age. For example, in Iowa, a 16-year-old boy met a 13-year-old girl who said she was 16 (Win, 2008). They began seeing each other and eventually had sex. The boy was convicted of lascivious acts with a child, a class D felony. He was expelled from high school and harassed by neighbors and strangers. He is now on the state public sex offender registry for life, prohibited from living within 2,000 feet of a school, day care center or park and from going to the movies or the mall with friends. In a similar case in Austin, Texas, a teenager was convicted of attempted sexual assault for having consensual sex with a 13-year-old girl when he was 17, and the girl lied to him about her age (KXAN-TV, 2008). He was placed on the state's sex offender registry, which forced him to quit school and made him unemployable. Because his probation required him to be employed, he was rearrested, and the state took action to revoke his probation and send him to prison. Also in Texas is the case of Robert Wyatt Evans, convicted of sexual assault and a charge of indecency with a child for having a sexual relationship with a 14-year-old boy when Evans was 18. Both charges are second-degree felonies and carry penalties of two to twenty years in prison.

There have also been reports of middle and high school students around the country arrested on felony charges of producing and disseminating child pornography as a result of taking and exchanging sexual pictures of themselves and their friends (CNN, 2008; NBC-13, 2008; Runbinkam, 2008; Winslow, 2008).

Although it must be recognized that some juvenile sex offenses are truly abusive and harmful, it must also be recognized that the prosecution of children and teenagers for nonviolent but illegal sexual behavior is just as harmful. It is unknown what proportion of juvenile sex offenses are noncoercive, but a Texas prosecutor recently estimated that at least half of the cases of "child sexual assault" filed with the district attorney involved consensual sex among teenagers (Stancil, 2005). An even more striking statistic was reported in Sheboygan County, Wisconsin, where, in 2006, nearly all of the thirty-one cases of "sexual assault" of a child between the ages of 13 and 15 involved consensual teenage sex (Litke, 2007). There have been several cases reported where both teenagers in a same-age sexual relationship (13 or 14 years old) have been arrested for "sexual assault" of each other (Abdul-Alim, 2003; Twohey, 2004; Manson, 2006). That a significant number of juvenile sex offenses are non-abusive is suggested by large-scale studies finding that most sexual offenses by teenagers involved no force at all, and that only 4 percent to 31 percent of those that did involve force involved some sort of weapon (Garfinkle, 2003). Teenagers who are prosecuted for engaging in consensual sexual activity with other juveniles can be placed on public sex offender registries (Garfinkle, 2003). In twenty-two states, a 17-year-old who engages in sex with a partner 14 or older, but under the age of consent, is placed on the sex offender registry (Carey, 2005).

Young teenagers are also convicted of "sexual assault," "battery," "abuse," or "child molestation," for annoying behavior or pranks. In Arkansas, a 13-year-old girl was charged with two counts of "sexual assault" for touching two 13-year-old boys over their clothing on the school bus (Wellner, 2008). In another case, a 13-year-old boy was convicted of "criminal sexual abuse" for grabbing a girl's breasts and running away as a prank (*Chicago Daily Herald*, 2008). When he reached 17 years of age, state law required that he be considered as having committed the offense on his 17th birthday, and he was placed on the sex offender registry. In Florida, two middle school boys were charged with registrable felonies for pinching and groping girls' breasts in class on a day that Myspace users had declared "National Grab a Boob Day" (Cormier, 2007). Two middle schoolers in Oregon were charged with multiple counts of felony sex abuse for participating in the practice—popular among both boys and girls—of going through the hallway slapping the behinds of members of the opposite gender (Michels, 2007). The boys faced the prospect of having to register as sex offenders for the rest of their lives.

Particularly egregious is the labeling or charging of preteens and young children for childish behavior or sexual experimentation. Human Rights Watch's (2007) report on the proliferation of irrational laws and destructive prosecution of juveniles recounts the story of a 12-year-old boy who invited friends aged 8 to 12 to watch pornographic videos he had found in his parents' bedroom. This led to mutual sex play. When caught, the boy was sent to juvenile jail for seven years and had to register as a sex offender when he reached age 19. In Kentucky, state police charged first and second graders in two different elementary schools with "first degree sodomy" for sex play at school (Sinovic, 2008). In 2007, 255 Virginia elementary students were suspended for "offensive sexual touching," and in Maryland, 166 elementary school children were suspended for sexual harassment, including three preschoolers, 16 kindergartners, and 22 first-graders (Schulte, 2008). A Denver councilman noted, "It's just getting to the point of ridiculousness where we're prosecuting kids for kissing," citing the cases of 5- and 6-year-olds referred to Human Services for kissing or making comments such as "You have a sexy booty" (Kass, 2008).

The unsurprising result of the redefinition of "sexual abuse" to include mutual sex play and romantic relationships, and the increased prosecution of such legal violations, is responsible for the inflated statistics regarding juvenile sex offenders. US courts have seen the number of juvenile sex offenses rise dramatically in recent years, not because of an increase in truly abusive behavior, but because of the proliferation of these draconian laws (*Taipei Times*, 2007). Both the US Department of Justice (Greenfield, 1997) and the Center for Sex Offender Management (1999) claim that one-third to one-half of all child molestation is committed by children themselves, and a leader in the sex offender treatment profession claims that one out of every twenty boys is or will become a child molester (Abel & Harlow, 2001). The US Department of Justice claims that of all ages seven to sixty, "the single age with the greatest number of offenders from the perspective of law enforcement was age 14" (Snyder, 2000). The US Office of Juvenile Justice reports that sexual "aggression" appears among children as young as 3 and 4, and that the most common age of onset appears to be between 6 and 9 (Righthand & Welch, 2001). Unsurprisingly, the report notes that "victims" of these deviant children typically are siblings, friends, or acquaintances.

The logical consequences of such alarmist statistics are refusals to back off from draconian measures as well as attempts to establish laws that are even more extreme. The governor of Illinois vetoed a bill that would have allowed a judge to eventually remove juveniles guilty of sex crimes from the sex offender registry if they pose no further danger (Hitzeman, 2007). The bill resulted from the case mentioned earlier where a 13-year-old boy grabbed the breasts of a 13-year-old girl and ran away as part of a prank. The Minnesota Court of Appeals affirmed a decision that requires juveniles convicted of felony sex offenses to register as predatory offenders, although they are not entitled to a jury trial in juvenile court (Behr, 2007). The decision arose from a case involving a 15-year-old boy accused of having uncoerced sex with a 13-year-old. Texas recently considered a bill to redefine "sexually violent offense against a child" to include indecency by contact, so that a 14-year-old could become a first-degree felon by touching the chest, even over clothing, of a 13-year-old. Doing so twice would make him a repeat violent offender, making him technically eligible for the death penalty (Hughes, 2007).

Perhaps most disturbing was the US Congress's passage in 2006 of what is called the Adam Walsh Child Protection and Safety Act. This act requires that all states place certain juveniles on a public sex offender registry and subject them to electronic monitoring. These provisions were included and the bill passed without debate, in spite of opposition from more than forty child health and justice organizations, such as the American Academy of Child and Adolescent Psychiatry, the American Psychiatric Association, the American Psychological Association, the Children's Defense Fund, the National Association for Children's Behavioral Health, and the National Mental Health Association (Letter to James Sensenbrenner, 2005; Letter to Arlen Specter and Patrick Leahy, 2005). The American Psychological Association objected to the "devastating impact these provisions will have on the lives of many children and youth" (American Psychological Association, 2006). The provisions not only apply to juveniles who have committed truly violent sexual acts, but to those age 14 and up who have had uncoerced sexual contact with other juveniles who are under 13 or who are more than 4 years younger.

If the other juvenile is under 12 or an offense is the second one, registration and monitoring will be for life.

The grave harm that such laws cause to children is clear. Of course, prosecuting, imprisoning, and monitoring children and teenagers who are not dangerous divert law enforcement and social services resources from real dangers to children and clogs the courts and corrections system. Imprisoning them steals years from their lives. Placing them on sex offender registries results in ostracism, harassment, violence, and inability to complete their education, find housing, or hold down jobs. One boy who was convicted of sodomy for having uncoerced oral sex with a 15-year-old when he was 17 was forced to move repeatedly because of residency restrictions for sex offenders. He ended up living in a camper in the woods without running water or electricity (Downey, 2007). Jill S. Levenson, southern regional coordinator for the Center for Offender Rehabilitation and Education, notes that housing restrictions are just the beginning of a lifetime of punishment and that the stigma and denied opportunities related to a sex offense will negatively impact juvenile offenders (Pierce, 2007). She asks:

> So what's going to happen when we have this whole population of teenage sex offenders on public registries who are not going to be able to live within 2,500 feet of schools, parks and playgrounds? They're not going to be able to live with their parents, who live in residential neighborhoods. Where are they going to go? They're not going to be able to be in a foster home. They're not going to be able to be in shelters. They're not going to be able to be in rehab centers or treatment facilities.

Being placed on a sex offender registry leads some teens to suicide. Michigan teenager Justin Fawcett, well-regarded for his kindness to others, was convicted of "sexual abuse" for consensual sex with a younger girl. When he found out he would be placed on a public sex offender registry, he committed suicide (Dickerson, 2005). In another case, an eighth grader in Delaware was harassed and threatened by other students at his school because he was on the public sex offender registry for an act he committed at age 11. Shortly thereafter, he made several suicide attempts (Jones, 2007).

Objecting to the Adam Walsh Act, also known as the Sex Offender Registration and Notification Act (SORNA), the Coalition for Juvenile Justice wrote,

> Research does not support the application of SORNA to children ... SORNA as applied to juveniles flies in the face of some of the core purposes, functions and objectives of our nation's juvenile justice systems in that it strips away the confidentiality and the overall rehabilitative emphasis ... SORNA as applied to children and youth will disrupt families and communities across the nation because SORNA does not just stigmatize

the child; it stigmatizes the entire family. (Letter to Attorney General Gonzales, 2007)

Human Rights Watch's (2007) report on sex offender laws notes that:

> [R]egistrants and their families have been hounded from their homes, had rocks thrown through their home windows, and feces left on their front doorsteps. They have been assaulted, stabbed, and had their homes burned by neighbors or strangers who discovered their status as a previously convicted sex offender. At least four registrants have been targeted and killed (two in 2006 and two in 2005) by strangers who found their names and addresses through online registries. Other registrants have been driven to suicide, including a teenager who was required to register after he had exposed himself to girls on their way to gym class. (p. 7)

Those who promote registration of juveniles seem unconcerned about a particularly ominous consequence of such policies: in cases where real abuse is perpetrated by a member of the family (a common form of sexual abuse), parents will remain silent to protect their children from decades on a registry rather than seek help that would benefit both the victim and the offender (Jones, 2007).

Garfinkle (2003) concludes that:

> Megan's Laws have the unique propensity to gravely harm some children in the hope of protecting an unknown few. Many child sex offenders are victims of sexual abuse themselves. Many more engage in common sexual behavior, sometimes healthy, sometimes inappropriate, that they will most likely learn to manage. Megan's Laws stigmatize and isolate these children, limiting their opportunities for normal growth and exacerbating the kinds of vulnerabilities that lead to future criminality, both sexual and nonsexual. When lawmakers vociferously declared that children were in more need of protection than convicted sex offenders, they never indicated that some of the sex offenders they were targeting were themselves vulnerable children. (p. 205)

For the reasons just cited, a number of sex offender treatment professionals are currently speaking out against placing juveniles on sex offender registries. However, it should be noted that the treatment profession has had a major role in promoting the harmful treatment of these children. Juvenile justice expert and Berkeley law professor Franklin Zimring (2004) offers a scathing critique of the emergence of juvenile sex offender treatment in the late 1980s. He notes that the National Adolescent Perpetrator Network (NAPN) based its highly influential 1993 report on 387 unproven assumptions and involved no input from researchers, the medical profession, or juvenile justice experts, nor were any of its recommendations based on psychological science or knowledge about treatment of violent nonsexual juvenile offenders. Claiming without basis that juvenile sex offenders were in a class apart from other kinds of juvenile offenders, NAPN recommended much harsher responses: prosecution, severe punishment, long-term registration, tracking as a part of treatment, the devaluation of the psychological well-being of the juvenile offender, and an adversarial relationship between therapist and juvenile. Zimring writes:

> There are powerful indications in the text of the 1993 report that adolescent offenders are regarded as enemies by the therapists.... blaming, the stigmatization, and the permanent labeling are the encouraged standard practice with offenders over age eleven.... It turns out that none of the solicitous attention to development that is usual in therapeutic relationships with children and adolescents is advocated by the Task Force. (pp. 85–86)

He also notes that NAPN defined all illegal sexual behaviors as "abuse" and "molestation" even when there was no coercion or harm. He writes:

> By the standards of the National Task Force on Juvenile Sexual Offending, a majority of American men and boys have committed multiple acts of child molestation by the time they reach their twenty-first birthdays.... This aggregation of such behavior into a single category of "child molestation" is an extraordinary abuse for an organization of therapists (p. 89).... The willingness of treatment staff to participate in punishment, in labeling, and in the denunciation of treatment subjects is a remarkable part of the 1993 Task Force's version of sex-offender therapy. (p. 92)

It is no wonder then that treatments for juvenile sex offenders and "children with sexual behavior problems" normally use a one-size-fits-all approach, regardless of whether the children's acts were actually coercive. For example, the state of Kentucky resisted a judge's order that juveniles who committed minor sex offenses no longer be placed in the same treatment programs as those who commit serious offenses (*Louisville Courier-Journal*, 2007). One popular workbook used in treatment encourages such indiscriminant therapy, saying, "Regardless of your specific problem, *Pathways* is for you" (Kahn, 2001, p. 2).

Furthermore, treatment uses methods that are never even used on aggressive or violent nonsexual juvenile offenders, and in fact would be deemed abusive and unethical in such cases. For example, peer group sessions and workbook assignments require participants to repeatedly provide detailed descriptions or draw pictures of their sexual behavior, feelings, and fantasies (and sometimes masturbatory habits), to admit how destructive they are (regardless of whether their crimes were actually coercive), to describe the devious methods they used to manipulate their victims (even if they did not), to accept blame for all harm that occurred to all people involved, and to admit that they engage in criminal thinking patterns and identify those patterns in their lives, all in an atmosphere of shaming and castigation. Failure to disclose sufficient aggression or deviance, or to admit sufficient guilt, leads to accusations of denial or minimization (Anonymous, 1997; Kahn, 2001; Kahn, 1999; Shaw, 1999; MacFarlane & Cunningham, 2003; Chaffin & Bonner, 1998).

Treatment essentially requires the child to take on a permanent identity as a sexual deviant. A treatment workbook for 11- to 21-year-olds (Kahn, 2001) tells its young readers, "Completing Pathways will not 'cure' you of your problem—there is no cure—but it will teach you how to recognize and control your problem behaviors" (p. 4). Its final exam contains the following questions:

- What have you learned about your sexual urges, and how have you learned to control your deviant sexual fantasies?
- How do your thinking patterns contribute to your victimizing other people, either in a sexual way or a non-sexual way?
- What is it about you (your personality) that allowed you to commit a sex offense in the first place?
- What are the factors that might eventually lead you to having sexual behavior problems in the future? (p. 289)

Such adversarial methods are never recommended as treatment for juveniles who commit violent nonsexual acts (e.g., those diagnosed with conduct disorder and who commit acts such as aggravated assault, robbery, or arson) (Steiner & Dunne, 1997). The field of psychology provides no scientific evidence of their therapeutic benefits (Zimring, 2004). Some therapists have noted the abusive nature of their profession's own practices:

> We have encountered young teenagers (13 to 15) who, as part of their treatment, have been compelled to recite daily lay-outs or creeds including phrases such as "I am a pedophile and am not fit to live in human society ... I can never be trusted ... everything I say is a lie ... I can never be cured." We have encountered residential programs where teenage boys were sanctioned if they looked at girls, were required to look at the floor when they passed females in the hall, and where the message was conveyed that all forms of teenage sexuality were offending. We have listened to teenage boys hesitantly confess that they admitted to offense histories and deviant fantasies they did not have, simply because it was expected and required before they would be eligible for release from residential programs. Our impression is that these incidents cannot be dismissed as isolated examples of overly zealous practice but are directly derived from an uncritical application of prevailing treatment models. (Chaffin & Bonner, 1998, p. 315)

In 1992, the *Arizona Republic* reported that a treatment program at Phoenix Memorial Hospital was using such methods on children as young as 10 years old (Young, 1992). It reported that the mother of a 12-year-old girl who had been sexually abused herself said that therapists required that the girl admit to being a rapist, and when she refused, therapists persisted until she tried to kill herself.

However, even more disturbing were the reported use on children as young as 10 years old of plethysmographs and ammonia aversion therapy—methods used on gay men fifty years ago, then abandoned as unethical and dangerous:

> *The Republic* learned that more than 100 children, more than one-third of them 10 to 12 years old, go through the program each year.... Many are tested for deviant sexual responses by a penile plethysmograph, a ring-like device slipped around the penis to measure changes in circumference as a patient views nude photographs. The program includes use of aversion therapy, in which patients inhale ammonia to prevent inappropriate arousal.... The hospital had told the girl to record a sexual fantasy. "Then every time she listened to it, she had to use that ammonia," the woman said. "It wasn't really a fantasy, it was just really bizarre. On the tape she was talking about hurting this child (in a violent, sexual manner). My daughter is very passive; she's never been violent." The woman is convinced that the fantasy came from the minds of therapists. "They told her she had to make this tape. She had to rewrite and rewrite until they were sure she'd get sexually aroused to it." (Young, 1992, p. A1)

Although public exposure of this program resulted in its being shut down, soon afterward, a similar treatment program was exposed in New York:

> At the clinic, the youth was told he would undergo "sexual behavior testing," and when he resisted, he was told that he would go to jail if he did not participate, the lawsuit states. According to the lawsuit, "his pants were lowered around his ankles and (he) was forced to place a round, mercury-filled plastic device around his penis, and further forced to wear earphones and listen to pornographic tapes including descriptions of sex between adults and children, and between children and children, violent rape, forced sex and other abnormal sexual acts." Afterward the youth was encouraged to masturbate, Paladino states. (Rivera, 1993, p. 6)

Disturbingly, aversion therapy and other forms of "arousal conditioning" are still used. A survey conducted in 2000 (the most recent year for which such figures are available) indicated that 81 percent of juvenile sex offender programs and 62 percent of programs for younger children use some form of arousal conditioning (Burton & Smith-Darden, 2001). The American Academy of Child and Adolescent Psychiatry (Shaw, 1999) describes various authors' recommendations for the use of phallometric testing (measuring of penile erection in response to different stimuli) to determine juveniles' sexual preference, and further details some of the arousal conditioning techniques used on juveniles:

Olfactory Conditioning. Sexually stimulating deviant imagery is presented which is followed by the presentation of a noxious odor.

Satiation Techniques. This involves either verbal or masturbatory satiation. The offender is first encouraged to masturbate to ejaculation in response to socially appropriate sexual fantasies with the concomitant feelings of affection and tenderness. After this experience the offender is required to masturbate to deviant sexual fantasies. If the offender becomes aroused, he or she is told to switch to an appropriate fantasy or in some instances exposed to an aversive stimulus such as ammonia. Verbal satiation requires the dictation on an audiotape of the most stimulating paraphiliac imagery for at least 30 minutes after masturbation 3 times a week. It is assumed that the paraphiliac fantasy becomes boring and subsequently extinguished. (pp. 66S–67S)

Abel and Harlow (2001), considered experts in sex offender treatment, believe that one out of every twenty boys is or will become a child molester. They urge parents to look for certain danger signs: sexual fantasies involving younger children, sexual victimization, or sexual behavior believed to be excessive or more extensive than normal (although researchers say that normality has yet to be defined; Haroian, 1985). Regarding the first danger sign, they recommend that parents ask their sons, when they reach age 11, about their sexual fantasies. If any of these signs is found, Abel and Harlow instruct parents to have their sons tested using a lie detector, a plethysmograph, or Abel's sexual interest test (which measures visual reaction time when shown photographs of males and females of different ages in swimwear). If test results are positive, parents are instructed to find a sex offender therapist who will use "covert sensitization, aversion, or satiation" on their son.

There appears to be no concern among many professionals of the harmful effects of these methods on children, although it is widely recognized that the use of arousal conditioning on adult gay men in the past could cause severe trauma, depression, nightmares, suicidal thoughts, and self-hatred—the very effects alleged of sexual abuse itself. That is, arousal conditioning can be considered a form of sexual abuse.

It is true that some treatment experts are retreating from the abusive practices just described, blaming such practices on a prior lack of knowledge and a lack of alternatives. However, such an explanation is disingenuous; after all, it has been recognized outside the sex offender treatment profession since the 1960s that such practices are abusive and unethical. In addition, much more humane methods have been available and used for decades on violent nonsexual juvenile offenders who are at least as dangerous as the minority of the sex offenders committing severe abuse and substantially more dangerous than the majority of juvenile sex offenders engaging in milder forms. It should be noted that no professional organization has made any statements rejecting the use of arousal conditioning methods on juveniles, and they continue to be used. Professionals who have promoted unethical treatment approaches and harsh punishment, such as Robert Emerick, who directed the abusive Phoenix Memorial program, and Toni Cavanaugh Johnson, who promoted the prosecution of young children without an understanding of childhood sexual behavior (see Johnson, 1989), have never been censured for their practices (Schultz, 1993); in fact they continue to publish and present in the field (e.g., Abel et al., 2004; Johnson, 2004), and their old writings are still promoted by the profession (e.g., Office of Juvenile Justice and Delinquency Prevention, 1999).

In summary, there are a number of facts that strongly suggest that legal and therapeutic responses to juvenile sex offenders are based partly or even mostly on other motives than a desire to protect children:

- Current laws and treatment methods used with juvenile sex offenders would be considered unethical and abusive if used on juveniles who commit violent nonsexual crimes.
- These laws and treatment methods harm minors substantially, arguably as much or even more than sexual abuse does.
- Politicians and treatment professionals generally show little or no concern about this harm.
- Professionals generally show far less concern about physical abuse and emotional neglect than about sexual abuse, even though the former two are far more common, in general have much greater frequency and duration when they do occur, and are more harmful on average (Rind, Tromovitch, & Bauserman, 1998; US Department of Heath and Human Services Administration on Children, Youth, and Families, 2001)

What might such motives be? An article in a Catholic publication may provide a clue (Lee, 2008). The article features Narda Beas-Nordell, the juvenile sex offender specialist for the Salt Lake County Attorney, who advocates serious prosecution of children who violate sex laws. A former junior high school dance teacher, she justifies her stance as follows:

> It should surprise and concern everyone that there are so many children having sex these days.... I was astounded at how sexually engaged students were in the hallways when I was teaching. I'm still shocked by the amount of nudity these young people are exposed to. I tried to uphold some moral standards for my dance students, but I wasn't always backed up by their parents.

Garfinkle (2003) suggests a different but related motive: "By applying Megan's Laws to juvenile adjudications, states throw out a century of juvenile justice jurisprudence and scholarship to protect an even older tradition of fear about childhood sexuality. In so doing, lawmakers perpetrate irreparable damage to the very children they claim to protect" (p. 205).

Such moralistic agendas do not form a sound basis for making public policy or dictating therapeutic regimens. Those who advocate ever higher age-of-consent laws and more draconian penalties justify their position by claiming that children under 18 are too immature to be capable of understanding the consequences of sexual activity and making responsible decisions about it. Nevertheless, the same legislators and therapists believe that children under 18 who do have sex, particularly with a younger child, are so morally culpable that they deserve "therapeutic" treatments so primitive and barbaric as to be rejected for any other class of behavior or crime, no matter how violent. In the growing number of states where it is required that juvenile sex offenders be placed permanently on sex offender registries, the punishment is nothing less than a life sentence.

References

ABC News. (2008). The age of consent. March 14, 2008. Retrieved from http://www.abcnews.go.com/2020/AgeOfConsent/

Abdul-Alim, A. (2003). Teens have right to have sex, lawyer argues. *Milwaukee Journal-Sentinel*, August 21, 2003. Retrieved from http://www.jsonline.com/story/index.aspx?id=163688

Abel, G., & Harlow, N. (2001). *The stop child molestation book*. Xlibris.

Abel, G. G., Jordan, A., Rouleau, J. L., Emerick, R., Barboza-Whitehead, S., & Osborn, C. (2004). Use of visual reaction time to assess male adolescents who molest children. *Sexual Abuse: A Journal of Research and Treatment*, 16 (3), 255–266.

American Psychological Association. (2006). Ensure that youth are not treated as adult sex offenders, APA Public Interest Policy Office, February 7, 2006. Retrieved from http://www.apa.org/ppo/ppan/sexoffenderaa06.html

Anonymous. (1997). Molested. *Salon Magazine*, February 1997. Retrieved from http://www.salon.com/feb97/molested970228.html

Behr, K. (2007). Appeals court upholds Winona County ruling regarding juvenile sex offenders. *Winona Daily News*, MN, June 7, 2007. Retrieved from http://www.winonadailynews.com/articles/2007/06/07/news/05winonaruling07.txt

Burton, D., & Smith-Darden, J. (2001). *North American survey of sexual abuser treatment and models 2000*. Brandon, VT: Safer Society Foundation.

Carey, C. A. (2005, November 17). Banishment or facilitated reentry: A human rights perspective. Presentation at the Research and Treatment Conference of the Association for the Treatment of Sexual Abusers, Salt Lake City, Utah.

Center for Sex Offender Management. (1999). Understanding juvenile sexual offending behavior. Retrieved from http://www.csom.org/pubs/juvbrf10.html

Chaffin, M., & Bonner, B. (1998). Don't shoot, we're your children: Have we gone too far in our response to adolescent sexual abusers and children with sexual behavior problems? *Child Maltreatment*, 3 (4), pp. 314–316.

Chicago Daily Herald. (2008). Justice finally prevails on youthful mistake. *Chicago Daily Herald*, April 9, 2008. Retrieved from http://www.dailyherald.com/story/?id=168630&src=

CNN. (2008). Naked photos, e-mail get teens in trouble. CNN.com. June 4, 2008. Retrieved from http://www.cnn.com/2008/CRIME/06/04/naked.teens.ap/index.html?eref=rss_tech

Cormier, A. (2007). 2 boys accused of groping at Sugg Middle. *Sarasota Herald Tribune*. September 25, 2007. Retrieved from http://www.heraldtribune.com/article/20070925/NEWS/709250545

Dickerson, B. (2005). A plea deal thwarted, a life is ended. *Detroit Free Press*, March 24, 2004. Retrieved from http://www.freep.com/news/metro/dicker24_20040324.htm

Downey, M. (2007). A sex law gone awry. *Atlanta Journal-Constitution*, October 21, 2007. Retrieved from http://www.ajc.com/opinion/content/opinion/stories/2007/10/19/offended_1021.html

Fielder, D. (2008). Denton County judge's son, 18, indicted in sexual assault. *Dallas News,* March 28, 2008. Retrieved from http://www.dallasnews.com/sharedcontent/dws/dn/latestnews/stories/032908dnmetassault.d40da07.html

Garfinkle, E. (2003). Coming of age in America: The misapplication of sex-offender registration and community notification laws to juveniles. *California Law Review,* 91, 163–208.

Greenfield, L. A. (1997). Sex offenses and offenders: An analysis of data on rape and sexual assault. *U.S. Department of Justice: Bureau of Justice Statistics.* Washington, D.C.Haroian, L. (1985). Child sexual development. Monograph prepared for student use at the Institute for Advanced Study of Human Sexuality. Retrieved from http://www.ejhs.org/volume3/Haroian/body.htm

Hitzeman, H. (2007). Governor nixes juvenile registry plan. *Chicago Daily Herald,* August 25, 2007. Retrieved from http://www.dailyherald.com/story/?id=25086

Hughes, P. R. (2007). Sex offenders: Fights over death penalty ahead. *Houston Chronicle Texas Politics Blog,* February 21, 2007. Retrieved from http://blogs.chron.com/texaspolitics/archives/2007/02/sex_offenders_d.html

Human Rights Watch. (2007). No easy answers: Sex offender laws in the US HRW Report, vol. 19, No. 4G. New York: Author. Retrieved from http://www.hrw.org/reports/2007/us0907/index.htm

Johnson, T. C. (1989). Female child perpetrators: Children who molest other children. *Child Abuse & Neglect,* 13, 571–585.

_____. (2004). *Understanding children's sexual behaviors: What's natural and healthy.* Self-published. Available at http://www.tcavjohn.com/

Jones, M. (2007). How can you distinguish a budding pedophile from a kid with real boundary problems? *New York Times Magazine,* July 22, 2007. Retrieved from http://www.nytimes.com/2007/07/22/magazine/22juvenile-t.html?_r=1&ei=5070&en=961acd3dc801260c&ex=1185768000&adxnnl=1&emc=eta1&adxnnlx=1185754330-Xs9g4EeJ3zKy8DyjnoxdUQ&oref=slogin

Kahn, T. J. (1999). *Roadmaps to recovery: A guided workbook for young people in treatment.* Brandon, VT: Safer Society Press.

_____. (2001). *Pathways: A guided workbook for youth beginning treatment.* Brandon, VT: Safer Society Press.

Kass, J. (2008). Kissing at school a crime? *Rocky Mountain News,* March 6, 2008. Retrieved from http://www.rockymountainnews.com/news/2008/mar/06/simple-kiss-at-school-may-morph-into-police-case/

Kitzinger, J. (1988). Defending innocence: Ideologies of childhood. *Feminist Review,* 28, 77–87.

Klein, M. (1928). Early stages of the Oedipus conflict. *International Journal of Psychoanalysis,* 9, 167–180.

KXAN-TV. (2008). Attorney withdraws from Williamson County teen sex case. KXAN-TV, Austin, TX, May 22, 2008. Retrieved from http://www.kxan.com/Global/story.asp?S=8363044&nav=0s3d

Lee, B. S. (2008). Sex abuse crimes with juvenile perpetrators a trend of growing prevalence says county prosecutor. *Intermountain Catholic News,* November 28, 2007. Retrieved from http://www.icatholic.org/indstory/2007/200742p03.html

Letter to Arlen Specter and Patrick Leahy from 15 national organizations and 21 state/regional organizations, October 14, 2005. Retrieved from http://www.nacdl.org/public.nsf/Legislation/SexOffender/$FILE/NJJDPC.pdf

Letter to Attorney General Gonzales from Nancy Hornberger, April 30, 2007. Retrieved from http://www.juvjustice.org/media/fckeditor/Comments%20on%20Interim%20Rule%20OAG%20Docket%20No%20117.pdf

Letter to James Sensenbrenner from 10 national child and mental health organizations, September 13, 2005. Retrieved from http://www.nacdl.org/public.nsf/Legislation/SexOffender/$FILE/MH_letter.pdf

Litke, E. (2007). Underage sex: Authorities grapple with consequences. *Sheboygan Press,* February 25, 2007. Retrieved from http://www.sheboygan-press.com/apps/pbcs.dll/article?AID=2007702250493

Louisville Courier-Journal. (2007). State must alter system for juvenile sex offenders, November 7, 2007. Retrieved from http://www.courier-journal.com/apps/pbcs.dll/article?AID=/20071107/NEWS01/711071052/1008/NEWS01

MacFarlane, K., & Cunningham, C. (2003). *Steps to healthy touching.* Indianapolis, IN: Kidsrights.

Manson, P. (2006). Teen, both a perpetrator and victim of sex offense, presents legal puzzle, *Salt Lake*

Tribune, Dec. 6, 2006. Retrieved from http://www.sltrib.com/ci_4787105 March 7, 2008. Retrieved from http://deseretnews.com/article/1,5143,695259607,00.html

Michels, S. (2007). Boys face sex trial for slapping girls' posteriors. ABC News, July 24, 2007. Retrieved from http://abcnews.go.com/TheLaw/Story?id=3406214

NBC-13. (2008). Porn pics problem in Walker County. NBC-13, Birmingham, AL, April 9, 2008. Retrieved from http://www.nbc13.com/gulfcoastwest/vtm/news.apx.-content-articles-VTM-2008-04-09-0029.html

Office of Juvenile Justice and Delinquency Prevention. (1999). A comprehensive bibliography of scholarly research and literature relating to juvenile sex offenders. Retrieved from http://ojjdp.ncjrs.org/juvsexoff/sexbibtopic.html

———. (2004). Juvenile arrests 2002, *OJJDP Bulletin,* September 2004, NCJ 204608. Retrieved April 5, 2008 from http://www.ncjrs.gov/html/ojjdp/204608/contents.html

Pierce, M. (2007). Next comes burning at the stake. *Cincinnati City Beat,* August 15, 2007. Retrieved from http://citybeat.com/gyrobase/Content?oid=oid%3A140906

Righthand, S., & Welch, C. (2001). Juveniles who have sexually offended: A review of the literature. Office of Juvenile Justice and Delinquency Prevention, Washington, DC. Retrieved from http://www.ncjrs.gov/html/ojjdp/report_juvsex_offend/contents.html

Rind, B., Tromovitch, P., & Bauserman, R. (1998). A meta-analytic examination of assumed properties of child sexual abuse using college samples. *Psychological Bulletin, 124,* 22–53.

Rivera, E. (1993). Teen sues clinic using penis device. *Newsday,* November 12, 1993, City edition, News section, p. 6.

Robinson, G. (2003). Juvenile sex offenders. *The Advocate, 24* (7), 61–63.

Runbinkam, M. (2008). Cell phone porn scandal hits U.S. school. MSNBC, January 25, 2008. Retrieved from http://www.msnbc.msn.com/id/22840727

Schulte, B. (2008). For little children, grown-up labels as sexual harassers. *Washington Post,* April 3, 2008. Retrieved from http://www.washingtonpost.com/wp-dyn/content/article/2008/04/02/AR2008040203463.html

Schultz, L. (1993). Review of *Assessment and treatment of sexualized children and children who molest,* by E. Gil and T. C. Johnson. *IPT Journal, 4.* Retrieved from http://www.ipt-forensics.com/journal/volume5/j5_4_br3.htm

Shaw, J. (1999). Practice parameters for the assessment and treatment of children and adolescents who are sexually abusive of others. *Journal of the American Academy of Child and Adolescent Psychiatry, 38* (12 Suppl.), 55S–76S.

Sheboygan Press. (2007). Boy, 17, faces sex assault charges. *Sheboygan Press,* WI, February 9, 2007.

Sinovic, E. (2008). First graders face sodomy charges. WFIE-TV, Evansville, IN, no date given. Retrieved from http://www.wfie.com/Global/story.asp?S=2931302&nav=3w6nWEna

Snyder, H. (2000). Sexual assault of young children as reported to law enforcement. US Department of Justice Bureau of Justice Statistics, July 2000.

Stancil, B. (2005). Attorneys deal with what is law. *Texas Examiner,* March 3, 2005, p. 8.

Steiner, H., & Dunne, J. E. (1997). Summary of the practice parameters for the assessment and treatment of children and adolescents with conduct disorder. *Journal of the American Academy of Child and Adolescent Psychiatry, 36* (10suppl), 122S–139S.

Stossel, J., Binkley, G., & Sullivan, A. G. (2008a). Parents turn to police when daughters have sex. March 14, 2008. Retrieved from http://abcnews.go.com/2020/Stossel/story?id=4444516&page=1

———. The age of consent: When young love is a sex crime. March 7, 2008. Retrieved from http://abcnews.go.com/2020/Stossel/story?id=4400537&page=1

Taipei Times. (2007). US court system sees rise in juvenile sex offender cases, June 10, 2007. Retrieved from http://www.taipeitimes.com/News/world/archives/2007/06/10/2003364620

Texas Examiner. (2005). Readers respond to story of young lives ruined. March 3, 2005, p. 9. Retrieved from http://www.theexaminer.com/files/03032005/Page%20009.pdf

Twohey, M. (2004). Teens who have sex charged with abuse. *Milwaukee Journal Sentinel,* March 7, 2004. Retrieved from www.jsonline.com/story/index.aspx?id=213082

US Department of Heath and Human Services Administration on Children, Youth, and Families. (2001). *Child maltreatment 1999.* Washington, DC: US Government Printing Office.

Wellner, A. (2008). 13-year-old girl arrested for alleged school bus assaults. Wasilla (AK) *Frontiersman*, January 17, 2008. Retrieved from http://www.frontiersman.com/articles/2008/01/17/local_news/doc478e89f9eccec212715178.txt

Win, H. I. (2008). Is Ricky really a sex offender? *Los Angeles City Beat*, February 20, 2008. Retrieved from http://www.lacitybeat.com/cms/story/detail/is_ricky_really_a_sex_offender/6726/

Winslow, B. (2008). Charges coming in Davis County over nude photos. *Deseret Morning News*, Salt Lake City, UT.

Young, A. (1992). Sex therapy nightmare or cure? *Arizona Republic*, July 26, 1992, p. A1.

Zimring, F. E. (2004). *An American travesty: Legal responses to adolescent sexual offending*. Chicago, IL: University of Chicago Press.

Chapter 9

THE SEX OFFENDER SYSTEM: PUNISHING *HOMO SACER*, THE NEW INTERNAL ENEMY

THOMAS K. HUBBARD

INTRODUCTION

In the featured article appearing in this volume, Dr. Rind noted that the harshness in legal treatment of persons committing sex offenses with minors has increased dramatically over the last thirty some years, but that no systematic study has tracked these changes. He did, however, mention a number of trends, including life sentences, the death penalty, civil commitment up to life, lifetime registration, and onerous zoning restrictions regarding living arrangements. He argued that these trends reflect a popular sentiment that has evolved into what historian Philip Jenkins (1998) has referred to as a "moral panic." Though his article did not elaborate further, it is important to consider contemporary legal changes more thoroughly in order to evaluate this "moral panic" and to better understand its nature and direction.

A systematic review of legal changes regarding sex offences is not possible at the present time, because the source material is too scattered and unorganized. Nevertheless, trends can be identified by surveying a diverse sampling of legal developments and specific cases. Thus, this review will attempt to flesh out trends in the response to sex offences involving minors, focusing mainly on the United States.

Results of the present survey verify that punishments moving in the direction of life sentences and the death penalty are indeed an emerging trend. The cases presented to illustrate this trend will suggest that the spiraling movement toward more and more severe punishments does reflect Jenkins's (1998) characterization of "moral panic," in which sentencing appears more and more to be grossly disproportionate to the underlying harm behind the crimes. To wit, both candidates for the U.S. presidency in 2008 offered, or felt the need to offer, a rebuke to a Supreme Court ruling that overturned the death penalty for certain kinds of sex with children, even though these crimes did not involve homicide and, upon closer inspection, did not have to involve violence, rape, or even actual contact (Andriette, 2008).

The attempt by a number of US states to resuscitate the death penalty for purely sexual offenses not necessarily resulting in physical or psychological harm does not come in a vacuum. After a generation of continually expanding laws and escalating punishments, long prison sentences, often including life terms, are now commonplace in the United States for adults, especially men, convicted of any sexual contact with minors. In addition, severe sentences are imposed on a range of often newly created offenses targeting not only physical acts, but merely the manifestation of possible erotic attraction to persons under 18. As well as prison, conviction for these crimes now entails in the US (and some other Western countries, especially the UK and Australia) permanent loss of various civil rights. Sex offenders now constitute a new and distinct legal class and are subject to never-ending sanctions in a separate and still quickly evolving legal system that functions outside conventional limits. More than simply a "moral panic"—a concept that implies temporal limits—the West's obsessive focus on sexual danger to minors, now a generation old, with no signs of abating, suggests a seemingly permanent *state of emergency,* to invoke the term of the authoritarian German political theorist Carl Schmitt,[1] in which sex offenders fill the role of an *internal enemy,* another Schmittian term. Those released from prison are condemned to lifetime public shaming via sex offender registries, which frequently have provoked threats and violence, and which have been linked to suicides and murders. Ex-offenders face nearly unlimited state surveillance and intrusions into their minds and bodies as well as control over their movements, living arrangements, and communications. Under civil commitment laws, persons deemed "likely" to commit sex crimes in the future can be incarcerated indefinitely. Demand for these measures and ever-stronger ones is a notable feature of contemporary public discourse. Sex offenders in the West, and especially in Anglophone countries, increasingly have a legal status like that of the ancient Roman *homo sacer,* a person exiled from civil and sacred obligation, whom anyone could kill without penalty. To illustrate these trends, this paper gives examples of the harsh punishments handed down for crimes following from sexual desire for minors, punishments that, by historically relevant criteria, have become more and more detached from sober appraisal of the harmfulness of the associated acts. Then it sketches the features, both structural and ideological, of this emerging system, of which harsh "headline" punishments are only one aspect.

A Crime Without Degrees

The core moral claim driving this new regulatory intensification is that sexual contact between adults and minors is among the most horrific of possible crimes, with permanent and severe damage to the younger person, irrespective of particular circumstance. It is "the worst evil I can think of," declared Andrews Vachss (2006), an attorney and frequent commentator in the US media on this issue. "[N]o mere words could ever truly describe the daily torture of victims...," he wrote in *Parade,* one of America's largest circulation magazines.

Sexual desire, like any human appetite, can occasion viciousness. Perhaps more than other biological drives, sexuality can fold cruelty or self-destructiveness into its own character. As well, violence and cruelty admit of sexual expression. But it would be a mistake to imagine that in the United States today harsh punishments in this area are only handed down in extreme cases involving force upon an unwilling victim, sadistic violence, physical harm, large numbers of victims, the very young, or even necessarily actual children.

In August 2007, a 41-year-old suburban mother from Round Rock, Texas, was sentenced to twenty-three years in prison for engaging in a consensual affair with a 16-year-old male neighbor, in the course of which, the woman gave the youth oral sex on three occasions. The woman helped the youth with his schoolwork, his grades improved during the affair, and the woman's two young children called the youth "dad," which pleased him immensely. The couple even talked about moving to California together once the youth reached 18, so that he could open a skateboard shop. However, when the youth's mother found out about the relationship, she compelled him to testify against his will, possibly motivated by rumors that her neighbor was about to inherit a large sum of money that could be extorted (*In the Pink,* 2007). Arguably, the result was four lives ruined: the woman's, those of her two young children, who were put into foster care after she lost custody of them, and that of the young man, who was compelled to give testimony that would ruin the lives of the woman and two small children whom he had loved. Arguably, the young man was victimized by his own parents and the system, far more than he had ever been by the three acts of oral sex.

Until recent times, heterosexual men have not been embarrassed to admit to a longing for attractive adult women when they were adolescent boys and youths; indeed, they frequently saw themselves as "lucky" when they actually had a sexual relationship with one. Movies such as the 1971 *Summer of '42* or the 1981 *Private Lessons* captured this sentiment well. In past times, a tradition was for fathers to introduce their teenage sons (around age 13 or 14) to sex by taking them to a prostitute. The panic over child sexual abuse, however, has extended to every form of adult-minor sexual relation, including consensual ones between mature 16- or 17-year-old male youths and women, which are far away from the coerced, incestuous sexual abuses that first aroused the attentions of child advocates in the early 1970s (cf. Jenkins, 1998). Until recently, women involved with teenage boys were not seen as the villains that men involved with younger children were. But the moral panic has come to be so pervasive that even adult female/adolescent male relations have come to be treated not simply as misdemeanors, as before the child sexual abuse revolution, but as heinous acts demanding draconian punishment.

When the perpetrator is a man instead of a woman, the punishment is likely to be much more severe, even if the circumstances of the sexual events do not involve aggravating elements such as violence or force. For example, in November 2006 in Naples, Florida, a 23-year-old man was convicted of oral sex and fondling involving a 9-year-old boy. The boy made no complaint; the events only came to light three years later when the man was discovered to possess child pornography (none of which he had himself produced), for which he received a twenty-six-year federal sentence. For the case involving the 9-year-old, he received two life sentences for two incidents of oral sex, which was automatic under Florida law, plus an additional thirty-year sentence for fondling the boy. In addition, the judge ordered that the man be castrated (Colby, 2006). Clearly, sex with 9-year-olds cannot be condoned in our society, but the perpetrator was a young man, only 20 when involved with the boy. Though he deserved punishment, what is the justification for two life sentences and castration, if sentencing is supposed to correspond in some meaningful way to actual harm as opposed to moral outrage and vigilantism?

Likewise, sex involving men and teenage boys is subject to severe penalties, even when the sex acts themselves are rather mild relative to acts that do involve aggravated sexual penetration. In Colorado in 2007, a 44-year-old former Catholic priest was sentenced to eighteen years to life in prison for horseplay accompanied by mild fondling with two male teenagers (aged 16 and 17), which had taken place eight and ten years earlier. He had caressed the 17-year-old under his boxer shorts, while wrestling with him on one occasion, and briefly grabbed his buttocks, while hugging him good-bye on another. The two youths each received settlements from the Denver diocese, with one reported to have been $300,000 (Barge, 2007; McPhee, 2008). The priest clearly violated the expectation that he keep his relationship with youths under his charge clean of sexual involvement and was deserving of some punishment, but the degree of punishment in relation to the physical acts devoid of anything resembling penetration, along with the enormous monetary awards, raises serious questions and concerns in relation to the proportionality of the punishment.

In another case, a 21-year-old man in Tyler, Texas, was sentenced to life in prison for sex with a 13-year-old boy, while dressed as a woman. After making contact in an Internet chat room, the two met at a theater and then had sex in the man's car. They met a second time and did the same. The boy did not complain about the contact: the matter came to light when a third party observed them together and contacted the authorities (Knaupp, 2008). Though the man's actions were criminal, the details of the case, with respect to issues such as violence and unambiguous damage, would seem to fall far short of what should entail a life sentence.

Sex between men and teenage girls can also be punished severely. In July 2003, a 43-year-old man from Springtown, Texas, was sentenced to 4,060 years for having sex with three teenage girls over a two-year period. Again, none of the girls had complained, and the events only came to light through other means: in this case, the man himself mentioned his affairs to a friend, who contacted Child Protective Services. Prosecutors said he would become eligible for parole in the year 3209 (Associated Press, 2008a). No overt force was alleged (Huffman, 2008), which brings into question the extremity of the sentence, an extremity that can be found in no other area of law and jurisprudence, including many homicide cases.

Even when a sexual crime is not sufficient to draw a life sentence, state authorities can turn it into one through civil-commitment laws. In Kansas, a 21-year-old man became involved in a consensual sexual relationship with a 14-year-old boy. When the boy was being harassed by an older teen, the 21-year-old man encouraged the boy to report the harasser to the police. The result, however, was that the harasser disclosed the sexual relationship between the other two. The young man was sent to prison for thirty-three months. However, just prior to his release, prosecutors successfully moved to have him civilly committed. For almost a decade now he has been committed to a state mental hospital without any prospect of release (D'Entremont, 2008). The complicating factor in this case was that he had been on probation for fondling his niece when he had the sexual relationship with the boy. But arguably, this aggravating circumstance does not warrant what appears to be lifetime civil commitment.

Even nonsexual contact (e.g., not involving genitals or breasts) can trigger prison for life. In July 2003, a 32-year-old man was sentenced to life in prison in California after being convicted of twenty-five felony counts of lewd acts with minors, charges related to sucking the toes of some twenty boys, aged 8 to 11, at a youth center, where he was supervisor. The boys themselves made no complaints; the authorities only learned of the events when a coworker reported the episodes. The man was popular with the boys at the center, and boys who testified said that the man did not touch their genitals or hurt them (Minaya, 2003). Again, the behavior was highly inappropriate, but the punishment arguably far exceeded any objective appraisal of harm.

In some of these cases, such as the priest and youth center supervisor, the aggravating circumstance of institutional authority is present, which justifiably adds concerns for intervention and punishment. But the seriousness of these cases is also mitigated by other considerations. In no instance was the sex accompanied by violence or overt force. Sometimes the sex continued for extended periods of time, suggesting a degree of mutuality. Most of these cases did not involve penetration in the canonical sense of penile-vaginal or penile-anal acts that could subject the minor to pregnancy or disease. In most of the cases, the activity did not rise to a level that prompted the minors to complain. In several of these cases, the offenders were young men, themselves only on the cusp of adulthood. In the case of the priest, financial motives complicate interpretation of the seriousness of his abuse. All these factors are circumstances that, in most cultural and historical contexts, would have mitigated the penalty meted out to the accused, had the cases been deemed worthy of prosecution in the first place. But in present-day America, these incidents are punished more severely than many crimes involving violence and entailing serious injury or even death.

In contrast to harsh penalties for adults having non-extreme sex with minors are the light penalties, in some cases, for those who attempt or succeed in murdering the adults so accused. In January 2007, a Wilmington, Delaware, man received a nine-month sentence in the beating death of 77-year-old man, who he believed had fondled his 5-year-old daughter. The Wilmington police said the girl's story seemed consistent, but that there was no physical evidence to support the allegations (Associated Press, 2007). In Baltimore in 2002, a 29-year-old man shot a former priest who he said had had sex with him over four years when he was a teenager. The priest was shot three times in the hip and hand, but survived. A jury acquitted the shooter of attempted murder, finding him guilty only on gun charges and urging the judge to show leniency. The shooter received eighteen months of home detention (Associated Press, 2005). In 1993, a mother walked into a courtroom, killing the man accused of molesting her son by shooting him five times in the head. In the end, she was only convicted of manslaughter and served only three years in prison (Associated Press, 2004). That cases such as these point to a trend is suggested by a headline in the *Telegraph,* a British newspaper, which read, "Parents who kill paedophiles can plead not guilty to murder" (Prince, 2008). The article discussed proposed changes to Britain's murder law, the first in fifty years. In these proposals, jealous husbands who kill their partners in a rage because they have been unfaithful would no longer be able to plead provocation. On the other hand, women who kill partners because they had been battered, or who feared future violence from their partners, could claim this defense. Likewise, those driven to kill in the most exceptional of circumstances, as in a confrontation with a pedophile, could similarly claim provocation as a defense.

Harsh Punishments for "Para-Sexual" Crimes

Morality, as conventionally understood in modern society, is fundamentally concerned with what happens to persons. Murder, for instance, is a foundational moral concern; but mere representation of murder, a staple of fiction and drama since time immemorial, is ethically indeterminate and indeed often held as cathartic or a fit subject for entertainment. Sexual contact between adults and minors is now oftentimes punished in the United States as equivalent to or worse than killing a person. But unlike murder, acts well short of such contact, for instance crimes of expression involving representations of sex depicting fictional minors or acts possibly indicating desire for young persons, are also punished with capricious severity.

In February 2007, the US Supreme Court let stand a 200-year sentence imposed on an Arizona man for possessing twenty pornographic images depicting boys. When he was arrested in 2002, the man was a 52-year-old married father of four and an award-winning public-school history teacher. His porn possession conviction was his first criminal offense. Arizona law requires a minimum 10-year sentence for possession of each single item of pornography depicting minors under 15, with sentences required to be served consecutively (Vicini, 2007). The man's conviction and punishment had earlier been upheld by the Arizona Supreme Court, with one justice partly dissenting and another upholding the punishment as legislative prerogative, but writing that were he a legislator, he would find the sentence "shocking to my conscience and vote for a less draconian sentencing scheme." The man would have faced a maximum of five years in prison had he been convicted in federal court. The only dissenting justice called the punishment "not merely disproportionate, but grossly disproportionate to the crime" and noted that the penalty exceeded that meted out to first-time offenders convicted of rape (Kilpatrick, 2006).

In the Arizona case, the charges related to the possession of sexually explicit images of actual minors, images the convicted man had downloaded from the Internet. But crimes involving no actual youngster, no matter how many degrees removed, also receive harsh sentences. The 47-year-old editor of the *Weekly Reader,* a well-known publication for schoolchildren, was sentenced to six years in prison and twenty years parole for crossing state lines to meet a (non-existent) 14-year-old boy (actually an FBI agent), with whom he had texted online (Associated Press, 2006a). In Arkansas, a 33-year-old chemistry professor was sentenced to ten years in prison for a sexually explicit chat on the Internet with an undercover police officer posing as a 15-year-old girl. The ten-year sentence was a new mandatory minimum set by the 2006 Adam Walsh Act, a federal statute (Satter, 2008). Under the same act, which applies retroactively, federal authorities can petition to have any federal inmate incarcerated indefinitely after his or her prison sentence is completed, if they are deemed likely to commit a sex crime.

In these cases, the defendants at least believed the minor in question was a real person. But life sentences are possible in situations where all parties involved know from the beginning that any minor represented is purely imaginary. In April 2004, a 52-year-old man was arrested for downloading twenty Japanese Anime cartoons depicting men having sex with girls. Someone had seen him printing out some of the drawings while using a public computer at the office of the Virginia Employment Commission and notified authorities. This man was the first person charged under a 2003 federal statute establishing harsh penalties for, as the US Attorney's office put it, "obscene drawings, cartoons, sculptures, paintings or any other obscene visual representation" depicting sex with fictional minors. The new law was an attempt to work around a US Supreme Court ruling reserving the category of "child pornography" only for depictions of actual minors. The man faced up to 1,160 years in prison and a fine of $18.5 million; he was sentenced to twenty years in prison (Campbell, 2005; US Department of Justice press release, 2006a).

If the operant moral concern is that sex between adults and minors is severely wrong, then, other things being equal, acts falling short should be less severe. Merely driving while intoxicated is punished less harshly than doing so and causing a fatal crash. A person getting angry at someone is distinct from one who murders, even if many murders are preceded by fights. Looking at pictures of the September 11 attacks is distinguishable from being their author or planning future terrorism. But in the current ideological environment surrounding sex and minors, the distinctions fade. What accounts for this confusion? Minimal acts lead to maximal punishments, because the act, or even the intention to act, is deemed as pointing to a certain kind of person defined as an *enemy* to be eliminated. "I consider it a war," declared then US Attorney General Gonzales in comments to law enforcement authorities in Pennsylvania in December 2006 (Associated Press, 2006b). The task, the US's top law enforcement official said earlier that month, was to "stop pedophiles and predators before they strike" (US Department of Justice press release, 2006b).

Are these harsh sentences exceptions? A search of news databases could yield hundreds of similar cases, but the question would still be left open as to what proportion of each type of charge ends in extreme punishment. Despite a continuing push since the 1970s to federalize sex crime, each US state has separate criminal statutes, used and interpreted by local prosecutors and judges in varied ways. A shift of power from judges to prosecutors, thanks to sentencing guidelines and "mandatory minimums," still leaves wiggle room. With many cases resolved by plea bargains seemingly unrelated to the original charge, it is impossible to isolate one category of similar acts, such as taking sexually explicit photos of 16-year-olds, and ascertain the average sentence. "If your state penalties are more aggressive, it should be a state-level case," urged Gonzales in December 2006 in a speech to prosecutors (US Department of Justice press release, 2006b). "If the federal law will put a pedophile behind bars for longer, I want it to be a federal case." Against Gonzales's advice, in August 2008, a federal judge in Tucson, Arizona, sentenced an 82-year-old man to six-and-a-half years in prison for possessing child pornography, after thirteen videos of his were discovered when rains eroded soil around a septic tank on the property that the elderly man managed (Marra, 2008). Had the case been prosecuted under local Arizona law, the octogenarian would have faced a mandatory 130 years. While sentencing discrepancies have shown a tendency to be resolved over time in the direction of uniform maximum terms, lingering variability complicates generalizations about how normal such extreme punishments may be.

THE "SEX OFFENDER SYSTEM"

Harsh "headline" sentences like those just sampled are increasingly the norm in the United States, even though exceptional by historical standards and even by those of contemporary Anglophone countries other than the United States, where there is also popular outrage over sex crimes. Part of the reason has been the powerful tough-on-crime attitude that has prevailed especially in the United States over the last three decades. Here, legislators compete to outdo each other in terms of who can be the "toughest" on crime. With respect to child sex, no politician "wants to be on the wrong side of a 15-second political spot on whether you're for or against [it]," as a professor at Washington and Lee University School of Law commented (quoted in Andriette, 2008, p. 10). A consequence of this political climate has been an increasing tendency in passage of federal and state laws imposing mandatory minimum sentences for nonviolent, nonpenetrative sex involving minors or for crimes of expression involving no clear victim. Another part of the reason is the willingness of US judges to give in to popular demands for vengeance, related to the fact, internationally unprecedented, that 87 percent of state judges are elected (Liptak, 2008). Popularly elected district attorneys determine which few cases their department selects to invest its resources into prosecuting before a jury; the promise of getting tough on child "predators" always wins votes among anxious parents (cf. Jenkins, 1998).

Long sentences are only one aspect of what is a parallel legal and regulatory system that has grown up within the United States and throughout the Anglosphere. This regime defines and targets a group of "predators," who are dehumanized, not least by the imposition of such a label, but even more by a concomitant net of restriction, surveillance, and criminalization cast over their lives. This regime in turn is lubricated with popular outrage, which is generated and focused by mass media and political rhetoric. This new and distinctive institutional and ideological apparatus might be called the "sex offender system." Harsh punishments and popular outrage are characteristic, but not sufficient features: the availability of execution as a punishment for sodomy over centuries under Christendom and Islam made the accusation often too terrible to invoke, helping make, in most times and places, prosecutions rare.[2] But the sex offender system is characterized by the presentation of sex crimes, especially when victims are young, as a crisis demanding a "state of exception" from ordinary legal norms, a crisis produced by an *internal enemy,* to again borrow from the terms used by Carl Schmitt to describe the German authoritarian regime. The threat is seen as a continuing, looming danger that demands the institutionalization and routinization of extraordinary measures. In public discourse, the threat is obsessively conjured up, and its vanquishing becomes a collective rallying point. The sex offender system maximizes the attention and symbolic weight given to this particular set of crimes, and it maximizes the duration for which a given malfeasance echoes, even exaggerating in public perception the frequency with which such crimes occur.

Kin perhaps to the ancient Romans' gladiatorial spectacles with captive criminals, a key feature of the US sex offender system is the "production" of sex crimes via sting operations, both public and private, with the lines between them sometimes blurring. Starting in 2004, the US television network NBC paid a vigilante group, Perverted Justice, to have its members pose online as minors, usually teens, in an effort to catch men who would approach them sexually. Sometimes the decoys themselves would steer discussion toward sex. If the men agreed to meet the decoys, they would be ambushed by NBC cameramen and police, who would arrest them, oftentimes flamboyantly (e.g., wrestling them to the ground; shooting them with a Taser). Between 2004 and 2007, some 300 men were caught. The resulting footage was broadcast on NBC's *Dateline*, in episodes that could draw more than 9 million viewers, a third more than usual for the program (Salkin, 2006). In November 2006, one of *Dateline*'s targets committed suicide, as police, with an NBC crew filming, broke down his door. A 56-year-old prosecutor in Terrell, Texas, had chatted with a decoy posing as a 13-year-old boy. But the prosecutor never went to the prearranged "meeting." At the request of the NBC film crew, police went to the prosecutor's home to arrest him, whereupon he shot himself in the head. In the wake of his death, his sister filed a lawsuit against the network, and in June 2008, settled out of court for an undisclosed sum. Two other men caught by *Dateline* died in police custody before their cases could be heard (Cohen, A., 2008; National Public Radio, 2007). Not all the men arrested in the sting were prosecuted, in part because of the sloppiness of Perverted Justice's online decoys, but those whose cases were tried received sentences ranging from probation to nearly twenty-two years (Associated Press, 2008b).

NBC's series is only the most visible of numerous stings run by all levels of US law enforcement, focusing on Internet sex chat, prostitution, and pornography involving minors. One FBI sting is notably minimalist: agents plant on a Web page a phony hyperlink whose name suggests it leads to sexual content depicting minors, but which in fact points nowhere. Those who click—as did a graduate student in history in a Northeastern university, who was convicted in November 2007—are traced, raided, and arrested, facing up to ten years in prison (McCullagh, 2008). Stings may expose intentions toward illegal behavior, but they also create crimes that would not have otherwise occurred and involve only notional victims. Though everyone has impulses to immoral and illegal acts, people frequently check urges to hurt others or steal. But leveraging minimal and inconsequential expressions of intention, such as clicking a mouse button, into acts with severe consequences only makes sense if the underlying impulse is seen as outing a distinct "other"—in this case a member of a sexually defined *enemy*.

Whereas persons released from prison are called "ex-convicts," those who break sex laws in the Anglosphere are now never, terminologically speaking, released: they remain "sex offenders" and do not pass to the status of "ex" anything. The conceptual robustness of this category is suggested by a headline in the *Boston Globe* (August 28, 2008) reporting the death sentence dealt to a man by an Idaho court. The man was convicted of murdering four members of a family, as well as kidnapping and raping two of the children. Only murderers, generally speaking, can be executed in the United States. But the headline seemed to assert the real source of the man's diabolical acts: "Sex Offender Given the Death Penalty," much as in another context it would have been grammatical to make the headline's subject "Negro."

The "sex offender system" buttresses the state's battle against an internal, sexually defined enemy. The system's key structural elements are the sex offender registry and civil commitment. The first helps forge a clearly delineated target class. The second, allowing indefinite incarceration of sane persons in mental hospitals for crimes they might commit in the future, enshrines the principle that the lives of those in this class are at the state's disposal outside of law, similar to those deemed "enemy combatants" in the state's never-ending war against "terrorism." In practice, these two structural elements meet at their edges. Not merely a passive list of miscreants, registries grow into fine-grained networks of total control, a form of "open" incarceration pitched always at the tipping point of becoming "closed." Together these structures have created a regime of internal exile for sex offenders.

California was the first US state to start a sex-offender registry in 1947. Five states followed in the 1950s and 1960s. Registries in their current form began in 1990 in Washington State and gained high-profile attention nationally after the 1994 murder of 7-year-old Megan Kanka in Hamilton, New Jersey, by a neighbor who was a twice-convicted child molester on parole. With some 400,000 New Jerseyans signing a petition demanding one, state legislators created a sex offender registry that year (Hellard, 2008). A federal "Megan's law" following shortly after led to registries in all fifty states and US territories. As of July 2008, some 645,000 people were registered sex offenders in the United States (National Center for Missing and Exploited Children at: http://www.ncmec.org). According to Human Rights Watch (2007), seven other countries as of 2007 maintain sex offender registries or conduct community notification when offenders move in: Australia, Canada, France, Ireland, Japan, Korea, and the United Kingdom. The European Union (EU) has encouraged their establishment by all member nations, and under legislation now pending in Congress, the United States will petition the United Nations to extend registries globally.

Registries are either public, or restricted to authorities, or some combination. Only registries in the United States are routinely public, listing on the Internet details such as the individual's name, home address, photo, place of work, car tags, and a gloss on the underlying crime. California's registry is among those offering maps that pinpoint offenders' places of residence. About half of US states now publicly list on the Internet all sex offenders required to register. Others keep data private on offenders who are juveniles, or those whose crimes are considered to fall beneath some threshold. In addition to offenses involving adults and minors, including crimes of expression, five states require registration for offenses relating to adult prostitution, thirteen states require registration for public urination, and twenty-nine states for consensual sex between teenagers (Human Rights Watch, 2007, p. 39). Kansas's registry has listed the name, photograph, and address of sex offenders as young as 11 (http://www.reformsexoffenderlaws.org), and Texas's registry has listed sex offenders as young as 10 (Freeman-Longo, undated, p. 13). The 2006 federal Adam Walsh Act established a national registry as well, required the listing of juvenile offenders, and federalized the offense of failing to register, with penalties of up to twenty years.

The sex offender registries lead to permanent disenfranchisement. For those marked, their crime never fades or is forgiven, but rather imparts a fixed identity tending to overwhelm their every other status and relationship. One-third of new registrants in a Florida study suffered a "dire event," such as physical attack, threats, harassment, property damage, or loss of a job, housing, or friends (Levenson & Cotter, 2005). In another survey, half said they had been forced to leave their home, and 44 percent said registry restrictions barred them from living with family members who would have taken them in (Levenson, 2005). Human Rights Watch (2007) reports a litany of death threats, violent attacks, arson, and attempted murders against registered sex offenders.

Registries are linked to at least six killings in the United States. In Whatcom County, Washington, in August 2006, a man posing as a federal agent went to a home where two registered sex offenders lived, shooting them both to death. Shortly afterward, the 35-year-old murderer confessed. In April 2006, a 20-year-old man murdered two men in their homes, whose addresses he had found on Maine's registry website. One of the victims, a 24-year-old, had confessed at age 20 to consensual sex with a girlfriend two weeks shy of her 16th birthday, for which he had to serve four months in county jail. On his laptop, the murderer had a list of more addresses from the registry, but committed suicide after the first two killings. In November 2007, a 29-year-old man stabbed to death his 67-year-old neighbor, after finding his name on California's sex offender registry. The victim had just been released after spending twenty years in prison. The killer had assumed wrongly that his neighbor had been imprisoned for sex with a minor, when his offences were confined to adult women (La Ganga, 2007). In November 2007, two teenagers killed a 26-year-old man, who was on Michigan's registry for sex with a 14-year-old girl when he was 17. The killers lured the man to a garage, where he was stabbed to death and decapitated (Fox News, 2007). Registries have also been linked to a handful of suicides, including a 19-year-old in Oklahoma, who had been convicted of exposing himself to a group of girls in his high school while on the way to the toilet, and a Michigan youth, who, after a conviction for consensual sex with a 14-year-old girl, was placed on the registry despite the efforts of the sentencing judge to keep the boy's name off (Human Rights Watch, 2007).

Registries serve as a trellis for a tangle of further regulations on sex offenders. Already regularly barred by landlords and banned from publicly funded housing, sex offenders increasingly are exiled de facto from whole towns and cities by state and local zoning ordinances requiring that they live some distance (1,000 or 2,500 feet are the most common) from schools, day care centers, parks, nursing homes, churches, and school bus stops. As of late 2007, some twenty-two states and hundreds of municipalities had passed residency restrictions (Levenson, Zgoba, & Tewksbury, 2007). In 2006 California voters, by a margin of more than 70 percent, approved Proposition 83, which barred the state's more than 90,000 sex offenders from living within 2,000 feet of schools and day care centers, with localities able to impose stricter limits. The cities of Los Angeles and San Francisco are effectively off-limits to registered sex offenders, though courts have allowed those already living in forbidden areas to stay until they leave their current addresses. In 2002, Iowa barred sex offenders from living within 2,000 feet of schools and other places children gather, leaving many with no legal domicile. "When users go to Iowa's online registry, they may be surprised to see a registrant's address listed as 'on the Raccoon River between Des Moines and West Des Moines,' 'behind the Target on Euclid,' or 'underneath the I-80 bridge,'" noted Human Rights Watch (2007). In 2006, an association of Iowa prosecutors declared the law a mistake, in part because it forced offenders underground: "The geographic areas included in the prohibited 2,000 foot zones are so extensive that realistic opportunities to find affordable housing are virtually eliminated in most communities" (Iowa County Attorneys Association 2006, p. 2). Iowa's highest court and the federal 8th Circuit Court of Appeals have upheld the law, citing public safety and noting that the restrictions still left offenders with some places to live. But despite second thoughts by Iowa officials, legislators have not revised the rules, and other states are imposing them.

Since 2007, Florida authorities have ordered sex offenders in Miami who could not find legal housing to sleep under highway overpasses. "[W]e have exhausted all efforts to locate affordable motels, rooming houses, street corners, abandoned junk cars, or any other location that could serve as a residence for sex offenders that are not in violation of the 1000-foot law or any ordinance," wrote a probation supervisor to her superiors (Thompson, 2007). An encampment under the Julia Tuttle Causeway has become home to dozens of offenders since then, including a deaf, 82-year-old man sentenced to ten years' probation for groping three children, and a man charged with oral sex with another child when he himself was 13. The men sleep in tents or shacks and maintain a generator, which is needed for lighting and to recharge the global positioning system (GPS) ankle bracelets that many are required to wear; allowing the device's batteries to run out is grounds for being sent back to prison (Thompson, 2007). A report on the settlement in the *Miami New Times*, the newspaper that broke the story, notes that many of the men forced to live there had been long-rehabilitated:

> "Increasing numbers of inhabitants have ... been out of prison for years, living and working without incident, until they violated probation (sometimes for something as simple as forgetting to re-register), were taken to jail, and then sent under the bridge. Nearly half the men would be out of here in a heartbeat if residency restrictions didn't prohibit them from living with their families" (Thompson, 2007)

Local officials say they are not troubled by the enforced homelessness. "I don't really care where they live," said the mayor of North Miami. "At this point I don't care if they live out of civilization" (Dennis & Waite, 2005). In June 2008, Dade County public defenders went to court arguing that the combination of state and municipal residency restrictions amounted to illegal banishment (Nesmith, 2008).

In some jurisdictions, the resulting inability of sex offenders to find housing can itself be grounds for declaring that they have not legally registered and must therefore go back to prison indefinitely. In August 2007, an offender from Augusta, Georgia, was convicted of failing to register for the second time, an offense carrying a mandatory life sentence. His failure to register, though, emanated from a Georgia law requiring a permanent address for registration, but he could not find one in Augusta that conformed to the legal requirement that it be 1,000 feet away from any church, school, park, swimming pool, school bus stop, or day care center (Dewan, 2007). He was not the only one: in December of the same year, a man from Atlanta also received a mandatory life sentence for trying, but failing to register a second time. His original offense was having consensual sex with a 15-year-old girl when he was 19 (Rankin, 2008).

Registries and the regulations they engender are recreating in a new guise the regime of "Jim Crow," the racial caste system that emerged in the post–Civil War US South. In 2006, Indianapolis banned sex offenders from coming within 1,000 feet of public parks and facilities where children gather, effectively criminalizing movement throughout the entire city. The law was struck down in federal court, though bans from visiting parks and other public facilities remain and are proliferating nationwide. In June 2008, North Carolina's Supreme Court upheld an ordinance banning offenders from parks, and towns around the state began rushing to impose them. In January 2008, in New Bedford, Massachusetts, a 26-year-old registered sex offender fondled and had oral sex with a 6-year-old boy in a library (Fraga, 2008). In reaction, authorities marked off many public facilities in the city as "child safety zones," banning offenders from any New Bedford "park, playground, recreation center, library, school, day care center, private youth center, video arcade, bathing beach, swimming pool or wading pool, gymnasium, sports field, or sports facility, including the parking area and land surrounding any of the aforementioned facilities, and school or camp bus stops" (Cohen, J., 2008). With new restrictions often triggered by crimes, offender registries in effect become a means of imposing collective punishments, in effect making the "author" of any new offense the demarcated, collective body of past offenders.

But, although treated as a group target for collective punishment, sex offenders, unlike Southern blacks, lack communal ties and face exile one by one. Banding together with other offenders for mutual support is itself made difficult. California's registry is open for viewing to all, except for sex offenders themselves, who risk six months in jail and a $1,000 fine for looking at it (State of California, undated). In August 2008, the town of Brookhaven, in New York's Suffolk County, banned more than two registered sex offenders from living in the same single-family house, on pain of a fine of $2,500 a week. Town officials passed what *Newsday* (2008) termed a *landmark measure* in order to break up group households that the men had formed in the limited areas in which they could live. Two months previously, the town had decreed a one-third increase in the distance offenders must live from schools, churches, day care centers, playgrounds, or nursing homes, from 1,000 feet to a quarter mile. There was already a severe shortage of housing available to sex offenders in Suffolk County. In February 2007, the *New York Times* reported that authorities were housing homeless offenders at night in mobile trailers secretly shifted around the county to avoid incensing neighbors (Kilgannon, 2007).

The state's assertion of control over registered sex offenders continues to grow more intimate, arbitrary, and absolute. For example, California's 2006 Proposition 83 mandates lifetime electronic monitoring of all sex offenders found guilty of felonies if and when they are released from custody. California joins other states expanding electronic tracking. Currently, GPS devices are permanently strapped on offenders, but some call for surgically implanted chips (Leppard, 2006). Paroled sex offenders in an increasing majority of US jurisdictions are required to submit to lie-detector tests, judged unreliable enough that their results are banned as evidence in the vast majority of US courts. Authorities ask questions that relate not only to actions, but thoughts as well. Failing the test (e.g., denying having had a thought when one in fact did, thus causing a rise in the lie-detector reading) can mean being sent back to prison, as happened to an Oregon man (Cohen, L., 2008). In Missouri, making official the informal policies of many jurisdictions, a 2008 law stipulates that sex offenders "shall be required on October 31st of each year to avoid all Halloween-related contact with children, remain inside his or her residence between the hours of 6 p.m. and 10:30 p.m.... [and] post a sign at his or her residence stating, 'No candy or treats at this residence'; and leave all outside residential lighting off during the evening 11 hours after 5 p.m" (Brecher, 2006). In another example, the National Conference of State Legislators warned of "ice-cream impersonators" in its July-August 2008 issue of *Stateline*. The group noted that some states and local governments were considering banning criminals from selling ice cream, adding that New York was the only state to have a statewide restriction for this for sex offenders (New York also bars sex offenders from obtaining real estate licenses). A 2008 Georgia law bans sex offenders from volunteering at houses of worship, on pain of ten to thirty years in prison. In June 2008, five men filed suit in federal court arguing that the law "effectively 'criminalizes fundamental religious activities' for sex offenders and bars them from serving as a choir member, a secretary, an accountant, or in any other role with a religious organization" (Associated Press, 2008c). In Schuylkill County, Pennsylvania, authorities seized a man's newborn son from the hospital, citing his conviction twenty-two years before for rape and sodomy of two teenage girls. They placed the baby in foster care, allowing his mother to visit, but banning all contact with his father (Parker, 2005). In one last illustration, the 2006 federal Adam Walsh Act declared that sex offenders forfeit their Fourth-Amendment constitutional protections against unreasonable search and seizure. Offenders' homes, workplaces, cars, and computers are declared subject to police search anytime without cause or warrant.

In the current political climate, scope for further imposition on sex offenders of regulations and prohibitions appears to be limitless. Resistance at any point can usually be politically leveraged and overcome. When the Missouri Supreme Court ruled that the new rules on residency, registration, and biometric data collection could not be imposed retroactively on offenders whose cases had been adjudicated before the new laws, the Missouri Senate in 2008 approved a voter referendum to amend the state constitution to deprive offenders of protection from ex post facto punishments (http://en.wikipedia.org/wiki/Sex_offender_registration; Missouri Senate SJR 34, 2008). When the New York State legislature resisted starting a civil-commitment program for sex offenders, then Governor George Pataki simply ordered offenders held after their prison sentences were over. When New York State's highest court ruled in November 2006 that this action was illegal, the governor called the legislature into special session to consider a civil-commitment bill, which passed in March 2007 (Johnson, 2006). Legislation introduced in Congress in April 2008 and embraced in the 2008 Republican Party platform effectively bans US sex offenders from traveling outside the country, establishing penalties of ten years in prison and fines for leaving the United States or crossing any international border without first giving US authorities twenty-one days' notice, so that the host country—which, under the circumstances, can be expected to deny the visit—can "properly identify and track the registered individual" (H.R. 5722 [110th]: International Megan's Law of 2008). As well, the proposed "International Megan's Law" [H.R. 5722] would bar foreigners who had been convicted of sex that is also illegal in the US or who merely admit having engaged in such acts, even if legal where and when they happened, from entering the United States without giving twenty-one days' notice to every jurisdiction they plan to visit. Foreigners as well would be subject to ten years in US prison for violating the notification requirements. The bill also instructs the United States to pressure foreign governments to start sex offender registries and offers aid toward this end to both states and nongovernmental organizations (NGOs) (Persico, 2008).

Revisiting the Status of "Sex Offender"

The totality with which the status of "sex offender" determines a person's existence—subjective and objective—suggests other subaltern statuses entrenched in Western societies, as Janus (2006) noted:

> [P]redator laws resurrect a concept that has properly fallen out of favor in US law: the notion of the "degraded other." In the past, we have used categories such as race, gender, national origin, sexual orientation, and disability to put people into reduced-rights zones. But the courts have, for the most part, put a stop to that. Now the predator laws have reversed that trend, reintroducing into our legal vocabulary the notion that we can designate a group to be put into this alternate legal universe where fundamental rights are diminished. (pp. 5–6)

Yet more than simply second-class citizens, the sex offender is a flashpoint of collective hate and demonization. The registries' power—most developed in the United States, where they are public—follows their form as a networked database. Until the era of information technology, large databases required infrastructure on a scale only the state or large organizations could muster. Even then, they were unwieldy, not readily duplicable, and so tended to reside only at "headquarters." Modern authoritarian regimes use databases to keep track of their internal enemies: Germany's Nazi state famously used IBM punch cards (Black, 2001). But the categories of persons whom the Nazis sought to liquidate (e.g., Jews) were age-old, however much they were newly recast in the foundry of totalitarian demonology.

What makes the sex offender unique is the extent the status itself is constituted by the database. Postmodern sexuality theory has called into question sexual categories—for example, "male," "female," "heterosexual," "homosexual"—and this notion of categorical fluidity is now widely embraced in mainstream Western culture. Sex offender registries (SORs) have ironically reconstituted, with a sharply negative valence, sexual absolutes. A homicidal rapist and someone who clicks on a link that says "Watch 16-year-olds do everything" do not constitute a single natural kind; it is their being in the same data pool that amalgamates them and binds their fates.

It is not simply the wide dissemination of the offenders' names, addresses, and photos that is relevant here. "Naming and shaming" of individual registered offenders, who US television stations now feature regularly in "public service" spots, is not enough; with some 645,000 registrants, the impact of such broadcasts comes at the margins. Rather than merely a means of publicity, the power of the US sex offender registries lies in the networked database's ability to keep vast quantities of data in play by tailoring its presentation to users' precise concerns. Registries are among US states' most popular websites; in January 2004, for example, Georgia officials reported 830,000 searches on the then 8,000 names on the state's online SOR (Chong, 2004). A primary reason for searching is to find out which offenders live or work nearby. Those looking will generally not know these offenders, and their crimes will be obscure (usually just a reference to the statute under which they were convicted). But local offenders tend to interest and frighten by their proximity. In previous regimes of demonization, locality of an individual in a demonized group could sometimes counteract the general fear; familiar or local Jews might be seen as friends or neighbors first, Jews second. But in this case, locality tends to amplify fear; to give the "monster" both a face and set him perilously right at the doorstep.

Yet another stream of fear that registries facilitate works at the most general level: sex offenders are lumped together without reason and may share little in common. So their group identity ends up being imparted by those committing the most notorious crimes. When a registered sex offender acts egregiously, it is the entire group that politicians and the media hold accountable, leading to collective punishment. Other examples abound of this group identity that races to the bottom. Michael Mullen, who shot execution-style two Whatcom County, Washington, registered men at their home in July 2005, said he did so to avenge murders and abductions that had been recently committed in Idaho by a man with a prior sex conviction. That the men who Mullen killed had not been found guilty of violent offenses—one had gone to prison for sex with a teenage boy—was irrelevant; apparently all that mattered was that they bore the label *sex offenders*. California had a registry since the 1940s—but it was only within two years of its going online that an overwhelming majority of voters felt the need to exile those listed from their communities (Rau, 2004). The impact of the United States's public SORs follows from how they create a distinct identity for those they mark, stereotyped by extreme cases, while, as a networked database, that "extremity" is funneled to those identifiable as local. From whichever perspective people look at the registry—close up, or "in summation" at a distance—the database works to present offenders in the most monstrous light. From the directions both of immediacy and generality, registries maximize fear.

For registered sex offenders, their status envelops them in a virtual prison, but as restrictions and penalties proliferate and intensify, the prison readily becomes actual. Details from two previously cited cases illustrate this point. Georgia bans all sex offenders, even residents of nursing homes, from living or working within 1,000 feet of any place "minors congregate," which for some makes finding housing or a job nearly impossible. At the same time, Georgia punishes with a mandatory life sentence a second instance of failing to complete all registration requirements, one of which requires having and reporting a permanent street address at all times. In August 2007, a 40-year-old man in Augusta, who in 1994 had been convicted of "indecent liberty with a child," was sentenced to life in prison. His first registry violation occurred several years before, when penalties were much less severe. His second missed registry resulted from being forced to live at a hotel, because all other places in his city of Augusta were off-limits, but not being able to afford it. Consequently he moved out, failing to notify the authorities, who could have then arrested him for not having a permanent residence. The sex offender system was not concerned with the unmanageable dilemma in which the man found himself; when it discovered he had moved out, it sent him to prison for life (Dewan, 2007). In the second case cited previously, another man in December 2007 received a mandatory life term after trying, but failing for a second time, to fulfill Georgia's registration requirements. The man was 19 when he was convicted of consensual sex with a 15-year-old girl, resulting in a five-year prison term. After his release, he moved in with his sister and properly registered as a sex offender. But the authorities made him leave, because he was too close to a recreation center. He then moved in with his aunt and correctly put her address on the registry. This time he was told to leave, because the home was within 1,000 feet of a Baptist Church. Then a relative connected him with a family friend, who offered him a spare bedroom in his single-wide trailer. The man registered once more, but provided the wrong address, inadvertently transposing two of the street numbers. An investigation by the authorities uncovered the mix-up, finding as well that the man did not move into the trailer within seventy-two hours of providing the address. In consequence, the beleaguered man received the mandatory life term (Rankin, 2008).

Cases such as these demonstrate the transformation of registries from a passive list to an instrument approaching total, arbitrary control. But if they have built up to this level in only just over a decade, the potential was present from the start. In 1996 the US Supreme Court overturned a ruling by Kansas's highest court and held in *Hendricks v. Kansas* that, uniquely in the case of sex offenses, people who were not mentally ill could be imprisoned indefinitely in mental hospitals for crimes they might commit in the future, so long as the state could demonstrate the person had a *personality disorder* or *mental abnormality,* terms that cover everything from caffeine addiction to depression and encompass as well adult sexual attraction to minors. Such imprisonment, coming after a sentence fully served, did not constitute extra punishment, the high court ruled. And, although there needed to be periodic review of a committed person's confinement, it was not required that an impartial court do it—a hospital committee would suffice. The ruling overturned a precedent from only four years earlier, in *Foucha v. Louisiana,* which held that both mental illness *and* dangerousness were necessary for commitment. In theory, detainees would receive "treatment" that, if successfully completed, would make them eligible for release. But the American Psychiatric Association opposed using mental hospitals to warehouse sane people. "This is not an attempt to gain treatment or anything close to that," said a Yale professor of psychiatry. "What this really is, is an attempt to extend prison sentences," he added (Andriette, 2007). By 2007, nineteen states had established civil commitment regimes for sex offenders (Davey & Goodnough, 2007), and some 4,534 men were being held (with 494 others having been discharged, and 85 dying in custody) (Washington State Institute for Public Policy, 2006). The 2006 Adam Walsh Act established civil commitment for *all* persons in federal custody, not merely those held for sex offenses, though the only basis for commitment is sexual dangerousness. In 2007, the US Department of Justice announced a policy to consider seeking civil commitment for federal inmates with HIV, in custody on any charge, who had ever engaged in sex without revealing their serostatus (Department of Justice, Bureau of Prisons, 2007). As of September 2007, the US Bureau of Prisons had identified some 12,000 inmates it would review for civil commitment. Proceedings have already been brought against inmates convicted of noncontact sex offenses, such as pornography possession, as well as bank robbery and possession of a firearm.[3] "What is to stop the state from assessing all of us for 'risk' and locking up prophylactically those whose RQ—risk quotient—is assessed above an arbitrary threshold?" asks Janus (2006, p. 5). These developments partially answer that question.

The threat of civil commitment leverages other regulations placed on sex offenders, because any event triggering an encounter with authorities—leaving a light on during Halloween, a form lost in the mail, entering a library—can transform into a life sentence. In Wisconsin in 2007, a man was civilly committed for his thoughts. A decade before, when he was 20, the man had received ten years' probation for relationships he had with two girls, who were, respectively, 16 and 14. "Both girls considered [him] their boyfriend, but they both were legally underage," according to the *Milwaukee Journal-Sentinel* (Doege, 2007). Earlier, when he was 16, the man had been found delinquent for sexual contact with a 9-year-old boy. In 1999, authorities revoked the man's probation on grounds of "inadequate participation in a treatment program for sex offenders." After serving five years, he was released from prison in 2004. Now the man participated in treatment more fully, but got in trouble precisely for doing so. As a consequence of these sessions, he was taken into custody several times over the next year for having deviant thoughts about children that he delayed reporting to his probation agent. Finally, he was sent back to prison because of his thought patterns, as well as improper visits to places such as shopping malls, where he might encounter minors. As he was about to leave prison, Wisconsin petitioned successfully to have him civilly committed (Doege, 2007).

Conclusion

No less than the Star of David, the Pink Triangle, or an "A" stamped on the forehead for adultery, the sex offender registry constitutes a permanent and public branding of the sexual outlaw, treating the crime, no matter how trivial or long ago, as a mark of Cain identifying the individual to everyone as a social leper and an irredeemable threat who may never be rehabilitated and who can always be located, should local police need to round up the "usual suspects." This panoptic regime of never-ending surveillance might be justified were there a demonstrably greater propensity to reoffend on the part of sex offenders, and especially child sex offenders (the ones whose possible proximity to schools, parks, and day care centers motivates the onerous residency restrictions). However, the recidivism rate among child sex offenders is lower than for felons generally, suggesting that these policies are not grounded in any rational assessment of the threat posed relative to other felons who had once been incarcerated for unambiguously violent crimes. The most comprehensive study of sex offender recidivism is the one commissioned by the US Department of Justice in November 2003. It tracked 4,295 child sex offenders released from prison in 1994 over a subsequent three-year period. Of those who had no previous convictions of any crime prior to the offense for which they were imprisoned, only 3.2 percent would be rearrested for another sex crime within the following three years (only 1.7 percent for another sex crime involving a child). Only 22.4 percent of those who had been imprisoned for sexual assault would be convicted of any other crime during the first three years following release from prison, compared with 47.8 percent of all those released from prison. Nevertheless, the principal finding that the Ashcroft Justice Department chose to highlight in its very brief public summary of the report was: "Compared to non-sex offenders released from State prisons, released sex offenders were 4 times more likely to be rearrested for a sex crime." This emphasis was despite the report's revelation that 87 percent of the sex crimes committed by released prisoners during this period were the work of those who had been imprisoned for something else (and were thus not listed on sex offender registries) (Bureau of Justice Statistics, 2003).

Arguably, by making life on the outside unendurable, the sex offender registry may so hinder reintegration of the offender into society that he will feel that he is no worse off in going underground with an assumed identity, or even in re-offending and returning to prison. As a *New York Times* (2006) editorial stated:

> The problem with residency restrictions is that they fulfill an emotional need but not a rational one. It's in everyone's interest for registered sex offenders to lead stable lives, near the watchful eyes of family and law enforcement and regular psychiatric treatment. Exile by zoning threatens to create just the opposite phenomenon—a subpopulation of unhinged nomads off their meds with no fixed address and no one keeping tabs on them. (A18)

Similarly, because the punishment for sex with a child is increasingly no less severe than that for murder, some particularly unstable child abusers may be tempted to try evading discovery by eliminating the witness. Rational penology recognizes that overly severe punishment becomes counterproductive after a certain point, no matter how great the public's thirst for vengeance.

But such rational calculus does not appear to be winning the debate. One appointment to the Supreme Court could change the balance of the 5–4 vote that ruled the death penalty for child abuse unconstitutional. On the same day the Supreme Court overturned Louisiana's death penalty, Governor Bobby Jindal signed into law S.B. 144, permitting judges to order chemical castration (and mandating it on a second offense) for aggravated rape, forcible rape, second-degree sexual battery, aggravated incest, or aggravated crimes against nature (Millhollon, 2008).

The fever pitch of anxiety over children is not unique to the United States, but has reached such a point in the UK that new legislation requires a criminal background check of any adult who comes into contact with children in any capacity; it is estimated that as much as one-fourth the adult population of England will have to register for such checks. Many child-related charitable agencies report a decline in volunteers because of the onerous requirements, and the press is rife with anecdotes of adults who refuse to help children in distress for fear of being accused of evil motives (Civitas Press Release, 2008). Despite occasional newspaper editorials and academic studies decrying the madness, there has been no serious effort by any elected officials to propose reforms in sentencing guidelines, the sex offender registry, residency restrictions, or the laws defining "statutory rape" and "age of consent" so as return to a system of punishments cognizant of and proportional to the presence or absence of consent and extent of harm. Such reforms do not poll well, and any legislator or jurist who might propose them would immediately open himself to attack as "soft on sexual predators." Instead, the "reforms" are all in the other direction, characterizing the sexual offender as not only "sub-human" and, thus, unworthy of various fundamental human rights, but more and more as "anti-human," forfeiting virtually all human rights (cf. Hilberg, 2003). As we see in the UK, the assumption that every adult is a potential pedophile has become so ubiquitous that official papers are now required to prove that one is not.

Humanity has been down this road before. The twentieth century witnessed repeated waves of ethnic cleansing and even mass annihilation of population groups that were out of favor with the political authorities. These waves tend to be spasmodic eruptions of irrational emotion fanned by partisans who would divert attention from the real and difficult problems of civil society. As Louis Crompton (2003) has documented in painstaking detail, earlier centuries witnessed orgies of mass hysteria and odium directed against a different sexual outlaw, the "sodomite." Whether in Renaissance Venice, Calvinist Geneva, the Spanish Inquisition, France during the religious wars, or England and The Netherlands in the eighteenth century, the "sodomite" came to represent almost a metaphysical threat to the survival of the state, fearing that its struggles could be divine punishment for excessive laxity toward the same sin that caused God to bury Sodom and Gomorrah. This collective anxiety led to a rapid increase in executions, often of the most gruesome sort, and systematic persecutions that sometimes played themselves out after a few years of carnage, but often lasted for decades. The sodomite, now known as *gay*, is today generally tolerated, but arguably a materialistic, career-obsessed society worried about the independence of its unsupervised children has found a new metaphysical threat in the "child predator." The recurrent, but never documented, accounts of widespread ritualized Satanic child sexual abuse from the formative decade of the 1980s suggest an apocalyptic religious dimension to the present panic as well (for comparison with the sexualization of other religious panics, see Frankfurter, 2006).

What is in the future for the sex offender? Andriette's (2008) report on the Supreme Court's ruling on the death penalty for child sex is relevant. In June 2008, the US Supreme Court ruled as unconstitutional the death penalty for non-homicidal child rape. A closer look at the laws involved, however, shows that the death penalty in three of the six states that had it actually extended well beyond violent acts of force normally associated with rape; it could apply to consensual acts and even to acts that involved no actual contact. Here, "consensual" means assenting, even if legally proscribed; legal rulings and courts do recognize "consent" in illicit sex with minors, even while judging them illegal for not being "informed consent." In Louisiana, as Andriette noted, an 18-year-old woman giving oral sex to a boy just shy of his 13th birthday, for whom she was babysitting and who was complicit in the sex act, would have been eligible for the death penalty before the Supreme Court ruling. Even after the ruling, she would still be subject to mandatory life in prison without parole. In Oklahoma, a 2006 law elevated "lewd molestation" with someone under 14 to a death-qualified level, such that looking upon a minor lewdly or lasciviously could put an adult at risk for this punishment. Chatting online with someone purporting to be a minor, but actually an adult, could also result in the death penalty.

Given the unabated public outrage over sex offenders, along with the ever-increasing dehumanizing treatments of them detailed in this review and the tenuousness of the Court's 5–4 decision, it is not hard to imagine that death sentences could eventually be imposed for acts that in the past might have resulted merely in probation. Hilberg's (2003) documentation of the transformation of German Jews in the 1930s from people with rights, to sub-humans with sharply limited rights, and finally to anti-humans requiring urgent elimination, arguably has parallels with the transformation of the modern sex offender.

It is not the purpose or intention of this article to defend or excuse the sexual acts of the persons labeled "sex offenders," but to confront the reader with the flip side of the offender's victimizing, which is the demonology that has emerged with respect to him (or her). A set of legal and social policies centered on demonology speaks not of any real progress, but of a dangerous backwardness not befitting a civilized society in the twenty-first century.

Notes

1. See: http://en.wikipedia.org/wiki/Carl_Schmitt (Accessed September 2, 2008).
2. Burg (1983) commented: "While murder, treason, bestiality, and serious crimes against property often brought their perpetrators to the gallows, the minor felonies—such as theft of restricted amounts of money or goods, shipping sheep across the sea, cutting purses, sodomy, or picking pockets—rarely cost anyone his or her life, at least until the application of excessive criminal penalties in the middle of the 18th century. The effect of the death penalty in earlier years was to mitigate the severity of the law rather than increase it" (p. 3). See also Greenberg (1988, p. 345).
3. "Adam Walsh Act III: It's Not the Sentence, It's the Commitment," by Amy Baron-Evans and Sara Noonan, memorandum from the US Office of Defender Services, available at http://www.fd.org/odstb_AdamWalsh.htm.

References

Andriette, B. (2007). America's sex gulags. *The Guide*, August.

_____. (2008). Iran, Nigeria, Sudan, Saudi Arabia, USA: In June, a divided Supreme Court struck the US off the list of nations where consensual sex can lead to execution. *The Guide*, August, pp. 9–12.

Associated Press (2004). Son of vigilate mother now subject of California murder probe, manhunt, July 29. Retrieved June 1, 2013 at: http://www.highbeam.com/doc/1P1-96949015.html

_____. (2005). Ex-priest guilty of molestation, February 18. Retrieved June 1, 2013 from LexisNexis Academic database.

_____. (2006a). Former children's editor sentenced for soliciting sex from minor, December 13. Retrieved June 1, 2013 from LexisNexis Academic database.

_____. (2006b). Gonzales visits Pa. officials combating Internet predators. December 12. Retrieved June 1, 2013 from LexisNexis Academic database.

_____. (2007). Father gets 9 months for killing molest suspect, January 5. Retrieved June 1, 2013 at: http://www.nbcnews.com/id/16488491/#.UauU2HakpEk.

_____. (2008a). Child abuser gets 4,060 year prison sentence, July 3. Retrieved June 1, 2013 from LexisNexis Academic database.

_____. (2008b). Man gets 262 month sentence in child porno case, July 24. Retrieved June 1, 2013 at: http://enewscourier.com/statenews/x1037416540/Man-gets-262-month-sentence-in-child-porno-case

_____. (2008c). Georgia: Sex Offenders Sue Over Church Ban, June 25. Retrieved June 1, 2013 at: http://www.nytimes.com/2008/06/25/us/25brfs-SEXOFFENDERS_BRF.html

Barge, C. (2007). Priest guilty of sexually assaulting youth. *Rocky Mountain News*, March 27. Retrieved June 1, 2013 at: http://www.rockymountainnews.com/news/2007/Mar/27/priest-guilty-of-sexually-assaulting-youth/

Black, E. J. (2001). *IBM and the Holocaust*. New York: Crown Publishes.

Brecher, E. J. (2006). Police target Halloween predators. *Miami Herald*, October 20. Retrieved June 1, 2013 at: http://newsstand.x10.mx/archive/0928.html

Bureau of Justice Statistics. (2003). Recidivism of sex offenders released from prison in 1994, November. Retrieved September 2, 2008 at: http://www.ojp.usdoj.gov/bjs/abstract/rsorp94.htm

Burg, B. R. (1983). *Sodomy and the pirate tradition*. New York: New York University Press. Campbell, T. (2005). Richmond man first convicted under expanded child-porn law. *RichmondTimes-Dispatch*, December 2. Retrieved June 1, 2013 at: http://www.timesdispatch.com/servlet/Satellite?pagename=RTD/MGArticle/RTD_BasicArticle&c=MGArticle&cid=1128768481527

Chong, J. (2004). Bill would permit posting facts about sex offenders on Internet. *Los Angeles Times*, February 22. Retrieved June 1, 2013 at: http://articles.latimes.com/2004/feb/22/local/me-megan22

Civitas Press Release (2008, June 26). Retrieved September 2, 2008 at: http://www.civitas.org.uk

Cohen, A. (2008). What's on TV tonight? Humiliation to the point of suicide. *New York Times*, March 10, A16.

Cohen, J. (2008). Child safety zone ordinance awaits New Bedford mayor's sign-off. *Standard-Times*, March 29. Retrieved June 1, 2013 at: http://www.southcoasttoday.com/apps/pbcs.dll/article?AID=/20080329/NEWS/803290337/-1/NEWS

Cohen, L. (2008). The polygraph paradox. *Wall Street Journal*, March 22. Retrieved June 1, 2013 at: http://online.wsj.com/public/article_print/SB120612863077155601.html

Colby, C. (2006). Judge orders chemical castration for convicted molester. *Naples News*, December 8. Retrieved June 1, 2013 at: http://www.naplesnews.com/news/2006/dec/08/judge_orders_chemical_castration_convicted_moleste/?local_news

Crompton, L. (2003). *Homosexuality and civilization*. Cambridge: Harvard University Press.

Davey, M., & Goodnough, A. (2007). Doubts rise as states hold sex offenders after prison. *New York Times*, March 4. Retrieved June 1, 2013 at: http://www.nytimes.com/2007/03/04/us/04civil.html?pagewanted=print&_r=0

Dennis, B., & Waite, M. (2005). Where is a sex offender to live? *St. Petersburg Times*, May 15. Retrieved June 1, 2013 at: http://www.sptimes.com/2005/05/15/Tampabay/Where_is_a_sex_offend.shtml

D'Entremont, J. (2008). No Wonder Dorothy wanted out—In Kansas, gay sex can mean life in jail. *The Guide*, May. Retrieved June 1, 2013 at: http://connection.ebscohost.com/c/articles/31782395/no-wonder-dorothy-wanted-out

Department of Justice, Bureau of Prisons. (2007). Civil commitment of a sexually dangerous person (proposed rule). *Federal Register*, August 3, Volume 72, Number 149. Retrieved June 1, 2013 at: http://www.gpo.gov/fdsys/pkg/FR-2007-08-03/html/E7-14943.htm

Dewan, S. (2007). Homelessness could mean life in prison for offender. *New York Times*, August 3, p. A13.

Doege, D. (2007). Man ruled sexual predator over thoughts of children. *Milwaukee Journal-Sentinel*, August 23. Retrieved June 1, 2013 at: http://www.jsonline.com/story/index.aspx?id=651629

Fox News. (2007). Head found, teens arrested in "thrill kill" death of decapitated sex offender, November 12. Retrieved September 2, 2008 at: http://www.foxnews.com/story/0,2933,310578,00.html

Fraga, B. (2008). Sex offender accused of molesting 6-year-old in New Bedford library. *Standard-Times*, January 31. Retrieved June 1, 2013 at: http://www.southcoasttoday.com/apps/pbcs.dll/article?AID=/20080131/NEWS/80131013&cid=sitesearch

Frankfurter, D. (2006). *Evil incarnate: Rumors of demonic conspiracy and ritual abuse in history.* Princeton, NJ: Princeton University Press.

Freeman-Longo, R. E. (undated). Revisiting Megan's Law and sex offender registration. American Probation and Parole Association: Retrieved September 2, 2008 at: www.appa-net.org/resources/ pubs/docs/revisitingmegan.pdf p. 13.

Greenberg, D. (1988). *The construction of homosexuality.* Chicago, IL: University of Chicago Press.

Hellard, P. (2008). Megan's Law would tell parents where pedophiles live. *Courier Mail*, July 9. Retrieved June 1, 2013 at: http://www.couriermail.com.au/news-unify/abusers-can-run-not-hide/story-e6freon6-1111114768851

Hilberg, R. (2003). *The destruction of the European Jews*, 3rd Edition. New Haven, CT: Yale University Press.

Huffman, D. M. (2008). Child sex crime trial continues. *Weatherford Democrat*, June 27. Retrieved June 1, 2013 at: http://www.weatherforddemocrat.com/archivesearch/local_story_179103356.html

Human Rights Watch (2007). *No easy answers: Sex offender laws in the US*, September. Retrieved September 2, 2008 at: www.hrw.org/reports/2007/us0907/us0907web.pdf

In the Pink. (2007). Getting his phill. Retrieved September 2, 2008 at: http://www.inthepinktexas.com/2007/08/14/getting-his-phill/

Iowa County Attorneys Association (2006). Statement on Sex-Offender Residency Restrictions in Iowa, December 11, 2006. Retrieved June 1, 2013. http://www.csom.org/pubs/Iowa%20DAs%20Association_Sex%20Offender%20Residency%20Statement%20Dec%2011%202006.pdf

Janus, E. S. (2006). *Failure to protect: America's sexual predator law and the rise of the preventative state.* Ithaca, NY: Cornell University Press.

Jenkins, P. (1998). *Moral panic: Changing concepts of the child-molester in modem America.* New Haven, CT: Yale University Press.

Johnson, M. (2006). Pataki and lawmakers hope to agree on civil commitment bill. *Associated Press*, December 10. Retrieved from LexisNexis Academic database.

Kilgannon, C. (2007). Suffolk County to keep sex offenders on the move. *New York Times*, February 17. Retrieved June 1, 2013 at: www.nytimes.com/2007/02/17/nyregion/17sex.html

Kilpatrick, J. (2006). Case of the 20 dirty pictures, September 20. Retrieved September 2, 2008 at http://www.mywire.com/pubs/uExpress/2006/09/20/1826887

Knaupp, C. (2008). Cross-dressing child molester gets life. *Tyler Morning Telegraph*, September 3, 2008. Retrieved June 1, 2013 at: http://www.tylerpaper.com/article/20080903/NEWS08/809030312

La Ganga, M. L. (2007). Megan's Law listing may have led to slaying. *Los Angeles Times*, December 10. Retrieved June 1, 2013 at: http://articles.latimes.com/2007/dec/10/local/me-molester10

Leppard, D. (2006), Police call for tracker chips in paedophiles. *Sunday Times* (London), July 16. Retrieved June 1, 2013 at: http://newsstand.x10.mx/archive2/2159.html

Levenson, J. S. (2005). Sex offender residence restrictions. Report to the Florida legislature, October.

Levenson, J. S., & Cotter, L. P. (2005). The effect of Megan's Law on sex offender reintegration. *Journal of Contemporary Criminal Justice, 21*, 49–66.

Levenson, J. S., Zgoba, K., & Tewksbury, R. (2007). Sex offender residence restrictions: Sensible crime policy or flawed logic? *Federal Probation, 71*. Retrieved September 2, 2008 at: http://www.uscourts.gov/fedprob/December_2007/sexOffendResRestrictions.html

Liptak, A. (2008). Rendering justice, with one eye on re-election. *New York Times*, May 25. Retrieved June 1, 2013 at: http://www.nytimes.com/2008/05/25/us/25exception.html

Marra, J. A. (2008) Sierra Vista man given prison in child porn case, *The Herald* (Sierra Vista, AZ), August 8. Retrieved June 1, 2013 at: http://www.svherald.com/content/julie-ann-marra/2009/09/20/61404

McCullagh, D. (2008). FBI posts fake hyperlinks to snare child porn suspects, Cnet News, March 20. Retrieved September 2, 2008 at: http://www.news.com/8301-13578_3-9899151-38.html

McPhee, M. (2008). Archdiocese settles sex-assault suit for $300K. *Denver Post*, April 10. Retrieved June 1, 2013 at: http://www.denverpost.com/news/ci_8879657

Millhollon, M. (2008). Jindal signs chemical castration bill. *The Advocate,* June 26. Retrieved September 2, 2008 at: http://www.2theadvocate.com/news/21656994.html?showAll=y&c=y

Minaya, Z. (2003). Case of man accused of sucking boys' toes tests definition of molestation. *Los Angeles Times,* May 15. Retrieved at: http://articles.latimes.com/2003/may/15/local/me-toes15

National Public Radio. (2007). Ethics of NBC's sting show *To Catch a Predator,* January 16. Retrieved September 2, 2008 at: http://www.npr.org/templates/story/story.php?storyId=6870926

Nesmith, S. A. (2008). Public defender challenges Dade's sex offender laws. *Miami Herald,* June 21. Retrieved June 1, 2013 at: http://www.sdp123a.com/index2.php?option=com_content&do_pdf=1&id=275

New York Times. (2006). Sex offenders in exile, December 30, A18.

Newsday. (2008). Brookhaven enacts landmark sex offender ruling, August 5. Retrieved June 1, 2013 at: http://www.sdp123a.com/index.php?option=com_content&task=view&id=378&Itemid=9

Parker, C. (2005). Schuylkill takes WolfHawk baby boy: Son of man who committed sex crimes is put in foster home. *The Morning Call,* October 20. Retrieved June 1, 2013 at: http://articles.mcall.com/2005-10-22/news/3641722_1_daishin-wolfhawk-custody-county-s-child-welfare-agency

Persico, J. (2008). Smith gets GOP to back international Megan's Law. *The Times* (Trenton, New Jersey), September 5. Retrieved June 1, 2013 at: http://sexoffenderissues.blogspot.com/2008/09/nj-smith-gets-gop-to-back-international.html#.UauHCXakpEk

Prince, R. (2008). Parents who kill paedophiles can plead not guilty to murder. *Telegraph,* July 28. Retrieved June 1, 2013 at: http://www.telegraph.co.uk/news/uknews/law-and-order/2466209/Parents-who-kill-paedophiles-can-plead-not-guilty-to-murder.html

Rankin, B. (2008). Fairness of law to be judged. *Atlanta Journal-Constitution,* June 29. Retrieved September 2, 2008 at: http://www.ajc.com/metro/content/printedition/2008/06/29/registry.html

Rau, J. (2004). Sex crime data to go on Web. *Los Angeles Times,* September 25. Retrieved June 1, 2013 at: http://articles.latimes.com/2004/sep/25/local/me-arnold25

Salkin, A. (2006). Web site hunts pedophiles, and TV goes along. *New York Times,* December 13. Retrieved June 1, 2013 at: http://www.nytimes.com/2006/12/13/technology/13justice.html?hp=&_r=0

Satter, L. (2008). Ex-professor draws 10-year sentence. *Arkansas Democrat-Gazette,* August 7. Retrieved June 1, 2013 at: http://www.highbeam.com/doc/1G1-182425106.html

State of California (undated). Penalties for misuse of sex offender registrant information. Retrieved September 2, 2008 at: http://www.meganslaw.ca.gov/registration/penalty.aspx?lang=ENGLISH

Thompson, I. (2007). Sex offenders set up camp. *Miami New Times,* December 13. Retrieved June 1, 2013 at: http://www.miaminewtimes.com/2007-12-13/news/sex-offenders-set-up-camp/full/

US Department of Justice press release. (2006a). Virginia Man Convicted for Possession of Child Pornography in the Form of Japanese Anime Cartoons, March 10.

_____. (2006b). Prepared Remarks of Attorney General Alberto Gonzales at the Project Safe Childhood Conference, December 4.

Vachss, A. (2006). Child pornography has expanded into a business so profitable it is no longer limited to pedophiles. *Parade,* February 19. Retrieved June 1, 2013 at: http://www.vachss.com/av_dispatches/parade_021906.html

Vicini, J. (2007). Court won't review 200-year child porn sentence, *Reuters,* February 26. Retrieved June 1, 2013 at: http://www.reuters.com/article/domesticNews/idUSN3034892420070226

Washington State Institute for Public Policy. (2006). Comparison of state laws authorizing involuntary commitment of sexually violent predators: 2006 update, revised. Retrieved September 2, 2008 at: http://www.wsipp.wa.gov/rptfiles/07-08-1101.pdf

Chapter 10

BLINDED BY POLITICS AND MORALITY—A REPLY TO MCANULTY AND WRIGHT

BRUCE RIND

In their critique published within this volume, McAnulty and Wright strive to paint as flawed and biased one of the building-block sections of my article on pederasty. In that section, I argued that the nonclinical evidence on gay and bisexual boys' pederastic relations with older males indicates that positive response in this population is common. In attempting to achieve their goal, McAnulty and Wright try to characterize all the evidence in it as untrustworthy, by selectively focusing on alleged weaknesses in a small subset of the evidence. For example, they cite the opinion of several non-scientist gay advocates (i.e., Burroway, 2006; Lauritsen, 1979), who critiqued two of the studies included in my review. But these critiques were explicitly directed at sanitizing gays from embarrassing matters, one being any association between gay and pederastic relations, so as to preserve the political gains made by gays since the late 1960s. In this regard, the chapters by Mader and Hekma and Yuill elsewhere in this volume are relevant, because they confront the political nature of current discourse on gay sexuality vis-à-vis pederasty, which has damaged scientific efforts to understand male homosexuality as a whole.

The McAnulty and Wright critique tries to characterize my article as not simply in error, but fundamentally biased and disingenuous—to wit, the critique's title "Blinded by Science ... ," presumably suggesting that my article was a deliberate attempt to confuse readers into accepting my conclusions through highly complex, but erroneous, streams of evidence.[1] In this reply, I turn the tables on McAnulty and Wright by demonstrating that each of their criticisms concerning evidence was flawed. At a deeper level, it seems to me, this controversy is not about evidence per se, but about the authority of clinicians, the guardianship of prevailing morality, and the political integrity of the gay movement, factors that can be substantially blinding in their own right with respect to scientific objectivity.

My current article on pederasty was revised and substantially shortened, per the current editors' and publisher's request, from the previously censored 2009 version (i.e., Rind, 2009). McAnulty and Wright's critique is directed at the 2009 version. Certain material that they criticized has been deleted or altered in the current version. It is important to emphasize that these changes were in response to the need to shorten the article, not to make corrections in response to McAnulty and Wright, because the 2009 version's section on gay and bisexual boys' pederastic experiences was sound as written, as I will show shortly. McAnulty and Wright's decision to stick with their original critique presumably reflects a conviction of having exposed serious error and bias and wanting such to be entered into the record. In rebutting their arguments, therefore, I shall include relevant passages from the 2009 version in the appendix or as quotes in the text that follows. This material will help readers more fully judge for themselves whether McAnulty and Wright are offering valid criticism or are carping.

Homosexuality, Pederasty, Discourse, Pseudoscience, and Science

In 1998 I published two sex-related articles, one achieving enormously widespread attention, the other being essentially ignored but quite germane to the present reply. The attention-gaining article was a meta-analysis of assumed properties of child sexual abuse (CSA), showing that the "properties" of pervasive, intense harm were highly exaggerated factoids, not scientifically derived facts (Rind, Tromovitch, & Bauserman, 1998). Criticisms not unlike those by McAnulty and Wright in tone and substance abounded. The meta-analysis withstood perhaps the most intense scrutiny ever paid to a psychological publication. The American Association for the Advancement of Science (AAAS) located the problem in the critics of the meta-analysis, not in the meta-analysis itself, as did a special issue of the *American Psychologist* in 2002. The meta-analysis was fully replicated and verified in 2008 by independent researchers, and we successfully rebutted all criticisms of it made by two sets of clinicians in *Psychological Bulletin* in 2001. In the end, the study remains a solid work of science, not the pseudoscience it was so often called by critics, who disagreed with its conclusions on ideological grounds.

My less noticed article from that year (Rind, 1998) is of special relevance for present purposes. It was a content-analysis of eighteen top-selling human sexuality textbooks, assessing their use or misuse of cross-cultural and historical examples of male homosexual behavior for perspective on the same in the contemporary West. All the textbooks condemned pederastic relations with males under age 18 as abusive and harmful, but endorsed gay relations between men aged 18 or older as normal and healthy, consistent with socially liberal values, morality, and politics that consolidated after the 1960s. Given these starting assumptions, then, it would clearly be inappropriate to use cross-cultural examples of institutionalized pederasty to argue that androphile gay relations in our society are normal and should be tolerated, while ignoring these same examples when considering pederasty in our society, using instead for perspective the incest model of crime and pathology. Yet almost every single textbook did exactly this. The mean measure of bias across the textbooks, using the correlation effect size, was huge ($r = 0.80$); an effect size of $r = 0.50$ is considered to be large. To put this result in laymen's terms for ease of comprehension, if we use the IQ scale, with a mean of 100 and standard deviation of 15, this effect size is equivalent to an IQ score of 60, that is, *scientifically* retarded. In terms of bias, it means, to rephrase McAnulty and Wright's expression, "blinded by politics and morality."

To illustrate this blindness, let us consider the top-ranked textbook at the time—Hyde and DeLamater (1997). In their chapter on homosexuality, providing perspective on gay sexuality between adult men in our society, in an attempt to show that it is a natural and normal phenomenon, they discussed ritualized homosexual behavior in Melanesia, which was, however, pederastic rather than gay. They quoted the anthropologist Schieffelin (1976), who observed:

> When a boy is eleven or twelve years old, he is engaged for several months in homosexual intercourse with a healthy older man chosen by his father.... Men point to the rapid growth of adolescent youths, the appearance of peach fuzz beards, and so on, as the favorable results of this child-rearing practice. (p. 124)

Hyde and DeLamater commented that we would surely term this behavior *homosexual* and added that it "is fortunate that anthropologists were able to make their observations over the last several decades to document these interesting and meaningful practices before they disappear" (p. 397). In a later chapter, when discussing pederastic relations in our society, they did not cite this cross-cultural example or any other one. Their language switched from *homosexual* to use of terms such as *child sexual abuse, victims,* and *perpetrators*. They no longer characterized these practices as "interesting and meaningful," but as intensely psychologically damaging in most cases, often leading to post-traumatic stress disorder.

This twisted approach was pervasive across the textbooks. One may be tempted to characterize it as hypocrisy. In my view, a master narrative emerged from political and ideological shifts in the 1970s, in which all adult egalitarian sexual relations became tolerated or esteemed, even if gay, and all unequal ones involving minors, including pederasty, were more vilified than ever before. This orthodoxy overwhelmed many textbook authors' logic and objectivity so completely that they comfortably and unconsciously committed their blatant errors. Though these authors presumed to be presenting valid science, deeper down they were simply rationalizing hegemonic ideals. They were blinded by politics and morality, as were many of the critics of the 1998 meta-analysis. It is this kind of blindness, not the one McAnulty and Wright attribute to me, that has plagued sexological science (Foucault, 1978; Kinsey, Pomeroy, & Martin, 1948; Szasz, 1990). The extremity of this bias evident with respect to pederasty indicates the need for an article such as mine, notwithstanding McAnulty and Wright's disapproval.

McAnulty and Wright's Critique Answered

In my 2009 pederasty article, the one McAnulty and Wright critiqued, I presented six gay men's personal accounts to illustrate that self-realized gay teens or preteens can respond positively at the time and in retrospect to sexual interactions with older males, interactions not infrequently initiated by the youths themselves. In the current revision, I retained only one of these cases for economy (the other five appear in the appendix to this reply). McAnulty and Wright argue that my drawing scientific conclusions from these six cases was "questionable, if not irresponsible." They attack my review of two nonrandom national samples of gay men, finding it "curious" that I concluded that these studies included "representative examples." They cite Ondersma et al. (2001) and Dallam (2001) to argue that critics are justified in questioning the "motives of scientists like [me]." They begin their critique with the title "Blinded by Science" and end it asserting that any "responsible and prudent discussion of such a sensitive topic [i.e., pederasty] requires balanced coverage." In other words, they imply that, although my treatment of the issue was biased and distorting, theirs and those of clinicians like them (e.g., Dallam; Ondersma et al.) are fair and accurate. In view of my earlier discussion on the bias that pervades the field on the issue of homosexuality vis-à-vis pederasty, readers might agree that skepticism regarding their attack is in order.

Fortune and Fame in the Six Case Studies?

In regard to my use of the six case studies, it is important to quote exactly what my conclusion was in the 2009 article:

> These case studies contradict in clear fashion *universalistic* claims or views, common in the popular media and professional discourse, that pederastic relations are, by nature, acts of violence that brutalize and leave emotional scars for life, or less dramatically, are *invariably* coercive, exploitive, and negative, irrespective of the minor's reaction at the time or afterwards. (italics added) (p. 31)

Methodologically and logically, it was proper to draw precisely this scientific conclusion from a series of counterexamples to a *universalistic* claim. For this conclusion to have been incorrect (which is different from being improper), one must argue that the case histories were, contrary to the gay men's accounts, in reality violent and brutalizing, or at least coercive and negative. To imply that they *all* were, McAnulty and Wright attempt to discredit them based on several recent autobiographies that were exposed as hoaxes: Margaret Jones, who falsely claimed to have grown up as a gang member in Los Angeles; Misha Defonesca, who falsely claimed to have survived the Holocaust; and James Frey, who vastly exaggerated his account of recovering from alcohol and drugs. Attributing these and similar hoaxes to the seeking of "fortune and fame" and claiming that such motives are characteristic of autobiographies in general, they deduce that my use of the six gay men's personal accounts was "questionable, if not irresponsible."

Are the "fortune and fame" hoaxes relevant to assessing the validity of the six gay men's personal accounts? First and foremost, it is important to note that McAnulty and Wright do not analyze *any* of the six accounts directly. Instead, they try to arouse suspicion based on a different work by one of the men (Augustin Burroughs's *Running with Scissors*), as well as the alleged support of NAMBLA by another (Harry Hay). Notably, they ignore the other four accounts entirely. I discuss Burroughs later, but note here that their attack on Hay is ad hominem and evidentially irrelevant to the validity of his personal account. Similarly, one might attempt to smear Frank Kameny, the other foremost key figure in gay liberation half a century ago, by noting that he recalled fondly that his coming out on his twenty-ninth birthday occurred when he was seduced by a boy aged 17, with whom he then spent "a golden summer" (O'Bryan, 2006). But that would be use of right-wing tactics, not science.

Regarding the three hoaxes McAnulty and Wright cite, it is important to discuss some of their details, so as to assess their relevance to the six gay men's accounts. First, it is arguably the case that all three *were* motivated by fortune and fame: Defonesca and Frey both made millions of dollars from their hoaxes, and Jones was on her way to fortune before exposure. Second, all three autobiographies dealt with topics resonating with contemporary American and European readers (survival and redemption amidst overwhelming adversity). Third, the details of all three are, on sober reflection, fantastical. Defonesca claimed to have wandered across Europe at age 6 after her parents were deported in 1941, to have been sheltered by friendly packs of wolves, to have killed a German soldier in self-defense, and to have found her way home after the war. Jones claimed to have been of mixed-race (white and Native American), to have become a foster child at age 8 to a stern but loving black grandmother working two jobs, to have been dealing drugs before reaching puberty, and yet to have found tenderness and love in this environment. Frey fabricated vomit-caked years as an addict and criminal and also invented survivorship in a deadly train crash.

McAnulty and Wright present no direct evidence that any of the six gay men's personal accounts reviewed in my 2009 article (Hay, Lambert, Beck, Savage, White, Burroughs—see the appendix) emanated from the motive to seek fortune and fame. In every single case, the details in their descriptions indicate that, instead, their reminiscences reflect the universal human tendency to recall cherished events. Additionally, Hay, Savage, and Burroughs presented their stories specifically to contradict entrenched stereotypes and to caution against uncritical generalizations so common in reference to pederasty. Burroughs's account of his interaction with the priest, for example, illustrated that priests, like laymen, are vulnerable to the force of sudden, unanticipated sexual opportunities, and that characterizing all "pedophile priests" as calculating predators is overly simplistic. Rather than casting a "negative light on the priesthood," as McAnulty and Wright claim, arguably Burroughs's account is better understood as shedding light on human nature and weakness, to which priests are not immune. In short, none of the boyhood pederastic accounts by the six gay men formed the foundation for multimillion-dollar book contracts, let alone even modest monetary payoffs. McAnulty and Wright ignore this consideration, but it is centrally relevant to their attempt to cast blanket suspicion on the six case studies.

Additionally, unlike the tales of struggle and redemption in the gangbanger, Holocaust, and drug recovery hoaxes, personal accounts of positive boyhood sexual experiences with adult men decidedly do *not* resonate with contemporary Western readers. Quite the contrary, such anecdotes are highly unwelcome and invite dismissal, personal attack, and social opprobrium. In my 2009 article, I noted journalist David Tuller's (2002) worries concerning writing about his own and other gay men's positive boyhood pederastic desires and experiences, and I discussed philosopher Jeremy Bentham's fear of publishing his writings on pederasty. The chapters in this volume by Mader and Hekma and Yuill reinforce these points.

Mader and Hekma note that biographical, autobiographical, and literary sources that are reworkings of autobiographical fact have become largely taboo in the gay community as a result of many writers' positive or mixed accounts of boyhood sexual experiences with men. As Mader and Hekma later argue, the gay movement became increasingly self-censoring in publishing personal stories for political reasons: after having made political gains in the 1970s, gays came under attack by homophobes like Anita Bryant, who used pederastic relations with boys to try to scandalize gays; so, to hold on to political gains, the gay movement had to join "the child protection clamor," which necessarily entailed discouraging or suppressing discussion of the common experience of positive pederasty in this population. Yuill notes that when one of his interviewees (Philip, a man in his 40s), who had had positive pederastic experiences as a gay boy, attempted to rebut a victimologist on the radio, he was abruptly cut off and characterized as having distorted thinking as a result of having been manipulated. Moreover, Yuill documents eight cases of academics pummeled for attempting to discuss adult-minor sex outside the dominant discourse of victimology. For years while completing his dissertation on pederasty, Yuill himself was hounded by the British gutter press and certainly did not achieve the fortune and fame that McAnulty and Wright imagine motivates non-victimological autobiography and writing on this subject. Finally, it is fitting to add that, in the aftermath of the censorship of the 2005 version of my pederasty article (i.e., Rind, 2005), I was attacked within my department at Temple University as conducting research "beyond the pale," and courses that I had taught previously were taken away from me (e.g., a scheduled course in meta-analysis was canceled, lest I "corrupt" the graduate students taking it). More realistic than discussing one's own or others' positive pederastic experiences as a means to acquiring "fortune and fame" is to characterize it as risking penury and infamy.

McAnulty and Wright's three examples of autobiographical hoaxes are all fantastical in their details, details that strained credulity to such a degree that all three accounts, even though initially embraced for their inspiring, uplifting tales, ultimately fell to sober reappraisal. McAnulty and Wright attempt to cast suspicion on the pederastic accounts of the six gay men in my 2009 article by noting that another work by Burroughs (his memoir *Running with Scissors*) had fabrications. This, however, is a straw man argument, because it does not concern his priest anecdote, the one that appeared in my previous article, which was written not to rake in fortunes, as his memoir may have been, but to give a counterexample to the exploding hysteria in the pedophile priest scandal. The central issue that McAnulty and Wright should have addressed is whether the details in the six personal accounts have the quality of being fantastical, as in the autobiographical hoaxes; they neglected to do such an analysis. For example, what in the six accounts corresponds to having been sheltered by friendly packs of wolves? Unlike this patently absurd claim by Defonesca, along with her other tall tales of Holocaust survival, one of my six accounts involved Gad Beck, a half-Jew in Berlin during the Nazi era, who actually did survive the Holocaust—and narrowly. His recounting of his initiating sex at age 12 with a man, with lifelong cherished memories of the event, was a sidenote in his memoir (see the appendix), clearly not included to increase sales of his book.

Arguably, the validity of the six case studies is indicated by their coherence as well as their consistency with gay men's personal stories in other sources reviewed in my 2009 article and elsewhere. For example, in my summary of Savin-Williams's well-conducted study (Rind, 2001, citing Savin-Williams, 1997), which I discussed in my 2009 article, I provided an appendix with fairly detailed descriptions of the pederastic relations of the twenty-six gay men in his study who had them. McAnulty and

Wright ignore this report in finding against the credibility of the six case studies, but readers can cross-reference and decide for themselves. Additional examples showing this consistency include Yuill's case study (Philip) in Chapter 3 and Mader and Hekma's essay, in which they present six more examples from the Netherlands of gay writers' autobiographies of positive age-gap boyhood homosexual experiences.

"Representative Examples" in Jay & Young (1977), Spada (1979)

McAnulty and Wright next attempt to show that the research studies I included, showing frequent positive reactions to pederastic experiences among gay men, are similarly untrustworthy. To do this, they focus on two older studies (Jay & Young, 1977; Spada, 1979), while ignoring the more recent ones (e.g., the well-conducted 1997 Savin-Williams study that I summarized in 2001, which had essentially the same results as the two studies they disputed). They complain:

> According to Rind, both reports include "representative examples" of adult-minor sex that is a positive experience for the younger person. However, Rind failed to mention any of the profound methodological problems with both surveys.

Regarding the first point on "representative examples," they note that Jay and Young (1977) themselves did not claim to have had a scientific or representative sample of lesbians and gay men. In consequence, McAnulty and Wright then write that they found it "curious" that I concluded that it did provide "representative examples of childhood and adolescent male homosexual experiences with both peers and older males." In their selective quotes, however, McAnulty and Wright misrepresent what I wrote, what I intended, and what is clear in the text and from the context.

To begin with, in the text, after introducing both studies, I wrote that "neither sample can be taken as nationally representative, but each is far more diverse and generalizable than any clinical sample." Then, and most central to McAnulty and Wright's misrepresentation, I wrote:

> Spada presented a subset of 52 descriptions from his respondents of their first meaningful sexual experiences, which *he* described as *representative* of the entire set of descriptions (italics added). (p. 35)

Simply put, I presented these fifty-two examples as representative of Spada's set of examples, not the population of gay men's pederastic experiences, as McAnulty and Wright allege. At the very beginning of the next paragraph, I turned to the second study, writing that "Jay and Young (1977) *also* presented representative examples" (italics added) (p. 36), which clearly continues the theme from the previous paragraph. That is, "representative examples" here clearly means examples that are representative of Jay and Young's set of examples. McAnulty and Wright put much weight on this issue in an attempt to demonstrate that I exhibited the very same bias (i.e., inappropriate generalization) that I attributed to clinicians in my 2009 article and other writings. But the full text and its context instead show misrepresentation on their part, not bias on mine.

They further accuse me of failing to mention any of the "profound methodological problems" with both surveys. First, let us review how the survey authors themselves justified their studies. In the 2009 version, I summarized their rationale:

> [B]oth Spada (1979) and Jay and Young (1977) complained that psychiatrists had created and sustained unwarranted stereotypes about gay people through use of anomalous clinical samples, and they both asserted that their studies were designed to correct for this bias by sampling a diverse group of gay people in the general population. (p. 34)

In other words, these researchers were never presuming to characterize the entire gay population. Instead, they were attempting to *un-characterize* a distortion of it by disassociating the whole from the anomalous part, whose association was the doing of clinicians. Given that clinicians had constructed their stereotypes of psycholopathology for all gay people by reliance on just the disturbed ones in treatment, Spada (1979) and Jay and Young (1977) correctly argued that surveying widely diverse samples outside the clinicians' orbit, regardless of representativeness, could only ameliorate the problem. The merits of their studies, then, done as they were in a time of harmful clinical hegemony, have to be judged in that context—as studies that improved knowledge about homosexuality, by expanding considerably the database, rather than as studies that failed to represent adequately the behavior and interests of the entire gay population. In short, McAnulty and Wright's complaint of "profound methodological problems" is misapplied, given that the goals of the two surveys were modest and adequately achieved.

In order to back their claim of profound methodological problems, it is important to add, they cite the criticisms of Burroway (2006) and Lauritsen (1979). Burroway described the Jay and Young survey as "statistically worthless," and Lauritsen called it "hopelessly inept." Additionally, McAnulty and Wright cite Lauritsen to argue that the scientific value of the Spada survey was seriously compromised by its data tables, which Lauritsen described as "shockingly bad" and "meaningless." First, neither of these commentaries was a peer-reviewed critique published in a scientific outlet (McAnulty and Wright simply retrieved them from the Internet). Second, both commentators were gay advocates, who were openly concerned to advance the gay agenda by distancing gays from politically embarrassing matters. Burroway wrote that "it's no wonder" that the Jay and Young book "has become a favorite resource for anti-gay activists," noting that the authors' report was cited by the ultra-right-wing Family Research Council as "showing that 73 percent of homosexuals surveyed had at some time had sex with boys sixteen to nineteen years of age or younger." Burroway wrote of "how potentially damaging to the gay liberation cause is the data presented in the study," with its reports not only of underage sex but of "gross promiscuity" (e.g., 35 percent had sex with 100 or more partners). Burroway criticized Jay and Young for publishing these "admissions," a criticism that is anachronistic. When we go back and read Jay and Young's rationale in their introduction, we see the context of the times; the respondents' responses were more "replies" than "admissions." It was a time when, as Jay and Young noted, gays were still disdained and continually subjected to "society's dehumanizing, biased, and yes, ignorant questions" (p. 1) about their sexual behavior, and they were too often kept in the dark themselves about their form of sexuality in a society that had isolated them and suppressed relevant sexual knowledge. They asserted that their survey was constructed to redress these problems. Though they noted the importance of going beyond sex to describe other aspects of gays and lesbians, they emphasized that this did not mean going *against* sex. To the contrary, they embraced sex as a positive good, even non-relational sex; this sentiment was in line with the times, though not before or since (Levine & Troiden, 1988). Specifically, they rebuked the idea of sanitizing their survey to appease those who would trade truth for comfort or political advantage:

> As compilers, we have resisted the temptation to present the well-scrubbed homosexual man and woman, hollow figures who are exactly like heterosexuals except for sexual proclivities. This image often makes certain "liberal" heterosexuals comfortable, or it fits the needs of some political ideology or movement rhetoric, but it serves to ignore diversity and cover up the life experiences that very often make gay people "different" indeed. (p. 5)

Lauritsen (1979) remarked: "I cannot feel that our cause is advanced by such seriously flawed 'research.'" He worked hard to show that the surveys are not representative of the gay population, but this criticism misses the point, as discussed above. He attacked the statistical tables as "shockingly bad" and "meaningless," which McAnulty and Wright seized upon. But I, as a researcher, statistician, and methodologist, found the tables quite useful and adequate for the modest goals of the surveys—and on par with those presented in many other studies on this topic. When McAnulty and Wright complain that I "did not mention any of these methodological limitations, contending instead that these surveys were devised in order to correct the misconceptions about pederasty derived from 'anomalous clinical samples,'" (p. 142 in this volume) it should first be noted that they err in specifying "pederasty" in place of "homosexuality." More importantly, it should be noted that they fail to inform us of the crucial fact that the methodological criticisms were authored not by scientists but gay advocates, openly and specifically concerned with deflecting what is embarrassing for the gay movement, even if it means unfairly trashing important evidence.

The Hooker (1957) study discussed in the main article on pederasty in this volume is relevant here owing to several key parallels. At a time when all homosexuals were thought to be maladjusted by mainstream clinicians, who drew upon clinical cases, Hooker examined the psychological adjustment of a sample of homosexuals, who were not in treatment and therefore not disturbed by definition. She found that they were as well adjusted as a matched sample of heterosexuals. She emphasized that the highly selected nature of her subjects was not a problem, because her goal was to test the universal claim of psychopathology. Later, her study came under attack by right-wing critics, who believed that her study facilitated gay liberation, which they abhorred. These critics ignored the logic behind her study, focusing instead on side issues to try to discredit it. In one attack, Landass (n.d.), a non-scientist advocate writing for the Family Research Council, argued that the study was flawed and untrustworthy because it contained errors such as: (a) in the text Hooker wrote that her subjects' IQs ranged from 90 to 135, but in a table the lowest IQ was 91; (b) Hooker wrote in the text that the average education of her homosexual sample was 13.9 years, but this number appeared as 14.0 in a table. In my 2009 article on pederasty, the six nonclinical anecdotes served to undermine the universal claim of trauma and harm—a claim largely constructed by clinicians drawing upon clinical cases. The empirical studies, including Spada (1979) with his tables, added to the anecdotes by substantially broadening the nonclinical database. These approaches achieved their goal: to provide a more realistic picture of the gay youth's pederastic experience than that offered by clinicians. So, to attack this method by ignoring its logic, distracting us with irrelevant hoaxes, confusing "representative examples" within a study with "representative samples" within a population, and caviling about tables is as scientifically specious as the attacks on Hooker's study.

INCEST MODEL IS WRONG FOR THE GAY EXPERIENCE

Contrary to McAnulty and Wright's charge of my being unbalanced by excluding clinical examples, I examined some such cases from Myers's (1989) report, detailing the extent of abuse and traumatic reaction that can occur. I stipulated that clinical reports do provide genuine cases of negative response. Notably, *never* do victimologists discuss positive cases as genuine: these are always rationalized to be cognitive distortions. My point was that clinical cases do not generalize, especially in the gay population, so focus on nonclinical research is called for.

From the 1970s onward, sexual victimologists have used the incest model of power exploitation and trauma involving very young girls to characterize all adult-minor sex, no matter how different. The gay experience *is* different, as so much empirical and anecdotal evidence indicates, and as critics of the incest model have repeatedly noted. The producer of a CBC radio series (*IDEAS*, 1999), documenting the sensationalistic media, political, and professional attacks on gay youths' sexual relations with men in one Canadian city in the earlier 1990s, summed it up this way:

> [T]he modern and useful feminist analysis of the reasons young women suffer in horrible incest cases—that analysis has been inappropriately used in an attempt to understand an entirely different set of circumstances. A blurring of motives and psychological effects has taken place, which has created a powerful and misleading narrative that produces neither justice nor happiness.

To highlight the radically different experience of many young gay males vis-à-vis adult men compared with that of young daughters vis-à-vis their fathers, I elaborate next on one of the references in the main article in this volume on pederasty. Trachtenberg (2005) compiled coming-of-age stories from named American contributors, typically notables. All contributors discussed the period when they first realized their homosexual attractions or nature. Of the twenty male contributors who specifically discussed awareness of emerging erotic desire (as opposed to other aspects of homosexual nature—e.g., being different, having effeminate tastes), this desire was focused on adult men in eighteen cases (90 percent). In fifteen of these eighteen cases, the age at which this age-gap desire emerged was provided or could be determined: the mean age was 9.73 ($SD = 2.81$). For example, movie star makeup artist Jeff Judd remembered watching Tarzan on TV at age seven: "I kept sliding closer to the TV, sort of looking under it, trying to see under Tarzan's loincloth" (p. 20). Television writer Jon Kinnally recalled: "As a kid, I became obsessed with the man on the Doan's Pills Box. His back was so sexy. When my mom's supply ran out and she threw the box away, I went to the drug store and stole another" (p. 32). Fashion designer John Bartlett recalled: "I knew at seven. My favorite pastime was shutting my eyes during *The Dating Game* and listening to the guys' voices to see if my pick would match that of the female contestant" (p. 58). Award-winning designer, theater and opera director, and accomplished painter Eugenio Zanetti recalled at age 11 seeing the Marlon Brando movie *Sayonara*: "when Brando leaned over to kiss Miyoshi Umeki, I realized that I was leaning over in my seat at the exact same angle Miyoshi was to receive Brando's kiss" (p. 83). Actor Chad Allen remembered as the "greatest job [he] had ever gotten" his role as an injured 9-year-old boy being given mouth-to-mouth resuscitation from a doctor played by a highly attractive adult male actor (Alec Baldwin) (p. 112).

These experiences are not part of the female world, and to use the latter to understand the former is procrustean. Since the publicity created by the 1998 meta-analysis, through networking and other means, I have had numerous conversations with older gay academics about their boyhood sexual milestones. The details differ, but the predominant recollections are of erotic desires for older males, attempts or wishes to be sexual with them, and positive reactions when such contacts occurred. In the present environment, with the omnipresent message that such relations are unspeakable acts of violence and abuse, and in which the generations are separated as at no time before in human history, I do not doubt that this pattern will present itself as substantially more negative for gay youths growing up during these times. But that is a cultural artifact. For gay men growing up before feminists and victimologists problematized these relations beyond any other childhood experience, the pattern was predominantly positive. I close this section with a didactic illustration, didactic because it is the story of one of the preeminent gay clinicians of the twentieth century in light of his significant, top-selling 1975 book, *The Homosexual Matrix*, at a crucial time during the gay liberation movement. It illustrates that clinicians need not adhere to the trauma and harm dogma, but can see the other side.

C. A. Tripp (1919–2003) was a gay clinician, scholar, sexologist, and expert on the Kinsey data (he began his career in sexology working for Kinsey and his own story is part of the Kinsey archives, because he was one of the thousand or so gay men interviewed). Because of my meta-analysis, Tripp became interested in communicating with me, and in the end, I visited him a dozen times. Regarding CSA's supposed impact, he asked critically during one of my trips, "What is the mechanism?" noting that victimologists have never provided one that is scientifically credible. He then discussed in detail his own childhood to rebut the CSA perspective anecdotally. When he was 5 years old, growing up in Oklahoma, one day his mother called a repairman to go under the house, which was raised up on stilts, to fix a leak. Tripp followed the man, whom he later referred to as Gandhi (his "liberator"), and could see his penis through a crack in his pants. Within one minute, Tripp reported, he "seduced" the man, performing oral sex on him "before he knew it." How did a 5-year-old know to do this? He answered that it emerged out of nowhere but just felt right; he had no prior sexual experience or knowledge. The man began pushing the boy away, but with "curiosity," in Tripp's perception, so the boy did not believe the rebuff and continued the sex act. He remembered that the man was "floored," but reported that he himself "loved it all." When he was a bit older, Tripp recalled sitting on the lap of several uncles, intentionally giving them erections without their seeming to know by just moving around. He said he would jump on their laps, asking them to teach him to read, for example, adding that "it was all subterfuge, a trick to get on their lap." He said he was always "on the prowl" during his boyhood, though he had little success. For example, he said he arranged it so that he could on many occasions ride in the wagon of a local iceman, a 25-year-old whom he found attractive because he was "very muscular." Nothing happened, he said, because he did not know quite how to seduce him. But he added that what he should have done was to have arranged to go home with him, upon which "his virginity would not have been safe."

These stories are a real and an important part of gay history and of the corpus of data on adult-minor sexual relations. It is not being "blinded by science" to consider them, discuss them, and use them to reevaluate and challenge hegemonic views of intrinsic abuse and trauma. It is the suppression of these stories, because they are politically inconvenient, or the rejection of them as unbelievable boasting or cognitive distortion when they are told, that is the real blindness, the blindness that allegiance to morality and political advantage can too easily produce.

NOTE

1. This is the message of several popular songs using this expression in their title.

REFERENCES

Andriette, B. (2002, December). Remembering Harry Hay. *The Guide*. Retrieved from: http://archive.guidemag.com/magcontent/invokemagcontent.cfm?ID=04B2069A-9937-4D06-8F9501675FA48931

Beck, G. (1999). *An underground life: The memoirs of a gay Jew in Nazi Berlin*. Madison, WI: The University of Wisconsin Press.

Burroughs, A. (2002a). *Running with scissors*. New York: NYU Press.

Burroughs, A. (2002b). A priest on his knees. Retrieved from: http://www.salon.com/sex/feature/2002/05/15/holy/index1.html

Burroway, J. (2006). The gay report. *Box Turtle Bulletin*. Retrieved from: http://www.boxturtlebulletin.com/Articles/000,005.htm

Carpenter, E. (1908). *The intermediate sex: A study of some transitional types of men and women*. New York: Mitchell Kennerley.

Dallam, S. J. (2001). Science or propaganda? An examination of Rind, Tromovitch, and Bauserman (1998). *Journal of Child Sexual Abuse, 9*, 109–134.

Foucault, M. (1978). *History of sexuality: Vol. 1. An introduction*. New York: Pantheon.

Hooker, E. (1957). The adjustment of the male overt homosexual. *Journal of Projective Techniques, 21*, 18–31. Hyde, J. S., & DeLamater, J. (1997). *Understanding human sexuality* (6th ed.). New York: McGraw-Hill.

IDEAS. (1999). *Victims of justice. Parts 1 and 2*. First broadcast May 13 and 14, 1999, on the CBC. (Audio file available at http://www.radio.cbc.ca/programs/ideas)

Jay, K., & Young, A. (1977). *The gay report*. New York: Simon and Schuster.

Kinsey, A., Pomeroy, W. B., & Martin. C. E. (1948). *Sexual behavior in the human male*. Philadelphia: W. B. Saunders.

Landass, T. (n.d.). The Evelyn Hooker study on the normalization of homosexuality. Retrieved from: http://www.frc.org/insight/is95elhs.html

Lauritsen, J. (1979). Reviews: The Gay Report by Karla Jay and Allen Young & the Spada Report by James Spada. Retrieved from http://www.williamapercy.com/wiki/index.php/Reviews:The_Gay_Report_by_Karla_Jay_and_Allen_Young_&_The_Spada_Report_by_James_Spada

Levine, M. P., & Troiden, R. R. (1988). The myth of sexual compulsivity. *The Journal of Sex Research, 25*, 347–363.

Myers, M. F. (1989). Men sexually assaulted as adults and sexually abused as boys. *Archives of Sexual Behavior, 18*, 203–215.

O'Bryan, W. (2006, Oct. 5). Gay is good: How Frank Kameny changed the face of America. Retrieved from: http://www.metroweekly.com/feature/?ak=2341

Ondersma, S. J., Chaffin, M., Berliner, L, Cordon, I., Goodman, G., & Barnett, D. (2001). Sex with children is abuse: The Rind et al. meta-analysis controversy. *Psychological Bulletin, 27,* 707–714.

Rapp, L. (2006). "Savage, Dan (b. 1964)". *glbtq: An Encyclopedia of Gay, Lesbian, Bisexual, Transgender, and Queer Culture.* Retrieved from: http://www.glbtq.com/literature/savage_d.html

Rind, B. (1998). Biased use of cross-cultural and historical perspectives on male homosexuality in human sexuality textbooks. *The Journal of Sex Research. 35*(4), 397–407.

Rind, B. (2001). Gay and bisexual adolescent boys' sexual experiences with men: An empirical examination of psychological correlates in a nonclinical sample. *Archives of Sexual Behavior, 30,* 345–368.

Rind, B. (2005). Pederasty: An integration of cross-cultural, cross-species, and empirical data. Unpublished manuscript.

Rind, B. (2009). Pederasty: An integration of empirical, historical, sociological, cross-cultural, cross-species, and evolutionary approaches. Unpublished manuscript.

Rind, B., Tromovitch, P., & Bauserman, R. (1998). A meta-analytic examination of assumed properties of child sexual abuse using college samples. *Psychological Bulletin, 124,* 22–53.

Savin-Williams, R. (1997). *"... And then I became gay: Young men's stories.* New York: Routledge.

Schieffelin, E. L. (1976). *The sorrow of the lonely and the burning of the dancers.* New York: St. Martin's Press.

Spada, J. (1979). *The Spada report.* New York: Signet.

Szasz, T. (1990). *Sex by prescription: The startling truth about today's sex therapy.* New York: Syracuse University Press.

Timmons, S. (1990). *The trouble with Harry Hay: Founder of the modern gay movement.* Boston, MA: Alyson Publications.

Trachtenberg, R. (2005). *When I Knew.* New York: HarperEntertainment.Tuller, D. (2002). Minor report: Sex between teenage boys and older men is not always coercive—and it can be more ecstatic than traumatic. Retrieved from http://www.sa-lon.com/mwt/feature/2002/07/22/coming_of_age/print.html

White, E. (2006). *My lives: An autobiography.* New York: HarperCollins.

Woodland, R. (2002). "White, Edmund," in *glbtq: An Encyclopedia of Gay, Lesbian, Bisexual, Transgender, and Queer Culture.* Retrieved from: http://www.glbtq.com/literature/white_e.html

APPENDIX: GAY BOYS' PEDERASTIC EXPERIENCES—SIX CASE STUDIES

Case 1

Harry Hay (1912–2002) is known as the father of gay liberation; he founded the Mattachine Society in 1951, which was the forerunner of today's gay movement (Timmons, 1990). In growing up, his father often inflicted severe punishments on him, including ear-boxings so frequent that Hay sustained permanent hearing loss in one ear. When he was older, Hay came to believe that his father's harshness was attributable to the father's realization that, in his son, he had spawned "a big sissy" (Timmons, 1990, p. 20). At age 11, he manipulated a librarian into leaving her post so that he could peak at a locked-away book, in which he expected to find pictures of naked men. The book, *The Intermediate Sex* by Edward Carpenter (1908), had no naked pictures, but did contain the word *homosexual*. Hay recounted this event, commenting that, "As soon as I saw it, I knew it was me. So I wasn't the only one of my kind in the whole world after all" (Timmons, 1990, p. 28).

At age 14, Hay met a merchant-seaman of about age 25. One evening, when the two walked alongside the moonlit ocean, Hay was swept up by the physical sensations. When Hay clasped the man's hand, the boy was afraid the sailor might respond violently. Instead, it turned into Hay's first lovemaking with an adult. When Hay revealed that he was only 14, the sailor panicked for fear of a lengthy prison sentence. Hay desperately tried to settle the man down, and when he did, the man gave the boy tips on how "people like us" should conduct themselves, which "inspired Harry almost as vividly as the erotic memory of [the man]" (Timmons, 1990, p. 36). This coming-of-age story was a favorite of Hay, which he repeatedly retold to audiences in later years and referred to ironically as his "child molestation speech," in order to emphasize how sharply different gay life is from heterosexual norms. On this point, his biographer Timmons (1990) elaborated:

> "As a child," [Hay] explained, "I molested an adult until I found out what I needed to know." He recalled that [the man's] promise of a new world and a future served as a life raft during the isolated period of high school. Far from being an experience of "molestation," Harry always described it as "the most beautiful gift that a fourteen-year-old ever got from his first love!" (p. 36)

Andriette (2002) summarized Hay's remarks from one of his "child molestation speeches," delivered nearly sixty years after this event. Hay recalled that this man was the first one he felt he could trust deeply and be trusted deeply by in return. Hay remarked, "Wherever he is, I want him to know that my love and gratitude followed him all my days, and all of his."

Case 2 (Gavin Lambert—see main article on pederasty in this volume)

Case 3

Gad Beck (1923–2012) recounted in his autobiography (Beck, 1999) how he perilously survived living as a half-Jew and homosexual in Berlin during the Nazi era, while many of his full-Jewish friends, some of whom were lovers, were arrested and sent off to death camps, and a number of his gentile homosexual friends were tortured and mutilated by the SS and Gestapo. He himself narrowly escaped torture and execution after being arrested by the Gestapo. After the war, he devoted himself to Jewish causes, first in Israel and then back in Berlin.

Beck (1999) recounted how his homoerotic hopes and experiences helped to partially counterbalance the chaos and terror produced by the Nazis. He related with delight his first homosexual encounter, which occurred soon after Nazi bigotry and policy began to impact him directly. This encounter was with his 22-year-old gym teacher when he was 12.

One day he and the teacher were the last two in the showers. Beck recalled that he "was overcome with unrestrained desire" (p. 22), walked over to the man while still naked, and snuggled into the bathrobe that the man had just put on. He embraced the man and noticed that the man was also aroused. Beck recalled that he "relished the feeling." They caressed and rubbed against each other and both orgasmed. Beck commented that the "nicest thing for me was that he reciprocated the affection by putting his arms around my shoulders. I had taken him by surprise, but when it happened, he wanted it too, there was no doubt about it." Beck then "ran home beaming with delight," breathlessly and naively telling his mother—his mother's reaction, surprising in retrospect, was, "Aha, I thought so [that young Beck was gay]." Beck commented that he "never had any feeling that it was wrong to accost my teacher in the shower. It happened spontaneously" (p. 22). Beck tried to initiate contact again when he was alone with the teacher, who was once again aroused, but did not permit it to go any further. Beck's overall reaction to the experience was: "He had done something for me. And I have never forgotten the happiness of that first encounter" (p. 23).

Case 4

Dan Savage (b. 1964) is best known for his nationally syndicated sex-advice column *Savage Love*; he has also authored books dealing with same-sex marriage and gay adoption (Rapp, 2006). In 1999, when the Rind et al. (1998) meta-analysis was being attacked by religious conservatives, victimologists, politicians, and talk show hosts, Savage commented on this affair in his nationally syndicated sex-advice column published in alternative newspapers, discussing his own boyhood sexual experiences (*Savage love,* July 29, 1999):

> Why is this controversial? Speaking as a survivor of CSA at fourteen with a twenty-two-year-old woman; sex at fifteen with a thirty-year-old man—I can back the researchers up; I was not traumatized by these technically illegal sexual encounters; indeed, I initiated them and cherish their memory. It's absurd to think that what I did at fifteen would be considered "child sexual abuse," or lumped together by lazy researchers with the incestuous rape of a five-year-old girl.

Case 5

Edmund White (b. 1940) is one of the most prominent writers in contemporary gay literature, both fiction and nonfiction (Woodland, 2002). White discussed some of his boyhood sexual experiences in an interview with journalist David Tuller (2002). Tuller noted how White recounted "with relish how he started cruising grown men from the age of 13 or 14 at beaches and public toilets in Chicago." Tuller quoted White:

"I was very oversexed, absolutely driven by wild desire. I would pick up men, and then they would abandon me as quickly as possible because they were worried that I was jail bait. The first one was a handsome architect, who actually had children older than me. I was absolutely fascinated by him, and I seduced him. I followed him to his car, walked right up to him and started talking with him. My mother was away and I said, 'Come back to my apartment.' And it was terrific."

In his autobiography, White (2006) added details to his teenage pursuit of men. While still underage, he would save up money by working during the week and then use it to buy the sexual services of adult men on the weekends.

Case 6

Augusten Burroughs (b. 1965) is a best-selling American author. His first book, a memoir entitled *Running with Scissors* (2002a), was a number one top seller for months and was later made into a movie. Shortly after the Catholic Church sex scandal involving priests sexually involved with boys began, Burroughs (2002b) retold his own involvement with priests to add some nuance to the invariant black-and-white presentations in the media. Burroughs noted that "Catholic priests have given me some of the best blow jobs of my life." The first was when he was 14 years old. Though his mother was not Catholic, nor even particularly religious, she frequented a Catholic church on Sundays for the symbolism, and young Augusten occasionally accompanied her. He would spend his time walking around the offices rather than attending the services. Often on his explorations he would pass by a priest, on whom he had a crush "because he was young and almost hunky." Eventually in the priest he could discern a hunger to match his own. At one point, Augusten passed the priest in the hallway and then walked into the men's room for the sole purpose of peeing. Then the priest walked in—Augusten thought the priest entered to scold him about some bad conduct. Instead the priest walked up to the urinal next to him and began staring at Augusten's penis in an absorbed, transfixed manner. For Burroughs, the unfolding situation was sudden and unexpected, but not unwanted. As Burroughs commented, he himself felt horny, so he dropped his pants and stepped away from the urinal, facing the man—and getting what turned out to be his "first excellent blow job from a Catholic priest."

The priest then began sobbing—he was fearful that his transgression would become known. Augusten, though, assured him he would never tell, and he never did tell anyone. He commented that he felt terrible—not for the sex, but for the priest's reaction. But for the sex itself, Burroughs provided the following analogy to convey his feelings: "He was a hunky young guy in the wrong career who got my rocks off. For a straight guy, it would be like being 14 and having one of the centerfolds from

Playboy step out of the magazine and hand you a bottle of mineral oil." Burroughs ended by noting that his own very positive experience with a priest was likely to be quite different from that of other boys, especially good Catholic ones, because he was not a virgin, and he was not Catholic. To Burroughs's qualification regarding other boys' sexual involvements with priests, it can be added that Burroughs had homoerotic desires at the time and was not under the authority of the priest.

Index

Adam Walsh Child Protection and Safety Act, 239–241, 257, 262, 266, 270
Alcoff, L., 130–131
Alger, J.R. *See* Coleman, A.L.
Angelides, S., xx, 40, 76

Bagemihl, B., 5, 42, 43, 50, 56–57, 59–60, 146–147, 153–154
Baurmann, M.C., 16
Bauserman, Robert. *See* Rind et al.
Beach, F. *See* Ford, C.
Bourdieu, Pierre, 92
Bullough, V.L., 3, 4,5, 17
Burroughs, Augusten, 140–141, 284, 285, 296–297

Clancy, Susan, xxi
Coleman, A.L. and Alger, J.R., 103–104
Crapo, R.H., 37–38
censorship
  in America vs. Canada, 97–98
  of pederasty scholarship, xxiii–xxvi, 1–2, 94–96, 193–195
  politics of, 91–93
  vs. "more speech," 102–105
child sexual abuse (CSA), xviii–xix, xxi–xxii, 110–113, 127–134, 216–219, 221, 280
consent, age of, vii–viii, 94, 179–180, 193, 198–200, 210–222, 235, 273–274
cross-species comparisons
  antelope, 50
  birds, 55–58
  bison, 54
  baboon, gelada, 47
    hamadryas, 47, 48, 49
    savanna, 49
  bonobo, 12, 47, 48, 49, 204
  dolphin, bottlenose, 50
  cat (feral), 54

  cavy, 54
  chimpanzee, 12, 204
  cock-of-the-rocks, Guinan, 55
  deer, 50
  elk, 50, 54
  elephant, 54
  gazelle, 50, 54
  gibbon, 43, 49
  giraffe, 54
  goat, mountain, 54
  gorilla, 47, 48, 49
  langur, Hanuman, 48
    Nilgiri, 49
  lyrebird, superb, 55
  macaque, bonnet, 48
    Japanese, 48
    pig-tailed, 48, 49
    rhesus, 43, 47, 48, 49
    stumptail, 47, 48, 49
    Tibetan, 43, 47, 49
  manatee, 50
  mona monkey, 48
  moose, 50
  seal, northern elephant, 50
  sheep, 54
  orangutan, 47
  sea lion, 50
  siamang, 47
  monkey, squirrel, 47
  walrus, 50
  whale, orca, 50, 51

de Waal, F.B.M., 44, 150–151

Enlightenment, The, 39, 133
Evans, D., 128

feminism, 39–41, 198–201, 206–207
Finkelhor, D., 9, 110
Ford, C. and Beach, F., 3, 4, 5, 17, 39, 42, 58, 59

Forouzan, E. and Van Gijseghem, H., 97
Foucault, Michael, 3–4, 39, 107–110, 133
Freeman, Gordon, 99–101, 102, 104

Gat, A., 2, 34–35, 64–65
Gilmore, D., 65–66
Goode, Sarah, xxi–xxii
Greece, Ancient, 8, 22, 28, 30, 32–33, 35–36, 197, 206

homosexuality, adult, 154–155, 161–163, 181–187
Hooker, Evelyn, 4–5, 289
Hutchinson, G.E., 59

Jay, Karla and Young, Allan, 14–15, 141–142, 286–288

Kincaid, James, xix–xx, 120–121, 127–128, 129
Kinsey, Alfred, viii–x, 3–5, 12, 78, 154, 236
Kirkpatrick, R.C., 61–62, 71, 155
Kohut, Heinz, 19–20

Lambert, Gavin, 17–19, 20
Levine, Judith, 122–123
Li, Chin-Keung, 121
Lilienfeld, Scott, 96, 104

Mackey, W.C., 62–64, 67, 147–148
McAnulty, Richard and Wright, Lester, 279–292
Melanesia, 21, 34–36, 66, 207, 281
mentorship, 32–35, 37–38, 61–62, 171, 182, 206
Mentorship-Bonding/Enculturation-Alliance Hypothesis, 62–72, 152–155
Mirkin, Harris, 123–125
Murray, S.O., 21, 37–38
Muscarella, F., 61, 154–155

Neill, J., 62, 67
New Guinea, 25, 34, 65, 204–205

pathology, 3–9, 20, 49, 55, 74, 76, 97, 196–197
Paglia, Camille, 40
pederasty
  as evolutionary adaptation, 58–72, 151–155, 201–208

case studies of, 17–20, 112–119, 120–127, 293–297
censorship of scholarship. *See* censorship
clinical approach to, 4,7
cross-cultural examination of, 21–30
definition of, 7–9
historical studies of, 163–173
homosexuality, relation to. *See* homosexuality
in material culture, 176–181
in other species. *See* cross-species comparisons
in poetry, 173–175
in premodern Japan, 33–34, 35
modern western attitudes toward, 39–41, 198–201
pedophilia, vii, x, 9, 15, 17, 41
phylogeny, 58–60, 148–149
Plato, 19, 33

Rind, Bruce, vii, xxiii–xxviii, 13, 107, 122, 139–143, 145–158, 161–163, 181–185, 193–197, 201–208, 215–218
Rind et al. (Rind, B., Bauserman, R. and Tromovitch, P.), xxii–xxiii, 77–78, 94–96, 97–98, 102, 104–105, 118–120, 122, 280
Rome, Ancient, 28, 197–198, 206
Rushton, J. Philippe, 98–99, 102

Saikaku, 33
Sandfort, T.G.M., 16
Savin-Williams, R.C., 13, 285–286
Schlessinger, Laura, xxiii, 94, 96, 102, 122, 123, 129
Schmitt, Carl, 252, 259
sex offenders, adult
  civil commitment of, 255, 266–267, 269–271
  sentencing of, 252–256, 256–259, 271–272
  registry of, 261–269
sex offenders, juvenile, 235–247
  registry of, 237–242
  therapy treatment of, 242–247
Sikes, Pat, 126–127
Sodom and Gomorrah (biblical myth), 36–37, 273
Spada, J., 14–15, 141–143, 286–287

Tindall, R.H., 16

Trivers R.L., 58
Tromovitch, Philip. *See* Rind et al.

Van Gijseghem. *See* Forouzan, E.
Vasey, P.L., 42, 43, 44–46, 48, 155
victimology, sexual, 9–17, 29–30, 39–40, 76–78, 110–111, 133–134
von Gloeden, Baron Wilhelm, 176–181

Waites, Matthew, 119, 120, 121–122
Wakefield, J.C., 5–6

Waugh, Thomas, 178–180
Werner, D., 2–3 60–61
Williams, C.A., 28–29
Wilson, E.O., 59, 67–68
Wright, Lester. *See* McAnulty, Richard

Young, Allan. *See* Jay, Karla
Yuill, Richard, 125–126, 284–286

Zimring, Franklin, 241–242

About the Contributors

Editors

Thomas K. Hubbard is professor of classics at the University of Texas–Austin. Among his books are *Homosexuality in Greece and Rome* (University of California Press, 2003), *Greek Love Reconsidered* (Wallace Hamilton, 2000), *Pipes of Pan* (University of Michigan Press 1998) and *Companion to Greek and Roman Sexualities* (Blackwell, 2013, forthcoming).

Beert Verstraete is professor emeritus in the Department of History and Classics, Acadia University.

Contributors

Eric Alcorn is an instructor in the Department of Biology, Acadia University.

Janice Best is professor in the Department of Languages and Literatures, Acadia University.

David Greenberg is professor in the Department of Sociology, New York University.

Gert Hekma is professor in the Department of Sociology and Anthropology, University of Amsterdam.

Andrew Heller is an attorney in private practice.

Thomas Hubbard is professor of classics at the University of Texas–Austin.

Donald H. Mader is assistant pastor at the Pauluskerk in Rotterdam, Netherlands.

Richard McAnulty is associate professor in the Department of Psychology, University of North Carolina–Charlotte.

Patrick O'Neill is professor emeritus in the Department of Psychology, Acadia University.

Bruce Rind is a former professor in the Department of Psychology, Temple University.

Daniel C. Tsang is Distinguished Librarian at the University of California–Irvine.

Lester Wright Jr. is associate professor in the Department of Psychology, Western Michigan University.

Richard Yuill is an independent researcher.

green press
INITIATIVE

Left Coast Press, Inc. is committed to preserving ancient forests and natural resources. We elected to print this title on 30% post consumer recycled paper, processed chlorine free. As a result, for this printing, we have saved:

3 Trees (40' tall and 6-8" diameter)
1 Million BTUs of Total Energy
234 Pounds of Greenhouse Gases
1,273 Gallons of Wastewater
85 Pounds of Solid Waste

Left Coast Press, Inc. made this paper choice because our printer, Thomson-Shore, Inc., is a member of Green Press Initiative, a nonprofit program dedicated to supporting authors, publishers, and suppliers in their efforts to reduce their use of fiber obtained from endangered forests.

For more information, visit www.greenpressinitiative.org

Environmental impact estimates were made using the Environmental Defense Paper Calculator. For more information visit: www.papercalculator.org.